The New American Chef has a refined and sophisticated style. There is a huge melting pot of techniques which draw on many cultures and regions, redefining old classics and creating new classics as well. Excellent reading!

—TODD ENGLISH, CHEF-OWNER, OLIVES AND FIGS

Like the great chefs they write about, Andrew Dornenburg and Karen Page bring to their work infectious enthusiasm, endless curiosity, and expansive knowledge. The breadth and depth of their passion makes this book at once a vivid education in the great cuisines of the world and a continuous treat to peruse.

—TONY SCHWARTZ, *NEW YORK TIMES* BESTSELLING CO-AUTHOR OF *THE POWER OF FULL ENGAGEMENT*

Andrew Dornenburg and Karen Page seek out—and offer—some of the best advice on pairing food and wines we've seen. Readers should expect imaginative and unexpected match-ups: Sherry and Cava for main courses; Pinot Noirs for tandoori. *The New American Chef* is relaxed, fun, and to the point.

—SAM PERKINS, EXECUTIVE EDITOR, *WINE ENTHUSIAST*

Drawing on a distinguished circle of America's leading culinary experts, *The New American Chef* is the first book to distill their wisdom to guide readers to cook more intuitively. This book provides the essence of each of 10 influential cuisines which will help you hone your gut instinct and guide you through the challenges of cooking with ingredients and techniques from around the world.

—LAURA DAY, *NEW YORK TIMES* BESTSELLING AUTHOR OF *PRACTICAL INTUITION* AND *THE CIRCLE*

Another remarkable book by Dornenburg and Page! Through numerous interviews with experts, *The New American Chef* provides insights into the basic concepts of ten different cuisines. This book is enlightening for both the amateur and the professional chef.

—KAREN AND DAVID WALTUCK, CO-OWNERS, CHANTERELLE IN NEW YORK CITY

The New American Chef is a groundbreaking work. It redefines and brings into sharp focus what is happening food-wise in America today. The book is filled with expert teaching and an abundance of mouth-watering recipes. The 'Dynamic Duo of Dining' has once again brought a fresh, vital, and immensely interesting work to the kitchen table.

—MICHAEL ROMANO, CHEF-PARTNER, UNION SQUARE CAFÉ IN NEW YORK CITY

The New American Chef thoroughly demonstrates that the zeitgeist of modern cooking in this country has shifted to the various ethnic influences that make up our populace. This glorious work literally sings with the excitement of what is our own culinary make-up: diversity, passion, exuberance, intrigue, and spice. You will be well served if you study these pages!

—CHARLIE TROTTER, CHEF-OWNER, CHARLIE TROTTER'S IN CHICAGO

The New American Chef demystifies the New American cuisine by gingerly getting you inside your favorite restaurants' kitchens and taking you out into the world's colorful fields, markets and villages—showing splendid sociological sensibilities throughout.

—GLENN CARROLL, LANE PROFESSOR OF ORGANIZATIONS AT THE STANFORD BUSINESS SCHOOL

"Before you tuck into Karen and Andrew's path-breaking portrayal of the future of American cuisine and its guiding chefs, look back for a moment at where we came from. It is impossible to grasp fully an emerging cultural phenomenon without a feel for its origins. A core component of human culture, cuisines were born of necessity and contingency—what food there was and when and how you could get it and prepare it—then shaped through ingenuity, formalized by custom, and cherished over generations.

"A meal is a physical as well as a cultural event, one that is repeated tens of thousands of times in a lifetime. But it is not a permanent cultural thing like Michelangelo's David. A cuisine must be recreated day after day by its practitioners. It comes into being before our eyes and palates and then vanishes. Experts can judge the authenticity of a Velasquez portrait or Shakespearean sonnet, but how does one evaluate what is becoming authentic American cuisine in the hands of the newer generations of chefs? Perhaps it would help to think back to the quintessential film about coming of age in America, 'The Graduate,' and the scene where an elder advises Dustin Hoffman that the future is 'plastics.' That may not be a bogus prediction when it comes to the New American chefs. Cuisine is a plastic art in that it is continually remolded and recreated from memory and recipes and reshaped and invented anew by creative minds. Or maybe it's *plastique*, since the international flavors chefs are incorporating into American cuisine are often explosive.

"I don't know what the twenty-first century's American cuisine will look like when it matures. The world is truly at the kitchen doorsteps of American 'FedEx' chefs, for whom locality and seasonality are diminishing as constraints on the availability of the world's finest ingredients—often as chefs simultaneously celebrate these conditions as virtues in their culinary aesthetics and menus. It is possible that in a rapidly changing society, the New American cuisine will never be codified into a classical, coherent tradition the way cuisines like French and Chinese or even our own Cajun have been. As Jean-Georges Vongerichten asserts in these pages, the perfection of new techniques as well as the adoption of new ingredients may lead to entirely new flavor experiences. Whatever their inventions taste like, the coming generations of American chefs will be plastic in the best sense of the word: their plastic artistic imaginations giving form and formal expression to this new cuisine, their food endlessly malleable and pleasurable."

—DENNIS RAY WHEATON,
CHIEF DINING CRITIC,
CHICAGO MAGAZINE

The New American Chef

The New American Chef

COOKING WITH THE BEST OF FLAVORS AND TECHNIQUES FROM AROUND THE WORLD

ANDREW DORNENBURG *and* **KAREN PAGE**

PHOTOGRAPHS BY MICHAEL DONNELLY

WILEY

JOHN WILEY & SONS, INC.

Published by John Wiley & Sons, Inc., Hoboken, New Jersey
Published simultaneously in Canada

Design by Vertigo Design, NYC   www.vertigodesignnyc.com

Library of Congress Cataloging-in-Publication Data
Dornenburg, Andrew.
    The New American chef/Andrew Dornenburg, Karen Page.
        p. cm.
    Includes bibliographical references and index
    ISBN 0-471-36344-8 (cloth)
    1. Cookery, International. I. Page, Karen. II. Title

TX725.A1 D57 2003
641.59—dc21

                                                                  2002031100

Printed in the United States of America

10 9 8 7 6 5 4 3 2

To those dedicated to preserving timeless culinary traditions around the world—as well as to the New American Chefs who are bringing new excitement and elevation to cuisine.

Contents

Introduction MEET THE NEW AMERICAN CHEF 1

Japan CELEBRATING THE SEASONS THROUGH ALL THE SENSES 24

While seasonality is a popular culinary touchstone throughout the world, the Japanese take their celebration of the seasons beyond the selection of produce in the market to the consideration of the flowers on the table, the types of bowls and plates used for serving the food, and the linens that dress the table. Seasonality is observed in every aspect of their lives—from the fabric of their clothing to the art on their walls.

Italy PROCURING THE BEST INGREDIENTS 60

The word "recipe" in Italian means "to procure"—and indeed, the most important aspect of good food in Italy starts with selecting the right ingredients. Learning to be as discriminating as an Italian chef will hold you in good stead when selecting ingredients from any part of the world.

Spain LETTING INGREDIENTS TASTE OF WHAT THEY ARE 102

While many countries are capable of serving and appreciating unadorned food, nowhere but in Spain is this taken to such an extreme. The classic dishes of Spain are the simplest ones that let the natural flavors of the ingredients shine through. It is the only country whose regions are actually named after dishes: stews, roasts, rice, and fried foods.

France WESTERN TECHNIQUES AND SAVOIR FAIRE 146

The French contributed a codification of recipes and techniques to professional cooking, which is why most American cooking schools teach French technique. These techniques are timeless and consistent, and mastering the classics will give your cooking a solid foundation upon which to build.

China EASTERN TECHNIQUES AND A YIN-YANG BALANCE 192

The underlying philosophy of Chinese cuisine is rooted in the concept of yin-yang: a constant balance. Balance in Chinese cuisine is raised to an art form, both within a single dish, as well as among dishes on a menu. Understanding the concept of yin-yang and how to apply it to your cooking—in any vernacular—will make you a better chef.

Acknowledgments

From our hearts, we'd like to thank the following people and places without whom and which this book would not exist:

JOHN WILEY & SONS: Natalie Chapman, Pam Chirls, Kate Fischer, Andrea Johnson, Edwin Kuo, Adrianne Maher, and Valerie Peterson

COPY EDITOR Judith Sutton

VERTIGO DESIGN: Renata De Oliveira and Alison Lew

ALL THE CULINARY EXPERTS who contributed their time and expertise for this book. We were heartbroken to lose Raji Jallepalli and Barbara Tropp over the course of this project, but are happy to see their culinary passion and influence live on in these pages.

KITCHEN ARTS AND LETTERS, especially Nach Waxman, for his recommendations of some of the best of the best culinary books for each country

OUR RESEARCH AND EDITORIAL ASSISTANTS Meeghan Truelove, as well as Dina Cheney (and Koby Rosenschein for his computer assistance), Julia Shannon, and Gail Simmons

PHOTOGRAPHER MICHAEL DONNELLY, and his photography assistant Stephanie Johnson (and Remy Amezuca) and producer Jennifer Lewis

FOR THEIR GOOD-NATURED MODELING, Mariano Aznar, Tony Bonner, Diane Forley, Michael Otsuka, Julie Sahni, Marja Samson, Amy Scherber, Hiroko Shimbo, and Corinne Trang, as well as Hemali Dessani, Michael Gelb, Billy Strong, and Steve Wilson for the same

ALL THOSE WHO OPENED THEIR DOORS TO US FOR OUR PHOTO SHOOTS: Alain Ducasse New York, Amy's Bread, Babbo, BuonItalia (and Mimo Magliulo), Restaurant Daniel (and Georgette Farkas), Corrine Trang, DiPalo's, Faicco's Pork Store, Florence Meat Market, Hiroko's Kitchen, Italian Wine Merchants, Joe's Dairy, Julie Sahni's Cooking School, Kalustyan's (and Aziz Osmani), Joy India, Lotfi's (and for that amazingly delicious feast that was fit for a king—literally!), Murray's Cheese Shop, Pho Bang, San Domenico (and Tony May and Magdalena Spirydowicz), SavorySojourns.com and Addie Tomei (yes, that's Marisa's mom) for our delicious tour of Italy right here in Manhattan and in the Bronx, Shun Lee Palace, Solera, Tabla, Taqueria Tulcingo (and Charlene Badman of Inside for sending us to Queens!), Vong (and Dan DelVecchio), Wild Edibles (and Jordy Rosenhek), and Zarela

FERN BERMAN PUBLIC RELATIONS: Fern Berman, Robin Insley

Preface

Happy families are all alike. . . . —TOLSTOY

JUST AS HAPPY FAMILIES ARE ALL ALIKE, so does all great food have in common a number of the same basic principles, including

Abundance	**Freshness**	**Regionality**
Aroma	**Harmony**	**Ripeness**
Balance	**Healthfulness**	**Seasonality**
Flavor	**Quality**	**Variety**

However, each country brings its own unique perspective and emphasis to its cuisine. This book seeks to celebrate the flavors and philosophies of ten global cuisines, which are increasingly an integral part of the contemporary American restaurant kitchen. Understanding and appreciating their foundational tenets can make anyone a better cook.

While the principles above advocate ideals such as regionality, even this is relative: in truth, *all* food is "fusion" food. At no point in time were the world's cuisines ever marked decisively into "authentic" and "fusion" categories. Instead, each has experienced an ongoing evolution. For example, can anyone imagine Italian cuisine without tomato sauce? Yet were it not for the Mexicans and the Spanish, the Italians never would have been introduced to tomatoes [in the 17th century].

Americans in particular have always been captivated by that which is new, explaining young cooks' affection for (and even preoccupation with) experimentation. And there's nothing wrong with experimentation—just with the too-common occurrence of ill-advised experiments ending up being served to paying customers!

The dilemma is simple: The dawn of the new millennium has brought with it the widespread availability of ingredients from around the world. However, their arrival on our grocery store shelves has far outpaced our knowledge of how to use and incorporate them into our daily cooking.

Before giving a presentation at the annual conference of the International Association of Culinary Professionals, we surveyed top chefs across the country, asking them what kinds of knowledge would help make the cooks in their kitchens even better at their jobs. From coast to coast, the answer we received was the same: young cooks need to develop a respect for the cuisines of other countries, and their component ingredients and techniques, before starting to experiment with fusion efforts.

We knew what they meant. While we were researching our third book, *Dining Out*, top restaurant critics voiced the same complaint to us. Ruth Reichl, then critic for the *New York Times*, described a shockingly ill-conceived dish of pasta with basil, white grapes, and gorgonzola she'd once seen offered at a restaurant.

ANDREW: Chefs love referring to the archetypal dish "Scallops with Blueberry Sauce" as a catch-all "Dumb Dish of All Time." The reference has become a not-so-delicate way of saying to a young cook, "Your dish makes no sense, and has no culinary reference point—and when you can roast a chicken a hundred times perfectly, *then* come back to me with your new ideas!"

As a young cook, I passed through my own "scallops with blueberry sauce" phase, which included my "creation" of goat cheese polenta with cilantro. I learned the hard way—by making a batch at home, and then realizing I had to throw the whole vile concoction in the trash—that sheer imagination is *not* a reference point: you can't simply combine favorite ingredients and assume that you'll love the end result. Every dish should have a specific reference point, which may be drawn from anywhere around the globe.

New American restaurants today are almost without exception influenced by regions beyond American borders. Take a glance at a sampling of menus from leading chefs across America and you will see countless global influences, from Indian and Italian influences on Michael Romano's menu at New York City's Union Square Café to Japanese influences in Charlie Trotter's cuisine at his Chicago restaurant to Moroccan influences in Gordon Hamersley's food at his upscale Boston bistro.

A dozen years ago, at the East Coast Grill in Boston, under chef-owner Chris Schlesinger, we drew on not only the American South, where he grew up, but also Asia, the Caribbean, and equatorial climates for our culinary reference points. This meant that on any given day in this New American "barbecue" restaurant, I might find myself making everything from a Korean chow-chow to serve with pork to a Kentucky burgoo (admittedly without the squirrel) to mahi mahi with pineapple salsa. We even used a very French consommé recipe straight from Escoffier, but then finished it with smoked chicken and cilantro leaves; it's doubtful that Escoffier himself would have recognized it!

At Lydia Shire's Biba, I worked both the tandoori oven and the wood-burning oven stations. I had to learn to roll out pizza dough by hand one minute and then brush a piece of naan bread fresh from the tandoori oven with flavored ghee the next, before roasting a suckling pig that was marinated in spices and wine from Spain. Three countries, three diverse culinary influences... and just another shift in the life of a New American cook.

Even Anne Rosenzweig, for whom I worked at Arcadia, one of the homes of "New American cuisine," drew on influences from outside the United States, such as Eastern Europe in dishes like kasha. During my tenure, the restaurant also featured a number of guest chefs, such as Barbara Tropp and Nobu Matsuhisa, who had me learning and applying ingredients and techniques from China and Japan for their special dinners.

While cooking at New York City's Judson Grill, in any fifteen-minute span I might adjust the seasoning of a soup with herbes de Provence, make a New Orleans pan roast with Tabasco and Worcestershire sauce, and then jump over to the sushi station to make yellowtail sushi rolls. During my tenure at 9 Jones Street, I worked with chef Marcey Bassoff, who'd previously cooked at The Quilted Giraffe, a Manhattan restaurant legendary for disregarding the rules of modern cuisine. She would put *nam pla* (Thai fish sauce) and chile-marinated tofu in the dressing of her Caesar salad (a dish invented in Acapulco, Mexico, and adopted by Italian restaurants).

On one hand, I believed there was merit in the cooking philosophy of some leading chefs that "if it tastes good, do it!" On the other hand, I was convinced that my cooking would be stronger if only I had a better grounding in the many cuisines I borrowed from so frequently. I can still hear Marcey's voice telling me to "take the culinary blinders off!" when I would rigidly recite that I tried to cook by the rule that "if it grows together, it goes together." But part of me still believes that mantra will rarely fail you, and one way to gain knowledge that will avoid the effort of reinventing the wheel is to go back to the ingredients' roots in their indigenous cuisines.

An understanding of culinary history provides a sense of how indigenous ingredients are used in their native regions. Chris Schlesinger has pointed out that "People have tried every combination of the ingredients that could be found in their areas over hundreds and thousands of years, and the process of evolution got rid of the sub-par combinations while retaining the combinations that came to be seen as 'classic.'" In other words, letting the cooks of history give the cooks of today a head start is a pretty smart thing to do. The Italians, for example, discovered the joy of pairing tomatoes with local herbs like basil. The Mexicans learned the joy of using chiles to spice up their diet. Why disregard centuries of research? We can learn from the chefs of yesterday, as well as from leading chefs and cookbook authors across America whose expertise lies in other parts of the globe.

In researching this book, we turned to some of the foremost authorities on ten popular world cuisines and asked them what makes their cuisines tick. Their answers comprise an around-the-world cooking school that promises to make anyone a better cook—no matter what they're cooking!

So, take a trip around the world with us, and with the culinary experts you'll meet in the pages that follow. Their passion and enthusiasm for these cuisines is infectious! And their insights into how you can best approach these cuisines, and even apply their lessons to *any* cooking you undertake, will make you smarter in the way you approach food. After speaking with them, we know that we'll never think about these cuisines the same way again.

Our goal was not to take a comprehensive, encyclopedic approach to these ten cuisines, which would doubtless require several lifetimes to accomplish. Rather, we hoped to share some of the underlying tenets each one has to offer.

Each country has a different emphasis that makes its cuisine sparkle, so understanding when and whether to apply certain techniques is critical. For example, a mastery of stocks will take you far in French cuisine, but heavy meat-based stocks would ruin the flavor of Mexican food, in which lighter broths are used. Toasting brings out the flavor of spices in Indian dishes, but that technique would spoil the more subtle seasoning of Moroccan cooking.

Our goal is to give you a feel for and practical knowledge of the cuisines from the perspectives of our experts. In the kitchen, we want you to feel like an actor inhabiting a role, knowing the motivation, the characteristics, the movements, the tone, the props—and when you can improvise. Our hope is to provide you with the context you need to understand how foreign influences can be united into something delicious in the New American kitchen—and to help ignite your passion to keep pursuing knowledge as a surefire way to guarantee your ongoing improvement as a cook!

Andrew Dornenburg and Karen Page

The New American Chef

Introduction

Food is part of our way of celebrating life. The ingredients will change, because we are becoming more aware every day. That means there is still such a possibility of discovery with food.

— PIERO SELVAGGIO, OWNER, VALENTINO, LOS ANGELES

IN THE LATE 1960s, when André Soltner of the four-star restaurant Lutèce in New York City charged $8.95 for fresh Dover sole, it caused a scandal. No chef had ever dared to charge so much for sole—but no customer had ever tasted sole in the United States that wasn't straight from a restaurant's freezer either. Without realizing it, Soltner—long considered the standard bearer for restaurant excellence in America—ushered in a whole new era of cuisine, and he can be thought of as a precursor to the contemporary "FedEx chef." Today American chefs think nothing of having the very best ingredients flown in from around the world, and of charging accordingly. Customers, too, have recovered from their initial sticker shock, and in tasting the difference for themselves, have come to appreciate and expect the very best and freshest ingredients.

Now, thirty-five years after Soltner's introduction of fresh Dover sole, the American restaurant scene has morphed into one where all professional chefs have the world to use as their pantry and where customers, in addition to demanding the best, are also looking to be entertained with something new. The global palette of flavors available from around the world provides never-ending inspiration from which chefs can draw to please their customers. Restaurant menus in the United States increasingly feature ingredients and techniques from beyond our borders, in a style that has become loosely known as "New American" cuisine.

To be sure, not everyone can even agree on what "New American" cuisine is. A sampling of definitions from media across America include:

- New World ingredients with European cooking techniques
- combining different cooking methods and ingredients from a variety of countries to create contemporary American dishes that are well balanced
- food prepared largely with American ingredients according to standard French methods, or simply,
- food not indigenous to any area or region.

Whereas a young professional cook may have had the opportunity in years past to develop a solid grounding in classic technique (most frequently French) before branching off into multiethnic experimentation, today the same cook has to work from day one with an extraordinarily wide variety of ingredients and techniques.

Home cooks today face the same challenges, as the ethnic sections of grocery stores have evolved from a single shelf (with taco sauce masquerading as salsa placed next to soy sauce free of any Asian lettering on its label) to entire aisles of the store devoted to ingredients from all over the world. While we've come to expect this in cosmopolitan cities like New York and San Francisco, which have become cultural mosaics, we've witnessed the same phenomenon in stores from the suburbs of Philadelphia to the outskirts of Tucson.

The widespread availability of international ingredients has outpaced our ability to assimilate them into our daily cooking. This represents both a major opportunity and a major challenge for the New American chef. On one hand, there is an exciting opportunity for experimentation and exercising creativity. On the other hand, experimentation—particularly in the hands of an inexperienced chef—can be disastrous.

When interviewing leading restaurant critics across America for our book *Dining Out*, one of the complaints we heard most often was how often young cooks' ill-conceived experiments ended up on restaurant menus. However, chefs are no different from other young people who have historically wanted to do things "their own way." Cookbook author and radio host Lynne Rossetto Kasper recalls, "Back in the 1960s, when college students were protesting everything, the cartoonist Al Capp—who was as zany as his comic strip, *L'il Abner*—would speak on university campuses, pointing out, 'You are protesting against wars you have never fought, and an establishment you have never been a part of.'

"This exactly echoes what needs to be said to recent culinary grads: Most of you are trying to cook things you know nothing about," she observes. "You might never have eaten at a great restaurant before you went to cooking school and maybe you still haven't had that experience. You might never have seen another country. You might not have any sense of how things grow. And you haven't yet worked like a dog in every kitchen you can get into to learn your craft. Once you have done all that, *then* you can 'play.'"

To help you master the challenges associated with being a New American cook, we hope this book will serve as your guide in learning:

1. the principles that underlie great cooking around the world;

2. an appreciation of and respect for the traditions of various world cuisines, and an understanding of how their ingredients, techniques, and recipes are customarily employed; and

3. discernment that will serve to guide your efforts, whether they involve the replication of a traditional dish, an experimental "riff" on it, or something in between.

Developing Your "Culinary Compass"

TO THIS END, we want to encourage you to develop your own "Culinary Compass," which will help guide your efforts in the kitchen and navigate the often challenging terrain of new and unfamiliar cuisines, ingredients, and techniques. Think of your Culinary Compass as being organized along two spectrums:

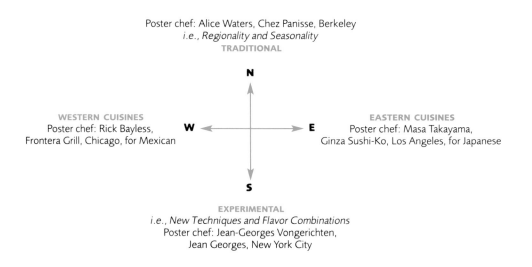

Poster chef: Alice Waters, Chez Panisse, Berkeley
i.e., Regionality and Seasonality
TRADITIONAL

N

WESTERN CUISINES
Poster chef: Rick Bayless,
Frontera Grill, Chicago, for Mexican

W ← → E

EASTERN CUISINES
Poster chef: Masa Takayama,
Ginza Sushi-Ko, Los Angeles, for Japanese

S

EXPERIMENTAL
i.e., New Techniques and Flavor Combinations
Poster chef: Jean-Georges Vongerichten,
Jean Georges, New York City

West to East: Choosing a Reference Point

All cooking begins with one's passion for and knowledge of a particular cuisine. If you want to learn the palate archetypes, you have to be on an exploration—and it has to be a long journey, not a short one.

—BARBARA TROPP, AUTHOR, *THE MODERN ART OF CHINESE COOKING*

The West-to-East spectrum includes the world of cuisines that exist from the Western to the Eastern hemispheres of the world. In this book, we address ten, including (from West to East) Mexican, Moroccan, Spanish, French, Italian, Indian, Chinese, Vietnamese, Thai, and Japanese.

Each cuisine, with its own unique set of flavor profiles and culinary philosophies, represents a possible reference point for your cooking. While two or more cuisines might be combined within a single dish (an approach typically referred to as "fusion") or within a single menu (often referred to as "eclectic"), the starting point is typically a single country.

French-born chef Daniel Boulud of New York has France as his reference point. Rick Bayless of Chicago has Mexico. Masa Takayama of Ginza Sushi-Ko in Los Angeles has Japan. Leading chefs agree that even with pan-ethnic efforts, one's food must have a reference point in which it is grounded. For Jean-Georges Vongerichten, his reference point varies by restaurant—at Prime, his steakhouse, it is all-American; at Vong, it is Thai flavors and classic French technique.

French technique has traditionally been the focus of leading cooking schools in the United States. However, Rick Bayless advises, "Cooks should start with a cuisine that they feel most comfortable with and that speaks most to their heart. While French cuisine can be a good place to start, it is important to realize how prejudiced it is in certain directions. It can really trip you up when you work with other cuisines. For example, in European cuisines, almost without exception, the cooking celebrates the flavor of meat. So when you go to cooking school, the first thing you learn is how to make and reduce stock, in order to get the flavor of meat in everything. However, if you do that in Mexican food, your efforts will be misguided because that is *not* the focus of Mexican flavors. Your dish won't taste French or Mexican. Stock in Mexican food is very light and is used to add a little richness, not to overwhelm a dish with the flavor of meat."

Mark Miller also underscores the limits that a traditional French-centric approach to cooking can place on chefs. "French society, from music to food, is highly codified. Codifying everything bonds the society together. It gives certain things a power and place, but also blocks other things out," he explains. Not developing an appreciation for the nuances of flavors outside one's native palate is a major limitation for a serious chef.

"If a French chef told me that he had a good palate, I would still doubt that he or she could tell me how to pair ten different sakes with ten different sashimi. He or she wouldn't understand the dynamics of that society," Miller asserts. "There are thirty-five different types of soy sauce used in one area of China. Three hundred different types of pickles are made in Kyoto, and some Japanese palates can differentiate among the types of spring water that are used to make them."

Just as it might take a multilingual traveler some time to shift fluently from one language into another, it can be a challenge to shift one's culinary reference point as well. "Our former sous-chef Paul Kahan, who is now the chef of Blackbird restaurant [in Chicago], came to us from Erwin restaurant, which serves American food with a real European base," says Rick Bayless. "After cooking here for a number of years, he returned to Erwin, where he found he had to struggle mightily. He said it took him almost six months to be able to cook the food at Erwin again because he had learned a completely different way to create, develop, and balance flavors here. Because he had changed his palate and ingredients , he felt as if he had forgotten how to cook! That was astonishing to him, but I understood completely. When I cook other cuisines at home, sometimes I feel like I'm all thumbs."

Bayless learned that taking the time to master different "languages" can allow one to develop greater appreciation of and fluency in each. "I love Thai food, but it has such a different sensibility of flavors and ingredients than Mexican cuisine," he says. "I feel like such a neophyte as I learn Thai cooking! The flavors are complex and well balanced the way the best Mexican food is, yet they get to that level with a completely different vocabulary.

"Now I'm able to understand what people mean when they say that Mexican food is 'Greek' to them," says Bayless. "I am happy to be going through the learning process myself, so I can reacquaint myself with what it's like on the other side of the fence."

The more you understand the reference point of whatever you're making, the more depth you can bring to your cooking. "For example, if you find yourself cooking Thai curries, ask yourself: Where did they come from? What was the 'mother lode' of the cuisine?" urges Barbara Tropp, author of *The Modern Art of Chinese Cooking*. "The truth is, when you look at Thai or Vietnamese food or any Southeast Asian cuisine, you have to consult the food of China and Japan, because they are the 'mother' and the 'father' of those cuisines. Without looking at that, your understanding would be extremely shallow—not only intellectually, but on the palate."

Choosing a reference point from the Western or Eastern side of the compass will provide you with a focus for your efforts in the kitchen. It will determine how you stock your pantry: Will your ingredients be from the Americas, Europe, Africa, or Asia, or a combination? It will help drive your decisions regarding seasoning: When you want to add saltiness to a dish, will you reach for *fleur de sel*, special French sea salt, or soy sauce? And it will even influence the techniques you apply to the ingredients and seasonings you're working with: When cooking with spices, will you toast them first or not?

For example, a beginning cook might mistakenly believe that "rice is rice." While rice is a key ingredient of both Mexican cuisine, which he has mastered, and Thai cuisine, which has more recently captured his interest, Rick Bayless underscores the importance of the myriad distinctions between varieties of rice.

"Once, when we had just returned from Thailand, I could not sleep, which is not like me at all. Because of the time change, my body clock was off, so I found myself in front of the refrigerator, peering in," Bayless recalls. "I saw some jasmine rice, which I had cooked the day before in Thailand. When I opened the lid of the container, the aroma was pure jasmine, and it perfumed the whole kitchen. I will never forget it," he says, "because it immediately heightened all my senses and helped me understand just how different the approach to rice is in Mexico. There it is a bland surface to which you add all these flavorings to embroider it. In Asian cooking, rice is its own thing—with its own flavor and aroma—that stands on its own the way it is."

Barbara Tropp observes that appreciating and respecting the differences in cuisines—and their component ingredients—makes one a much better cook. "How many chefs don't taste their salt because they think 'salt is salt'?" she asks. "Yet sea salts from France, Italy, and Japan taste quite different from one another. Processed salt tastes different from unprocessed salt. Understanding salt is a whole topic unto itself, but it is one more example of how far you have to go to really understand cuisine. Sea salt doesn't even work with great effectiveness in Chinese food because it is too strong and competes with the archetypal aromatics of the cuisine."

The application of proper technique is important in getting the flavors and textures true to the classical versions. "People in Asia eat poultry with its head on, and pork on the bone," observes Mark Miller. "In America, people describe good ribs as having 'the meat falling off the bone.' But in Asia, people like to chew the meat off the bone so that they're interacting with it and enjoying the visceral experience of holding a bone and tearing the meat off it. It doesn't sound pretty, but it is pleasurable and sensual when you become part of that process."

This appreciation for the "gestalt" of a cuisine and its flavors are of critical importance in being able to duplicate them successfully. "For example, in Mexican food, there is a 'wildness' to the flavor," Miller continues. "It comes from the oregano and cactus. The edges are not 'rounded off' as they are in French cooking. Mexican food cannot be domesticated. When you cook it, that sensibility needs to be recreated."

Choosing a reference point and rooting your cooking in it is the first step to becoming a better chef. But focusing your cooking doesn't have to be a limitation.

North to South: Expressing Your Point of View

The Culinary Compass also allows for a range of expression. The spectrum from North to South symbolizes the range of approaches to cuisine, from Traditional to Experimental. Traditional (North) represents the principles that underlie classical cuisine. Many of these concepts, including regionality and seasonality, have become the oft-heard mantras of the New American kitchen. At the South end of the spectrum is Experimentation, or "breaking the rules"—the recognition that there might be times when you want to pair ingredients that don't necessarily "grow together," or when you might intentionally forgo balance for decadence. The key point, again, is that you've got to first understand the rules before you can break them successfully.

Each approach is accompanied by its own set of expectations on the part of the diner. "In Italy, dishes are divided two ways: something is either *tradizionale* or it is *fantasia,* and to call something *fantasia* can either be insulting or complimentary," explains Lynne Rossetto Kasper. "If you improvise, people will judge you on the merits of the dish. But, if you are going to do a risotto Milanese from Milan, heaven help you if you don't do it *right!*"

The same is true around the world, where exacting standards of excellence exist for specific dishes. For example, "tempura is actually very difficult to prepare," says Mark Miller. "The oil has to be at the perfect temperature. A great tempura restaurant will use a separate oil for each style of food: one for fish, another for vegetables, and so forth, and in some places they change the oil every two hours."

In Japan, the ritual of certain dishes is so revered that some chefs will devote years—even a lifetime—to their perfection. "I go to a tempura bar that is 136 years old. The chef has been there 37 years and is only the fourth chef in the history of the restaurant. The restaurant has eight seats and he works there five nights a week, making only tempura," revels Miller.

Even with so much tradition in place, it is possible to bring a "South-driven" sensibility to the same dishes. "El Bulli [a Michelin three-star restaurant] in Spain represents the opposite extreme," Miller explains. "The chef, Ferran Adrià, makes a tempura of caviar and it's amazing. His technique is perfect; technically, you can't have warm caviar, but his caviar tempura works. I respect what he is doing because he is pushing conceptual boundaries."

Still, Miller, like other leading chefs, is a proponent of mastering tradition before taking the step of deviating from it. "It is problematic that chefs and customers are not learning to read and understand the importance of the cultural experience in its original context," he argues. "They need to see beyond what they can derive from it. People are doing too much filtering and not enough learning."

North

On the culinary compass, North represents the Traditional principles of a cuisine—classic flavor combinations, preparations, dishes, and menus—all of which can be counted on because they are the result of centuries of trial and error. These include such principles as:

- **Balance and Harmony:** achieving a pleasing marriage of flavors and textures both within a dish and throughout a menu
- **Regionality:** following the adage that "if it grows together, it goes together"
- **Seasonality:** serving food at its peak in the height of its season when it has optimal flavor (e.g., tomatoes in August)
- **Simplicity:** serving uncomplicated dishes so that essential flavors shine through without being muddled

The "poster chef" of New American cuisine, exemplifying the code of the North, would be Alice Waters of Chez Panisse in Berkeley, California. While Waters herself readily admits to influences on her menu from outside the United States, from Mexico to the Mediterranean, she has inspired a legion of New American chefs to embrace the principles of cooking regionally and seasonally.

Leading chefs are insistent that any aspiring cook must first master the principles of the traditional North. "I see this as the role of cooking schools—teaching the very basics, from seasonality to classic techniques," says Jean-Georges Vongerichten. "If someone comes out of school and does not know to fry something at 375 degrees, forget it! When I was at the Lafayette Hotel [in New York City, where he earned four stars], I would sometimes give cooks an onion and ask them to cut it three ways. I swear, they could hardly ever get past 'chop' and 'slice'!"

South

South on the Culinary Compass represents Experimentation, where some of the traditional principles of the North may be intentionally disregarded. With experience and judgment, the results can work—or even prove extraordinary. While simplicity is a precept of the North, a dish inspired by the South might feature challenging flavors juxtaposed against one another.

In the United States, Jean-Georges Vongerichten would be cited as the chef who exemplifies excellence at the South end of the North-South spectrum. Abroad, the aforementioned Ferran Adrià of El Bulli in Spain, who applies innovative techniques to transform foods into unexpected consistencies (e.g., from bacon foams to vegetable sorbets), is one of the foremost examples of a chef rooted firmly in the principles of the South.

Two dishes we were recently served at Jean Georges demonstrate that breaking the rules can be breathtaking: scallop tartare with chunks of black truffles, and a crepe filled with caviar, tied with a scallion, sitting atop a sliver of lime. No region of which we are aware could have produced those combinations of ingredients, uniting the pearls of the ocean with the jewels of the forest! Why did these dishes work? Vongerichten grew up in France and lived in Asia while working at several top restaurants, so his entire résumé was visible on our plates. He drew on flavors of countries in which he'd lived and worked and therefore had much firsthand experience.

Like his fellow Experimental chefs, Vongerichten eschews the notion that Traditional always equals quality. "If you go to many Thai restaurants in Thailand, you'll get overcooked food—because that is the way they cook, or what's 'traditional.' At Vong, I wanted to do something 'halfway.' We organize the menu for people so that they see things they recognize, like salmon or chicken, which we cook with great care—and then take them on a trip with their flavors that are 'out there'! A native Asian might recognize the flavors of coconut or lemongrass, but not any of the dishes," says Vongerichten.

In a master's hands, even the most traditional of cuisines can be tweaked, which Vongerichten proved through reinventing the steakhouse. "At Prime in Las Vegas, we use a seven-spice mix for one steak and we cook another one with six different peppercorns," he says. "We also offer a tray of mustards with different infusions ranging from peppercorns to Thai herbs. We use the traditional technique of making a mustard, but instead of using mustard seeds, we use coriander seeds to make something a little more unusual.

"You see, it's still a steak! People recognize familiar meat like rib-eye, shell, or T-bone, and we figure out the best complement for it. Same steak, new flavors. We offer ten different potato dishes, including one flavored with curry, raisins, and cumin seeds, as well as wasabi mashed potatoes. We even have fries made of chickpeas. Even at a steakhouse serving 'meat and potatoes,' you can do something different.

"It is like seeing a movie the second time, where you see things you didn't see the first time," muses Vongerichten. "You can make a dish for ten years using the same combination of ingredients, and it becomes routine. But with one little change, it can take on a whole new dimension."

The better you understand the rules, the more effective you can be when you choose to disregard them. A delicious example that comes to mind is the solid grounding in the traditional Italian dish of *vitello tonnato* (veal with tuna sauce) that led Boston chef Lydia Shire of Biba to her inspired, whimsical take on the flavor combination as tuna with veal sauce.

Even the traditional structure of menus is being revisited. "To me the whole concept of a meal with appetizer, entrée, and dessert is antiquated," says Mark Miller. "It is like saying every single symphony should have three movements: exposition, development, and denouement. However, modern music doesn't follow classic form. In the same vein, many people eat with the idea of classic or Western form. So, when Ferran Adrià at El Bulli puts sweets at the beginning of the meal, many people don't like it.

"But being strange and wonderful is not enough," Miller is quick to point out. "An experience has to be life-enlarging. As a chef, you have to learn to appreciate another type of consciousness and aesthetic, even if you don't like it."

Whether they actually like it or are simply intrigued by it, as we mentioned in our book *Chef's Night Out,* chefs around the globe are finding themselves inspired by Ferran Adrià's cuisine. "Everything worked at El Bulli," says Jean-Georges Vongerichten. "I had twenty (small) courses. It was delicious yet experimental. I saw it as Asian at times in the way he worked with contrast, texture, and temperature. He did a pea soup that was very hot on top, the next layer was warm, and the bottom was ice-cold. The same pea soup with three different temperatures, which made for three flavors in the same soup. It was brilliant! He also served a puree of squash with what he called a 'bacon foam.' He took a vegetable broth and smoked it, then he put it in a canister and foamed it, so the dish had bacon flavor that had nothing to do with actual bacon.

"He also served a poached quail egg wrapped in a paper-thin sheet of caramel. The quail egg had a bit of salt and vinegar flavor from the poaching liquid, the yolk was liquid, and the caramel exterior was bittersweet. He gave me one, and I could have eaten twenty! It was very balanced.

"I am not going to copy anything, but a meal like this will wake me up to new ideas and flavors," says Vongerichten. "I see techniques as creating the new flavors of the future."

The Third Dimension

There's a third dimension to the concept of the Culinary Compass, one that can be thought to measure a dish's effectiveness in achieving that subjective state of "deliciousness." In the best cooking, a dish transcends its status as a classic or as an experiment, and is found to be either pleasing or not. It is the dimension where the selection of ingredients, seasonings, and techniques unites with the chef's cooking talent and—ideally—the diner's pleasure.

This dimension is a reflection of the success of one's effort, no matter where it falls on the other two spectrums. "I don't give two hoots if something is authentic or experimental, as long as it tastes good," asserts Barbara Tropp. "Authenticity, for me, is not where it's at. I just want food to taste delicious. Nobu Matsuhisa makes food I adore that has nothing to do with authentic Japanese cuisine. Some of the food that Jean-Georges Vongerichten serves at Vong would not be recognized by a Thai person—but it is so good, who cares?"

In addition to how it pleases the tongue, quality in food can also be judged by how it moves the heart. "The food experience extends beyond one's palate," says Mark Miller. "It is not enough just to have information and cook well, nor is it enough to simply run a restaurant. You need to bring passion and soul to it, which doesn't come easy. Alice Waters has it. She runs Chez Panisse restaurant emotionally. It is not a restaurant built out of logic.

"The dining experience is about more than just the flavor of the food, and more than just plunking down a credit card and ordering off the menu. One of its most important aspects is the human element," Miller asserts. "There is a process: an ingredient came from a farm, then maybe a market, then made its way to a chef who respects it and serves it with love and attention to someone they know."

Capturing this human element in one's food is what can elevate it to the stratosphere. "We can write cookbooks all day long, but until you make the food and share it with other people, it does not become a living, breathing thing," agrees Rick Bayless. "When I hear people talk about starting culinary museums, I just want to laugh. It is so opposed to what the role of food really is. Food takes on its full potential only when it is shared between people."

Learning as a New American Chef

TO BE A NEW AMERICAN CHEF means to be part explorer and part detective. While a sense of adventure will propel you on your journey, a sense of curiosity about everything you see and smell and taste will drive your learning.

In *Chef's Night Out*, we told the story of how four-star chef André Soltner had the curiosity and the humility to go into the kitchen of a diner to ask the short order cook how his perfectly poached eggs had been prepared. On a recent taco expedition, we noticed that the tacos were served on two delicious tortillas, not one, and that this made the tacos easier to eat. (A single tortilla has the tendency to fall apart, especially with a very moist filling, while the reinforcement of a second tortilla makes the taco sturdier and capable of holding up through each and every bite.) Now our refrigerator is stocked with the same tortillas, and we serve our tacos on two tortillas.

The most important lesson for any cook is to keep learning. The best way to learn is to open your mind to what you don't know.

"For me, learning is completely gestalt," says Rick Bayless. "When I was a young cook, I wanted to take classes in France, and the woman I was working for gave me some sage advice. She said, 'You know a lot about techniques and if you decide you know

how to make all the dishes, you will get absolutely nothing out of it. Empty your mind completely and go in with a clean slate. Whatever they tell you to do, do it without question. Take in the whole experience, like you have never done it before. Then you will really learn.' I've never forgotten that. It is true in all of life that a little knowledge can turn out to be a dangerous thing."

Bayless' wife and partner, Deann, adds, "It is funny how many people come to Rick's classes and think they know more than he does! They are not willing to empty their minds. So many people think they already know everything, and as a result, they'll never learn the most basic things. They don't ever come to understand why they should take the time to follow the steps of the dish."

Rick Bayless has observed that cooks' impatience results in major knowledge gaps. "Where cooks get off base in America is that often they don't build from a thorough knowledge of a cuisine, so that when they want to experiment with 'fusion,' they are doing it at more of a surface level," he says. "What you find is a chef trying to use sixteen different cuisines and mastering none. It takes a lifetime to master something. I wish more chefs who came out of cooking school had this pounded into them."

Barbara Tropp agrees that surface imitation is simply that—and that to succeed in replicating the real thing, you've got to do your homework and bring an authentic sensibility to whatever it is you're aiming for—whether dressing a salad or dressing yourself. "If you are not French and want to look like a French girl, you can't pull it off just trying to dress like a French girl," she explains. "Instead, you have to get your mitts on every French magazine and watch movies and study Jeanne Moreau, Brigitte Bardot, and Catherine Deneuve. You have to go to Paris and soak up French culture before you can turn around in your bedroom and look French. Food is exactly the same way: You can't just put fish sauce in your *beurre blanc* and call it an Indochine dish!"

Have an Open Mind

Being an explorer and a detective takes some courage. Barbara Tropp has shared the good advice that diners should always order at least one unusual dish at a Chinese restaurant (taking any leftovers home to be polite, even if they didn't like it), because it will start to build a trusting relationship with the restaurant. Your explorer sensibility in ordering an exotic dish will impress the restaurant staff, and you can use your detective skills to analyze the dish: Is the dish "wacky" in a good way or in a bad way, and why? Is it similar in any way to anything you've ever tasted before? Can you imagine why other people might consider this dish to be a delicacy?

"Part of the joy of food is learning to stretch what you like," says Mark Miller. "If somebody else likes a dish, there is a reason to learn it. I never allow my cooks to simply say that they don't like something—they have to explain why. Otherwise, they are limiting themselves as chefs. They are personalizing their food without opening themselves up to experiences that they can learn from. By doing so, they can lock themselves into a culinary corner."

When tasting a dish, it is important to let go of any expectations of what it "should" be and to experience it for what it *is*. Otherwise, you can miss some important, and pleasurable, learning experiences. Charles Phan, chef-owner of the Slanted Door in San Francisco, tells the story of offering Hainan chicken, a popular dish from Southeast Asia, to his customers with little success. "The dish celebrates chicken very simply: The chicken is blanched, and it is served cold, with bones and skin, with a bowl of broth and vegetables. The dish is all about perfect chicken. However," he says, "I found that I couldn't put it on the menu because customers who order chicken always expect to see it served piping hot with crispy skin. People come in with their preconceived notions of what chicken is or should be, and that's that," Phan laments.

In terms of educating people about their food, some chefs have found that simply giving someone a bite of a dish can teach them more than a long explanation of it. "It has been scientifically proven that the brain responds most quickly to taste, more so than to words or pain. So let someone taste the food of your country, then let their mind do its job. Their mind will analyze it and connect them to that era or civilization," says Rafih Benjelloun, chef-owner of Imperial Fez, one of the first Moroccan restaurants in Atlanta. "If I cook you a dish that I learned from my mother, you will taste the history of both my mother and *her* mother, which will be an extension of our philosophies and of Morocco."

Occasionally, however, chefs will need to use their marketing skills to get someone to "open up," as it were. Benjelloun recalls, "At one charity event that had guests walking around to sample various chefs' dishes, I served a fish dish called *pell pell*. The dish contains many different types of fish, tomatoes, and spices. People would ask what it was, and if we told them '*pell pell*,' they'd walk away. But once we started describing it as 'Moroccan jambalaya,' people couldn't wait to try it!

"When I teach schoolchildren about food, I tell them that a person can be just as 'racist' about food as he or she can be about people," he continues. "I may use the same ingredients as another person, such as fish or tomatoes, but since the dish I make is Moroccan, others may turn their noses up at it. That is discrimination. You should taste something and open your mind; then, you will learn. The racist mind is one that is not open—and that is a lesson for adults as well as children."

Focus on the Whole Learning Process

It is important to not have blinders on when you cook, but rather to look at the entire process. Take a salad: What could be more simple than making a salad? You merely combine the best available raw ingredients—no cooking whatsoever. However, if the greens are not rinsed properly, or the dressing is too strong or too tame, or there is too much or not enough dressing coating the leaves, the salad is a failure. What will happen when you attempt something even more complex?

Understanding your ingredients is critical. "If I work with rice noodles, I have to learn how long to cook them, and what will happen when I combine them with other things," emphasizes Rick Bayless. "There is a learning curve, because I have no previous experience with rice noodles. I have even had to relearn rice! Again, rice in Thai cooking is completely different than it is in Mexican cooking—so much so that I don't even see them as the same basic product. It has taken me a month to choose a rice cooker for Thai cooking."

However, "often, young cooks are too focused on ingredients," Mark Miller says. "Philosophically, they have been brainwashed to believe that cooking is only great ingredients. In fact, it's technique—not ingredients—that creates a lot of flavor profiles. Finding out exactly what is in a recipe is not always as important as the steps that were used to achieve it. How dark were the chiles roasted? Was it on clay or metal? How long was the mole stirred—twenty minutes, two hours, or eight hours?"

Travel

Travel has always been a great inspiration for chefs, and a means of learning as well as rejuvenation. The experts we've interviewed are all passionate advocates of travel as a means of understanding and enjoying a cuisine.

"After reading a great deal about the country and its cuisine, if I had the resources, I would travel to the country itself," says Barbara Tropp. "Asia is accessible to travelers on a shoestring. I would eat street food, not the food in fancy restaurants. Taste and absorb as much as you can: the closer you get to street food and home cooking, the closer you are to the soul of a cuisine."

Mark Miller agrees. "One reason that chefs should travel now is that street food is disappearing," he says. "When I went to Shanghai twelve years ago, I could wander for six hours, never see another tourist, and eat twenty or thirty different street foods. Now there are only a few blocks of street vendors left, and restaurants are primarily in hotels and aimed at business travelers."

Mario Batali, chef-owner of Babbo, Lupa, and Esca in New York, sums up advice that has enabled him to get the most out of his travels through Italy. "Read a book first, then go to Italy—even if it is only for a week," he recommends. "It will clarify the food for you and empower you to make it yourself. I'd also suggest that you get off the beaten path: eat in a little trattoria, shop at a local market, and make a dinner based on some local produce. And keep your eyes and ears open—to be there is to understand the culture!"

Learn the Breadth of a Country's Cuisine

In the United States, it is next to impossible to sample all of the various regional cuisines of another country. You might find dishes of a few different regions on a Chinese or Italian restaurant menu, or find a restaurant that specializes in a specific region, but you are only scratching the surface of what's out there. On your first visit to another country, of a few days or weeks, you might be overwhelmed to see so much that is new to you. It is only through extended repeat visits that you'll get to know a country's nuances.

"Find an area that speaks to you, and then go back to that area," advises Mark Miller. "I have seen chefs go to Spain on two or three ten-day vacations, then open a Spanish restaurant. I have been to Spain twenty-five times. I go two or three times every year and find out that I know less and less.

"As a chef, you are not just working from a taste memory, but from the 'philosophical memory' of the place and the people," says Miller. "You need to understand the rationale of a cuisine to cook it correctly, and that can't come if you visit a place only once or twice.

"There are successive levels of learning," he continues. "The first time you are too excited. The second time you are a little disappointed because everything is not a surprise like it was the first time. The third time you find the subtleties. The fourth time you know the ingredients, you are asking for certain dishes, and you know that certain places only make certain things. In Spain, for example, the tapas you'll taste in Barcelona, San Sebastián, and Madrid are completely different."

Getting off the beaten path can prove more memorable than going to the places that all the guidebooks recommend. "When you travel, there is a sense of randomness that you get from just following your nose," says Miller. "Years ago, I remember walking by a coffee roaster who was roasting almonds in his olive wood–fired oven in Spain, and I can still smell the incredible aroma that led me there. These sensations are not something you can read about or see in a restaurant; they are about moments in time.

"In Istanbul, there is an Egyptian spice market and you could walk through it a hundred times and have a hundred different experiences. I guarantee you could walk through a hundred different malls in America and have pretty much the exact same experience every time! I was in a bakery in Beijing and counted 142 types of rolls made of flour," he continues. "If you go to a Chinatown in the U.S., you won't see anything like that! That is why you travel, to see the complexity and creativity of a people."

Just as visiting a winery to see how wine is made can be more memorable and educational than simply tasting a wine, there is much to be learned about food outside of markets and restaurants. "If possible, try to go to factories where ingredients are produced: it could be a rice cracker factory in Kyoto, a sugar factory in India, or a chocolate factory in Mexico. You want to see the simple ingredients that make up a complex recipe. That will help your palate," says Miller.

Su-Mei Yu has been chef-owner of Saffron, the top-rated Thai restaurant in San Diego, for more than sixteen years, but she still returns to Thailand every year to continue her education. "I will learn from anyone," she asserts, "family, friends, acquaintances, or restaurateurs. From them, I have learned not only how to cook, but also the culture, history, and social customs of the country.

"If you are truly interested in a cuisine, you should experience an authentically prepared dish in that country," she says. "If you're not adventurous, you don't have to have a whole mouthful—just a taste will teach you about the dynamics of the food. Then, you'll know if it's right or off-balance when you have it again."

Through all they learn through travel, Yu believes, chefs can play an important role in safeguarding a culture's culinary customs. "It is important to preserve many of these beliefs, techniques, and theories of tastes and textures, which are soon going to disappear," she says. "Young children are so attracted to fast food, and their taste buds are no longer trained to eat and appreciate the kind of food that was once renowned as Thai food."

Mark Miller agrees that cooking with people in their own country brings an important dimension of reality to one's experience of food. "It's so easy to pick up food magazines and look at travel articles thinking, 'I'm as good a cook as the people in this article!'" he observes. But those who go to the country and taste the food that is made in some of the villages can find it humbling. "There is a woman in Oaxaca who sells tamales for forty cents that are better than anything I will ever make," Miller swears.

By taking some time for a class or to ask the chef at a favorite café if you might be able to spend an afternoon in his kitchen, you will be able to get much closer to the heart of the cooking of the country you are visiting. "I studied with a woman who lives eight hours outside of Oaxaca," he continues. "She uses a *metate* that she got when she was married at sixteen, as well as corn from a five-hundred-year-old field. This woman has been grinding her corn every day for almost sixty years and when you taste her tortillas, it is as if you have never eaten them before. When you travel, you realize that you have a lot to learn.

"I sometimes travel with my cooks and managers," says Miller. "We recently went to the Yucatan, where we had roast suckling pig tacos at seven in the morning. We had watched them being made from the beginning: slaughtering the pig, digging the pit, roasting it for eight hours. As a result, we experienced a connection to that street food.

"While I was there, I wanted to make a classic soup of garlic broth and wild turkeys. I bought a live squawking, biting turkey and I had it slaughtered, then plucked it myself, which I had never done. The experience was very humbling, because it had looked so simple," Miller recalls. "These kinds of experiences demand that you pay attention to how the dishes worked—not just the recipes, but the gestalt and concept behind the flavor and how expressive the food is."

Study the Culture and the Language

Barbara Tropp and Rick Bayless both believe there is much to be gained by learning at least a little of the language. "You can learn the basics of how to cook a cuisine, but if you really fall in love with a cuisine and want to master it, you must learn the country's language," says Tropp. "There is a barrier when you don't know the language. Take a night class or listen to a couple of language tapes. Then, when you go into a restaurant, if you use a few phrases and ask if you can spend time in their kitchen, you are more likely to be embraced."

Bayless finds learning the language of a foreign country essential to going below the surface. "When you go to another country, you might learn a few words that will help you say 'hello,' 'good-bye' and 'thank you' and things like that, but that doesn't mean you can converse—it only means you can be polite. That is a nice nod to the culture, but you can't say that you've internalized that culture at all. When you speak another language, you learn grammar and the rules of the language. It is not until you do that and learn the whole vocabulary that you can put ideas together."

Learn Within Your Borders

Travel is without question a great way to learn about other cuisines and cultures, but it is not the only way. More than ever, there are countless opportunities across America to educate yourself, from bookstores to cooking schools to restaurants. "When you are dealing with a foreign cuisine, there are books, people, and restaurants that can help you learn more about it," says Nina Simonds. "Get a book that gives the basic seasonings and techniques. Or take an introductory class and speak with chefs. I really like the idea of going to an ethnic supermarket first. That way, you learn the basic pantry of the country. Then, when you go to a restaurant and taste the food, you already have some knowledge. That knowledge may enable you to identify certain flavors that are in the dishes you're tasting."

"To learn about Thai food, some people would start by going to as many Thai restaurants as possible," observes Barbara Tropp. "However, I'm a reader, so I would go to the library and pull out all the books on Thai food, as well as books on Thailand's geography and culture. I would want to understand the country's regions, because its geography gives rise to its food. For example, you can't really understand the food unless you know whether it comes from a mountainous or a coastal region [as the latter emphasizes seafood]."

In addition to reading cookbooks, even the best chefs learn a great deal through reading and following recipes. "It is important to go into something with a completely open mind and to do what you are told," comments Rick Bayless. "People laugh when I tell them that when I cook from other people's books, I literally follow every single direction. I measure everything out, cook exactly the way they say for as long as they say, and try to experience what they are trying to teach me. That is the way to learn a cuisine."

Tropp suggests another approach as well. "If I wanted to learn the food of another country within the borders of mine, I would probably visit the home of an elderly person," she says. "If you want to learn Chinese cooking, find someone to teach you who is in their seventies or eighties. Someone who is that old was brought up before the Cultural Revolution. It's important to realize how big an impact that had, and that the real cuisine that existed before it is quickly disappearing."

Shop the Markets

Going to a market is more important than going to a fancy restaurant.
—BARBARA TROPP

Our culinary experts believe that one should approach learning about ingredients much as one would approach learning about wines. "It is unfortunate that as Westerners we think there is only one flavor to *hoisin* sauce, while we know that there is a who le range of balsamic vinegars," says Tropp. "We have a simplistic view of Asian ingredients that is further enhanced by grocery stores, where you will find a plethora of mediocrity."

Tropp took a very structured approach to learning about the ingredients of the Chinese kitchen. "After I came back from Taiwan, every time I went to Chinatown, I would buy as many things as I could. Then, being an academic, I kept file cards on what stuff was good and what I thought was drop-dead awful. I approached learning about any new item by sampling different versions and brands and keeping careful tasting notes," she recalls.

"I became interested in fish sauce, and, I tell you, that is something to try 'in the nude'!" she laughs, referring to tasting the ingredient right out of the bottle. "Line up seven types together and taste them straight up. After the initial shock, you'll start to discriminate not between what is 'best' and 'worst,' but between what your tongue perceives as 'good' and 'bad.' Saying 'I don't know what it should taste like' has some validity, but the ultimate validity is that it should taste *good*. If something doesn't taste good to you, it doesn't mean that it is incorrect—it means you don't like it, which will get you a long way. When you taste fish sauces, if you like one and an expert likes the other, your palate may be immature, or just different. So you work with the sauce you like best and then later retaste your basic ingredients to determine if the one you originally liked still appeals most to you.

"Tasting doesn't have to be an expensive proposition. You can do an extremely involved soy sauce tasting for under twenty dollars," she notes. "I use three to four soy sauces. For consistency, Kikkoman remains the brewed soy sauce of choice. I prefer light soy sauce because it contains more flavor notes due to the removal of some of its salt. I liken it to a woman of a certain age who is wearing a dark lipstick. All you can see is the lipstick, but when you look beyond it, you see that she has beautiful eyes and lovely hair. When salt is taken out of a very complex ingredient like soy sauce, you suddenly become aware of many other flavor notes.

"Tasting soy sauce is no different from tasting wine," she continues. "You want a proper flavor balance, and good beginning, middle, and end notes. Once you learn to segregate the flavor notes in your perception and keep an eye on balance, you will end up with something that tastes good even if you can't pronounce it.

"I love doing an anthropological trip to a grocery store," she says. "My motto is: 'Never buy just one brand—buy one of every brand available.' I do have some parameters, as I am a big believer in the theory that the less English and the more tawdry the language on the package, the better the ingredient. These are not absolutes, but they rarely steer me wrong.

"Unfortunately, quality control can be iffy, so you may have a great batch of something and a not-so-great batch wearing the same label. People who cook Chinese food seriously know this. You may buy an extraordinary brand of hoisin sauce that tastes better than any you have ever tasted, then it disappears from the market and you are stuck with Lee Kun Kee, which is the Skippy peanut butter of hoisin sauce; it is always the same: bland and sweet. You can rely on its mediocrity. Unfortunately, these products are often given free of charge to cooking schools in the United States, so students too often learn these mediocre flavors as benchmarks, not even realizing that there are better versions out there."

Dine

After you have researched a cuisine in other ways, top culinary experts recommend dining in restaurants serving the food of that country. However, doing so in the United States can be tricky, because so many restaurants serve "Americanized" food that hardly suggests the individual cuisine's traditional flavors.

"In the United States, the food products and cultural norms are different from those in the cuisine's home country," says Tropp. "Maybe abroad you crack a coconut, but here you open a can. In a Thai restaurant here, the spices used may be ground and come in bags. That is a totally different sensation on the palate than tasting spices that have been pounded and ground in a mortar and pestle. Part of the beauty of living in a large metropolitan area is that sometimes you can go to restaurants where the owners and cooks have not yet learned that you can buy coconut milk in cans!"

Still, dining has the potential to offer important instruction and inspiration. "There is that moment when you taste a dish that you have had many times before and it is perfect. That's when you realize why it is a great dish," observes Mark Miller. "You may have to eat a lot of bad couscous until you find one that inspires you. It may not happen for years, you have to have that passion that says, I am going to continue to look. It is out there!

"At the first meal I had at Fredy Girardet in Switzerland, I ordered a *petit pois* terrine. For every four slices cut, they could only use one because it was so fragile," Miller enthuses. "I have never had anything like that in my life again—but it's out there, and I am still looking!"

Conclusion

YOUR AROUND-THE-WORLD JOURNEY—either literally in the years to come, or virtually in the pages that follow—will lead you to experience new flavors and culinary philosophies from around the globe. Enjoy the adventure and the process of learning! Use the profiles of these ten cuisines as your starting point to develop new skills in the kitchen that can serve you no matter what, or where, you are cooking. Don't be content with a dilettante-like approach to your experimentation: Dig deep into these and other resources (recommended at the end of each chapter), and strive to master the cuisines that you'll be drawing on throughout your lifetime. Through embracing the principles shared by these experts, you'll be better equipped than ever to move toward achieving your potential as a New American chef.

Japan

CELEBRATING THE SEASONS
THROUGH ALL THE SENSES

*A Japanese meal is a
communion with nature.*

—HIROKO SHIMBO, AUTHOR, *THE JAPANESE KITCHEN*

WHILE "SEASONALITY" IS a mantra for chefs the world over—a determination to cook with only those ingredients seasonally available in the market—the Japanese elevate the idea to a whole new level. They make it a point to celebrate the seasons not only with the cuisine itself, but throughout every aspect of the environment in which a meal is served. This is reflected in everything from the materials and colors of the plates, bowls, and other serving dishes to the fabrics of the placemats and napkins to the flowers on the table to the artwork on the walls.

No other people go to such extremes to ensure that their food as well as their surroundings are in harmony with the seasons. Every Japanese meal alludes to the natural world. (Even take-out sushi features a plastic cut-out of grass, separating the pickled ginger from the sushi!) To the Japanese, the dining experience should be not mere sustenance, but an aesthetic encounter that nourishes *all* the senses.

"Japanese food is very sensuous," confirms Hiroko Shimbo. "The seasons in Japan are very distinct, so we're very aware of the changing of the seasons and take care to 'mirror' that in both the food and the environment."

Every sense is to be pleased—never startled or jarred. Appealing visuals create an environment that is welcoming to guests, and food is made attractive through careful presentation. The subtle use of scents provides further scintillation. Finally, the taste of the food is pleasing to the taste buds, while its array of textures and temperatures provides a variety of tactile experiences—from mouth-meltingly soft to chewy to crunchy—the sounds of which can hold their own enjoyment.

Influences on Japanese Cuisine

THE RITUALS OF JAPANESE CUISINE derive from those of the tea ceremony (*cha-no-yu*), which itself evolved from the Chinese tea code. In fifteenth-century Japan, the Zen Buddhist tea ceremony was perfected, detailing exact specifications for everything from the proper utensils to be used for preparing and serving the tea to the importance of including a natural component, such as a single blossom, on which to meditate. Its characteristic spirit, as suggested by the four Zen principles—harmony, respect, purity, and tranquility—permeates Japanese cuisine today.

The fact that Japan is a relatively small, mountainous country made up of small islands (four main islands plus thousands of smaller islands) has also had a marked impact on its cuisine. Notably, it lacks the often-distinctive regional variations observed in other countries, and its mostly coastal terrain explains the predominance of seafood. In addition, as only 15 percent of Japanese land is farmable, historically there has been a scarce

supply of food available to feed its population. Instead, Japan has managed to make the pragmatic necessity of small portions of food aesthetically desirable. By focusing on exquisite ingredients and presentations, Japanese cuisine has converted this limitation into a compelling and meaningful aesthetic that expresses an almost-reverential attitude toward food.

In individual dishes, the essence of each ingredient, as opposed to a blend of flavors, is emphasized. "Variety and interest in a Japanese dinner are achieved through serving an array of many different dishes," explains Hiroko Shimbo. "It is important to keep the flavors separate, which is why we use so many dishes. Each flavor plays a role in the meal."

The design of the Japanese bento box (a lunch or picnic box featuring individual compartments) is a ubiquitous example of these intentions. Each compartment in these lacquered wooden boxes contains a different food item with a unique presentation. The foods range from raw to cooked, including such items as sushi, blanched vegetables, steamed dumplings, grilled teriyaki, and crispy tempura.

Food is meant not only to be enjoyed on the palate, but also to be appreciated on the plate. Dishes are presented with larger pieces of food ("mountains") to the back and smaller pieces ("water") to the front. With sushi, the Japanese serve pickled ginger and wasabi arranged in mounds whose shapes echo the country's mountainous and hilly terrain. Vegetables are carved into shapes from nature, such as leaves and flowers. Garnishes, too, may be chosen not necessarily to complement the food but to accent the season, and might include, for example, actual tree leaves.

Even a small amount of a particular food can take on large significance. "When you eat a ten-course Japanese meal, a single pickled vegetable can provide a note of drama," says Mark Miller. "The drama comes from the pickle being so intense and the rest of the meal being so pure. That level of subtlety often escapes non-Japanese people, so they are not always able to fully appreciate a Japanese meal."

Bringing Nature Indoors

THERE ARE MANY WAYS in which nature is reflected indoors for the comfort and enjoyment of guests. "For example, we always take into account the weather in selecting a dish's preparation method and the temperature at which it's served," Hiroko Shimbo explains. "During the cold months, more hot dishes are served. In the summer, the main course will often be served cold—though not ice-cold, because that would cause the dish's flavor to suffer."

While Westerners are more likely to seek to conquer nature, the Japanese seek contact with nature—and to express their reverence for it. "We work hard to bring the seasons into our home and kitchen as a way of showing appreciation," says Shimbo. "Every season, my mother would change everything from the carpets to the art on the walls. Even the chair and floor cushions would be changed: In the warm months, they would be white and blue linen, while in the colder months, they would be dark red and brown wool.

"My mother also had four sets of dishes, whose patterns related to the four seasons," Shimbo recalls. "Now I own multiple sets of dishes as well. My spring dishes are ceramic with cherry blossoms, and the summer dishes are white, blue, and clear glass. My autumn dishes are earth-colored, and the winter dishes are even darker than those."

Masa Takayama of Ginza Sushi-Ko in New York uses his entire restaurant as a canvas on which to celebrate the seasons. "Atmosphere is very important to me, and I'm involved in every aspect of creating it at Ginza Sushi-Ko," says Takayama. "I visit the flower market every morning, and that can be a real inspiration. Recently, I constructed large bamboo stems connecting both walls, then cut holes in them and filled them with water to make little pools. In the spring, I use tiny cherry blossoms. I want to express to the customer that it is springtime, so they should wake up!"

After being shown to one of his restaurant's nine seats, a customer is taken further into Takayama's expression of the seasons. He is as serious about his presentations as he is about the food, paying careful attention to the plate chosen for serving each dish. "I am always thinking about flavor and visual contrast, combined with my own feeling about what is 'right,'" Takayama explains. "I even design my own plates and then have an artist make them for me. I know one who is very talented and can make anything that I come up with.

"My plate choices depend on the season," he says, echoing Hiroko Shimbo. "In winter, I like using brown or clay, which are earthy colors. In the summer, when diners

are hot, I will get them to think cool by making 'ice dishes'—literally, dishes carved from ice. I'll also use more white or turquoise plates, since I consider those to be summer colors. I'll even change the cups used for sake: in summer, I will take a piece of bamboo, cut a hole in it, and freeze it, then fill it with sake!

"I also like to play the plate's color, depth, width, and texture off the fish I'm serving. For example, *toro* is a little pink, so I like to serve it on a dark green dish. I like to wrap sea urchin around shrimp, and for that I prefer a brown dish. *Hamo* is a white fish, so it needs a colored plate; I may pair it with a red or sour plum color, then add a little broth to make it softer. If I am starting with caviar, I like to use a crystal plate.

"I don't have an artistic background," Takayama points out. "I just like combining visuals and featuring contrasts on my plates and in my restaurant. Some chefs don't care; they just slice the fish and put it on the plate. Not me. This is my own creation. Art and food are the same to me."

Pillars of Japanese Cuisine

MANY THINK OF PRISTINE FISH so perfect that it should be eaten raw as the star of Japanese cuisine. Yet rice is every bit its equal in importance. To a great extent, what make the fish, rice, and other ingredients that define Japanese cuisine shine so brightly are a handful of other key flavor enhancers—including *dashi, mirin, miso, sake,* and *shoyu* (soy sauce). These ingredients add depth of flavor while ensuring subtlety in Japanese cuisine.

Unlike cooks in other parts of the world, the Japanese use few spices; their seasoning is very delicate and refined. Although wasabi and mustard are used as condiments, they are relatively minor players. As contradictory as it sounds, the Japanese focus on adding layers of subtlety to their dishes.

Rice

Rice is a critical part of Japan's self-identity. It has been the staple grain for centuries and at one time was a sign of wealth. During the Middle Ages, real estate values were given in *koku,* a volume of rice, and samurai continued to be paid in *koku* even after cash became common.

Rice is eaten in its whole-grain form, but it is also widely consumed as flour, sake, and vinegar. "New rice," fresh from the fall harvest, is considered the best, and the source of each year's best new rice is hotly debated. For whole-grain rice, the short-

HIROKO SHIMBO ON SEASONAL HOLIDAYS

In Japan, we don't celebrate holidays such as Thanksgiving or Christmas. Instead, we celebrate the seasons. In fact, seasonality is so revered that there are not merely four seasons: each season is further divided into six subseasons, making twenty-four *sekkus*. Our holidays throughout the year include:

- **JANUARY:** New Year's is the most important national holiday in Japan. The day is one of joyful celebration, auspicious for the rest of the year. We always prepare a special dinner. *O-zoni*, New Year's soup, contains *mochi* (sweet rice cake) and vegetables such as daikon, carrot, and taro. *Osechi ryori* is also representative of New Year's dinners, which are packed and served in layered lacquerware boxes, containing an appetizer, grilled dish, simmered dish, and vinegared salad dishes.

- **FEBRUARY:** In this month, we celebrate the Sun Goddess, or the origin of Japan in 660 B.C. On *Setsuban* (February 3–4), which marks the beginning of spring, dry-roasted soybeans are thrown into every room and corner of Japanese houses to drive away evil

spirits and to welcome health and good fortune into the home for the new year. Each person eats one soybean for each year he or she has lived, plus one.

- **MARCH:** On Goddess Day, which is also known as Girls Day, we make a special dinner for our daughters to wish them a healthy and safe year. My mother prepared "doll sushi" (sushi rice wrapped in a thin omelet as a body, topped with a quail egg on which she placed two black sesame seeds as eyes and painted a red line for a mouth—it was cute sushi!) for us, as well as clam soup (as clams represent chastity; other clams such as abalone were eaten as sushi or steamed).

- **APRIL:** In celebration of bamboo shoot season, we serve lots of dishes made with bamboo shoots. You'll also see *hanami* (cherry blossom) bento boxes or dinners, with dishes made from seasonal ingredients, such as *tamagoyaki* (Japanese omelet), *tori no kara-age* (fried chicken), chicken and shrimp dumplings on skewers, and simmered spring vegetables such as bamboo shoots, fiddlehead ferns, and daikon radishes.

- **MAY:** Boys get their turn in May, when we prepare a special dinner for our sons, including such items as *kashiwa-mochi* (a rice cake wrapped in an oak leaf, as oak symbolizes strength and a successful life) and carp, a fish known as having a fighting spirit, as it climbs upstream. Foodwise, bonito is the highlight of the month, made into *tataki* (browned outside, with skin on, cut into sashimi slices, and served with herbs such as scallions, ginger, shiso, garlic, and/or daikon radish).

- **JUNE:** Plums become ripe, and about half of the population makes plum juice or plum wine. A sweet freshwater fish called *ayu* is also enjoyed. June is also rice-planting season.

- **JULY:** June and July represent the rainy season, which is terribly uncomfortable in Japan. The hottest part of Japanese summer falls on or around July 20, when it is recommended that *unagi* (eel) be eaten. Eel is rich in nutrients, and it is said to help one regain energy, both mentally and physically, in order to survive the hot and humid summer.

- **AUGUST:** This is the month we pray for a good harvest of rice, and all through Japan you'll see shrines for rice, which people carry through the streets with lots of shouting. Throughout the summer, cold dishes and preparations are enjoyed, from cold noodles to chilled soups. August 15 is thought to be the most beautiful moon of the year, and is celebrated at night with taro and special "moon-viewing dumplings," as well as the seven fall flowers: bush clover, Japanese pampas grass, Chinese bellflower, fringed pink, *ominaeshi, kuzu,* and *fuji bakama.*

- **SEPTEMBER:** This is the new moon, so we celebrate with a dinner for it. You'll see edible chrysanthemum flowers (which are traditionally eaten for longevity, in salads, tossed with cooked rice, and added to soups and simmered dishes) start to appear in food stores.

- **OCTOBER**: We not only have the harvest celebration to enjoy autumn delicacies such as chestnuts, gingko nuts, persimmons, and fish such as pike and sardines, but this is also the season of the matsutake mushroom, which is very prized. It has a wonderful bouquet and one piece can cost a hundred dollars. It is cooked with rice or soup to stretch the flavor because it is so expensive.

- **NOVEMBER**: On November 15, we celebrate *Shichigo-san,* on which day children aged seven, five, and three are dressed in traditional kimono costumes and visit the shrines to offer a prayer for protection and normal growth. At home, mothers prepare a special "7-5-3" dinner that includes *sekihan* (rice with azuki beans), salt-grilled sea bream, simmered seasonal vegetables, Japanese omelet, and

clear soup. This is the season of yellowtail tuna, cod, monkfish, lobster, and oysters, as well as *mastsuba-gani* crab. The crab has a small body and long legs and is very sweet. We also celebrate the change of colors in October and November.

- **DECEMBER**: We have lots of banquets in December, gearing up for the New Year, where you'll see all your friends and family. We call the parties "Forget-the-Year" parties: whatever you did wrong during the year, you're encouraged to forget it for the New Year. December is the month of *nabe-mono,* or hot-pot dishes. On the last day of the year, we finish our day eating *toshikoshi soba,* which literally means "crossover-the-year buckwheat noodles." Because of the noodles' length, they symbolize longevity. At midnight, the bells of the temples ring 108 times, representing the 108 sins to avoid in the New Year.

grain varieties are often preferred because they are quite moist when cooked, remaining firm yet sticky enough to be picked up easily with chopsticks. Masa Takayama, however, prefers *koda,* which he considers "the perfect long-grain rice." Except for glutinous rice, which is steamed, Japanese rice is usually boiled. It may be served plain (*gohan* or *meshi*); cooked with something else, such as beans or chestnuts (*takikomi-gohan*); mixed with other things after cooking (*maze-gohan*); made into a gruel (*okayu*); or vinegared for use with sushi (*sushi-meshi*).

"The bottom line is that to master Japanese cooking, you have to know how to cook rice," asserts Kaz Okochi, chef-owner of Kaz Sushi Bistro in Washington, D.C. "In America, rice is a side dish. In Japan, it is *the* dish. A good bowl of rice is very important. As a professional cook, I wash rice before cooking it. The rice comes out nicer that way, although it takes away some of the nutrients. The most important thing about cooking rice is the amount of water you use. Every bag of rice cooks differently, so you need to be aware of this, and to taste and adjust.

"Freshly harvested rice from the fall cooks differently from older rice," he explains. "A bag of the harvest rice will have a sticker on it indicating that it is from the 'new crop.' With new-crop rice, you cut back on the water. Later in the year, as the rice dries out, you increase the amount of water. After one bite, we know how to adjust it, which is something that comes from experience. You must realize that growing up in Japan, we eat rice 365 days a year. I would compare it to working with bread. Once [Washington, D.C., chef] Roberto Donna was pointing out the subtleties of good and bad bread to me, but I couldn't tell the difference because I didn't grow up eating bread."

Understanding the nuances of rice doesn't come naturally to most Americans either," says Mark Miller. "Americans don't respect rice. In Japan, rice has a milling date and, by law, can only be sold for a certain period of time, then must be removed from the shelves. In America, we have been eating stale rice all our lives."

Dashi

A good way to get a sense of the Japanese palate is to make a dashi broth or some miso soup.

—KAZ OKOCHI

In Japan, *dashi,* a fish-flavored broth made primarily from dried bonito (a type of tuna) and kombu, a seaweed, is the equivalent of stock in the Western kitchen. In American restaurant cooking, chicken stock is most commonly used. However, as the Japanese diet relies far more on fish, fish stock is more appropriate to the Japanese marriage of flavors.

In Japanese tradition, the soup course reveals how well a cook has made dashi, the key component for all the dishes that will follow. Aside from its use as a stock, dashi is also used in many other ways, such as to poach vegetables. "When you order vegetables in a restaurant, they will be cooked in a light dashi broth with a little soy sauce," says Kaz Okochi. "They would never be poached in just water. Dashi is good for poaching vegetables because the vegetables will absorb its flavor. Spinach is commonly eaten in Japan, and it is great poached in dashi with a dash of soy. Dashi is very delicate and very healthy."

Mirin

Mirin is a sweet golden-brown wine made from rice, used exclusively for cooking. "It is a source of sweetness that is more refined than sugar," explains Hiroko Shimbo. "We use mirin in almost every food preparation, so the body is satisfied and doesn't crave sweet foods.

"Mirin is the most important ingredient for a marinade," she continues. "It is used in teriyaki and for basting eel, and it makes for a rich, glossy sauce. It is important to get authentic, not synthetic, mirin, so be sure to check the label."

Miso

Miso is a soybean paste that has a texture similar to creamy peanut butter. It is made from fermented soybeans combined with one of three different bases—barley, rice, or wheat—and a special yeast. There are many types to choose from, and they range in flavor and color intensity. Darker misos have been fermented longer and tend to be saltier and more robust-flavored, while lighter misos are less salty and more delicately flavored. Miso is not an ingredient that needs to be replaced often, as it will keep in the refrigerator for up to a year after opening.

"Miso, which was developed in the seventeenth century as a preservative, is a source of salt, but it has more amino acids," explains Hiroko Shimbo. "It is very versatile, and used in soups, dressings, marinades, and sauces. There are two basic types of miso, light and dark, with light used most often for soups and dark for marinades. A good dark miso should be fermented for at least a year, and some are aged for up to three years. Most light miso is only fermented for three to six months. I recommend Miso Master brand, which is made in the U.S. and can be found in health food stores."

"Miso is great to work with," enthuses Kaz Okochi. "While making soup from miso is very common, it is also great in a marinade for beef or fish." Shimbo echoes Okochi, pointing out that miso-marinated beef is a good place for a beginning cook to start, because it's an easy way to taste how miso adds a great deal of flavor. "Marinate a steak overnight in miso and cook it medium-rare, then add a little more miso, sugar, and brandy to the pan," she instructs. "You will have a great dish!"

Sake

Sake is a clear wine made from rice that is becoming increasingly popular in the United States. It can be very fragrant, with flowery or tropical aromas. Not only is it traditionally Japan's most popular alcoholic beverage, but it also plays a large role in the country's cooking. While it was initially used by the Japanese for its food tenderizing properties, it is valued as a flavor enhancer and balancer (especially as it subdues saltiness).

"Sake is like a great wine used in French cooking, in that it has the ability to soften flavors," Hiroko Shimbo points out. "Sake is used for marinating, braising, poaching, simmering, and steaming foods. It is especially good for steaming fish, as it is such a delicate medium that it manages to add flavor without overpowering the fish. As with any wine you would use for cooking, the rule of thumb is to use a sake you would also be willing to drink."

Soy Sauce

Because soy sauce is used so frequently in Japanese cooking and is always on the table, it is important to learn how to choose one. "Soy sauce, or *shoyu*, is made from toasted

WASABI is the bright green condiment commonly served alongside the pickled ginger with sushi or sashimi. It has a very strong flavor that is a cross between dried yellow mustard and horseradish, so a little goes a long way. There are two types of wasabi available, dried and fresh, but in the United States the dried version, which is reconstituted by being mixed with a little water, is by far the most common. Wasabi powder is easy to find and keeps well. Fresh wasabi can be found in the Pacific Northwest (e.g., Oregon and Washington), as well as imported from Japan.

"The perception is that fresh wasabi is hotter than dried wasabi, but that is not the case," Kaz Okochi explains. "The easiest comparison would be fresh herbs to dry herbs; they simply have different flavors. Fresh wasabi is grainier and has a slightly milder, sweeter taste. Dried, or powdered wasabi, as it is more commonly known, has a flatter and spicier flavor."

Masa Takayama cautions on the proper use of wasabi: "Some people put wasabi into their dish of soy sauce and stir it around. However, at our restaurant we use fresh wasabi, and if you stir it around in the soy sauce, you lose all of its flavor. It is important that the fresh wasabi never touch the soy sauce. So if you like wasabi, just rub a little on the fish." (Hiroko Shimbo recommends the Oregon-grown wasabi available from Pacific Farms, which can be reached at www.freshwasabi.com or 800–927–2248.)

soybeans, and the best ones have lots of flavor," says Hiroko Shimbo. "Nothing marries better with raw fish than a good soy sauce! I recommend buying a Japanese brand, one that has been aged about one and a half years. It is wise to go to the expense of choosing a good soy sauce, because a cheap one will not have much flavor."

"In Japan, there are many different brands of soy sauce," says Kaz Okochi. "In addition to the big producers you'll find small soy sauce breweries. In the U.S., we don't have much variety. I like Yamasa soy sauce, which I'll use as a base, adding dashi and sweet sake to it to make my own milder blend."

At Ginza Sushi-ko, Masa Takayama actually blends different "levels" of sauce for each fish he serves, as well as for his sushi and sashimi. "I will use a stronger soy blend for fattier fish like tuna, while for white fish I like a lighter blend," he explains. "For sashimi, I will blend soy sauce with ponzu. For sushi, I'll blend soy with sweet sake."

Kaz Okochi is dismayed by the quantity of soy sauce used by many Americans, which can overpower some foods' delicate flavors. "It is funny that we get requests from customers for low-sodium sauce, and then we watch the same people drown their sushi in the sauce," he laments. "In Japan, we pour just enough soy into the dipping dish to cover the bottom, then we dip just a corner of our food into the sauce. When you pick up a piece of sushi, you should touch only the fish side to the soy sauce. If you dip your sushi rice side down, the rice breaks into the sauce, and it's terrible."

Techniques for Japanese Cooking

Japanese cuisine depends gently on water.   **—JAPANESE CHEF'S PROVERB**

AS A GENERAL RULE, Japanese food is cooked only lightly. Fresh ingredients are sliced into thin or small uniform pieces, then cooked quickly to maximize and celebrate, not hide, their flavors. Ingredients are most frequently simmered, steamed, fried, or cooked quickly over very high heat. With the exception of grilling, the most common cooking techniques don't impart their own strong flavors.

"While we started with a strong influence from China, over the centuries our food became 'Japanized,'" says Hiroko Shimbo. "We describe our cuisine as 'cooking by water.' That means we employ lots of blanching, steaming, and boiling. The Japanese also use very little oil. Chinese cooking, in contrast, can be represented as 'cooking by fire.' They use lots of oil in, and very intense heat under, their woks."

Soup is a good example of the Japanese cooking philosophy in action. Because the base is made from dashi, rather than a slowly simmered poultry- or meat-based stock, it does not require a long cooking time. Japanese soups are often bulked up with such items as noodles, eggs, or thin slices of pork, all of which go in at the last minute and require only brief cooking time.

Steaming

Steaming is a universal cooking technique, valued the world around for the same reason: it is an efficient way to cook evenly and quickly, to lock in flavor, and to retain moisture. The Japanese steam vegetables, chicken, and some (nonfatty) fish. In addition, steaming is ideal for dumplings, such as *shu mai*. As in simmering, water may be used, but more often the Japanese will employ a flavored liquid (such as dashi), the components of which will be tailored to enhance the flavor of the specific ingredient being steamed.

Steaming, like simmering, is loaded with technique. Some items are steamed over high heat (e.g., vegetables), while others are best steamed on medium or low heat (e.g., custard, tofu, ground meats). The steaming vessel used is a matter of choice, though Hiroko Shimbo recommends a Chinese bamboo steamer because it cooks food so evenly.

Simmering

Simmering, a very delicate cooking technique, underscores the ability of the Japanese cook to create subtly flavored dishes. "Simmering is used a lot in home cooking," Kaz Okochi says. "We don't use much oil at home. Instead, we will make a simmering broth from soy sauce, dashi, sake, mirin, and sugar. Those ingredients are the base, but the proportions will vary depending on what you are cooking. It can be used for chicken, fish, or beef. One of the most popular simmered dishes in Japan is thinly sliced beef, onions, and potatoes cooked in that broth. It is great, and I don't know why it is not more popular in the U.S."

There are a dozen subcategories of simmering, many of them with their own sub-subcategories. What differentiates the categories is the combination of liquids used, which depends on what is being cooked. A broth that is appropriate for pork, for example, will not necessarily be appropriate for chicken or duck.

Other techniques also come into play. In Japanese cooking, simmering is not simply a matter of ingredients being dropped into a pot of flavorful broth over low heat. Poultry, such as duck or chicken, may be seared first to render its fat before being placed in the broth, and vegetables are often blanched before they are finished off in the broth. And, in the final step, other ingredients may be added to the broth, turning it into a sauce.

Note that the lid used for simmering is also important. Its circumference should be a little smaller than that of the pot, so it keeps the food submerged in the liquid but also enables steam to escape, so that the pot does not boil over.

Yakimono: Grilling, Broiling, and Panfrying

The term *yakimono* encompasses grilling, broiling, and panfrying. It essentially refers to cooking quickly over (or under) high heat so that the interior of the food remains tender while the outside takes on a characteristic crispiness. Most often the food has been marinated, and for broiling and grilling, it is often put onto skewers before it is cooked.

The Japanese grill a variety of foods, from shellfish and meats to vegetables and bean curd on skewers. One of the most popular dishes using this method is *yakitori* (skewered bite-sized pieces of chicken). Just as you will find restaurants specializing in noodles or sushi, there are yakitori restaurants in Japan. Yakitori items are often marinated and then continually basted with a mixture of sake, soy, and mirin. This not only infuses the chicken with great flavor, but also imparts color and shine.

Deep-Frying

Deep-frying is a common Japanese technique. The Japanese have taken deep-frying to an art form in that fried food doesn't taste greasy; rather, it tastes of the ingredient, and its crunchy light crisp exterior or coating. A tempura batter used for frying may contain ice cubes to keep it light. The temperature and depth of oil are very carefully monitored, to ensure that the ingredient will cook quickly and not have a chance to absorb the flavor of the oil.

The Japanese also coat fried dishes with *panko*, coarse dried bread crumbs, which add an additional layer of crunch. The resulting texture is almost an airy, fluffy crispiness. Hiroko Shimbo explains that this breading helps to lock in juices, keeping the meat moist. Panko are available in most Asian markets.

DEVELOP YOUR DEEP-FRYING TECHNIQUE

BY MAKING *TONKATSU* (DEEP-FRIED PORK CUTLETS)

Katsu is a hundred-year-old fusion dish originating from when Western [including German] influences flooded Japan. Tonkatsu was made by French chefs in Western-style restaurants. —HIROKO SHIMBO

This is a good, uncomplicated dish that doesn't require many ingredients.

USE pork cutlets sliced ½ inch thick. First, dip each one into flour and then into beaten egg, then repeat. Next, dip into panko. Coating the pork so many times makes for a crispy crust.

DEEP-FRY the pork in 360-degree oil for 8 to 10 minutes.

DRAIN the pork, and slice it into ½-inch-wide strips.

SERVE with tonkatsu sauce, which can be store-bought or made at home from roughly equal parts Worcestershire sauce, sugar, soy sauce, and ketchup, reduced over heat by one-fifth, then seasoned with French mustard and a pinch of allspice.

SHREDDED cabbage is tonkatsu's traditional accompaniment. While it was originally served with other vegetables, one day a chef grabbed cabbage instead. It turned out that cabbage was a great match—it is an antioxidant and cuts the fat of the dish.

42

NOODLES are almost as ubiquitous in Japanese cuisine as pasta is in Italian. Typical noodles include *soba,* made from buckwheat, and *udon,* made from wheat. Soba tends to be more popular in eastern Japan, while udon predominates in western Japan.

Soba noodles are revered not only for their flavor, but also for their distinctive texture. The quality of the soba noodle is said to be dependent on three things: *hikitate* (how the dough is kneaded), *chitate* (how the noodles are formed), and *yudetate* (how they are boiled).

"Noodles are my favorite!" Kaz Okochi enthuses. "To me, though, the worst food in the world is bad, overcooked noodles. At our restaurant, we don't even work with them, because they are such a specialty, and I don't want to do anything halfway. It is funny that in the U.S., people expect restaurants to have everything. However, in Japan, restaurants specialize in only one thing. I believe in that, which is why we stay focused on what we do best: sushi.

"When I was growing up, I had a favorite restaurant that made ramen noodles [Chinese-style soba noodles] with three or four toppings, and that was it. If you wanted soba or udon noodles, you had to go to a different restaurant. In the United States, I like the noodles at Honmura An restaurant in New York City, where they make their own."

Time to Eat

Japan has embraced many foods of the West, and their influence can be seen in the home as well as in restaurants. "Only about a third of the cooking done at home today is traditional Japanese," says Hiroko Shimbo. "Mothers make their kids lots of spaghetti, curried rice, and hamburgers—and some easy stir-fried dishes."

Breakfast

"In the countryside, people still eat a more traditional Japanese-style breakfast, such as a bowl of rice, miso soup, an omelet, possibly some dried fish and pickled vegetables," says Shimbo. "However, in the cities, 75 percent of the people eat a Western breakfast of a very thick piece of toast. The bread in Tokyo is great. They have very good bakeries, and you can get good heavy German breads, French baguettes, and Italian breads. In other parts of Japan without good bakeries, people eat what would best be described as really thick Wonder Bread.

"People drink tea, but coffee is very much a national drink. You will also find bagels, but they are much smaller than American bagels."

Lunch

While noodles are often enjoyed for lunch, the bento box is also very common in Japan. "It is even used by kids to take their lunch to school," says Kaz Okochi. "My mother made my lunch all through junior high and high school. I actually had two bento boxes. The first would have a piece of grilled fish, potato croquettes with beef, crab, or shrimp, an egg, and some spaghetti. My mother would do daily variations on this. The second box would be just for rice, because I was a big eater!"

Dinner

"Many other cultures like one-pot food," observes Hiroko Shimbo, "but in Japanese cooking, that is not done very often. Instead, we prefer twenty different ingredients to get a variety of nutrients on the plate. To keep the meal balanced and light, you would not serve two dishes that were both deep-fried. This meal could be typical of dinner or lunch, but at lunch the portions would be smaller."

- Bowl of rice
- Soup: miso or clear dashi
- Protein: a small portion of about four ounces of meat or fish
- Vegetables: two to three dishes, including a tofu dish that will be simmered, fried, stir-fried, or blanched, with dressing
- Pickled vegetables: always
- Dessert: fruit is served as dessert, and always reflects what is best in season. Even if it is just a grape, the grape will be peeled, seeded, and presented.

Beverages

What is drunk with a Japanese meal? "Beer is very popular with meals and is inexpensive," says Shimbo. "While sake is drunk, it has been falling in popularity. People are drinking more wine now, but sake actually pairs far better with the food of Japan. Sake is subtle and goes with the delicate flavors of the fish and food."

"It is nice to drink beer with a Japanese meal, then to switch to sake," recommends Kaz Okochi. "We have a wine list at our restaurant only because there is such a demand for it."

Restaurant Dining Traditions

THE JAPANESE CULINARY TRADITION of respect for the senses and the seasons is not just the responsibility of the chef in a restaurant; it is important for the diner as well to show respect and appreciation for what the chef has created and shared.

The Japanese won't do business with anyone until they've shared a meal with them. "The way the dining ritual works in Japan is that meals will be spread out over a year or so," explains Mark Miller. "If you are an American in Japan, the first meeting will be at your hotel. The second will be at a Japanese restaurant where your hosts take lots of other Westerners. The third might be for tempura, because they know Westerners like fried things. It is not until the fourth or fifth meeting that you will get to go to a 'real' Japanese restaurant. That only happens if you have a real passion for the food and interact well with your hosts. You must show good etiquette—for example, by pouring the sake or tea for everyone else, by not talking about business, and by being sure to mention how much you like everything, because your hosts want you to like everything. The first meetings are just to find out who you are and what you like.

"I once went with my host and business colleague Mr. Yamada to a restaurant where there were two seats at the bar and eight seats total in the restaurant. They served wild raw black chickens with hot oil poured on top as a sashimi course. Some people who have worked with him for fifteen years had never gone to that restaurant. Americans would never be able to find the restaurant, because they wouldn't know the right people and they wouldn't be allowed in if they stumbled upon it. The restaurant experience is not something you buy. Rather, you have to earn the right to go to a great chef's restaurant. You have to be educated. Just because someone has money and eats out in New York and France doesn't mean they will behave correctly in Japan. This is about the culture of a cuisine. Not only do you have to respect the people, but you have to respect yourself."

The same standards apply when dining at Japanese restaurants in the United States. "When someone calls Ginza Sushi-Ko for a reservation, we ask if this will be their first visit to the restaurant," says Masa Takayama. "Then we explain what we serve and the price [easily several hundred dollars per person]. I try to get a sense of the person and may not take their reservation if I don't think they will 'get' what we do, only because that kind of person can be scary. I never want to ruin the experience for my other guests.

Chopsticks should always be placed horizontally, parallel to the dish.

—HIROIKO SHIMBO

RESTAURANTS most often use wooden chopsticks. Everyday ones for at-home use are lacquered, and more formal ones are made from plain cedar. When food requires two or more bites, the piece generally remains grasped in the chopsticks while each successive bite is chewed and swallowed. It's impolite to point or gesture with chopsticks. Never stick chopsticks upright in rice, and never use chopsticks to grasp something from someone else's chopsticks—both actions are related to Japan's funeral traditions and are taboo during dining. When serving oneself from a communal bowl, use the other ends of the chopsticks.

"I define my success by having my favorite customers at the sushi bar, with perfect ingredients from Japan, serving my favorite dishes in season and watching people enjoy them," he continues. "A terrible night is having people who refuse to use chopsticks or who say, 'What's this? I don't eat this.' One night, the bar was nearly full of people having such a good time that they had become one. Two people walked in at nine-thirty and before the woman had even sat down, she said, 'I don't eat any fish.' The mood was broken. I explained that this is a sushi restaurant, and sent her away to get a hamburger!"

Customizing the Meal to the Customer

Once guests are deemed "welcomed" through the informal rituals described by Mark Miller above, it is an important part of Japanese hospitality to learn what one's guests like, so they can be pleased. This sometimes presents cultural challenges.

"Customers are a little different in the U.S. than they are in Japan," notes Kaz Okochi. "In Japan, they expect the freshest seasonal fish, done in a simple way. In the U.S., they always ask for something 'different' or unique. In Japan, a beautiful plate with a piece of grilled sardine on it is considered done, and that alone could be served in the best restaurant in Japan. If you put that sardine on a white plate in a fancy restaurant in the U.S., the customer would ask, 'What is this?'"

How does a chef design a menu to please a customer he doesn't know well? "There are no textbook answers," Okochi says. "What is nice about the sushi bar is that you give the person his food piece by piece, so you have time to think about the menu in your head as you go along. A sushi chef is kind of like a sommelier, but instead of matching wine to food, chefs match food to the customer. They have to look at the customer, then vary the menu by matching ingredients to the customer's taste, all while keeping in mind the ingredients that are at their peak that day.

"When making sushi for a customer, you vary the fish according to their taste," he continues. "Some people really like white fish, which is very subtle. Others like things spicy. You need to create a variety within those boundaries. Some fish tastes very fishy, so you don't want to serve sweeter fish before that. Also, vary the textures. All that comes from your imagination and experience. The key is to think about it before you send it to the customer."

The Changing Constant

JAPANESE CUISINE IS ONE of the world's most distinctive cuisines because of its unique history. Japan underwent a period of self-imposed isolation from the 1600s until the mid-1850s, during which time it was impervious to outside influences. It was not until the mid-nineteenth century, when borders were re-opened, that such Western practices as the public consumption of meat were adopted. The Portuguese introduced the Japanese to fried foods, resulting in the welcome addition of tempura to the array of dishes for which Japanese cuisine is known.

How can today's chefs respect the cuisine's traditions while also experimenting with it? The experts we interviewed have been able to explore these boundaries after coming to America to cook, which forced them to look anew at their own criteria for how far their native cuisine should be stretched.

THE ORDER OF A FORMAL MENU

A basic Japanese menu consists of soup, sashimi or sushi, a simmered dish, and a broiled dish. At an informal dinner, a small number of dishes are presented at the same time. Traditionally, though, there are seven courses of the Japanese tea ceremony, and while there may be more or fewer dishes served individually at intervals during a formal meal, it will typically be an odd number of dishes. In accordance with the Japanese proverb that "a stomach four-fifths full knows no doctors," portions are small, each consisting of just a bite or two. The order of a formal dinner:

appetizer

clear soup

sashimi

grilled dish

steamed dish

simmered dish

deep-fried dish

vinegar-flavored salad dish

rice (*gohan*)

miso soup (*miso shiru*)

pickled vegetables

green tea

When a course does not feature either hot soup or tea, sake is typically served.

CREATING A MENU AT GINZA SUSHI-KO

IN OUR BOOK DINING OUT, Ruth Reichl (then restaurant critic for the *New York Times* and now editor of *Gourmet* magazine) describes Ginza Sushi-Ko as "the only restaurant where the food is as good as you get in Japan." *Gourmet*'s restaurant critic Jonathan Gold refers to it as "being seasonal, as only a Japanese restaurant can be: they have things that are in season just two days!" So how does a chef who owns what some consider to be the most expensive restaurant in America decide what to serve his guests? Chef-owner Masa Takayama explains:

I get 90 to 95 percent of my fish from Japan. Sometimes, if there is a typhoon in Japan and the fishermen can't go out, I will have to close for the night. I will have to cancel the reservations, and it can be very disappointing because people come from New York and Europe to eat here.

Fish from California does not taste the same as the fish from Japan. It is not bad; it is just not the flavor I am looking for. The Kobe Sea off

Japan has warm water, like the Mediterranean, and is filled with good plankton. Small fish eat the plankton, then larger fish eat them, and so on. It does what good soil does for produce: fish that eat good fish are better fish! In California, the water is cold and does not have the same plankton.

The French and Italians sauté or grill fish and finish it in a butter sauce or an oil, which is fine. My style

Many agree that some popular American "innovations" aren't necessarily good for the cuisine. "I hate it when people try to 'Americanize' Japanese food, or when people come in and ask for things like California rolls," says Takayama. "I have to explain to them that we don't serve those kinds of things."

Hiroko Shimbo recalls an American chef who took a class with her, mentioning that the most popular dish at his restaurant was a "Japanese" dish. "He said it was called

is lighter because my food is simply fish with a little soy or wasabi. You can taste the difference and the nuances, so I need fish with the most flavor possible.

The menu depends on how I am feeling and what I want to eat. I will start with something light and then go to some small richer dishes. The dinner will be about seventeen courses, and since we are a sushi restaurant, the menu will feature sushi and sashimi.

- Most people come in hungry, so I like to start with a little punch! I might begin with Russian or Iranian caviar on grilled *toro* [a fatty tuna].

- Then, I might serve white truffle with the sperm sac from a cod that has been steamed, strained, and mixed with a little rice to make it creamy.

- Next, maybe raw fish, depending on the season. Today we have sweet shrimp. It is bright red, very tiny, and very sweet.

- I would follow that with blowfish in a salad, then fried blowfish.

- Then I would move on to sushi, like *toro* or white fish.

- For dessert, I would serve only one flavor of sorbet, like grapefruit or pomegranate.

To drink, I recommend sake or a white wine like a Chablis or a Riesling. It should be a light white. I have a small wine list with white and red Burgundies. Some of my regulars will call and ask what I am serving and bring something from their own cellar.

'drunken shrimp,' for which he made a shrimp tempura, topping it with mayonnaise and a spicy sauce before broiling it," she winces. "But shrimp should not be tortured that way! Tempura should be very fresh shrimp, fried quickly."

Kaz Okochi notes that his early cooking had international influences even before he left Japan's borders. "When I was a teenager, part of what inspired me to want to pursue cooking as a career was watching a French chef on TV every week," he says. "I

SPRING	SUMMER	FALL	WINTER
Bamboo shoots	Abalone	Apples	Cod
Bonito	Cherries	Chestnuts	Crab (matsuba-
Daikon	Corn	Chrysanthemum	gani)
Fiddlehead ferns	Cucumbers	flowers (edible)	Daikon
Green tea (new	Eel	Ginkgo nuts	Lobster
green tea, or	Eggplant	Grapes	Monkfish liver
shincha, appears	Loquats	Melon	Oysters
in April/May)	Noodles, served	Mushrooms	Sake, especially hot
Kiwi	cold	Pears	Soba noodles,
Loquats	Octopus	Persimmons	especially hot
Melon	Okra	Pike	Spinach
Short-necked clams	Peaches	Rice (new)	Stews
(asari)	Peppers (green bell)	Salmon and salmon	Tangerines
Strawberries	Pineapple	roe	Yellowtail
	Plums	Sardines	Preparations: hot-
	Tofu		pot dishes, stews,
	Tomatoes		long noodles
	Watermelons		

attended culinary school in Osaka, and at school I was also taught classic French cooking. The teachers were at the top of their professions, and Michelin three-star chefs often came to teach.

"But in 1988, I came to Sushi-Ko in Washington, D.C., which was one of the oldest sushi restaurants in town. I was stubborn about what I would make for a guest. If I didn't think a guest's request would work, I refused to do it. However, now that I own my own restaurant, I am a little more flexible."

Okochi is clear as to the time and place that's right for experimentation. "Sometimes, inspiration will come from a flavor combination I had elsewhere," he says. "But, to be honest, I would guess that 90 percent of my experiments don't work. So if I am creating something for the customer in the moment, I don't gamble." He keeps a few rules of thumb in mind. "For example, I don't like mixing fish—I would not want to put tuna, salmon, and yellowtail together. What I think about is what texture or spice will best accent a particular fish. I believe that what I cook now is 'Japanese' food," he says, "because I am Japanese, I am from Japan, and my training is Japanese."

Takayama never deviates from the time-tested principle of designing a menu around the season and pleasing the senses. "However, I'll change the menu for my regulars, some of whom come in every week," he says. "Sometimes I'll use white truffles and other non-Japanese ingredients. But I always use them with a traditional touch that keeps the overall effect within the realm of Japanese cuisine."

NachWaxman's Recommended Reading on Japanese Cooking

In Japan, there are different restaurants for different kinds of foods: you'll go to a sushi restaurant for sushi and a soba restaurant for soba noodles; there are even eel restaurants! Likewise, many of the books on Japanese cooking tend to segment by specialty, so there are relatively few general Japanese cookbooks.

One fine one, however, is ***Japanese Cooking: A Simple Art*** by Shizuo Tsuji, which provides good coverage of all types and styles of cooking. He was a master teacher in Japan who also ran the country's largest professional cooking school. It is a good, large, and important book.

I'd also recommend Hiroko Shimbo's ***The Japanese Kitchen,*** which has a somewhat different outlook. Her book covers a range from traditional dishes to new-style Japanese dishes, including some of her own modest, decorous fusion dishes.

For a further departure from traditional Japanese cuisine, there's ***Tetsuya: Recipes from Australia's Most Acclaimed Chef*** by Tetsuya Wakuda. We carried the Australian edition of this book for eight to ten months before it was published in the United States, and it flew off the shelves, catching people's imaginations as few books do, with its emphasis on advanced, innovative Japanese cooking.

There's an interesting book called ***A Taste of Japan*** by Donald Richie. It doesn't have any recipes, but it gives a nice overview of the many styles of Japanese cuisine, offering enriching detail on its traditions, customs, and etiquette.

Lots of people ask me about sushi books because they want to try their hand at making sushi at home. In truth, no book can teach you how to cut fish so that it sings on the plate. That only comes from a sushi apprenticeship—during which you may spend the first five years of your career sharpening knives. While we have lots of books on sushi, I particularly recommend the ***Book of Sushi*** by Kinjiro Omae, which will at least give you a good foot in the door. It addresses the styles, techniques, etiquette, and history of sushi.

Ichiban Dashi
Primary Dashi

4 cups cold water

1 ounce *konbu* (giant kelp)

1 ounce dried bonito flakes
(*hana-katsuo*)

MAKES 1 QUART

FILL A MEDIUM POT with the water and konbu. Bring to just below a boil: it is very important not to let the water boil! If the mixture boils, the konbu will be too strong. Remove the konbu from the pot and insert your thumbnail into the fleshiest part of it. If it is still tough, return it to the pot for 1 or 2 minutes, adding approximately ¼ cup of cold water to keep the stock from boiling.

AFTER REMOVING THE KONBU, bring the stock to a full boil. Add ¼ cup cold water to bring the temperature down quickly and immediately add the bonito flakes (you don't need to stir them). Bring to a full boil again, and immediately remove from the heat. The bonito flakes shouldn't boil for more than a few seconds, or the stock will become too strong and bitter. (If you happen to make this mistake, use the stock as a base for a thick soup or simmered dish.)

ALLOW THE BONITO FLAKES to start to settle to the bottom of the pot (30 seconds to 1 minute). Skim off the foam, then strain the dashi through a cheesecloth-lined sieve, leaving the bonito flakes behind.

Ebi Suimono
Clear Soup with Shrimp

1 small piece dried wakame seaweed

4 medium shrimp, shelled but tails left intact, deveined, rinsed, and patted dry

Salt

Cornstarch for dredging

2½ cups Primary Dashi (page 52)

About 1 tablespoon light soy sauce or slightly more dark soy sauce

4 slivers lemon rind

SERVES 4

SOAK THE WAKAME in cold water for 20 minutes to soften; drain. Cut out any hard parts and discard, then cut into 1-inch lengths. (If desired, to bring out its bright green color and ensure tenderness, first blanch the wakame in boiling water for 30 seconds, then drain and quickly plunge into cold water.)

SALT THE SHRIMP LIGHTLY and dredge in cornstarch. Blanch in boiling unsalted water for 2 minutes; drain.

IN A MEDIUM SAUCEPAN, bring the dashi to a simmer over medium heat; do not allow to boil. Gradually add about 1½ teaspoons salt, dissolving it little by little; stir frequently and taste so you don't add too much.

GRADUALLY ADD THE soy sauce, again stirring and tasting frequently. (The higher quality the dashi, the less soy sauce required.)

WARM INDIVIDUAL SOUP BOWLS by filling them with hot water and allowing to stand for 1 to 2 minutes, then drain thoroughly and wipe dry. Arrange 1 shrimp and a small amount of seaweed in each bowl. Ladle in the seasoned stock, and add a sliver of lemon rind to each bowl. Serve immediately.

53

RECIPES INSPIRED BY Japan

Masu no Agemono
Deep-Fried Fillet of Trout

2 rainbow trout (6–8 ounces each), cleaned, scaled, and filleted (skin left on), or 4 skin-on rainbow trout fillets

2 cups bamboo shoots

½ medium carrot

5 dried shiitake mushrooms, soaked in hot water until softened, drained, and trimmed

4 snow peas, strings removed

3 tablespoons vegetable oil

2½ cups Primary Dashi (page 52)

2 tablespoons rice wine vinegar

2 tablespoons sugar

2½ tablespoons dark soy sauce

Flour for dredging

Vegetable oil for deep-frying

2 tablespoons cornstarch, mixed with 2 tablespoons water

SERVES 4

SCORE THE FLESH SIDES of the trout fillets with shallow cuts at ¼-inch intervals to allow the heat and flavoring to penetrate quickly and to keep them from curling in the hot oil. Set aside.

CUT THE BAMBOO SHOOTS, carrot, and shiitakes into slices about the same size as the whole snow peas (to equalize the cooking time).

IN A LARGE SKILLET, heat the 3 tablespoons oil until hot. Add and stir-fry all the vegetables until thoroughly coated with hot oil and beginning to soften (about 2 minutes). Add the dashi, stir, and add the vinegar, sugar, and soy sauce. Simmer, uncovered, for 3 minutes, until the dashi has reduced somewhat. Remove from the heat and set the pan aside.

DUST BOTH SIDES of the trout fillets with flour. Heat 2 to 3 inches of oil to 340 degrees F in a heavy pot or deep-fryer. Deep-fry the fillets two at a time for about 2 minutes, until the skin is crisp; the flesh should still be moist. Remove with a slotted spoon and drain on paper towels.

MEANWHILE, RETURN THE vegetables to medium heat and bring to a simmer. Add the cornstarch mixture and stir until the sauce thickens, about 1 minute.

SERVE IN SOUP DISHES or deep plates. Place one fillet in each dish and cover with the vegetables and hot sauce. Serve immediately.

Kabosu no Zeri
Kabosu Gelatin

½ to ⅙ ounce ito kanten (a Japanese gelatin), soaked in cold water overnight (using the larger amount produces a firmer gelatin)

2 cups water

½ cup sugar

½ cup kabosu juice (preferably) or a mixture of fresh grapefruit and lime juice

1 cup raspberries

1 cup blueberries

1 cup blackberries

FOR THE SAUCE

¼ cup kabosu juice or fresh lime juice

1 cup fresh grapefruit juice

½ cup sugar

9 small mint leaves

SERVES 9

Kabosu is similar to yuzu, a variety of citron; both are acidic citrus fruits similar to lemons and limes. Kabosu juice is used in Japanese dressings and sauces. Unsweetened juice is available bottled at Japanese food stores. Kabosu juice makes a very refreshing, tart gelatin, perfect for hot summer days.

DRAIN THE *ito kanten* and squeeze it firmly to remove excess water. In a pot, combine the kanten and water. Bring to a boil over medium heat, and cook, stirring constantly, until the kanten is dissolved. Add the sugar and stir to dissolve it. Continue cooking over low heat for 3 minutes more.

STRAIN THE LIQUID through a sieve set over a bowl. Add the kabosu juice and stir. Let stand at room temperature until the gelatin is almost set.

ADD THE BERRIES to the gelatin and stir until well mixed. (Do not worry about breaking up the set gelatin.) Scoop the gelatin into individual dessert bowls and refrigerate until chilled.

FOR THE SAUCE

IN A SMALL SAUCEPAN, combine the kabosu juice, grapefruit juice, and sugar. Bring to a boil and cook over low to medium heat until reduced by one-third. Chill the sauce in the refrigerator.

SERVE THE GELATIN garnished with mint leaves and a little sauce poured over.

55

Japan

Namban-zuke

Fish and Vegetables in a Sweet
Vinegar–Namban Marinade

FOR THE MARINADE

⅔ cup rice vinegar (see Note)

⅓ cup dashi (see Note)

¼ cup sugar

2 tablespoons soy sauce

1 teaspoon salt

2 *akatogarashi* or other small dried red chile peppers, stemmed and seeded

Vegetable oil for deep-frying

¼ kabocha squash, seeded but not peeled, cut into 12 slices about ¼ inch thick

2 Japanese eggplants (preferably), quartered lengthwise, or ½ large, purple eggplant, stemmed and cut lengthwise into 8 wedges

1 zucchini, cut lengthwise in half, and then into 1½-inch pieces

1 red bell pepper

½ cup all-purpose flour

1¼ pounds skinned and boned swordfish steaks or boneless, skinless chicken breasts, cut into 1½-by-3-inch pieces

6 to 8 sprigs flat-leaf parsley

SERVES 6 TO 8

Several Japanese dishes have the word namban *in their names.* Namban *literally means "southern barbarian." The word was applied to the Portuguese and Spanish, the first Westerners who came to Japan, during the sixteenth century. The word* namban *reflects the shock the Japanese felt upon encountering Europeans, who had, by comparison, large noses and eyes, hairy bodies, and astonishing height.*

The Portuguese and Spanish brought both new foods and cooking techniques. These included kabocha pumpkins, potatoes, corn, watermelons, chile peppers, figs and sugary sweets, and deep-frying. Dishes prepared namban-*style typically call for red chile peppers and the combined techniques of deep-frying and marinating.*

In this dish, cooked fish or chicken and vegetables are marinated in a sweet vinegar marinade and served chilled or at room temperature. This appetizer is always a hit with my guests and students.

FOR THE MARINADE

IN A MEDIUM POT, combine the vinegar, dashi, sugar, soy sauce, and salt. Bring to a boil, stirring. Add the chile peppers, and pour the marinade into a medium flat-bottomed container; set it aside.

IN A LARGE DEEP POT, heat 2 inches of vegetable oil to 320 degrees F. In small batches, cook the kabocha until slightly golden, about 2 to 3 minutes. Drain, and while it is still hot, transfer the kabocha to the marinade.

INCREASE THE HEAT of the oil to 350 degrees F. Cook the eggplant and zucchini in small batches, until lightly golden. Drain, and while the vegetables are still hot, transfer them to the marinade. Carefully set the pot of oil aside.

ROAST THE BELL PEPPER over a gas flame, turning frequently, until blackened on all sides, or roast it under the broiler. Let cool slightly, then remove the skin, core, and seeds and cut into thick strips. Add to the marinade.

PUT THE FLOUR in a shallow bowl, and dredge the swordfish or chicken in it. Let stand 2 minutes.

HEAT THE VEGETABLE OIL to 350 degrees F. Add the fish or chicken, in small batches, and cook until light golden, about 4 to 5 minutes, maintaining the oil temperature at 350 degrees F. Drain the fish or chicken briefly on a rack, then add to the marinade. Marinate for at least an hour before serving, turning the fish or chicken several times. (The dish can be prepared a day in advance to this point, covered, and refrigerated.)

REMOVE THE CHILE PEPPERS from the marinade, and cut them into thin rings. Serve the fish or chicken and vegetables drizzled with the marinade and garnished with the chiles and parsley.

Note
For a less tart flavor, decrease the amount of rice vinegar to ½ cup and increase the amount of dashi to ½ cup.

Gyuniku no Misozuke
Miso-Marinated Beefsteak

FOR THE MARINADE

7 ounces brown miso

¼ cup mirin (sweet rice wine)

¼ cup sake

Three boneless 6-ounce sirloin steaks, 1 inch thick, excess fat cut off

1 scallion (green part only), thinly sliced

10 shiso leaves, julienned

½ cup grated daikon radish, blanched briefly in boiling water and cooled in ice water

½ cup Ponzu Sauce (recipe follows)

SERVES 4

As fish was once preserved in a miso marinade, so was beef. The technique of marinating beef was developed in the domain of Hikone, now Shiga Prefecture, during the Edo period (1600 to 1868).

Beef can be marinated in either sweet white miso or salty brown miso. I prefer brown miso, whose very rich flavor complements the robust flavor of beef. In contrast to the Edo period, today the marination time can be short, from only five hours to overnight. Marinating meat longer dries it out and toughens it. When you remove the meat from the marinade, however, you don't have to cook it right away; it will keep for up to 3 days in the refrigerator, stored in a container with a tight-fitting lid.

The marinated beef is placed on skewers and broiled, then sliced and served with grated daikon radish and ponzu sauce, with scallions and shiso leaf on the side.

FOR THE MARINADE

IN A MEDIUM BOWL, combine the miso, mirin, and sake to make a soft paste. Spread one-third of the mixture in the bottom of a large baking dish in which the steaks will fit without overlapping. Place a tightly woven cotton cloth or two layers of cheesecloth over the miso mixture and place the steaks on top. Cover them with another cloth or two more layers of cheesecloth, and spread the remaining miso mixture over it. Cover the pan with plastic wrap, and let the beef marinate for at least 5 hours, or overnight in the refrigerator.

REMOVE THE CLOTH from the beef and then the beef from the dish (reserve the marinade in the refrigerator for a later use, if desired, but use it within a few days). If there is any miso residue on the surface of the beef, gently wipe it away with a paper towel; do not rinse the beef.

PREHEAT THE BROILER or prepare a fire in a barbecue grill. Meanwhile, cut the steak into 1-inch cubes and thread the beef on skewers. Place the beef on the broiler pan or grill and cook until browned on the first side. Turn over and cook until the other side is browned. Check the doneness by pressing the meat with your fingers: when it is resilient on the outside but feels softer as you press a little deeper, it is still rare. The 1-inch-thick cubes of steak will take about 8 minutes to cook medium-rare.

TRANSFER THE BEEF to a warmed plate. Remove the skewers and cover the meat to keep warm.

IN A BOWL, toss the scallions and julienned shiso. Arrange one-quarter of the vegetable mixture on each dinner plate. Place a generous mound of grated daikon next to the greens. Arrange the beef next to the greens and daikon radish. Serve with the ponzu sauce in individual small saucers on the side.

Ponzu Sauce

3 tablespoons rice wine vinegar

2½ tablespoons mirin (sweet rice wine)

2 tablespoons yuzu (preferably) or good quality rice wine vinegar

5 tablespoons soy sauce

6 tablespoons dashi (see page 52 for a recipe)

MAKES ABOUT 1¼ CUPS

COMBINE ALL THE ingredients in a small pan and bring to a boil. Let cool, then refrigerate until ready to serve.

Italy

PROCURING THE BEST INGREDIENTS

Italian cooking can be considered,
for all the countries of Latin Europe,
as a veritable mother cuisine.

—LAROUSSE GASTRONOMIQUE

WHAT'S THE SECRET TO great Italian cuisine? Our first clue comes from the fact that the word for recipe in Italian is rooted in the verb meaning "to procure"—the secret of a great Italian dish begins with procuring the best possible ingredients.

"The fundamentals of Italian cooking are using the best and freshest ingredients possible, with the shortest distance from the garden to the table," agree George Germon and Johanne Killeen of Al Forno in Providence, Rhode Island. "We never stray from using our regional products and produce. It sounds clichéd because everyone says the same thing in every cookbook you pick up these days, but it is nevertheless true: the quality of the ingredients is vital to the success of Italian cooking."

Mario Batali, chef-owner of Babbo, Lupa, and Esca in New York City, adds, "When Italians buy food, they don't worry if they have to pay ten percent more to go to a better purveyor. They think about food the way Americans might think about prescriptions: most of us don't want to put something in our bodies unless we know everything about it. Italians are the same way about food.

"The average American might decide to make veal with mushrooms, go to the store, and see that the veal and mushrooms there aren't great, and then make the dish anyway. But Italians figure out what dish to make by going to the store to first find out what looks best. They see what the store has to offer and create backwards: they buy the ingredients, then go home and create the dish. They realize that the quality of the ingredients will reflect the quality of the final product."

In fact, this chapter could almost be one long shopping list, one that would change depending upon the season. After selecting the choicest ingredients, you do as little as possible to them. That is not to say that technique is not important, but Italian cuisine is defined to a greater extent by its simplicity and the pure flavors of its ingredients.

Batali points out, "The simplicity of a dish is also its greatness—that is the most important thing. Perfect peas don't need anything else. For example, if you make pappardelle with peas, it is *not* pappardelle with peas, mint, onions, pesto, and four kinds of cheese. It's pappardelle with peas, butter, and, maybe, some Parmigiano-Reggiano cheese.

"People need to understand that the regional diet of Italians changes twelve times a year. When it is asparagus season, they do a full-on attack, serving asparagus in everything for three or four weeks—and when it is gone, they move on to the next thing. They don't drag out a season. Everyone's diet should change throughout the year," he concludes, "and that is the biggest step for most Americans to take."

"Even if you're just cooking a handful of wonderful asparagus," concurs Lynne Rossetto Kasper, author of *The Splendid Table* and host of the radio show of the same name, "all you need to do is steam them lightly, and put a pat of good butter and a sprinkling of Parmesan on them—and you are eating like an Italian!"

Location, Location, Location

THE CUISINE OF ITALY is dictated by its regions and regional products. It is almost a wonder that highways were ever built. What did they need to trade or transport? Since Italians are so fanatical about the freshness of their ingredients, it certainly was not food.

Lynne Rossetto Kasper relates how three words—*nostrano, campanilismo,* and *sisposa*—explain the focus on regional foods. "*Nostrano* literally means 'local,'" she says. "The labels of products from Italy often include variations of this word. The root *nostro* means 'ours' or our part of the world—and we are not messing around with it!

"*Campanile* is the bell tower in every Italian town and village, and *campanilismo* refers to the mentality associated with that area. The term defines your home, which is within hearing distance of the bell. Those not from that town or village are treated as outsiders; Italians are deeply dubious of and not very open to them.

"*Campanilismo* is a deep affiliation with the products and collective mentality of your town or village, of the experiences and food that are shared by the residents of the village or town. How you eat within hearing distance of the bell is different from how someone would eat twenty miles away. Even though the food in a village just over the hill may seem similar, it's not the same. Italians also feel that the products from their town or village should be used together, a principle explained by the word '*sisposa,*' which means, literally 'it marries.' It's a more poetic way of saying, essentially, 'What goes together grows together.'

"One of the great misunderstandings about Italian cuisine is that there are two cuisines, 'Northern' and 'Southern,'" she continues. "But, in fact, here is how it works: there are twenty different regions, they all eat differently, and there is no blanket statement you can make about them!"

"In order to cook really good Italian food, you need to understand micro-regions," agrees Mario Batali. "And you need to understand all of them, not just Emilia-Romagna or Bologna, or a specific grandma or individual cook. Then you will realize how different Italian cooking is from French, where they make a classic béarnaise sauce the same way in Paris and Lyon as they do in Monte Carlo."

Americans—even experts in Italian cuisine—can underestimate the regional variations of food in Italy. Says Lynne Rossetto Kasper, "I was confident that I knew my stuff when it came to Italian food. I was in Bologna, where everywhere you go, you are served handmade meat-filled tortellini, usually in a beautiful capon broth or with a ragù, or cheese and butter. So I drew the conclusion that the traditional first course in Emilia-Romagna was tortellini.

"I was taken to Parma, which is two hours away by car but still in the same region. I was seated at a dinner with the head of the region, and the owner of the restaurant was acting as my personal waiter. Both men were addressing me by my full name—so gracious! I was feeling pretty full of myself, living in Europe, writing about some of the world's best chefs. I was cocky!

"The owner asked me what I would like as a first course, and I replied, 'Tortellini in broth, of course.' My host leaned over, addressing me with my full title, 'La Signóra la giornalista Kasper, we don't eat tortellini—it is a foreign food.' It turns out that, so to speak, the food in Parma is completely different from that of Bologna! There is a meat-filled pasta in Parma, but *anolino* is made and served differently, and it has nothing to do with the tortellini in Bologna. Never tell someone from Parma what great food you had in Bologna!"

The food changes so much from valley to valley that the term "North," as mentioned earlier, is really almost meaningless when it comes to discussing regional food variations. Kasper continues, "When people say they love 'Northern Italian' food, I ask, 'What do you mean? Are you talking about Tuscany, with its grilled flavors, caramelization, its use of olive oil—and the sense that this food comes directly from the earth? Are you talking about Milan, with its incredible combination of great risotto, saffron and broth, and beef marrow? Or the polenta from Friuli? The dumplings that are made of bread up near the Tyrole, where pasta is a foreign food? Or do you mean Venice, where you still find influences from the Arab world, such as sweet-and-sour flavor combinations? These are all 'north' in Italy."

What Happens When American Chefs Don't Do Their Homework

I don't want to sound like a grouch, but while I welcome innovation, I wish chefs would do some homework first and have respect for what they are cooking. —LYNNE ROSSETTO KASPER

DESPITE THE POPULARITY of Italian cuisine outside of Italy, experts have observed the difficulty of moving a cuisine that is deeply rooted in locality and values to another part of the world. "What gets messed up here in America is that no one does any homework," laments Lynne Rossetto Kasper. "Italian food is so approachable that everyone thinks they can just start cooking it, which has unfortunately led to some pretty harrowing dishes in restaurants! This is not just snobbishness in the 'it is never done in Italy' school. If you are going to open an Italian restaurant, do me a favor—read a book, even if it is just one."

Piero Selvaggio of Valentino in Los Angeles shares Kasper's discouragement over seeing how foods have been misinterpreted or mistreated. "It took a long time for risotto to be appreciated as risotto and not parboiled rice," says Selvaggio. "Unfortunately, once Italian food became so popular, everyone began interpreting it in their own way, and we lost the sense of authenticity. I don't mind that people open Italian restaurants, but I wish they would do some homework beforehand to ensure that their products are authentic! To serve a pasta with Kraft Parmesan cheese is not right."

"I once went to a 'Tuscan' restaurant in Minneapolis where there was *nothing* on the menu that had anything to do with Tuscany," relates Kasper. "The featured pasta was orecchiette with wilted greens. That pasta comes from the heel of the boot in Italy. The dish was closer to Africa than Tuscany! That told me that the people in this restaurant had not done any homework. If you ever served this dish in Tuscany, you would be laughed off the street!

"Ten years ago, what was being taught as 'Italian cuisine' in cooking schools was horrendous," she continues. "At a top culinary school, the students were making braised chicken in tomato sauce with polenta, pasta, and spinach in their Italian class. No Italian ever eats pasta as a main dish; it is a separate course. And no Italian, or anyone else in their right mind, would want to eat pasta and polenta at the same time. When I asked him why the students were cooking this way, the Swiss chef-instructor said, 'It's Italian— you can do anything.'"

Mario Batali finds that the best intentions of cooks can sometimes prove to be their worst enemies. "There is a lot of bad food masquerading as Italian food out there. Fortunately, thanks to Giuliano Bugialli, Lidia Bastianich, and Marcella Hazan, the awareness of what regional Italian food is has been brought into the public eye in the last ten years. People are no longer trying to do 'Italian' dishes with kiwi."

Capturing Authentic Regional Flavors

Ask for Bolognese sauce in 200 different Italian restaurants, and you will get 200 different versions of ragù.

—ENRICO GALOZZI, ITALIAN GASTRONOMIC EXPERT

BECAUSE ITALIAN DISHES EMPLOY so few ingredients, each flavor counts a lot and there is no hiding inferior, or inauthentic, ingredients. If, for example, you use olive oil from Liguria in a Genoan dish, the dish will not be authentically Genoan—and that fact would be discernible to knowledgeable diners. Basil from Genoa is not basil from Liguria is not basil from southern California. Still, despite the limitation of not being in the Italian region whose food you are cooking—and not having access to such ingredients as Genoese basil—you do have some options for preparing an authentic regional meal.

As much as possible, use ingredients in your pantry from the appropriate region. "When making a regional Italian dish, prepare it with the olive oil of its region," recommends Mario Batali. "If you are doing Ligurian-style food, you should use Ligurian Taggiasca olives and wine. Each region's oil has its own flavor, nuance and feel. If you are making a dish from Puglia and you use a light oil, you will never get the flavor right."

"Every area's olive oil has a different taste profile," echoes Lynne Rossetto Kasper. "If you are going to make a great pesto true to the spirit of Liguria, you should use oil from that area. Ligurian oil tends to be very buttery, gentle, and flowery. Oil from Tuscany has none of those characteristics; a Tuscan oil is very green-tasting, peppery, and can be robust."

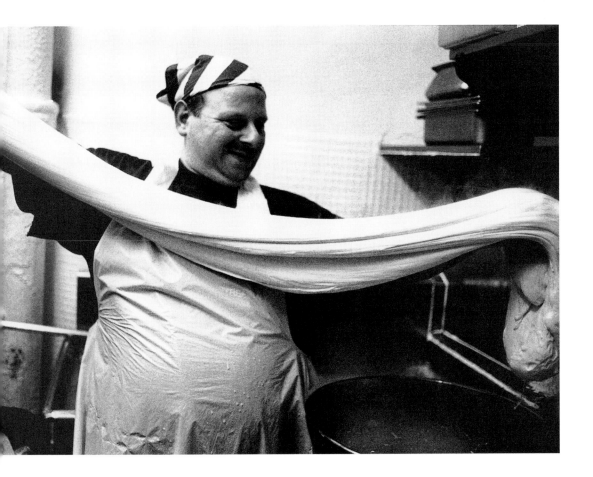

In addition, as Batali points out, you can certainly experience regionalism in your own backyard. "You want to catch that regionalism—even if we're not talking about a field in Italy, but about your own backyard in the United States," he says. "If the basil you're using is grown in Washington State in August, that basil becomes a personalized version of basil. If you grow your basil next to your string beans and it gets the flavor of the bean plant in the middle of a hot day, that basil has taken on an additional flavor component. If you think of basil as a musical chord, it can play five notes. Basil can taste like fennel, mint, soil, rain, or the hot sun. When you mix these tastes together, you get a dish that is a little more sexy and personal," he says.

Lynne Rossetto Kasper notes that while pesto is made all over Liguria, the best is thought to come from basil grown in Genoa's micro-climate. "In Genoa, they say that the best pesto comes from a little suburb outside the city, where the key is that they don't use fully mature plants," she explains. "The leaves are picked before the plant has flowered. They pluck the leaves off plants that are six inches high. Young leaves are sweeter. If you grow your own plants, stagger the planting, then harvest early and move on to the next plant as each matures. I did that and I would say my pesto could be a stunt double for Genoese pesto. When I mix those sweet leaves with a flowery, buttery olive oil, it is a beautiful marriage!"

Choosing Your Favorite Ingredients and Brands

WITHIN EVERY REGION, THERE is a great variety of ingredients and brands. There is not just one olive oil in Tuscany, or one brand of canned tomatoes from San Marzano. When we asked our experts for recommendations, they all had the same response: "The important thing is to find out what *you* like best!"

Determining your favorite ingredients and brands and then trusting those distinctions is vital to your cooking. If you don't start with your own personal preferences, you will be correcting the dish all the way through the cooking process, trying to match it to your palate. Instead, at the outset, make sure that all the ingredients you are using reflect your taste.

For example, because Andrew prefers kosher salt, he takes some with him whenever we travel. Friends and family members even have kosher salt on hand when they know that he will be in their kitchens. And in a recent cooking class, when we hosted a black pepper tasting, we were struck by the differences between different varieties, and we realized we'd developed our own preferences among them as well.

"Great ingredients turn cooking into a whole new game," says Mario Batali. "Realizing how important those initial decisions are at the beginning is a radical idea. You should try five different versions of an item to find what tastes best to you," he advises. "If you're trying to find an olive oil, go to a few stores and buy a bunch of different oils and try them side by side."

"It is so important to figure out what you like best," agrees Lynne Rossetto Kasper. "For instance, canned tomatoes are very important because you will use so many in Italian cooking. The best thing to do is taste different brands straight out of the cans with a pinch of salt and see what you like best. I recommend buying every kind of canned whole tomato you can find in your local supermarkets and gourmet stores. Line up your cans and taste the contents of each one to see what you like. (Then make a big batch of tomato sauce out of all the tomatoes and put it in your freezer.) Don't buy crushed or pureed tomatoes—they are often thickened with a very cheap tomato paste, which can start to taste metallic as it cooks." At the end of the chapter, we offer some guidelines for your own shopping.

The Art of Shopping

GETTING GOOD INGREDIENTS ISN'T about luck. You need to develop relationships with the people from whom you buy. Chefs know this: if you look at the menu of many top restaurants you will see purveyors' names, from Jamison for lamb to Coach Farm for goat cheese, in the descriptions of the dishes. While you're getting to know your butcher and grocer, be suspicious of imported products with fancy, "authentic-sounding" names and no taste. You need to shop with your eyes, nose, and loyalty to get the best.

"If there is one thing I would really recommend, it is becoming a good customer of the people you buy from," says Mario Batali. "Be faithful to them, and buy regularly, and

you will get better products, because they want to reward their most frequent customers. It is the same thing in Italy; there, the grandmothers go to the stores where they have been shopping for thirty years. If they need the right piece of meat, they are going to get it! The same thing is not true if you shop at giant grocery stores and go to the butcher maybe once a month for something special."

Batali continues, "It is easy to go to the fancy grocery store and get white asparagus in February and strawberries in March and melons in January. That is science doing its best job to create and give the market what it wants. But the best way to learn about produce is from the store guys themselves. They know what is best and what is in season. One key thing with produce is to look at where it was cut from the plant. If the root is slightly firm, you can be sure it is pretty fresh—or that your produce guy has one up on you because he is trimming and moistening the root! If the root is dry like a tree branch, you know the produce guy is not on the ball and that what you're buying is not great."

Freshness First

Your best source will always be organic, at your local farmers' market. Radicchio imported from Treviso is not going to make the trip. It would not be what an Italian would buy. If an ingredient doesn't grow in your area, don't worry—you will find something that works. . . . The real key is a sense of "urgency of taste." With the best food, there's the sense that if you wait twenty minutes, an ingredient will change and then you won't want it anymore. **—LYNNE ROSSETTO KASPER**

THE ITALIAN PHILOSOPHY of procuring the freshest ingredients travels beyond the borders of the country. It is simply the way in which Italians approach cooking, whether they are in Tuscany, Liguria, or the western United States. If Italians in America have to choose between a high-quality Italian-style cheese freshly made in California and a high-quality cheese made a few weeks earlier in Italy, they'll certainly choose the former.

"Thank God 'artisan' and 'heirloom' have become blessed words in the American food glossary," says Piero Selvaggio. "There are better tomatoes now than there were ten years ago. The vegetables we get from the farmers' markets have been picked that morning, as opposed to some at the supermarket that have been sprayed and are old. I get incredible radicchio from Salinas, which is just a few hours away. The radicchio I would get from Italy would be days out of the ground by the time it arrived here.

"The other major development at farmers' markets is the arrival of artisans who hand-make different products. We use an Italian cheese called *burrata*. If we were to import it from Italy, it would be pasteurized [because of USDA regulations] and live for a few days. Now we have a local artisan who makes it for us every morning, so we can serve something that is traditionally Italian with the same quality level."

Adds Lynne Rossetto Kasper, "If an Italian cook won't drive forty miles for cheese, should we be eating imported buffalo mozzarella—especially when someone down the road makes really good mozzarella, or a similar cheese? Mary Faulk from Love Tree Farm makes a great pecorino cheese, which I use in Italian dishes all the time. That's what an Italian would do!

"Just remember to keep it simple. If there are great green beans and green garlic in the farmers' market, I will use them to make a pea and garlic soup finished with a fresh sheep's cheese, like one I had in Sicily. Are the garlic and are the peas the same that I had in Sicily? No. Am I going to buy imported sheep's cheese that won't be fresh when it gets to me? No. I'll use a great local sheep's cheese—and if I can't find one, I'll use something similar. Does the food change? Yes. Does the integrity change? No. Spirit is the whole thing."

Simplicity

The idea behind Italian cooking is to try to catch the smell of the wind, the flavor of the rain, and the way things taste on the perfect day.

— **MARIO BATALI**

IN ORDER TO CELEBRATE the flavors of their fresh, high-quality ingredients, Italians prepare them very simply. "When you get to Italy, you realize that 'true simplicity' is the shining star," says Mario Batali. "They are not trying to re-create the wheel. They make simple food, serve it without a huge amount of fanfare, and understand that good food comes more from the field than it does from the sauté pan. I visit Italy at least five or six times a year, and whenever I return to Babbo, I always simplify the food."

Sometimes creating a sublime dish is as simple as combining two or three ingredients. "*Aglio e olio* with peperoncino [spaghetti with garlic oil and hot pepper] is a great dish that cooks overlook," says Batali. "They are busy trying to make something complicated to expand their horizons, especially when they are entertaining. When you become confident enough to serve *aglio e olio* with peperoncino in your home, then you have developed the ability to shop."

"The first time I had carpaccio was magical," remembers Piero Selvaggio. "It was sliced Piedmontese beef—which is incredibly delicate—with a touch of mustard, a sprinkle of olive oil, and a little salt. My palate was not very evolved at the time, so the idea of eating raw meat wasn't that appealing to me. I almost thought that I should close my eyes to eat the carpaccio, but when I put it in my mouth, all I could think was, 'This is so good!'

"I was halfway through the dish when the waiter came over to shave on some white truffle that had just arrived in the kitchen. I went from, 'This is so good,' to, 'I've just died and gone to heaven!' The point is that with simple ingredients, you can create a spectacular Italian dish. You don't need a lot of ingredients, a long cooking process, or a sauce to make a straightforward statement." (See the recipe on page 98.)

Mario Batali encourages cooks to grow herbs on their windowsills to provide them with the proper inspiration. "Grow the 'Simon-and-Garfunkel' for your Italian herb pantry: parsley, sage, rosemary, and thyme. Make sure they get lots of sun, then cut them as you need them," he advises. "Let's say it is August or September and you decide to make *caprese* [sliced tomatoes, fresh basil, and mozzarella, with a drizzle of olive oil]. You should not be using hothouse basil. If you have gone to the trouble to find heirloom tomatoes and great extra-virgin olive oil, then use basil from your backyard that tastes like the rain from three days ago. That is when you enter into the poetry of what a dish can be."

The Importance of Balance

"THE BEAUTY OF ITALIAN COOKING is its restraint and balance," Batali elaborates. "It is about everything—the noodles, condiments, cheese, herbs—being in the right place in the pasta dish. Or it is about braising osso bucco with just tomatoes, onions, and celery—try not adding the carrots. Suddenly you might find that without them, the dish is cleaner, lighter, and even better than you remember."

A touch of acidity is a key component of this balance. "One of the trademarks of Babbo's cooking is the bright acidity in every dish," says Batali. "The acidity emphasizes the flavors and helps the food match with wine. At the last moment, we drizzle an acid over the top of the plate. It may be red or white vinegar, or some orange or fresh lemon juice. This makes a huge difference in how the flavors are perceived.

"This is a fine line, of course, because the acid could hurt the wine, but what we are doing is balancing the flavors. Often it is so subtle that most guests would not consciously pick it out. Three drops of orange juice added at the last second to a dish with tomatoes will bring out the intensity of the tomato flavor. It is not overpowering; it is accenting."

Italian-American Food: Beyond Canned Parmesan

NO ONE WOULD DISPUTE that Americans *love* Italian food, despite the fact that some Americans' stereotypical idea of what is actually Italian-*American* food is a far cry from simple, fresh Italian cooking. "Italian is supposedly the Western world's favorite foreign food, and has been for the last thirty or forty years," says Lynne Rossetto Kasper. "I can't think of any major city in the entire Western world where you can't find pizza or pasta."

Why have pizza and pasta become as popular as—if not more so than—hamburgers and fried chicken in this country? According to Lynne Rossetto Kasper, "We react to it so emotionally for two different reasons: one, it tastes like home cooking, regardless of our backgrounds, and two, it is easy to like. You don't have to know anything to enjoy a pizza! Plus, pizza and pasta pair tomatoes with wheat. We get a creatine buzz from that combination.

"People love the taste combinations of sweet/tart and sweet/tart/salty/savory. If you break down the food of Thailand, India, China, and, in fact, most of Asia, you see those profiles. So with the sweet from the tomato and the tart from the wheat, you have that door opened. And don't forget the cheese, which is fat—and we all love fat. Invariably with that pasta or pizza, you will have cheese."

Describing the development of Italian-American food, George Germon and Johanne Killeen concur. "Most of the Italian immigrants who arrived in the northeastern United States came from Southern Italy. There are communities in Rhode Island made up of the immigrant descendants of people who came only from a single, small village. When they arrived here many years ago, the products they were used to—good olive oil and cheeses, for instance—were unavailable. They adapted to what was here and the food morphed into a cuisine of its own, 'Italian-American.' The rules of the kitchen changed, but that is not to say that they necessarily changed for the worse. One of our favorite restaurants in America is Mike's Kitchen [in the VFW Hall in Cranston, Rhode Island], which is one of the finest examples of just how good Italian-American cooking can be."

Along with Americans' growing love of Italian food came a bevy of misconceptions. "When Italian cuisine arrived in America, it was called 'Southern Italian' because the immigrants were from the south," explains Piero Selvaggio. "So when butter, cheese, and creamy sauces were introduced, people assumed they were from the north and were somehow more noble."

"Misconceptions about 'Northern' and 'Southern' food have created a lot of confusion about Italian food," adds Selvaggio. "Italian food started out as an immigrant cuisine and has now made it into the mainstream. It was always considered second to

French food, but it has slowly shown itself as an equal. Unfortunately, there are times when the food is still not considered 'haute' because of the popularity of such things as pizza and pasta."

"Many people still think they are eating Italian food when they go to spaghetti and meatball houses or heavy red sauce emporiums, but that is such a big misconception," lament George Germon and Johanne Killeen. "Worse still are the bottled spaghetti sauces available at the supermarket. Does Ragu resemble any real Italian food? I don't think so. Not to mention canned spaghetti and meatballs!"

"Like Chinese food, Italian food is misconstrued as a cuisine based on cheap, poor-quality ingredients," says Selvaggio. "You can make a pasta that will feed a lot of people inexpensively if you want, yet when you look deeper, Italian food is much more serious than that. When we opened Primi restaurant fifteen years ago, we were offering risotto, porcini mushrooms, polenta, and so forth, and it was a real struggle. When I started in the restaurant business, mozzarella was Mozzarella Marinara, which was cardboard cheese that had been breaded, deep-fried, and served with anchovy and tomato. When I first served buffalo mozzarella, the response from customers was, 'I am paying *how much* for something made of buffalo?' Now, there is a clearer idea about Italian products and food. No one needs to ask what balsamic vinegar, porcini mushrooms, or extra-virgin olive oil are. Everyone knows about *insalata caprese,* a wonderful creamy salad of buffalo mozzarella that only needs a gorgeous slice of tomato and a drizzle of olive oil.

"This is part of my joy," he continues. "Twenty years ago, I couldn't give away a bottle of San Pellegrino! Now, it is part of the dining experience. Back then, I was the only person who had an espresso machine in the area. It was a treat! Yet I had to explain to guests that they were not going to get a big American cup of coffee so that they would not feel cheated. Only people who had been to espresso bars in Italy understood that espresso is part of the culture, and is about the essence of the bean. Thank goodness Starbucks has now made it impossible for Americans to get up without a latte! I love it that they've made espresso a staple in America."

Room for Interpretation According to Your Taste

AS MARIO BATALI POINTS OUT, everyone in Italy improvises. "A *ragù Bolognese* is different at either end of Bologna, in two houses next to each other, or even made by two daughters of the same mom. There is a framework into which an Italian dish fits, but each individual cook's interpretation becomes more valid than any single recipe could

ever be. Some Bolognese sauces may have veal, others porcini mushrooms, and others pork, veal, and beef simmered in white wine. Someone else will use red wine. It goes on and on. The recipe becomes far more personalized after any cook has experimented according to individual taste."

Thus, because of the collective individual "tweaks" to various dishes, Italian cuisine is always evolving. "I see it in homes as well as restaurants, even when people are cooking dishes from their heritage," says Lynne Rossetto Kasper. "At some point, someone will be making the family sauce and add a little chicken liver to it because it tastes good. There will be a boycott at the table that might go on for a year. Then suddenly the classic family sauce has chicken livers in it!"

Simply put, every dish you make is an interpretation. "Most dishes are based on another, then interpreted within your own style," as Piero Selvaggio points out. "Fortunately, Valentino is not a regional restaurant. We describe ourselves as 'contemporary.' We look for the best products in season. If I want to serve truffles in the winter, that doesn't mean I want to necessarily serve strictly Piemontese cuisine. If I serve bottagga [pressed tuna roe], that does not mean I am serving strictly Sardinian cuisine. I take the best ingredients and interpret them 'in the Italian manner.'

"Revisiting and taking a fresh look at traditional Italian cuisine is a great deal of fun for me," he adds. "For instance, we love to marry rich ingredients with poor ingredients.

Sautéed liver, sweet onions, and vinegar is a classic dish called 'liver Venetian-style.' I revisited the dish by doing it with foie gras, Maui onions, and balsamic vinegar. I am keeping true to its spirit by using similar components, but I found a way to take it to the next level. We also pair *burrata* cheese, an artisan cheese that is creamy and buttery, with caviar. It's one of the greatest things you will ever put in your mouth. I also like to stuff small cannoli with caviar and present it with all the traditional garnishes."

In the same spirit, "At Al Forno, we deconstruct and reconstruct many traditional dishes," says Johanne Killeen. "The perfect example is George's grilled pizza. It tastes Italian and is made with Italian ingredients—and attitude—but it is cooked over live fire on a grill rather than in a conventional oven. With a total lack of modesty, we think it is better than any pizza we have had in Italy.

"We have also reworked the *castagnaccio,* an unleavened Tuscan cake made with chestnut flour, rosemary, olive oil, raisins, and pine nuts. The traditional cake resembles

the heaviest clafoutis you have ever come across. You could charitably call it a 'sinker.' It is a cultural experience, an acquired taste we now appreciate, but for our customers at Al Forno it would have little to no appeal. So, we modernized the recipe by making it into an American-style upside-down cake. The topping is made with rosemary, raisins, and nuts with melted butter and sugar. The cake is made in the style of a butter cake, with eggs whipped into creamed butter and sugar. The batter is lightened by substituting cake flour for a portion of the chestnut flour and adding baking powder for extra leavening. A small amount of olive oil stirred into the batter makes the cake really moist. All the original, unusual ingredients of the *castagnaccio* are used, so the integrity of the original cake remains, but they are used in a way that appeals to today's tastes."

There is no place on earth where the clock stops. "Food, like everything, evolves over time," says Lynne Rossetto Kasper. "Before a dish is a classic, it is an innovation—but there must be a logic in moving from the one to the other. I was in Bologna twelve years ago, eating in a restaurant that had a new chef. Everybody was shocked because he put orange zest in the tomato sauce for his scampi dish. Well, all the shocked people cleaned their plates because it was delicious. The logic is that 'tomato likes orange.'

"When it comes to Italian food in America, the question for me is, does it work? If you transport me with a dish, I will follow you anywhere. If a dish doesn't fly, you can taste it. If a dish works, it means that the chef's instincts are pretty good and that he or she is fairly sure in the craft of cooking. A really good chef can zero right in on what makes something work or not. He or she will be instinctively true to basic premises.

"Innovation never stops," she adds. "One of the chefs who does the best riffs on Italian cooking is Wolfgang Puck. He has a real feel for what the food is about. Would an Italian put lamb sausage on pizza? Not likely, but it worked for him because he understands what works on the palate."

Recipes: Following a Winding Road

IF A LITTLE OF YOUR favorite ingredient is good, will more make it better? "The tendency is to create your own dish by adding more of what you like—more garlic, more basil, more whatever," observes Mario Batali. "You basically create your own dish from someone else's list of ingredients. That makes your food taste like you."

"When you cook, it is important to realize that a recipe is a guideline," agrees Piero Selvaggio. "Nothing is meant to be followed verbatim. Once you become a more skilled cook, you should use your logic. You need to keep the end in mind, but along the way you can exchange one acid for a different one or substitute one pungent ingredient for another pungent ingredient. Sometimes you need to make changes for one reason or another."

As Batali concludes, "When you are trying to define the best of something, using your own personal taste is most important. Learn to trust yourself," he urges. "Empowering yourself to make decisions is a huge part of understanding Italian cooking."

The Italian Larder

Have these things on hand, then work with the freshest and best ingredients you can get your hands on. —LYNNE ROSSETTO KASPER

THERE ARE certain key ingredients that anyone who wants to cook Italian should stock in their kitchen. Choosing the very best products in each category—and using them as the base for your cooking—has the power to elevate the food you serve to a realm far beyond the ordinary.

Olive Oil

Olive oil is the foundation of Italian cooking.

—LIDIA BASTIANICH, CHEF-OWNER, FELIDIA, NEW YORK CITY

While in the United States olive oil might be generally thought of as a substitute for butter as a cooking medium or complement for bread, in many regions of Italy where it is produced it is used as a seasoning. "Good olive oil is used to finish a dish," points out Lynne Rossetto Kasper. "There is nothing better than a lovely vegetable soup finished with a crack of black pepper and a drizzle of really good olive oil." However, as she adds indignantly, "A big misconception is that you can't cook with extra-virgin olive oil. Whoever started that idea had no clue. That's simply not true!

"Two primary ways in which olive oil is misused in the U.S. are the use of inferior olive oil and the practice of putting olive oil on the table," Kasper continues. "Olive oil on the table is a nice thing, but I have never seen it in Italy. Never! If you have great olive oil you are not going to waste it on someone who will not appreciate it. In restaurants here, the olive oil on the table is usually not very good."

In fact, Piero Selvaggio recently removed olive oil from the tables at Valentino. "It is really more of a trattoria touch than a fine-dining one," he says. "Some restaurants have also gotten carried away. Instead of a little oil on the plate, it has become a ceremony, with the pouring of the oil and cracking of pepper tableside. Or else oil is served with all sorts of herbs inside it. A very special bottle of extra-virgin olive oil will cost at least $25. If I put it on the table and someone uses and abuses it, or sends a full plate back to the dishwasher, it breaks my heart!"

What's the secret of choosing a good olive oil? It depends in part on whom you ask. "If you wanted to get fanatical about olive oil, I would recommend buying a Sicilian oil like Ravida or Olio Verde, along with the great Tuscan and Ligurian oils," says Kasper. "But you shouldn't turn up your nose at California olive oil. McEvoy and Lila Jager are very good."

"Aspirator olive oil is one of the greatest things a person will ever taste," says Piero Selvaggio. "It is produced by Alfredo Mancianti in Umbria (www.mancianti.it). It is the oil that results from the olives' very first contact with one another after they've been picked but before they have gone to press. We have paired this with soppressata, which is earthy salami, on grilled bruschetta. It can be that simple. If you crave a simple taste, this is better than any caviar."

"Capezzana, Castella d'Ana, and DaVero are my current three favorites this year," says Mario Batali. "My list changes every year because, like wine, olive oils have good years, OK years, and grand years. My palate for olive oil is aggressive. I like a powerful oil, nearly peppery, deep dark green. That is a Tuscan-style oil. But if I am cooking fish, I like the oil of Liguria or of Carso, which is a micro-climate at the top of the Adriatic Sea on the border of Italy in what used to be Yugoslavia. DaVero is from Healdsburg, California, and it has been on my list for three years running."

When building your pantry, you can buy a variety of small bottles of olive oil from different regions. Having them on hand will help you cook more authentically and become familiar enough with them to determine your personal favorites.

Sea Salt

Batali is partial to sea salt from Sicily. "It has a great mineral component to it," he explains. But, he goes on to say, "Different salts bring out different elements of a dish. At our seafood restaurant Esca, our chef Dave Pasternack has eleven different salts in his pantry. He will use different ones on different fish. It makes a huge difference in the *crudo*. There is nothing better to use as a canvas for how different salts affect something than a piece of raw fish with a little olive oil. People wonder why food tastes better at a chef's house than at their own home. It's because chefs pay attention to everything. In a chef's home, salt is not just salt."

Parmesan Cheese

Although Parmigiano-Reggiano comes from only one region, it is used throughout Italy. "It is a glorious cheese to have in the house and it keeps very well," says Lynne Rossetto Kasper.

Parmigiano Reggiano

Accept no substitute, for no substitute exists. Italy's most famous cheese. Many try to Imitate, nothing comes close to its complexity of sweet, salt, and nuttiness of flavor. Worth It's Weight in Gold.

$10.99lb

Parmigiano Reggiano delle Vacche Rosse

This particular Reggiano has met all the rules set forth to be called Parmigiano Reggiano; but is set apart from the rest by the fact that milk from the "vacca rossa" breed of cow is used. This beautiful straw Reggiano is nutty and rich. It is extremely high in protein and is a meal. Enjoy anytime with just about anything!!!

aged 36 months

$18.99l

Finding a great Parmigiano-Reggiano—or Taleggio or Fontina, for that matter—is not something to be left to chance. "There is a huge difference in quality among cheese stores," cautions Mario Batali. "You have to develop trust with your cheesemonger. The most important thing about cheese, beyond where it comes from, is whether the producer and purveyor has ripened it well. When you buy a well-made and well-aged cheese, it is an amazing thing."

Pasta

"Some French people say there is no technique to Italian food, but that is not true!" says Lynne Rossetto Kasper. "Take pasta making, for example. Rolling it by hand is really difficult, but if you use a machine to roll pasta in Italy, they will politely put you in the car and drive you to the border! Pasta is hand-rolled for a reason; then its texture marries with sauce like nothing else."

As for dried pastas, "There are always the old workhorses DeCecco, which I use in my restaurants, and Barilla," says Mario Batali. "But what I like are more artisanal pastas that require a little bit longer cooking time. What that means is that they have been

dried longer. Some factories dry pasta for twelve hours, while others dry them for seventy-two hours. The longer a pasta is dried, the more of a window you have when cooking. With the artisanal pastas, if you go over by thirty seconds, you are still OK. But if you are using Ronzoni and go over by thirty seconds, you get Cream of Wheat. My two favorite artisanal pastas are Rustico and Pagano."

"There are tons of industrial pasta makers," adds Piero Selvaggio. "But when you start going up the pasta-making pyramid, you get the pioneers and artisans. Your ultimate choice will be personal, but for me the tip of the pyramid is two makers: Carlo Latini and Martelli. Both companies share the same philosophy, which is achieving perfection when growing the wheat. Then they age the pasta for three days to take it to another level of perfection. I assure you, when you try these pastas, they will taste better than any pasta you have ever had. They box their pasta with a date. They want to make sure you get the intense yeast flavor. We do a dish with Latini *la gataria* pasta with summer onions and pecorino cheese. Words cannot describe how good it tastes!"

Prosciutto and Other Salumi

"Some of the top producers of prosciutto are in the regions of Parma and San Daniele," says Selvaggio. "However, I personally like prosciuttos from Carpegna, which may be the best producer there of all. They make small quantities so they can age it better, and you can really taste the difference. Culatello may be the ultimate Italian cured ham, but it is hard to find; if you see it, you are in for a treat."

"There is a rebirth of artisanal salumi makers happening right now," says Mario Batali. "You see this happening around the country, in Chicago, Philadelphia, Kansas, you name it. The website gratefulpalate.com has a Bacon-of-the-Month Club. They find beautiful handmade stuff from all around the country that is mindblowingly great. I would also recommend my father's store [Salumi, in Seattle's Pioneer Square] because he has really great stuff. The Seattle *Zagat Survey* gave him a 27 food rating. He called and asked what a 27 meant, and I said, 'It means you're one point ahead of me, Dad!'"

Tomatoes

"Canned tomatoes or fresh? I am picky about both," Mario Batali says. "For my palate, I find that the Californian and Chilean canned tomatoes lack acidity as well as flavor. I like the San Marzano tomatoes packed in Essai. I like heirloom tomatoes for a raw tomato salad. We get our fresh tomatoes from the Union Square Greenmarket and serve them from the end of July to the end of September only."

"People are stunned when I talk about canned tomatoes," says Lynne Rossetto Kasper. "I find most Italian imports disappointing. If every can of 'San Marzano' tomatoes

MARIO BATALI ON BREAD

Because bread is eaten throughout the meal, it affects everything else you eat. "If you get really good bread, everything you are eating is taken to a whole new level," asserts Mario Batali. "Many people tend to just buy the *'Eye-talian'* bread in the supermarket, which is really a glorified, overblown baguette. If you get an interesting artisan bread, like those we have in New York from Amy's Bread or Tom Cat or Sullivan Street, then the whole table changes. This is especially key at the cheese course, because cheese and bad bread can't be matched together—it wrecks the whole experience."

What makes a great bread? "A good Italian bread is cooked long enough to get a deep, dark golden brown, almost burnt crust. It has a soft crumb with good texture," Batali notes. "Tuscans don't like salt in their bread, but most Italian breads have salt in them, and yet they're still not oversalted."

were really from there, the area would have to be the size of California! We have wonderful canned tomatoes in the United States. Contadina makes a very respectable tomato. There are some very good Italian brands, but they are double the price and not superior. Red Gold tomatoes are also good, and they come from that Italian area known as Ohio."

Vinegars

Batali believes that anyone serious about Italian cooking needs to have a stock of really good red and white wine vinegars. "My favorite vinegars are made by Lidia Bastianich in her garage, so I'm afraid they are not widely available," he admits. He even recommends making your own vinegar. "Go to a wine or brew shop and purchase 'vinegar mother'— it looks like a jellyfish—and use it to start your own vinegar. Buy some acceptable inexpensive red wine, pour it over, and continue adding other leftover wine. This makes for an interesting, rich vinegar. Homemade vinegar will be the next big thing in America," Batali asserts, "because it is so easy to make. Italians have been making it forever.

"We don't cook with balsamic vinegar in my restaurants," he says. "Rather, we 'anoint' a perfectly grilled piece of meat, or some beautiful strawberries, or some great

Parmigiano-Reggiano, with just a drizzle. There is a 'DOC' [Controlled Origin Denomination] for balsamic vinegar [just as there is for wine]. Samples submitted by vinegar makers are rated. The ones that are approved—called gold-standard vinegars—all go into the same shape bottle and get stamped. There are a couple of alternatives that are substantially less expensive:

- Compagnia Del Montale is a good vinegar. It has depth and viscosity, and a permanence of flavor that I really like.

- Villa Manodori is made by a friend of mine. It takes twelve years to make a batch. When he submitted it, he got 221 points from the DOC, and you need 225 to get approved. So he sells it for $32, as opposed to $65, and it is great!" (It is available at www.finefeast.com/villaman.html.)

Other Flavor Enhancers

"There are three Sicilian items that will radically improve how your food tastes," says Batali:

- *Salt-packed anchovies:* "Rinse the anchovies and put them in spaghetti with garlic. You will realize why that dish tastes so good in Italy! It is all about the anchovies."

- *Bottarga (dried salted roe of tuna or mullet):* "Grate it over the top of spaghetti *aglio e olio* with peperoncino. Or shave it with a truffle slicer over a salad of thinly shaved fennel and blood oranges. It is the essence of the foamy sea flavor, so you use it for anything in which you want the essence of the sea. It is so versatile; people use it on pasta, bruschetta, or carpaccio."

- *Capers:* "Soak them for twenty-four hours. A caper that is treated like this tastes like the fruit of a plant—not like a pickle, which is how most taste."

Simplicity of Technique

BROWNING IS A SIMPLE yet delicious method of bringing out lots of flavor in Italian cooking. It might be said that no one understands browning the way an Italian cook does. Lynne Rossetto Kasper explains, "Ninety percent of savory dishes in the Italian repertoire, whether they are braised, grilled, or sautéed, are based on caramelization. It is not done quickly, but by controlling the heat over a long cooking time so that there is a slow, gradual buildup of an incredibly delicious deep brown taste. Watching an Italian cook at home or in a restaurant is fascinating; the art of caramelization, which is not easy to do, is almost in an Italian's blood."

She continues, "There is always a multiple-layer reduction over a browned base, which is a fancy way of saying: Take a piece of chicken, cut it up, and pat it dry. Salt and pepper it. Film some olive oil in a large wide pan and start browning the chicken slowly. Get it crusty and brown. Keep turning it, scraping up that brown glaze from the pan. Add some sage and a branch of rosemary. Then add some onion, carrot, and minced celery leaves. As that slowly gets brown, you might add a little splash of red wine, but don't boil the wine—just let it slowly cook away. Then add a little tomato and a few black olives. It is all about the building of flavors."

(Andrew followed Kasper's advice and cooked chicken according to these guidelines. He slowed down, browned everything, and did not boil the wine—and blew everyone away at the dinner table!)

A Final Toast with Italian Wines

WINE HAS CHANGED EVERYWHERE, and Italy is no exception. "Italians used to make wine in a low-tech way, and that has changed," Piero Selvaggio points out. "Chianti is no longer associated with cheap wine in a straw bottle. A 1997 Solara was rated the best wine by *Wine Spectator* magazine. It is a victory for any of us who have been supporting Italian wines for so long. You see great depth in Piedmont and Tuscany, and people now know what a Brunello and a Chianti are capable of. Italian white wines have also come very far. They are now aged in better wood and can take some age."

The importance of matching wine with food can't be overstated. "Frankly, it is a book unto itself," says Mario Batali. When you choose a wine, it is important to understand the intensity of the dish. "When you are drinking an old Barolo, you need to make the food simple so that the wine stands up by itself. If you are having a simple Chianti, then you want something more complex to eat. The adage 'If it grows together, it goes together' also applies here. The best thing to do is ask your waiter or sommelier a lot of questions about the dishes you have chosen when selecting your wine.

"Say you are making food from Campagna. *Alici marinati* (marinated fresh anchovies) goes perfectly well with a Falanghina or a Greco Di Tufo from that region," he continues. "Yet those two wines would fall very short if you were drinking them with a chicken liver crostini with capers, chiles, and anchovies. The intensity of the dish needs to be matched or complemented by the wine.

"I regularly establish relationships with people who have a greater knowledge about a more specific product. It doesn't matter if it is wine, cheese, meat, or apples. Don't be afraid not to know; let someone help you. Then your palate becomes more evolved and you are more capable of doing what you want to do."

NachWaxman's Recommended Reading on Italian Cooking

If you're looking for a general introduction to Italian cuisine, the kinds of books recommended for French cuisine simply don't apply. There are no "canons" of Italian cuisine, no culinary academies whose rules and standards must be upheld. Rather, Italian cooking is a derivative of home cooking. And it's almost invariably regional, as there is no culinary center of Italy, the way Paris serves as the center of France.

Marcella Hazan's first two books, **The Classic Italian Cook Book** and **More Classic Italian Cooking,** are both out of print in their original form, but they were somewhat revised and combined in **Essentials of Classic Italian Cooking,** which is available. Marcella set out to produce a collection of authoritative, reliable recipes for the standard dishes of Italian cooking, believing that one should be able to find a good recipe for almost anything that might appear on an Italian menu. This book remains immensely reliable.

While Giuliano Bugialli has written numerous cookbooks, **The Fine Art of Italian Cooking** is the book. It takes a respectful, richly historical look at Italian cooking through his Florentine lens.

Beyond that, there are a number of books with a regional emphasis: Lynne Rossetto Kasper's **The Splendid Table: Recipes from Emilia-Romagna, the Heartland of Northern Italian Food,** Colman Andrews' **Flavors of the Riviera** (on the Liguria region), Mary Taylor Simeti's **Pomp and Sustenance: Twenty Five Hundred Years of Sicilian Cooking,** Benedetta Vitali's **Soffrito** (on Tuscany), and Carlo Middione's **The Food of Southern Italy.**

Also recommended is **Cucina Essenziale: Essential Cooking** by Stefano Cavallini, the talented young Italian chef cooking in London.

Braciolona
Braised Pork Roll with Ziti

3 pounds boneless pork shoulder or leg, butterflied and pounded to yield a large piece ½ inch thick and 12 inches square

Kosher salt and freshly ground black pepper

½ cup plus 2 tablespoons finely chopped fresh flat-leaf parsley

¼ cup pine nuts, toasted

½ cup dried currants

¾ cup freshly grated young pecorino cheese

16 slices prosciutto di Parma (about 8 ounces)

4 hard-boiled eggs, peeled and quartered lengthwise

Freshly grated nutmeg

¼ cup dried oregano

¼ cup extra-virgin olive oil

2 red onions, cut into ¼-inch dice

4 garlic cloves, thinly sliced

2 cups dry white wine

Three 28-ounce cans plum tomatoes, crushed by hand, with their juices

2 teaspoons hot red pepper flakes

2 pounds ziti, cooked until al dente (optional)

SERVES 8

The most difficult part of this dish might be finding a piece of pork big enough to stuff and roll. Few supermarkets stock a piece of pork shoulder this large, so you will probably need to special-order it. This is when it definitely pays to have a good relationship with a local butcher. The sauce from this dish is generally used to dress ziti, which is served as a pasta course. The meat is held in a warm place and served as a se-condo, or main course.

LAY THE PORK ON A cutting board and season with salt and pepper. In a small bowl, stir together ½ cup of the parsley, the pine nuts, currants, and ½ cup of the pecorino. Season with salt and pepper. Lay the prosciutto slices over the piece of pork, covering the meat completely. Sprinkle the parsley mixture evenly over the prosciutto. Arrange the egg quarters in two rows across the meat. Grate nutmeg over the meat and sprinkle with 2 tablespoons of the oregano, rubbing it between your fingers to release the essential oils. Carefully roll the meat up like a jelly roll and tie firmly in several places with butcher's twine. Season the roll with salt and pepper. (The roll can be refrigerated for a day or two.)

IN AN 8-QUART Dutch oven, heat the oil until smoking. Carefully brown the pork roll on all sides, taking your time to get it a deep golden brown; this should take 15 to 20 minutes. Remove the meat and set aside.

ADD THE ONIONS, the remaining 2 tablespoons oregano, and the garlic to the pot and cook until the onions are light golden brown and soft, 9 to 11 minutes. Add the wine, tomatoes, and pepper flakes and bring to a boil. Return the pork to the pot, reduce the heat, and simmer, partially covered, for 1 hour and 20 minutes, turning the pork occasionally to avoid sticking.

TRANSFER THE PORK to a cutting board and carefully remove the twine. Slice the *braciolona* into ¾-inch slices. Arrange, overlapping the slices, on a warm platter and sprinkle with the remaining ¼ cup grated pecorino and 2 tablespoons chopped parsley. Serve, or cover and keep warm if serving after the pasta with the sauce.

Gamberoni al'Acqua Pazza
Shrimp in "Crazy Water"

90

6 tablespoons extra-virgin olive oil

1 medium Spanish onion, cut into ½-inch dice

4 garlic cloves, thinly sliced

2 tablespoons chopped hot chiles

1 fennel bulb, trimmed, fronds reserved, and cut into ½-inch dice

One 28-ounce can tomatoes, crushed by hand, with their juices

2 cups dry white wine

½ cup seawater, or ½ cup water plus 1 teaspoon sea salt

16 jumbo shrimp, heads on, peeled, but tails left on and deveined

Freshly ground black pepper

SERVES 4 AS AN ENTRÉE, 8 AS AN APPETIZER

The southern Italian cooking liquid known as acqua pazza— *literally, "crazy water"—is traditionally seawater and seasonings, although it has come to include tomatoes, hot peppers, and any number of additional ingredients. If you can't get fresh shrimp, flash-frozen shrimp from the Gulf of Mexico are a great product; buy those with the heads and tails still on and thaw them in the refrigerator overnight (as opposed to blasting the frozen block with water).*

IN A 6-QUART SOUP POT, heat the oil over medium heat until smoking. Add the onion, garlic, chiles, and fennel and cook until soft and light golden brown, 8 to 10 minutes. Add the tomatoes, wine, and water and bring to a boil. Lower the heat and simmer for 10 minutes.

ADD THE SHRIMP and simmer until cooked through, about 5 minutes.

POUR INTO A SOUP TUREEN and garnish with the reserved fennel fronds. Serve with plenty of freshly ground black pepper.

Affogato al Caffe
Coffee Semifreddo "Drowned" in Coffee

2½ cups whole milk

6 tablespoons very strong espresso

6 large egg yolks

1 cup sugar

1 tablespoon pure vanilla extract

2 cups heavy cream

8 cups strong decaffeinated coffee, cooled

¼ cup unsweetened cocoa powder

SERVES 8

IN A 3-QUART SAUCEPAN, bring the milk to a boil over medium-high heat. Remove from the heat and add the espresso.

IN A MEDIUM BOWL, beat the yolks until pale yellow. Gradually add the sugar and beat until light yellow ribbons form when the beaters are lifted. Gradually stir in half of the hot milk, then stir the yolks into the remaining milk. Cook over low heat, without boiling, until the mixture thickly coats the back of a spoon, about 4 to 5 minutes. Remove from the heat and stir in the vanilla. Transfer to a bowl, set in a larger bowl of ice, and chill for 30 minutes.

WHIP 1½ CUPS of the cream to stiff peaks. Fold into the custard mixture. Transfer to an ice cream machine and freeze according to the manufacturer's instructions. Pack into a container and freeze until ready to serve. (The semifreddo can be made up to 2 weeks in advance.)

WHIP THE REMAINING ½ CUP cream to soft peaks. Place a scoop of semifreddo in each of eight tall glasses. Pour 1 cup cooled coffee over each scoop, dollop with whipped cream, and dust with cocoa. Serve immediately.

Mushroom Salad with Shaved Parmigiano

12 ounces white mushrooms

¼ teaspoon kosher salt

½ to 1 teaspoon fresh thyme leaves or 24 to 30 fresh flat-leaf parsley leaves

One 4- to 6-ounce (at least) piece Parmigiano-Reggiano

2 lemons

6 to 8 tablespoons virgin olive oil

Freshly cracked black pepper

SERVES 4 TO 6

We're fanatics about the preparation and presentation of salads, which are emphasized at our restaurants. First impressions are always important, and a great salad is a great way to begin a meal.

If you happen to have a fresh white truffle, by all means shave it over the mushrooms, but you needn't go to the expense to enjoy this lovely salad.

When you buy the Parmigiano-Reggiano, select a piece that is larger than the specified 4 to 6 ounces. You will be shaving the cheese over the mushrooms with a vegetable peeler, and it will be much easier to do this if you have a larger piece.

WIPE THE MUSHROOMS to remove any dirt clinging to them, trim the stem ends, and cut the mushrooms into paper-thin slices.

DISTRIBUTE HALF the mushrooms among four to six individual salad bowls. Sprinkle with a pinch of salt each and the thyme. With a vegetable peeler, shave a layer of Parmigiano-Reggiano over the mushrooms. Repeat with the remaining mushrooms, salt, and Parmigiano.

CUT 1 LEMON INTO 4 to 6 wedges for garnish. Squeeze the juice of the other lemon into a small bowl.

DRIZZLE 1 TO 1½ TABLESPOONS olive oil over each salad, pour on the lemon juice, and sprinkle with pepper. Serve garnished with the lemon wedges.

Johanne Killeen and George Germon

Grilled Onion Salad with Shaved Parmigiano

4 yellow or red onions (about 12 ounces each)

7 tablespoons virgin olive oil

About ½ teaspoon kosher salt

½ cup fresh flat-leaf parsley leaves

One 3- to 4-ounce piece Parmigiano-Reggiano

Juice of 1 lemon

SERVES 4

Buy large yellow or red onions for this recipe. Large onions are much easier to work with and will give you a nicer presentation than small ones. In the summer, we do our grilling outdoors. In the winter, we set up a grill in our fireplace. It doesn't require any special equipment: we put a stack of bricks on each side of the fire basket, lay a grill rack over the bricks, and we're in business!

PREPARE A MEDIUM-HOT charcoal fire, setting the grill rack about 4 inches above the coals.

TRIM THE ENDS OFF the onions and cut them horizontally into ⅜-inch slices; do not peel them. Brush the onion slices with 2 to 3 tablespoons of the olive oil and sprinkle them with the salt.

GRILL THE ONION SLICES for 6 to 8 minutes per side, or until the outsides are charred and the insides are completely cooked through. Transfer the slices to a platter and allow them to cool enough to handle.

REMOVE THE SKINS from the onion slices and separate the slices into rings. Put a layer of overlapping rings into each of four individual salad bowls, and garnish with some parsley leaves. With a vegetable peeler, shave a layer of Parmigiano over the onions. Repeat the layers until all the onion slices are used. Dress with the remaining olive oil and the lemon juice, and serve.

Johanne Killeen and George Germon

Crunchy Fennel Salad with Shaved Parmigiano

2 lemons

4 large fennel bulbs

½ teaspoon kosher salt

One 4- to 6-oz piece Parmigiano-Reggiano

½ cup fresh flat-leaf parsley leaves

6 to 8 tablespoons virgin olive oil

SERVES 4 TO 6

CUT 1 LEMON into 4 to 6 wedges for garnish. Squeeze the juice of the other lemon into a bowl. Set aside.

CUT OFF THE feathery leaves and fibrous stalks of the fennel. (You can chop the leaves and use them as a fresh herb. The stalks are not tender enough to eat, but they will lend a delicate flavor and fragrance to a homemade chicken stock.) Trim the root ends. With a sharp knife, cut the fennel lengthwise into paper-thin slices.

DISTRIBUTE HALF of the fennel among four to six individual salad bowls, and sprinkle with a little salt. With a vegetable peeler, shave a layer of Parmigiano directly over each salad. Garnish with half the parsley leaves. Repeat with the remaining fennel, salt, Parmigiano, and parsley. Drizzle the salads with the olive oil and lemon juice. Serve garnished with the lemon wedges.

Lynne Rossetto Kasper

Maccheroni with Tomato Sauce Mellowed by Simmering

5 large garlic cloves, coarsely chopped

12 large fresh basil leaves, torn

¼ medium onion, coarsely chopped

⅛ teaspoon salt

⅛ teaspoon freshly ground black pepper

¼ cup fruity extra-virgin olive oil

3½ pounds mixed ripe delicious tomatoes, cored and possibly peeled (do not seed), or two 28-ounce cans whole tomatoes, drained

1 pound modest-sized maccheroni, such as gemelli, strozzapretti, casareccia, zita, or penne, or substantial string pasta such as perciatelli, spaghetti, linguine, or bucatini

1½ to 2 cups freshly grated Parmigiano-Reggiano (6 to 8 ounces) (optional)

SERVES 6 TO 8 AS AN APPETIZER, 4 TO 6 AS AN ENTRÉE

Italian cooks make this sauce with unpeeled fresh tomatoes or canned ones, passing it through a food mill once it's cooked. My preference is for a more rustic, juicy sauce with bits of tomato, so I roughly chop it in a blender or food processor. Only if the fresh tomatoes' peels are tough or bitter do I peel them. This is a matter of personal choice.

IN A 4-QUART SAUCEPAN, combine the garlic, basil, onion, salt, pepper, and oil. Heat over medium-high heat for 1 minute, no more. Add the tomatoes, breaking them up with your hands as they go into the pan. Bring to a lively bubble, uncovered, and cook for 30 minutes, or until the sauce is thick and reduced by half. Stir often, watching for sticking and scorching. Remove the pan from the heat, cover, and let stand for 15 minutes.

PASS THE SAUCE through a food mill or chop it in a blender or food processor until in small pieces. (The sauce can be cooled and refrigerated for up to 2 days, or frozen for up to 3 months.)

COOK THE PASTA in 6 quarts fiercely boiling salted water, stirring often, until tender yet firm to the bite. Drain, toss with the reheated sauce, and serve immediately, with grated cheese, if desired.

Lynne Rossetto Kasper

Pollo a Due Tempi, Il Vecchio Molinetto
Erminia's Pan Crisped Chicken

One 3½-pound frying or roasting chicken

A 3-inch branch fresh rosemary, leaves only, or ⅓ teaspoon dried rosemary

1 small garlic clove

¼ teaspoon salt

⅛ teaspoon freshly ground black pepper

2 tablespons fresh lemon juice

6 tablespoons extra-virgin olive oil, plus a little extra for the second cooking

½ cup water

2 to 3 branches fresh rosemary for garnish (optional)

SERVES 4

At Erminia Marasi's trattoria Il Vecchio Molinetto in Parma, this dish is the specialty of the house.

Cooking the chicken in two stages and weighting it as it sautés draws off most of the bird's fat while crisping it perfectly. (The weight is improvised with what is available in the kitchen.) The two-step cooking also makes this good company food, as it needs little last-minute attention. First the chicken is sautéed, then hours later, just before dinner, it is reheated and given its final crisping.

This is an easy recipe, but it uses a technique unfamiliar for most of us. Follow the timing for the two-step cooking carefully, and you will have no difficulties. The chicken is excellent eaten cold or hot. If serving it hot, do not refrigerate it between cooking and reheating.

FOR THE BEST FLAVOR, season the chicken 18 to 24 hours before cooking. Rinse the chicken. Cut it into 8 pieces, halving each side of the breast and eliminating the wings and backbone. Pat the pieces dry. Blend the rosemary, garlic, salt, pepper, and 1 tablespoon of the lemon juice into a paste and rub over the chicken. Set the pieces on a platter, lightly cover with plastic wrap, and refrigerate.

FOR THE FIRST COOKING

HEAT THE OLIVE OIL in a 12-inch sauté pan over medium-high heat. Slip in the chicken pieces skin side down. Turn the heat to medium. Cook for 1 minute to lightly sear them, then turn the pieces to coat them with oil.

ARRANGE THE PIECES in a circle in the pan's center. Set a 9-inch cake pan on top of the chicken and weight it with several heavy cans. The breast pieces will cook faster than the thigh and leg pieces. Cook the weighted chicken, turning the breast pieces after 8 minutes and the thigh and leg pieces after 10 minutes, putting the pan back on the chicken after each turning; sprinkle the chicken with the remaining 1 tablespoon lemon juice before returning the weighted pan. Cook the breasts another 8 minutes, and remove. Cook the thigh and leg pieces another 10 minutes.

CRISP THE CHICKEN to a rich dark brown by turning the heat to medium-low, arranging all the pieces back in the pan skin side up, and cooking under the weighted pan for another 2 minutes. With a slotted spoon or tongs, immediately remove the pieces to a platter (set the pan aside). Cool for about 10 minutes, and then lightly cover the chicken with plastic wrap or foil. Set aside, or cover and refrigerate (see headnote).

POUR AWAY ALL THE FAT and replace the sauté pan over high heat. Swirl in the water and boil down by half while scraping up the brown bits with a wooden spatula. Turn the pan juices into a small bowl and put in freezer for 2 hours; then lift off hardened fat.

FOR THE SECOND COOKING

HAVE A SERVING DISH warming in a low oven. Film the bottom of the sauté pan with a little olive oil. Have the heat at medium when you slip in the chicken pieces skin side down. Top with the cake pan and weights, and heat for 5 minutes. Then remove the weighted pan. Turn the chicken pieces, moistening each piece with the defatted pan juices. Lightly cover with aluminum foil and heat for another 5 to 8 minutes.

PILE THE PIECES on the platter and garnish with rosemary sprigs, if desired. Serve hot or cold.

Carpaccio alla Piemontese

14 ounces beef tenderloin, very thinly sliced (see Note)

Salt and freshly ground black pepper

¼ cup extra-virgin olive oil

Juice of 1 lemon

3 ounces Parmigiano-Reggiano, very thinly sliced

4 celery stalks, very thinly sliced

1 ounce white truffles, if in season

SERVES 4

PLACE THE SLICES of beef between two sheets of plastic wrap and beat gently with a meat mallet until very thin.

ARRANGE THE MEAT on four large plates, without letting the slices overlap. Season with salt and pepper, then brush with the oil and lemon juice. Sprinkle the thin slices of Parmigiano, celery, and, hopefully, truffle over the beef, and serve.

Note
One way of obtaining very thin slices of beef is to freeze the meat slightly first.

Fusilli con Olive, Piselli, e Pecorino
Fusilli with Olives, Peas, and Pecorino

1 pound fusilli

½ cup olive oil

1 cup fresh peas, steamed until tender

1 pound spinach, trimmed, washed, steamed, and chopped (to equal ½ cup)

Salt and freshly ground black pepper

2 garlic cloves

Crushed dried chile peppers (optional)

½ cup dry white wine

5 fresh basil leaves, finely chopped

½ cup imported black olives, chopped

½ cup grated aged Pecorino

SERVES 6 TO 8

This recipe is typical of Southern Italy—strong flavors but intriguing in the mouth, especially if you match it to a nice robust wine.

IN A LARGE POT of boiling salted water, cook the fusilli until just al dente. Drain and toss with 1 tablespoon olive oil to keep the pasta from sticking together. Set aside to cool.

IN A FOOD PROCESSOR, combine half the peas and half the spinach with 5 tablespoons of the olive oil. Puree until smooth. Season with salt and pepper to taste and set aside.

IN A LARGE SKILLET, brown the garlic in the remaining 2 tablespoons oil over medium heat. Discard the garlic. Add the chiles, if using, and sauté. Add the wine and let it evaporate. Add the remaining peas and spinach and the basil, and sauté for another minute. Season to taste and set aside to cool.

IN A LARGE BOWL, combine the pasta, sautéed vegetables, olives, three-fourths of the pureed vegetables, and the Pecorino and toss well. Add more of the vegetable puree if needed. Serve at room temperature, within 3 to 4 hours.

Wine Recommendation
For this dish, we need a complex wine of rich fruit to cut through the saltiness of the ingredients and cleanse the palate with renewed sensations. I would try a robust Merlot (Matanzas Creek, Lewis Cellars, or St. Francis) or a Chianti riserva (Antinori, Fonterutoli, or Castello di Ama).

Torta di Formaggio con Fragole e Vecchio Balsamico Mascarpone Cheesecake with Strawberries in Balsamic Vinegar

1 Sponge Cake (recipe follows)

4 ounces cream cheese

1 cup sugar

1 teaspoon pure vanilla extract

½ cup mascarpone cheese

2 large egg whites

1 pint strawberries, stems removed and cut into quarters

2 tablespoons balsamic vinegar

SERVES 8

This is my variation on traditional cheesecake, with mascarpone added for its more distinguished flavor and lovely creaminess. This version is not mile-high, it's smaller in scale, with a slim layer of filling between the cake crust and the fruit.

PREHEAT THE OVEN to 325 degrees F.

SLICE A ½-inch-thick layer from the sponge cake; reserve the remaining cake for another use. Line the bottom of a 9-inch cake pan with the thin layer of sponge cake.

IN THE BOWL of an electric mixer fitted with the paddle attachment, beat the cream cheese and ½ cup of the sugar on medium speed until smooth, 2 to 3 minutes. Beat in the vanilla and mascarpone cheese. Set aside.

IN THE CLEAN DRY mixer bowl, with the whisk attachment, whip the egg whites on medium-high speed while slowly adding ¼ cup of the sugar. Beat for a few more minutes, until semi-stiff peaks form. Fold the whites into the cheese mixture. Pour or spoon the cheese mixture into the cake-lined pan.

PLACE THE CAKE PAN in a water bath. Bake for approximately 1 hour. Let cool, then refrigerate.

HALF AN HOUR before serving, prepare the strawberries: Put the fruit in a large bowl and toss with the remaining ¼ cup sugar and the balsamic vinegar. Allow to marinate for 20 minutes.

SLICE THE CHEESECAKE into individual portions and serve with the strawberries.

Pan di Spagna
Sponge Cake

1 cup plus 1 tablespoon cake flour

¾ cup plus 2 tablespoons sugar

6 large eggs, separated

2 tablespoons water

1 tablespoon pure almond extract

¾ teaspoon cream of tartar

MAKES ONE 9-INCH ROUND CAKE

PREHEAT THE OVEN to 350 degrees F. Lightly butter a 9-inch springform pan.

SIFT THE FLOUR and 3 tablespoons sugar together.

IN THE BOWL of an electric mixer, whisk the egg yolks and ½ cup of the sugar on high speed until very pale. Turn the mixer down to low and add the water and almond extract. Beat for 1 minute. Gently fold in sifted flour mixture. Set aside.

IN A CLEAN, dry mixer bowl, with the clean whisk attachment, beat the egg whites with the cream of tartar on medium-high speed until soft peaks form. Gradually add the remaining 3 tablespoons sugar and continue to beat until stiff peaks form. Gently fold the whites into yolk mixture until incorporated.

POUR INTO THE prepared pan and bake for 30 to 35 minutes, until a toothpick inserted in the center comes out clean. Allow the cake to cool on a wire rack.

RUN A SPATULA around the side of the pan and release the springform. Wrap the cake in plastic.

Spain

LETTING INGREDIENTS TASTE OF WHAT THEY ARE

*When cooking in Spain, we use very simple products, because
that's what customers want. You can serve them plain
shrimp with no sauce. In the United States, customers don't
even want just shrimp and sauce—they want three sauces!*

—MARIANO AZNAR, CHEF, SOLERA RESTAURANT, NEW YORK CITY

SPANISH CUISINE IS AN ENIGMA wrapped in a riddle. How did its food manage to stay so simple? Perhaps more than any other country in history, Spain has had the opportunity to become the fusion food capital of the world. It is only seven miles from Morocco, was inhabited by the Arabs, neighbors on France, and is situated across the sea from Italy. It is the home of Columbus and Cortés, who in turn made it a gateway from the New World. Chocolate and gold were welcomed, but chiles must have stayed on the boat—and the spice blend *ras el hanout* must have been sent back to Morocco. Instead of embracing the influences of other cultures, Spanish cuisine celebrates the purity of its native ingredients in simple dishes like boiled octopus sprinkled with paprika and salt, or seared chorizo, which is so good that the Spanish don't even bother to serve it with a sauce.

This is not to say that Spain has let the world pass it by. The country's most acclaimed contemporary restaurant, the Michelin three-star El Bulli, is known for employing the most inventive techniques anywhere in the world today. Yet, this cutting-edge food still shows its Spanish roots. The dishes don't rely on combining flavors from other cultures, but rather on celebrating the true essence of ingredients in creative ways. Chef Ferran Adrià will serve you a local turnip or beet—but it may be in the form of a "turnip foam" or "beet sorbet" offered as your vegetable course.

Spain's restaurant philosophy is similar to that of a country one might least expect: Japan. The Japanese go to different restaurants for specific dishes—from noodles to sushi to tempura—because each restaurant has its own specialty. The Spanish do the same, hopping from one tapas bar to the next for a specific dish. They will savor the olives at one spot and the calamari at another. Like the Japanese, the Spanish also want their food to be simple. They want a high-quality ingredient with as little done to it as possible. In Japan, you'll be served tempura with a dipping sauce, whereas in Spain you'll find fried calamari with alioli.

As in neighboring Morocco, Spain features one of the most pleasure-loving food cultures in the world. The three-hour lunch is so sacred that even former dictator Francisco Franco could not do away with it. The Spanish think nothing of having tapas for a couple of hours with friends around 8 P.M., then having dinner at 11 P.M. In fact, Spain is so food-centric that it identifies its regions in terms of foods and food preparations, such as roasts (central Spain), fried foods (south central), stews (north), and rice dishes (east, or Mediterranean).

How has a country with so many influences managed to stay this purist course? "Our gastronomy begins with the people," explains Jose Andres, chef-owner of Jaleo in Washington, D.C. "It is not like France, where the cuisine came down from the monarchy. Spanish food is more homey. If you analyze our food dish by dish, you will see that we have many similarities to the French, but we have a different perspective in our approach."

"The Spanish will take simple ingredients and combine them in unusual, delicious ways," explains Penelope Casas, author of *The Foods and Wines of Spain*. "The Spanish tortilla is a perfect example: All it consists of are eggs, potatoes, and olive oil—yet people go crazy over it! The same is true for the Basque sauce known as *pil pil*, which is garlic, oil, and a little gelatin. It comes out like a mayonnaise and tastes great."

When simple ingredients can be so great, it is good to keep a sharp eye out when dining, no matter where you are. "In Spain, a family will sometimes run a restaurant and live in the same building," says Jose Andres. "We stopped once at a roadside tavern, where the restaurant was in the front of the house. The son was the waiter and the menu was simple. I asked for the bathroom and had to go through the house to get there. While on my way, I spied some peppers on a table, and when I got back to my table, I asked about them, because they were not on the menu. It turns out that they were for the family's dinner, but they served them to us instead, and they were delicious!

"You could not judge that meal on a scale of one to ten. How do you compute the smell of bull being fried in a pan in the bull region of Spain or the father of a family serving you his own food? This, to me, is Spanish cooking again—it gets back to the people."

Penelope Casas has led tours through Spain for Americans, who, she has found, are always surprised to taste the flavors that the Spanish coax from the simplest ingredients. "We once stopped at a winery with a tour group, and they served us some potatoes," she recalls. "They had been stewed with a little tomato, smoked paprika, and pork ribs. It was the cheapest thing you could eat, just simple country food, but the

Americans went crazy for it! It was especially funny because by that time they had eaten in some of the finest restaurants in Spain."

The simplest dishes of Spain are also the ones closest to the hearts of its people. "I traveled across Spain and asked chefs what their favorite dish was when they were little," says Casas. "I talked to chefs cooking everything from fine cuisine to simple cuisine, but they all had the same answer: fried eggs! It is important to note that Spaniards never eat fried eggs for breakfast; they eat them for lunch or dinner. You fry them in olive oil until they get crispy, and then you serve them with some ham or chorizo. When it's my husband's birthday, this is the dish he wants!"

A fried egg for a birthday dinner? That is the essence of Spain! It is not about long, involved techniques or hard-to-find ingredients. Think of Spanish ingredients in dishes as a long-married couple—a husband and wife who have been together for so long that they complete each other's sentences and communicate in simple, uncomplicated harmony!

Spain Is Not in Latin America

SEVERAL SPANISH EXPERTS LAMENTED what they saw as Americans' confusion about the cooking of Spain, given the relative scarcity of Spanish restaurants here compared to the number of those serving other cuisines. "They confuse it with the cooking of Mexico, Cuba, and South America," observes Penelope Casas. "But, they are getting the idea, slowly."

The problem stems in part from the way Americans use the word "Spanish," according to Jim Becker, former chef-owner of Rauxa in Boston. "Most Americans associate the word with Latin America. In the U.S., you may hear someone described as Spanish when they are actually Colombian, Mexican, or Puerto Rican. When I hear 'Spanish' used that way, I'll ask the person if he or she is from England. They will inevitably say 'no,' and I make the point that speaking English does not make you British any more than speaking Spanish makes a person Spanish.

"Even relatively educated food people make false generalizations about Spanish food," he continues. "They think the food is spicy, or that it contains rice and beans. I cannot stress enough that traditional Spanish food is not spicy!" Jose Andres agrees: "Spanish food is *not* spicy! It should not be hot. We have a few dishes that are a little spicy, but that's it."

Not wanting to add to the confusion about Spanish cuisine, Andres sometimes hesitates to put certain Spanish dishes on his menu. "At Jaleo, we make empanadas from the area of Asturias, but we do it with some reluctance, even though it is a great local dish," Andres admits. "The dough is made from wheat and corn flour, and I'm afraid the public will see corn and think, 'Mexican food.' However, corn is used in small amounts in the north of Spain."

Another popular misconception is that sangriá is the drink of choice to accompany Spanish cuisine. "You would *never* find a Spaniard in Spain ordering sangriá in a restaurant," Jim Becker points out. "It is not meant to accompany your meal. They do drink it, but not seriously. You might make it for the beach or at a picnic. I had the hardest time when I opened my Rauxa convincing people that they did not want sangriá with dinner!"

Culinary Map of Spain: Regional Simplicity

To describe Spanish cooking is a big challenge. To describe Spanish regional cooking is easier. Spanish cooking is the sum of all its regional cooking. It is the art of many regions. —JOSE ANDRES

SPAIN IS ONE OF THE more difficult countries to divide into just a few general regions. Many countries can be divided into North, South, East, and West from both a geographical and a food perspective—but not Spain. Experts and the Spaniards themselves classify the gastronomic regions of Spain in a variety of ways, which do not always neatly correspond with one another.

"The regions of Spain are very different," says Penelope Casas, "so much so that sometimes it feels like you are entering different countries. Food that you were just eating can completely disappear when you change regions. When you go to Asturias, everyone is drinking hard cider, but this disappears as soon as you cross into the next region."

If you were to drive from Asturias, in the north, to Valencia, in the south, in one day, you could start by listening to bagpipes while drinking cider, stop to watch a bullfight in the center of Spain, and then sip sherry and eat paella while admiring the Mediterranean Sea. Still, this trip would leave out so many other regions, like the Basque area, which possesses its own language, and a preponderance of male-only cooking clubs.

"Spanish food is rooted in history, religion, and geography," continues Casas. "The country is divided by several mountain ranges, which historically have been difficult to cross, so people tended to stay in their areas. Also, the climates of the regions are very different. Because of this, it is exciting to travel in Spain. If you want *paella*, you have to go to the coast, to Valencia. If you eat paella in another area, it can be pretty bad, because they have no tradition with the dish."

The definitions of the food regions might seem a little simplistic to the passionate palate. A good comparison would be the generalities of "Northern" and "Southern" Italian food, which are far too vague given the twenty-one regions of Italy and all the subdivisions within them. Spain is no different. "Spain is much like Italy. A dish may come from a certain town and five miles away they have never heard of it! It's amazing, and you find that throughout the country," says Jim Becker.

Despite the culinary differences between the regions of Spain, the rule of simplicity reigns. Many of the most famous dishes rely on well-combined ingredients rather than elaborate techniques or seasonings.

North or Atlantic Spain: Stews

You always feel some attachment to the region where you were born, and for me that place is Asturias. I walk into a restaurant there and smell the smells and immediately think "I belong here."

—JOSE ANDRES

Ingredients in Spain take on critical importance because the preparations are so simple. "Compare a French *cassoulet* to a Spanish *fabada*, the classic bean stew of the north of Spain, in Asturias," suggests Jose Andres. "I am sorry, but it is very easy to make a cassoulet taste good. Fabada is so simple that the challenge is much more difficult. However, while the dish is made with only white beans, three pieces of pork, and two sausages, it is the best dish you'll ever eat in your life! The beans are ten dollars a pound, and they are the ultimate bean: white, skinless, big, and buttery. They are so delicate they taste as if they are from heaven! They have to be cooked very slowly, for almost five hours."

The Galicia region of the north is very different from the rest of Spain. "It actually has a Celtic heritage," Jim Becker explains. "When you think 'Spain,' you probably think of sunshine and flamenco dancers, but Galicia is wet. The men wear kilts and play bagpipes. Hard cider, not wine, is the beverage of choice. Galicia's food is very similar to that of Portugal. The wines they drink are similar to those of the *vinho verde* [green wine] region in Portugal, light and refreshing. Some have a little effervescence and a touch of sweetness.

"Empanadas are, literally, very big in Galicia. They are large pies, unlike the more common half-moon turnovers, and are typically stuffed with meat or shellfish. They are delicious and one of the most popular dishes in the region," he says. "Picón, considered by many to be the best blue cheese in Spain, is from here. The cheese is a mix of cow's, sheep's, and goat's milk, which is then wrapped in chestnut leaves to age and cure in caves."

One of Spain's most famous dishes is from the north of Spain: boiled, sliced *pulpo* (octopus) finished with paprika oil and garlic. Cooking octopus could be compared to roasting a chicken—simple in theory, but hard to get right. For some chefs, the secret is boiling the octopus with corks, which is said to tenderize the meat.

The north is also known for baking the best bread in Spain. The loaves are large and have a thick crust. Wheat predominates, while little to no rice is grown here. This is the area of the famous light Albariño white wine and Spain's other noteworthy blue cheese, Cabrales. Fish, especially salmon, trout, and hake, are a huge part of the diet. This area may rely less on spices than any other part of Spain; instead, apples, onions, and wine are used frequently as seasonings.

Central Spain: Roasts

Our regions are about the products that are grown within them. The area known as "The Roasts" is also the land of Rioja. The Rioja vines are used for the roasting and the wines are drunk with the roasted food, so everything goes together.

—JOSE ANDRES

The harsh climate of Spain's central region calls forth the winter-season staples of hearty foods like pork, wild game, and legumes, and heat-generating cooking techniques like roasting. It's no wonder that in this region, roasted meats are elevated to an art.

"The central region produces what is considered poor man's food—you see lots of beans and sausages," says Jim Becker. "However, poor man's food does not equate to bad food! Madrid, which is the culinary melting pot of Spain, is known for a stew called *cocido madrileño,* which is made with chickpeas, meat, potatoes, and leeks and served in separate courses, like a French pot aú feu."

South of Madrid, one will find lots of beans, chickpeas, lentils, and potatoes employed in dishes, including lots of soups. The egg and potato *tortilla* hails from this region. The area of La Mancha is a saffron capital of the world, and saffron and cumin are frequently used spices. *Garbanzos con espinacas* (chickpeas with spinach and saffron) is a classic dish of central Spain. You also see Arabic influences, such as *escabeches* of pickled partridge or other game. The area is also known for Manchego cheese, which might be the most well known Spanish cheese outside of the country.

"In the area known as Extremadura, a cookbook written by Benedictine monks was reputedly stolen and taken to France during the Napoleonic invasion," says Jim Becker. "Two of Escoffier's famous recipes came from this book, one for partridge and one for the first *consommé,* known in Spain as *consuido.*"

South Central Spain: Fried Foods

The south central region extends across the bottom of Spain. Reflecting its rich food history, it faces the Atlantic Ocean on the west, Morocco to the south, and the Mediterranean to the east. Most of this area is part of the region of Andalusia.

"When people think of Spain, they usually picture Andalusia," says Jim Becker. "Andalusia is the southernmost region of Spain, of which Seville is the capital. This is where you find flamenco dancers, bullfights, and gazpacho, and where most people believe tapas originated, before being exported to other regions.

"Andalusia has the strongest North African and Middle Eastern influences of any region in Spain," he continues. "People don't realize that couscous was eaten here up to

GAZPACHO

The first gazpachos were made before the arrival of peppers and tomatoes from the New World. "Known as white gazpachos, they're made with almonds, garlic, vinegar, bread, and grapes, and can still be found in the southern part of the country," says Jim Becker. "Gazpacho is a very regional dish, and every cook makes it differently. Some are made completely with pureed vegetables, while others will be tomato broth with raw cucumbers and peppers. With the tomato broth versions, you will be served the chopped vegetables on the side to put in your own bowl."

Jose Andres believes that gazpacho is the perfect dish to introduce you to Spanish cooking. "The dish depends on good ingredients, and ingredients drive Spanish cooking," he says. "The secret is to follow the rules: Use the best possible ingredients! Use only fresh tomatoes, cucumbers, peppers, and garlic. Use a good Spanish olive oil, and a good sherry vinegar. Do not add anything spicy—no Tabasco. It seems that nine out of ten gazpacho recipes that I see call for Tabasco, but this is wrong. The dish is not spicy. Blend everything together, add some salt, and enjoy." (See the recipe on page 130.)

two hundred years ago. Along with Catalonia, Andalusia is home to some of the oldest documented food in Spain, dating back to the thirteenth century."

In Andalusia, you will find more olive oil than anywhere else in the world; the area is host to 165 million olive trees. No wonder this area is celebrated for its fried foods, which range from fried fish to *croquetas* (potato croquettes) to *empanadillas* (small sweet or savory pies). Other common foods in the region include red and white gazpachos, shellfish, and oranges. Sherry, Spain's most famous wine, is also produced here.

The best of Spain's famed salted and semi-dried hams are also from Andalusia, which provides an ideal climate for curing the hams. The vast majority of the cured ham made in Spain is serrano, which is made from pork, but about ten percent is Iberian,

TAPAS

The word "tapas" has been borrowed freely in recent years to refer to any food served in small portions in restaurants. "As a result, you are starting to see restaurants offering 'authentic Spanish tapas.' I would define authentic tapas as small bites of food that accompany the drinking of sherry or wine before a meal," says Jim Becker.

"*Tapa* means 'cover'," he continues. "The old wives' tale is that bartenders used to put a piece of bread on top of a person's sherry or wine glass to keep the flies out. Eventually, they started putting food on top of the bread. The story is colorful, but it's more likely that bartenders served food to entice customers and it then blossomed into a custom.

"Tapas are simple foods meant for small bites. Traditionally, there are two sizes, the larger being big enough for two people to have a bite. Tapas can be something as simple as skewered or fried food or as elaborate as clams cooked in broth."

Seville is often considered the capital of tapas. Rufino Lopez, owner of the tapas restaurant Solera in New York City, reports, "People in Seville divide tapas into three categories: *á liño,* marinated tapas, which may be a little salty or acidic, such as olives or sardines; *chacina,* pork products, like ham or chorizo, and dried meats; and *cocina,* cooked foods, which are usually more elaborate."

"Nowadays, there are some tapas that you find all over Spain," adds Solera's chef Mariano Aznar. "The most common are *boquerones* [marinated anchovies], cheese, chorizo, serrano ham, marinated olives, sardines, and anchovies. Tortilla is made everywhere—in bars, restaurants, and homes. Other tapas, such as *pulpo* [octopus] in Galicia, fried fish or fried croquettes in the south, romesco sauce with fish in Catalonia, and brandade, salsa verde, clams, and bean stew in the north, are regional."

Accompanying beverages differ from region to region as well. "In Barcelona. you would find cava paired with tapas, and in the south, you would find sherry," says Ron Miller, sommelier and general manager of Solera.

"Enjoying tapas is a social activity," he continues. "It is a healthy way to eat, because the portions are small and are meant to be shared. Don't try to taste everything all at once: one bar may have upwards of twenty different kinds! Some tapas bars are known for doing one thing really well, so you might go from bar to bar, eating tortilla at one and then progressing to another for olives or mussels, another for cod, and maybe another for the best sherry selection. People will come to Solera just for our olives, which we marinate for at least a week.

"If you are having tapas for the first time," he advises, "the key is to open yourself up to trying different things. Start with a few cold things and progress from there. Start with things that are familiar to you, but then ask the bartender for some recommendations. Try some traditional tapas, such as tortilla, or *patatas bravas,* which are fried potatoes

served with chile sauce and alioli. The great thing is that if you do get something you don't like, it will only have cost you five or six dollars. It's not like you're paying thirty dollars for an entrée, so you can be open to experimenting."

"A good progression for tapas is to go from lighter to heavier," suggests Mariano Aznar. "Some light cold tapas are almonds or olives. An example of a light hot tapa would be fried calamari or shrimp. Brandade is also good. Next, move on to shellfish or shellfish stews, then progress to the meats and meat stews, starting with rabbit and moving to heavier ones, such as oxtail, or a cold tapa such as peppers stuffed with meat."

At Solera restaurant you can finish a tapas meal with sweet tapas. The most unusual yet delicious choice is *picatostes,* mounds of bittersweet chocolate on toast points, drizzled with extra virgin olive oil and a sprinkle of salt.

which is made from wild boar. The most prized is, without question, *Ibérico de bellota*, which is made from exclusively acorn-fed boar.

"Having the boar feed on acorns gives the ham great flavor," says Becker. "I have compared a great many hams, and I still find Spanish-cured ham to be superior to Italian prosciutto. Serrano ham has a sweeter, nuttier taste."

Mediterranean Spain: Rice Dishes

When you go to Barcelona, it is all about seafood. Spain has a variety of seafood to which probably only Japan can compare. France and Italy do not come close!

—JOSE ANDRES

Mediterranean Spain runs north to south along the country's east coast facing the Mediterranean Sea and Italy, with part of the region bordering on France. "The food of Mediterranean Spain is especially known for its simplicity," says Jose Andres. "If they can do less, they always will. The seafood is very simple, just cooked with a few drops of olive oil, or baked in salt, or fried with just a dusting of flour. Soups are also very popular in this region." One of the most famous dishes is *zarzuela de mariscos*, a spicy shellfish stew. The region is also known for tangy sauces and its generous use of saffron, as well as its wines and produce.

"The fish in America are very different from the fish in Spain," says Mariano Aznar. "Mediterranean fish are from warmer waters. The fish in the Mediterranean are also much saltier; you really notice these differences in sardines, shrimp, and lobster. I have noticed that the cold waters of the Atlantic, however, make for better cod and bass.

"Cod and hake are the staples of Spain. Hake is one of my favorite fish, especially when it is properly caught and forty to sixty hours old. Hake is like cod, only a little lighter in texture. You can't fillet it, so you cut it into steaks, and the best way to serve it is with a little oil or sofrito."

Catalonia and Valencia are the two prominent regions of Mediterranean Spain. Catalonia has some of the most sophisticated cuisine in the country, and Valencia is the home of paella.

Catalonia

"Culturally, linguistically, and gastronomically, Catalonia has more in common with southern France than with the rest of Spain," explains Jim Becker. "The Catalan culture actually extends into France. There is an area there known as the Roussillon, and its capital city, Perpignan, is also considered the second Catalan capital.

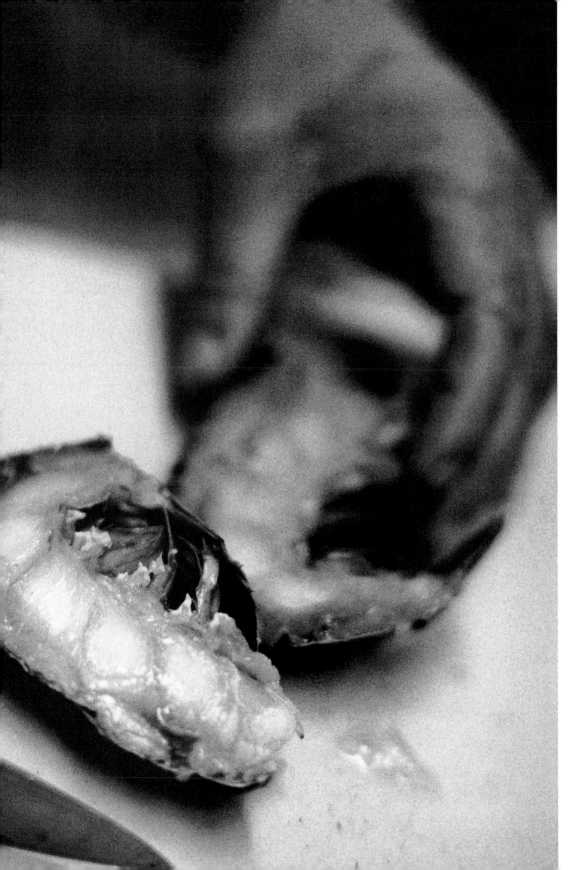

"Many dishes that people consider Provençal are actually Catalonian. You will find the same dish with a different name in Catalonia. Ratatouille, for example, is called *xan-faina,* which means 'symphony.' You will also find fish stews called *bullabesa* instead of bouillabaisse. The Catalans eat more aïoli than the French do, and there is strong evidence that it originated in Catalonia. The other thing Catalonia shares with France is meat dishes with fruit. You will find things like duck with figs and goose with pears, which you don't find in the rest of Spain. The sauces in these sweet and savory dishes are flavored and thickened with almonds, pine nuts, or hazelnuts.

"Catalonians," Becker continues, "finish dishes with *picada,* which is made with bread, garlic, and nuts, all pounded to a paste in a mortar and pestle. Some versions may include bitter chocolate or saffron. It is added toward the end of the cooking to thicken the dish and add flavor, and it is cooked just long enough to cook out the raw garlic flavor. *Picada* adds a whole different dimension to a dish. Catalan food is very medieval in its cooking style, with techniques dating back to the Middle Ages. If you look back in thirteenth-century Catalan cookbooks, you'll find that some of the recipes are still made the same way today."

Valencia: The Area of Rice

Paella is a unique and magical dish. Its simplicity is part of its sophistication.

—JOSE ANDRES

"In Valencia, they speak Catalan and have Catalan-influenced dishes, but the area is best known for rice," says Jim Becker. "They say that Valencians eat fifty pounds of rice per person per year. This is where paella originated."

"If paella were a person, he or she could make a lot of money suing people for defamation of character!" jokes Jose Andres. "This is a dish that has been completely disrespected. It has come to mean any dish with rice. It gets made with everything from Uncle Ben's to jasmine rice.

"Paella does not have to be yellow," he continues. "I don't know where that started, but it is wrong. I once had a customer send back paella because it was not yellow and I could not convince her that this was the correct way. Saffron may or may not be in the dish, but if you notice the flavor of saffron, it is definitely wrong.

"Paella needs to be made with good stock, a *sofrito* (see page 134), and only one or two ingredients, like rabbit, chicken, or lobster," adds Andres. "It should not be made with thirty ingredients, and it should not be made with chorizo."

Andres is not the only chef with strong opinions about this classic dish. "Don't get me started on paella!" says Jim Becker. "In the United States, or even in touristy restaurants in Spain, you will see lobster, sausage, and chicken together in paella, which is definitely not traditional. Paella is prepared all over Spain, but the original from Valencia traditionally contained rabbits, eels, and snails. A true Valencian will tell you that you never mix meat and shellfish together in paella. You make either a meat or a fish paella. In Valencia, paella is eaten at room temperature, not hot, because the Valencians believe it tastes better that way. People go to a shop where a large pot of paella has been prepared, and they buy a portion to take home."

    "When I was working on my paella book, I went from place to place eating rice," recalls Penelope Casas. "Americans think paella is always the same dish, but that is a big misconception. Paella is anything you want it to be. There is no one 'right way' to make it, but there are some guidelines. Spaniards believe that each ingredient in a paella should stand out and be highlighted. If you have too many ingredients, it is just a jumble.

"My favorite, after all the research for my paella book, was black rice paella, especially when eaten with a strong alioli (see page 143). I ate a great many researching my book, but the good news is that I liked the last paella of my research as much as I liked the first!"

The most important thing to remember is that paella is about the rice, not the other ingredients. "It should be made with Bomba rice, a short-grain rice that absorbs less water than Italian Arborio, which looks similar," says Jose Andres. "Paella also needs to be cooked in a paella pan, because the shallow pan means the rice can better absorb the cooking liquid."

A paella pan is wide and shallow, so that as much rice as possible is in contact with the hot bottom of the pan. One of the signs of a good paella is the *socarrat,* or the crunchy layer of rice on the bottom of the pan.

The Basque people inhabit the mountainous region between Spain and France. "You find French Basques and Spanish Basques, but the bulk of the Basques live in Spain," explains Jim Becker. "The Basques are a little mysterious, because their language is not related to any other language. It was as if they were plopped down in the middle of the mountains, with no relationship to any other culture around them.

"Another unusual thing about the Basques is their men-only gastronomic societies, which are basically cooking clubs," he continues. "They are made up of men from many different economic levels and backgrounds, and they have cooking competitions. Each week a different member of the club will prepare a different dish.

"The cuisine is considered, along with Catalan, to be the most refined in Spain, though Catalan cooking is more elaborate. Basque cooking celebrates the qualities of perfect fresh ingredients; hake with clams and peas is a perfect example. *Piperade*, garlic and peppers cooked with scrambled eggs, is a traditional dish. Pimientos stuffed with fish and pork and mushrooms with Idiazábal, a sheep's milk cheese, are also popular. And the Basque region is known for producing the best beef in Spain."

The Basques make one of the most unusual sauces in the world, called *pil pil*. Jose Andres enthuses, "It is amazing! It is as thick as a velouté made with flour, or a béchamel, but there is nothing like it in France. It is made with cod, olive oil, garlic, and chile pepper—that is it! The secret is the gelatin of the cod. The gelatin mixes with the olive oil and is amazingly stable. It can take almost a half hour to blend the sauce, and it then gets paired with a piece of cod. This is the great white sauce of the Basques, and it is the ultimate in simplicity."

The Basques have traditionally been deep-sea fisherman, so fish—including tuna, crab, and cod—are an important part of the cuisine. Salt cod is usually prepared with dried peppers, fresh peppers, onions, and salt pork.

Time to Eat

WHEN RON MILLER SAID, "Enjoying tapas is a social activity," he could just as easily have been referring to the Spanish way of life, much of which is conducted in or around restaurants.

"I was a Spanish major at Vassar, and when I was nineteen, I went to Spain to spend a summer with a family," recalls Penelope Casas. "When I got off the plane, the son was there to meet me—little did I know I was meeting my future husband! That same night, he and I went out to bars to meet his friends, who played guitar and sang, and we stayed out until two or three in the morning. I was completely transported by this world! I would do it every night and somehow make it to class by seven the next morning.

"Food goes hand in hand with the lifestyle, in which a lot of time is spent over meals. It is said that there are more bars in Spain than in all the other European countries put together," continues Casas. "That is what the Spanish do! They love to be out meeting friends. Home entertaining is almost unheard of. Also, people in Spain do not eat in motion. They wouldn't dream of drinking their coffee in the car. You want coffee? You stop in a bar, have your coffee, and chat for a while. Then get back on the road."

The Spanish Day of Meals

I grew up on a farm, so breakfast would always include milk still warm from the cow!

—RUFINO LOPEZ

A day in Spain revolves around several meals, most of which are taken in a social context. Most days begin at around eight o'clock, with a light breakfast consisting of a roll or slice of ham, with coffee or juice. After starting work, it is common to stop at around eleven for a light snack at a bar, such as a sandwich on crusty bread with a slice of ham and cheese.

"Most Spanish work from 9 A.M. to 1 P.M.," explains Rufino Lopez. "At one o'clock, everything closes for three hours, and after lunch people take a siesta. Then they go back to work from four until eight. Around nine, they go out for tapas, and then get to dinner around eleven. I personally don't know how they do it!"

Lunch is typically eaten between one and three and consists of appetizers, a main dish, and dessert. Around six, it is time for a light snack. After work, from around eight until ten or so, depending on the region, it will be aperitivos and perhaps more tapas.

"The Spanish eat extremely late," says Jim Becker. "You eat dinner no earlier than ten o'clock at night, but more commonly it is eleven or eleven-thirty."

"At Botin, the oldest restaurant in Madrid [which dates from 1725]," says Lopez, "they have the American seating at six o'clock, the German seating at eight-thirty, and the Spanish seating at midnight!"

Setting Up Your Spanish Kitchen

GETTING STARTED COOKING SPANISH FOOD is relatively easy, as no elaborate equipment is required. "You can still make a pretty good paella without a paella pan," says Jim Becker. In addition, "You don't need anything truly exotic," he continues. "It is not like walking into an Asian market, where there are so many things you may not know. Most Spanish ingredients are familiar to Americans." Becker adds that there are a few things you can't find easily in the U.S., such as certain sausages, but even those can be mail-ordered.

"A mortar and pestle are key to Spanish cooking," insists Penelope Casas. "Every household has one, and they use it! Mashed ingredients are very important. Mash up some garlic, nuts, and parsley, and you have the base for a sauce."

"Almost all Spanish dishes are started with a *sofrito*, which you also see used in Italy [but there it is spelled *soffrito*]," says Becker. "In Spain, sofrito is made with onions, peppers, and garlic, cooked slowly in olive oil until the mixture becomes jam-like. You start a dish with the sofrito and then build on it. Soups or stews are started with it, as well as many everyday dishes. It is something you can make a batch of to have on hand."

Your Spanish Larder

There are no complex spice blends. Spain essentially relies on two spices: paprika and saffron.

—JIM BECKER

"Spain does not rely that heavily on herbs and spices, points out Penelope Casas. "Traditionally you really only see coriander, parsley, saffron, and herbs that grow wild, like rosemary and thyme. Most Spanish cooking relies on very basic ingredients, so it is not hard to reproduce it in America," she says reassuringly.

Bread: "It may sound silly to list bread as an ingredient, but it gets added to many dishes," says Becker. "Spanish breads are similar to French baguettes, though recently whole wheat bread has become popular. As in France, you buy it fresh every day, and then turn it into bread crumbs the next. You might even buy bread twice a day, because it doesn't have much of a shelf life."

Sausages: "Chorizo is used in bean stews, where it is cooked for a long time and imparts an incredible taste to the dishes. Each region in Spain has its own style of sausage," says Casas. "Sausages are vital to the Spanish kitchen," agrees Becker. "I get them from a company in California called La Espanola." (www.donajuana.com)

Dried chickpeas: "This is something you see a lot of in Spain," says Becker, "especially in the central region, where they are used in soups, stews, and salads."

Nuts: Almonds are most common, and are served fried as tapas and ground into sauces such as romesco (see page 141). "Hazelnuts and pine nuts are also used in some regions," says Becker.

Smoked paprika: *"Pimentón de La Vera,* smoked paprika, is what makes Spanish food so identifiable to me," says Becker. "I once had a vegetarian customer who insisted her paella had meat in it, but what she was tasting was the paprika. I let her smell it, and she finally believed me." (It is available through www.kalustyans.com.)

Olive oil: "Olive oils are produced all over Spain. The key is to get a good one, so you need to spend a little money," says Becker. "Spain produces more olive oil than any other country. Much Italian olive oil, in fact, is Spanish oil imported into Italy and bottled there. I use a Catalan-style oil with a peppery quality, made from Arbequina olives."

"Rafael Salgado has a great fruity-flavored olive oil," says Casas. "I must admit that I would love this olive oil even if it weren't made by my husband's cousin. *Saveur* rated it as one of 100 best ingredients. I also like the oils of Andalusia and Catalonia."

A TRADITIONAL CATALAN MEAL WITH JIM BECKER

Like anywhere else in Spain, you would have some olives and almonds with sherry to start. Then you might have some serrano ham and cheese, followed by fried calamari with romesco sauce.

For a main course, a typical dish would be pork with a fruit sauce, such as one of pomegranate. Traditionally in Spain, you won't get a dish composed of a protein, a starch, and a vegetable on the same plate. Typically, if you go to a restaurant and want a vegetable, you'll have to ask for it separately.

Salads, however, are considered part of the meal. A traditional Catalan salad would include some anchovies, either fresh or canned, with tomato, lettuce, onion, hard-cooked egg, and dressing. The salads of Spain are not too exciting—you don't see a large mixture of greens like you do in Italy or France.

Dessert would be *crema Catalana;* "burnt cream" is the older name for it. I always laugh when our crema Catalana is described as similar to a *crème brulée,* as the Spanish version of the dessert is older than the French.

RON MILLER OF SOLERA RESTAURANT ON SHERRY AND CAVA

Unfortunately, many people have had bad sherry experiences, either from sneaking some of the cooking sherry or drinking sweet cream sherry. There is nothing wrong with cream sherry; it is just not anywhere near as food-friendly as dry sherry. When we do a tasting menu, sherry will be served throughout the meal.

With tapas, the drier sherries are better because they stand up to the high acids of most tapas food. Red wine is not the best match with tapas, because high-acid vinaigrettes are often used in tapas. Think about salty cheese paired with red wine—you have a war in your mouth.

For drier sherries, start with a manzanilla or fino. They are the same type of sherry, but manzanilla is from the coast and has a slightly tangier, lighter style. We will serve fino and manzanilla sherries with tapas of seafood, fried foods, or sliced ham.

A dry sherry, for those trying one for the first time, is like a dry white wine. It will be on the yeasty and minerally end of the flavor spectrum, with the saltiness of the sea.

There will be fruit overtones, such as green olive, and a hint of raw almond. The almond note will become stronger as the sherry ages. As a fino sherry ages, it becomes an amontillado. The wine takes on nutty notes, such as almond and hazelnut.

We will serve amontillado with things like simple chicken, duck, or rabbit. Stews are also very good with this style of sherry, as are snails. Some cheeses also work really well with it, especially a dry cheese such as a young Manchego or a smoked sheep's milk cheese from the Basque country.

Oloroso is the richest, most full-bodied sherry, but it is still dry. It has characteristics of caramel, apricot, and orange. Oloroso is good with richer flavors like lamb, beef, or venison—or even ostrich! Softer

south of Barcelona. The wine is light and fruity, and can be either dry or slightly sweet. It is festive and sprightly, and its acidity factor makes it a good match for tapas. It also works well with the famous Spanish blue cheese Cabrales. Serrano ham and fresh figs are also really nice with cava. It is a fraction of the cost of Champagne, and equally good. You can find an eighteen-dollar cava that is comparable to a Champagne in the fifty- to sixty-dollar range. There are over two hundred producers of cava.

A few recommended brands:

- **MANZANILLA**: La Gitana, La Guita Osborne

- **FINO**: La Ina, Tio Pepe

- **AMONTILLADO**: Lustau, Sanchez Romate

- **OLOROSO**: Lustau

- **CAVA**: Codorniu, Llopart Brut, Leopardi

cheeses are nice with this sherry, such as torta del Caser, a buttery sheep's milk cheese.

Cava also matches nicely with food. It is a sparkling wine made using the *méthode champenoise*. Cava is made from three or four grapes that are indigenous to the Penedès, just

JIM BECKER ON CREATING A SPANISH MEAL

If you were trying to learn about Spain in a general way through cooking a meal, this would be a good representation.

TAPAS: Start with a couple of easy tapas, one skewered and one fried. For example, skewer some serrano ham and Manchego cheese and serve it cold, then deep-fry salt cod fritters and serve them with alioli (garlic mayonnaise). To drink, a fino sherry.

SOUP: You might serve a cold gazpacho in warmer weather, or a traditional garlic soup with a poached egg if the weather is cold. With this, you could drink sherry or wine.

MAIN COURSE: Try a seafood paella, because they are so interesting. To drink, a young white from Penedès.

DESSERT: Flan, with an olorosao sherry to drink.

CHEESE: Or, if I wanted to skip dessert, I would serve some cheese. There are many wonderful Spanish cheeses now available in the United States, though there are still a great many that you can't get here because they are not made in large enough quantities to export. The group below, however, you can find pretty easily:

Mahón is a cow's milk cheese from Majorca. It has a Gouda-type quality to it and is considered one of the best cheeses in Spain.

Garrotxa is a goat's milk cheese from Catalonia. It is a semi-hard cheese with a tangy flavor.

Cabrales is the best-known blue cheese in Spain. Valdeon, which is similar to Roquefort, would work in place of Cabrales.

Idiazábal is a lightly smoked cow's milk cheese from the Basque area.

Pequillo peppers and dried sweet red peppers: "There is nothing like pequillo peppers [which have a rich flesh, a mild spiciness, and a slightly woody flavor when roasted and are available both bottled and canned]," says Casas. "Dried sweet peppers are a little harder to find, but you can substitute guajillo or another chile that is not too spicy."

Rice: "You need a short-grain rice from Valencia," says Casas. "I think the two best types are Bomba and Calasparra. They are considered the best for paella because they are difficult to overcook. You *can* overcook them, but they take a long time to become mushy."

Saffron: Spain is one of the leading producers of saffron in the world. Most people know that saffron is the world's most expensive spice, if not ingredient—more so than even caviar. Saffron is made from crocus stamens, all of which have to be picked by hand, and each flower produces only three usable stamens. After the stamens are picked, they are toasted, which increases their flavor; however, it reduces their weight by almost two-thirds, and so it takes more than ten thousand flowers to produce a gram of saffron. "The saffron from La Mancha is my favorite," says Becker.

Serrano ham: "When we take Americans to eat in restaurants in Spain, they take one bite of ham and leave the rest," says Penelope Casas. "In Spain, that is a crime! It is almost a religion, the eating of ham. Serrano ham is just starting to get imported into the United States. Prosciutto and serrano ham are similar, but they are not the same. They both come from the white pig and are cured in similar ways, but the Spanish ham has an earthier taste to it. In restaurants in Spain, every meal begins with ham."

Fish: "When I get off the plane after landing in Spain, I crave two things: one is baby lamb and the other is seafood," says Penelope Casas. "I especially like fresh shrimp grilled in the shell and sprinkled with coarse salt, and hake that has been very simply sautéed. Spaniards are very passionate about their fish. They're fanatical about its quality and freshness, and they don't compromise, even in land-locked cities like Madrid. They love their seafood and pay the highest prices in order to get the best quality. If you go to a market in the U.S. and see the fish case filled with fish, you know it will probably be there for a while. In Spain, the fish is gone by lunchtime!"

Sherry vinegar: "Use dry sherry for cooking shellfish dishes, and sherry vinegar for any recipe calling for vinegar," advises Becker.

Vegetables: Some of the most common are eggplant, garlic, green peppers, onions, spinach, Swiss chard, and tomatoes. Mushrooms are also popular, but they are very regional; Catalonians, for example, are huge mushroom eaters.

A Pinch of Salt, a Pinch of Change

A man must eat a peck of salt with his friend before he knows him.
—MIGUEL DE CERVANTES, *DON QUIXOTE*

WHILE LETTING THE FLAVOR of the ingredients shine through is of primary importance, American cooks can take a little latitude in adjusting Spanish cuisine for local palates and lifestyles.

"I've now spent ten years cooking in Spain and ten years cooking in New York, and I've found two main differences between Spanish and American palates," observes Mariano Aznar. "In Spain, they prefer flavors stronger and a little more salty. The American palate is more delicate.

"Some traditional Spanish food can be a bit heavy for our lifestyle today," he acknowledges. "People are not only farmers or fishermen anymore, and if you work in an office for ten hours a day, your body does not crave the fats that it would if you had toiled all day in the sun.

"*Zarzuela,* which is like a Spanish bouillabaisse, is an example of a traditional dish that I have changed a bit. Traditionally, the fish would be seasoned with flour and fried, then added to the dish. Now I make a reduction of fish stock, and I simply sear the fish, which makes the dish much lighter. You can eat it and not feel too full," says Aznar.

Sometimes no adjustment in the cooking itself is even necessary—just a little ingenuity in its application. "Romesco sauce was originally used for leeks," Aznar points out, "but I've come to love it with seafood like mussels. In this case, I haven't changed the way the sauce is made, but I've applied it to something else." You'll enjoy discovering your own uses for this delicious sauce.

NachWaxman's Recommended Reading on Spanish Cooking

Penelope Casas's **Foods and Wines of Spain** does what a book should do: it covers the subject well, in a seemingly intelligent manner. Not all Spaniards have embraced its representation of Spanish cuisine, however—which I myself cannot judge, as I am less familiar with Spanish food.

Catalan Cuisine by Colman Andrews is a wonderful book, with headnotes and anecdotes that provide a terrific sense of place and history.

While no longer in print, **The Flavors of Andalusia** by Elizabeth Luard—a fine English writer—is worth seeking out. (Incidentally, her two-volume memoir, **Family Life: Birth, Death, and the Whole Damn Thing,** and **Still Life** are wonderful reads.)

For new-style cooking in Spain, there are Spanish-language books not yet published in English by cutting-edge chefs like Andres Madrigal, Sonti Santamaria, and Ferran Adrià that are worth checking out.

Gazpacho Andaluz

3 cups very ripe tomatoes, medium dice

1 garlic clove

1 cucumber, peeled and diced

1 green bell pepper, cored, seeded, and diced

5 ounces bread, torn into small pieces

¼ cup extra-virgin olive oil

2 tablespoons sherry vinegar

Salt to taste

1 cup spring water, or more as needed

FOR GARNISH

Croutons

Olive oil

SERVES 6

IN BATCHES, PUREE ALL the ingredients in a blender until very smooth reserving 1 tablespoon each of the diced tomato, cucumber, and green pepper to use as garnish. Strain through a sieve and chill.

TO SERVE, LADLE THE gazpacho into bowls. Garnish with tomato, cucumber, green pepper, and the croutons, and drizzle with olive oil.

Arroz Negro
Catalan Black Rice

¼ cup extra-virgin olive oil

2 cups cleaned squid—bodies cut into squares, tentacles chopped

3 cups finely diced onions

3 garlic cloves, minced

3 cups pureed and strained tomatoes

⅓ cup dry white wine

1 teaspoon pimentón (see page 123)

4 cups fish stock

1 bay leaf

2 tablespoons squid ink

½ teaspoon saffron threads

2 cups Calasparra rice (or other medium-grain rice)

1 teaspoon chopped fresh flat-leaf parsley

Salt

SERVES 6

At the restaurant, we like to serve this paella with alioli. (See page 143 for Penelope Casas's alioli recipe.)

HEAT THE OLIVE OIL in a paella or other wide, shallow pan until very hot but not smoking. Add the squid and sauté until the juices released by the squid disappear. Transfer the squid to a plate and set aside.

LOWER THE HEAT TO medium, then add the onions and garlic. Cook, stirring, until translucent, about 15 minutes.

ADD THE TOMATOES and cook until the liquid has evaporated. Add the white wine and cook until it has almost cooked away. Add the *pimentón* and stir constantly for 1 minute. (We call this preparation of onion and tomato *sofrito*. It is one of the traditional base sauces of Spain.)

RAISE THE HEAT TO high and add the fish stock, bay leaf, squid ink, and saffron. Once the liquid comes to a boil, add the rice and stir to distribute it evenly in the pan. Cook, stirring often to prevent the rice from sticking to the bottom of the pan, for 5 minutes. Turn down the heat to medium-low and cook, *without stirring,* for 10 more minutes, or until the liquid evaporates.

REMOVE FROM THE HEAT and allow the paella to rest for about 5 minutes.

SPRINKLE WITH THE chopped parsley, salt to taste, and serve.

131

RECIPES INSPIRED BY Spain

Canalones Barcelona-Style

1 medium onion, minced

2 garlic cloves, minced

2 ounces button mushrooms, sliced

½ cup olive oil

8 ounces boneless pork butt, cut into ½-inch cubes

8 ounces boneless veal shoulder, cut into ½-inch cubes

8 ounces boneless, skinless chicken thigh, cut into ½-inch cubes

4 ounces chicken liver, cleaned and cut into ½-inch cubes

2 ounces bread, cut into ½-inch cubes

¼ cup milk

¼ cup fino sherry

Twelve 3-by-2-inch rectangles cut from lasagna noodles, cooked until al dente

4 cups Béchamel Sauce (recipe follows)

4 ounces Manchego cheese, grated

MAKES 12 CANALONES

This is perhaps the most traditional dish on our menu. It is a staple at restaurants along the Ramblas in Barcelona (an area akin to the Champs-Élysées of Paris).

IN A LARGE SAUTÉ PAN, sweat the onion, garlic, and mushrooms in the olive oil for 8 to 10 minutes. Add the pork and cook for 15 minutes. Add the veal and cook for 15 minutes more. Add the chicken, chicken livers, bread, and milk and simmer for 2 hours.

ADD THE SHERRY to the pork mixture, remove from the heat, and allow to cool.

PROCESS THE MEAT MIXTURE in a food processor to a thick paste, or pass it through a meat grinder.

ROLL UP THE MIXTURE in the noodles, removing the excess from the ends. (If you have a pastry bag, put the mixture in the bag and pipe it out.) (The canalones can be frozen if desired or used immediately.)

HEAT THE CANALONES in the microwave or a moderate oven. Top with the béchamel, sprinkle with Manchego, and place under the broiler until the cheese has melted and the béchamel is beginning to turn golden brown. Serve immediately.

Béchamel Sauce

4 pounds unsalted butter

1 small white onion, minced

4 cups milk

1 sprig rosemary

1 sprig thyme

1 bay leaf

4 cups all-purpose flour

Freshly grated nutmeg

Salt and freshly ground black pepper

MELT THE BUTTER in a heavy pot or sauté pan. Add the onion and cook over very low heat until softened, 10 to 15 minutes, but do not brown.

MEANWHILE, COMBINE THE milk and herbs in a saucepan and bring to a boil. Let simmer over very low heat so the flavors infuse while the onion cooks.

ADD THE FLOUR to the onion mixture, whisking constantly, and cook, whisking, for 10 minutes.

STRAIN THE MILK and add to the onion mixture. Cook, whisking, for 20 minutes. Season with nutmeg, salt, and pepper.

Note
I often like to add pureed pequillo peppers to béchamel, to give the sauce a nice flavor and color.

Suquet de Rape
Fish Stew

FOR THE SOFREGIT (SOFRITO)

¼ cup olive oil

2 large onions, minced

2 large red bell peppers, cored, seeded, and minced

1 pound ripe tomatoes, peeled, seeded, and chopped

FOR THE FISH AND POTATOES

¼ cup olive oil

Twelve 4-ounce monkfish steaks

Flour for dredging fish

3 large garlic cloves, minced

2 tablespoons chopped fresh flat-leaf parsley

½ cup full-bodied Spanish brandy, such as Torres Tres Torres

4 cups fish stock

1 pound white potatoes, peeled and thinly sliced

Salt and freshly ground black pepper

SERVES 6

Every Catalan cook along the Costa Brava, north of Barcelona, has a different way of preparing this dish. The name suquet *is the diminutive of "suc," which means "juice," from the appearance of this soupy fish stew.*

This is traditionally served with alioli; for a recipe, see page 143.

FOR THE SOFREGIT (SOFRITO)

IN A LARGE CASSEROLE (preferably made of clay), heat the oil. Sauté the onions and peppers over medium-low heat for 45 minutes to 1 hour, stirring frequently, until the onions are golden brown and almost caramelized. Toward the end of the cooking time, you may have to add a bit of water to the pot to keep the mixture from burning.

ADD THE TOMATOES and cook over low heat until the juices have evaporated. Remove from the heat and set aside.

FOR THE FISH AND POTATOES

HEAT THE OIL in a skillet large enough to hold all the fish. Dredge the fish in flour, and sauté lightly on both sides over medium-low heat. Remove from the pan and drain on paper towels.

FOR THE PICADA

1 tablespoon olive oil

1 thin slice white bread (about 1 ounce)

¼ cup skinned almonds, toasted

2 large cloves garlic

ADD THE GARLIC and parsley to the skillet and sauté until the garlic is soft. Add the brandy and cook over high heat until the pan is almost dry. Transfer the contents of the skillet to the casserole with the sofregit. Add the fish stock and potatoes and bring to a boil. Reduce the heat to medium-low and cook until the potatoes are tender. Season with salt and pepper.

MEANWHILE, MAKE THE PICADA: In a small skillet, heat the oil. Fry the bread, turning once, until golden on both sides.

TRANSFER THE BREAD to a food processor, add the almonds and garlic, and grind very fine.

TO FINISH

WHEN THE POTATOES are tender, stir in the picada. Add the fish steaks and cook for 10 minutes, or just until the fish is done.

SERVE HOT IN BOWLS or soup plates, with alioli.

Chilled Tomato Consommé

FOR THE CONSOMMÉ

4 beefsteak tomatoes, peeled and seeded

4 cups water

Salt and freshly ground black pepper

3 sheets gelatin

¼ cup fino Montillia-Moriles wine or fino sherry

FOR THE GARNISHES

2 cups olive oil

3 thin slices serrano ham, cut into thin strips

4 garlic cloves, thinly sliced

1 cup diced white bread

3 tablespoons chopped fresh flat-leaf parsley

1 teaspoon hot pimentón (see page 123) or paprika

6 quail eggs, poached, fried, or hard boiled—your choice

I have several different ways of garnishing this consommé. The garlic chips, croutons, and oils should be constants, but you can experiment with different oil infusions, such as basil, cilantro, or chive. In addition, try adding ingredients such as poached shrimp, scallops, lobster, sardines, or smoked salmon to the consommé. When serving this consommé, I find it looks best in chilled martini glasses.

PUREE THE TOMATOES with the water in a food processor. Transfer to a saucepan and cook over low heat for 1 hour. Season with salt and pepper.

POUR THE MIXTURE into a fine sieve or cheese-cloth-lined strainer set over a bowl. Don't press the liquid out of the puree, just allow it to slowly drain out; scoop the puree up from the bottom of the sieve from time to time to allow the liquid to drain more easily. This process may take a couple of hours.

SOAK THE GELATIN in 2 cups cold water to soften it, about 2 minutes.

HEAT 2 CUPS of the consommé in a small saucepan. Drain the gelatin and add it to the hot consommé to dissolve. When the gelatin has dissolved, pour the mixture into the remaining consommé. Refrigerate until chilled.

FOR THE GARNISHES

HEAT THE OLIVE OIL in a small pot. Add the ham and fry until crisp. Remove with a slotted spoon or skimmer and drain on paper towels. Add the garlic slices to the oil and fry until golden brown. Transfer to paper towels to drain. Fry the bread cubes until golden brown. Transfer to paper towels to drain. Allow the oil to cool.

PUT HALF THE OIL in a blender and puree with the parsley. Add the *pimentón* to the oil in the pan. You now have two infused oils.

TO SERVE, PLACE AN EGG in the center of each of six chilled soup bowls or martini glasses. Add the wine to the consommé and whisk to break it up. Add to the soup bowls, and garnish with the ham, garlic, and croutons. Drizzle with the parsley and *pimentón* oils and serve.

Crema Catalana

4 cups milk

2 cups sugar

1½ teaspoons grated lemon zest, or to taste

1½ teaspoons grated orange zest, or to taste

1 cinnamon stick

1 teaspoon pure vanilla extract

3 tablespoons cornstarch

10 egg yolks

Sugar for caramelizing the custards

SERVES 6 TO 8

COMBINE 3 CUPS of the milk, 1 cup of the sugar, the lemon and orange zest, the cinnamon stick, and vanilla in a large saucepan and bring just to a boil. Reduce the heat to low and simmer gently for 3 to 4 minutes.

MEANWHILE, PUT the cornstarch in a medium bowl. Gradually add the remaining 1 cup milk, whisking constantly until well blended and smooth. Whisk in the egg yolks, then whisk in the remaining 1 cup sugar.

GRADUALLY ADD the egg yolk mixture to the saucepan, stirring constantly with a wooden spoon or spatula. Cook, stirring constantly, until thickened, 10 to 15 minutes; do not allow to boil, or the egg yolks may curdle. Strain the custard through a fine-mesh sieve into a bowl.

POUR OR LADLE the custard into six or eight ramekins or custard cups. Refrigerate for at least 2 hours.

JUST BEFORE SERVING, sprinkle a thin layer of sugar evenly over the top of each custard. Using a blowtorch, caramelize the sugar (or caramelize under a hot broiler, carefully turning the ramekins as necessary so the sugar does not burn).

Chocolate con Churros
Fried Fluted Dough with Chocolate Dipping Sauce

FOR THE CHURROS

1½ cups water

Pinch of salt

2 cups all-purpose flour

6 to 8 cups peanut oil, for deep-frying

About 1 cup sugar, for coating

FOR THE HOT CHOCOLATE

1 cup water

½ cup sugar

2 tablespoons unsweetened cocoa powder

2 cups semisweet chocolate, chopped

½ cup bittersweet chocolate, chopped

2 cups milk

SERVES 6

FOR THE CHURROS

COMBINE THE WATER and salt in a medium saucepan and bring to a boil. Add the flour all at once and stir vigorously with a wooden spoon until smooth, about 2 minutes. Remove from the heat and let cool.

MEANWHILE, FOR THE HOT CHOCOLATE

COMBINE THE WATER, sugar, and cocoa powder in a large heavy saucepan and bring to a boil, stirring to dissolve the sugar. Reduce the heat to low, add both the chocolates and the milk, and heat, whisking or stirring constantly, until the chocolate is melted and the mixture is smooth. Remove from the heat and set aside until ready to use.

TO FRY THE CHURROS, heat the oil in a large saucepan or a deep fryer to 360 degrees F. Put the sugar in a shallow bowl. Fill a pastry bag fitted with a large star tip with the dough. When the oil is hot, squeeze four 5-inch lengths of dough into the oil and fry until the churros puff and turn golden brown. Using a wire skimmer or tongs, transfer to paper towels to drain. Skim any particles of dough from the oil, and continue frying churros in the same fashion, making sure the oil returns to the proper temperature between batches. Toss the warm churros in the sugar to coat.

JUST BEFORE SERVING, reheat the chocolate in a microwave or over very low heat, preferably in a water bath.

POUR THE CHOCOLATE into six small cups, and serve the churros on dessert plates, with the cups of chocolate for dipping.

Jim Becker

Barcelona-Style Flounder with Raisins, Nuts, Lemon Butter, and Anise

2 tablespoons unsalted butter, softened

1 tablespoon minced lemon zest

2 tablespoons olive oil

Flour for dredging

Spanish paprika

Salt and freshly ground black pepper

8 flounder fillets (about 4 ounces each)

½ cup raisins

½ cup mixed almonds, hazelnuts, and pinenuts, lightly toasted

¼ cup minced orange zest

2 tablespoons chopped fresh flat-leaf parsley

Dry anise (a Spanish anisette liqueur, available in better wine shops)

SERVES 4

PREHEAT THE OVEN to 350 degrees F.

COMBINE THE BUTTER and lemon zest in a cup, blending well.

HEAT A LARGE SKILLET over medium-high heat. When hot, add the olive oil. Meanwhile, season the flour with paprika, salt, and pepper. Dredge the flounder fillets in the flour, shaking off the excess. Sauté the fillets in batches—don't crowd the pan—until lightly golden on both sides.

PUT THE FILLETS on a baking sheet and place in the oven for 3 to 5 minutes to finish cooking.

MEANWHILE, POUR OFF the excess oil from the skillet and reheat the pan. When hot, add the raisins, nuts, orange zest, and parsley. Remove the pan from the heat and carefully add the liqueur. (Note: Never add alcohol to a pan directly over the flame, and always add it from a measuring cup, not the bottle.)

RETURN THE PAN to the heat and flambé, using a long-stemmed match. When the flames die down, add the lemon butter and shake the pan back and forth to incorporate the butter.

REMOVE THE FILLETS from the oven and place on four plates. Spoon the sauce over the fillets and season lightly with salt. Serve with a green vegetable, such as sautéed spinach or Swiss chard.

Jim Becker

Romesco Sauce

2 red bell peppers, roasted, peeled, and seeded

2 ancho chiles, softened in hot water, drained, stemmed, and seeded

2 plum tomatoes, roasted until slightly blackened

2 small red onions, roasted and peeled

3 tablespoons hazelnuts, toasted and skinned

3 tablespoons blanched almonds, toasted

1 slice bread, toasted

1 tablespoon mild Spanish paprika

2 tablespoons sherry vinegar

1 bulb garlic, roasted

¾ cup olive oil

Salt and freshly cracked black pepper

MAKES ABOUT 1½ CUPS

Serve romesco sauce with grilled or fried fish or shellfish.

IN A FOOD PROCESSOR, combine the bell peppers, chiles, tomatoes, red onions, nuts, bread, paprika, and vinegar, and pulse to a coarse puree.

CUT OFF THE TOP of the roasted garlic and squeeze the garlic pulp into the mixture in the processor. With the machine running, add the olive oil in a thin, steady stream until the mixture forms a chunky paste. Season to taste with salt and pepper.

Arroz Negro Tasca del Puerto
Black Rice Paella

8 ounces medium shrimp, peeled and cut crosswise in half

1½ pounds small cleaned squid with tentacles

1 pound monkfish fillet, cut into ¼-inch cubes

Kosher or sea salt

3 ripe tomatoes

Six 4-gram packets squid ink

½ cup dry white wine

½ cup olive oil

1½ cups finely diced green bell peppers

12 garlic cloves, minced

6 tablespoons Alioli (recipe follows), plus extra for serving

1½ teaspoons imported sweet paprika

5½ cups fish stock

¼ teaspoon crumbled saffron threads

3 cups short-grain rice

1 pimiento, cut into ½-inch strips

SERVES 6 TO 8

SPRINKLE THE SHRIMP, squid, and monkfish with salt; set aside.

SLICE THE TOMATOES in half and squeeze out the seeds. Using a coarse grater, grate the tomatoes down to their skins; discard the skins. Drain off excess juice.

COMBINE THE SQUID INK and wine, and strain several times.

PREHEAT THE OVEN to 400 degrees F.

HEAT THE OIL in a paella pan measuring at least 17 to 18 inches; you may need to put the pan over two burners on the stove. Add the shrimp, squid, and monkfish and sauté over medium-high heat for 2 minutes; rotate the pan as necessary to make sure you are frying evenly. Add the green peppers and sauté for 2 more minutes. Add the garlic and sauté for 1 minute.

ADD THE 6 TABLESPOONS alioli and the paprika and cook for 1 minute. Add the tomatoes and cook for 3 minutes. (The dish can be made in advance to this point.)

MEANWHILE, BRING THE fish stock to a boil. Stir in the saffron.

ADD THE RICE to the paella pan, stirring to coat well.

POUR THE STOCK over the rice. Stir in the squid ink mixture and boil over medium heat for 5 to 10 minutes, or until the rice is no longer soupy. Adjust the salt.

ARRANGE THE PIMIENTO STRIPS over the rice. Transfer to the oven and cook, uncovered, for 10 minutes or until the rice is almost done. Cover the pan loosely and let the dish rest for 10 minutes on top of the stove. Serve with alioli.

Alioli

8 garlic cloves

¾ teaspoon salt

1 egg

1 teaspoon fresh lemon juice

2 cups olive oil

2 tablespoons hot water

MAKES ABOUT 2 CUPS

MASH THE GARLIC with ¼ teaspoon of the salt in a mortar and pestle (or use a garlic press). Transfer to a food processor. Add the egg, the remaining ½ teaspoon salt, and the lemon juice and blend for about 30 seconds. With the motor running, slowly add oil and then the water.

COVER AND REFRIGERATE until ready to use; bring to room temperature before using.

Tortilla a la Espanola
Spanish Potato Omelet

1 cup olive oil or a blend of olive and vegetable oil

4 large potatoes, peeled and cut into ⅛-inch slices

1 large onion, thinly sliced

Coarse salt

4 large eggs

SERVES 8 TO 10

This is the all-time tapas classic! It tastes better if it has been made in advance and can be cut more easily if it has had a chance to sit at room temperature.

HEAT THE OIL in an 8- or 9-inch skillet. Layer the potatoes in the pan, adding the slices one at a time and alternating each layer with a layer of onions; salt each layer. Cook slowly over medium heat (the dish involves more simmering than frying), lifting the potatoes occasionally so that they do not brown, until tender. The potatoes should remain separated.

DRAIN THE MIXTURE in a colander, and reserve about 3 tablespoons of the oil for the omelet. (You will want to save the rest of the oil for other uses, because it has such a great flavor.) Wipe out the skillet, making sure there is no residue; it must be completely clean for cooking the omelet. Set aside.

IN A LARGE BOWL, beat the eggs until slightly foamy. Add salt. Add the potatoes, pressing down so they are all covered. Let stand for 15 minutes.

HEAT 2 TABLESPOONS of the reserved oil in the pan until it smokes. Add the potato mixture and spread it out evenly. Lower the heat to medium and cook, shaking the pan occasionally to make sure the omelet doesn't stick. When the eggs begin to brown on the bottom, cover the pan with a plate and invert the potatoes onto it.

QUICKLY ADD THE REMAINING OIL to the pan and heat until smoking. Slide the omelet back into the pan to brown the other side, and lower the heat to medium. Once the second side has browned, flip the omelet two or three more times, cooking briefly on each side. This helps it finish cooking and gives it shape. Turn the omelet out onto a plate and let cool.

TO SERVE, CUT INTO WEDGES or small squares so it can be picked up with toothpicks.

145

France

WESTERN TECHNIQUES
AND SAVOIR FAIRE

I would contend that French cooking is so great in part because nobody strayed from the basic French cooking techniques and recipes throughout the centuries. A French dish with elements of Southeast Asia woven into it is still obviously a French dish.

—RICK BAYLESS, CHEF-OWNER, FRONTERA GRILL AND TOPOLOBAMPO, CHICAGO

FRANCE'S ENORMOUS CONTRIBUTION to the development of fine cuisine is rooted in several factors, but might well be boiled down to two. First, the great chefs of France codified the techniques and classic recipes that represent the building blocks taught in most of the Western world's leading culinary schools. French cuisine reflects an extraordinary precision and perfectionism that is an invaluable foundation for any cook. France's second major contribution is its corresponding emphasis on savoir faire, which has led to the cuisine's evolution and elevation.

After mastering the tenets of the cuisine through their own education and training, the great chefs of France—from Antonin Carême to Auguste Escoffier—left the past behind without even a glance over their shoulders. Carême improved cuisine's aesthetics by bringing the arts to the culinary arts through his innovative and elaborate presentations. After perfecting the four classic sauces of French cuisine, Escoffier had the nerve to condemn two of them as unnecessary, and to refocus on simpler sauces based on the juices of the meats being served.

In much the same fashion, the French chefs who made their way to the United States found their new home an inspiration for further culinary refinement. André Soltner rejected the tired "French cuisine" served in too many restaurants and flew in the freshest Dover sole from Europe to serve at Lutèce in New York City. In Washington, D.C., Jean-Louis Palladin searched out and supported local purveyors long before it became fashionable. Jean-Georges Vongerichten originally fused French and Thai flavors at New York's Lafayette, and he then expanded this effort through multiple Vong restaurants around the globe. Daniel Boulud combines the best of all possible worlds: While celebrating classic French cuisine at his four-star Restaurant Daniel, he celebrates everything from vegetarian menus to international influences at Café Boulud—and has fun stuffing foie gras into his burger at DB Bistro Moderne.

A French chef's mastery of the rules is the prerequisite for knowing how to break them to improve the end result.

"For restaurant cooks, French cuisine certainly offers the broadest foundation. It is a cuisine that has been devoted to restaurants longer than any other," Bayless points out. "It's where I got my start after graduating from barbecue. I threw myself completely into French cooking by reading every book and cooking my way through them. Despite not going through cooking school, I got a lot of that basic experience. French cuisine shows you the breadth of cooking. If you are braising, whether the food is French or Thai or Indian, you are employing more or less the same elements."

"Today, French cuisine is expressed in its techniques and professionalism, and it is done on a worldwide level," says Alain Ducasse, chef-owner of Alain Ducasse in New York City. "I tell my students that if they learn French techniques, they can take them to any country," adds André Soltner, former chef-owner of Lutèce. "The cuisines' ingredients will vary, but one can apply the French techniques anywhere."

For a cook, mastering a French dish is a moment in time, a feeling that one has donned history's toque by matching the standards of the culture that set the bar. In our book *Chef's Night Out,* Boston chef Lydia Shire mentions how proud she felt after she'd painstakingly mastered *soupe de poisson,* the base for bouillabaisse. Countless chefs can recall their first visits to three-star Michelin restaurants and how profound the experiences were for them. And one of the most influential restaurants in American history—Chez Panisse in Berkeley—originated with Alice Waters's desire to capture the fresh flavors and cooking of France!

Whether French cuisine is the starting point, the ending point, or a point along the road in between, it clearly offers a path along which there is much to learn.

Setting Pen to Paper and Passion to Pan

THE FRENCH DIDN'T INVENT TECHNIQUE, and they didn't invent enthusiasm for food. However, they were the first ones in the West to formalize cooking and set recipes and techniques down in books.

"Other countries were braising, so it's not as if the French invented braising," says Hubert Keller of Fleur de Lys in San Francisco. "Similar techniques had been used in other cuisines for a long time, but the French put them into cookbooks—pinpointing them and explaining each in great detail. Then, when someone wanted to learn the cuisine, it was there to learn.

"Italian, Spanish, and other Mediterranean cuisines used the same techniques. They also employed a similar combination of ingredients, because these ingredients were being traded throughout the region. What made the French different was that they turned cooking into a real profession by organizing everything. When people talk about techniques, they refer to the French or the Chinese, who were also leaders in documenting their recipes and techniques.

"Urban DuBois' books from the 1850s are amazing. If you look up something simple like a pineapple, you will be shocked by all the variations," Keller says. "In the book, first they trim it, then chop and mix the rind with sugar to macerate it, then put it through a tamis [drum sieve]. You haven't even touched the best part of the fruit yet! The pineapple was so precious that they figured out how to get everything they could from it. It's amazing that this was all analyzed, formulated, and documented in this manner. It is inspiring to me, and it should be inspiring to young chefs. When I read DuBois' books, I feel 'small' because, a hundred fifty years ago, it seems they were already thinking of everything!

"Cooks can find countless old books like this on French and Chinese cuisines," continues Keller. "However, when they want to learn one of the 'New World' cuisines, it is more difficult because most have just come into the professional kitchen. That is the big difference."

The Legacies of Carême and Escoffier

BECAUSE FRENCH CUISINE WAS formulated and recorded by professional chefs, it could be taught. The influences of two chefs in particular, Antonin Carême and Auguste Escoffier, are still very visible. Before Carême, recipes were largely passed down in the oral tradition. Carême published books that contained not only recipes, but also menus and sketches of his legendary presentations and dinners.

Escoffier may be the most influential French chef of all. His book *Le Guide Culinaire*, first published in 1902, featured a staggering five thousand recipes. Escoffier simplified dining in several important ways. First, he limited the size of his menus and popularized the practice of serving food in courses rather than all at once on large platters, banquet-style. As a result of the smaller number of dishes, quality, rather than quantity, became the emphasis.

In addition, Escoffier organized the restaurant kitchen creating a model that is still used today: the "brigade system," in which cooks are assigned specific cooking stations. In more formal restaurants, this system, or some variation on it, is still the norm, usually with a meat or grill cook, fish or sauté cook, vegetable cook, garde-manger cook, and pastry chef.

"French cuisine is more than the food. One of the reasons it's so successful is the brigade system," Keller says. "The chef and sous-chef are generals and lieutenants. The structure came via the Romans through Napoleon's army."

Molding the French Chef

French savoir faire is a combination of things: technique, as in the actual hand movements and procedures we use to carry out the physical work, but also professionalism, discipline, and respect for hierarchy.

—ALAIN DUCASSE

THE FRENCH ARE KNOWN not only for codifying recipes but also for their methods of training professional cooks. "We try to keep our cooks on a particular station for a year," says Daniel Boulud. "Unless you stay a year to see the full cycle of the seasons, it is hard to understand that station completely. I want them to master one thing before they do anything else. Consistency is what makes a great cook, no matter what you're making. How many cooks can make a perfect salad or roast chicken or steamed fish? It is very hard to find that cook."

During their tenure at a station, cooks learn more than technique. They are also training their palates. "All the chefs I worked for were extremely strict about quality," says Hubert Keller. "If you were standing with the chef when the orders were delivered, he wanted you to taste everything. If he asked what you thought of the berries and you made a face, he knew they were sour. Back they would go! A chef knows that a beautiful berry is not always a good berry.

"When I started my apprenticeship, the first things we learned were to taste and to season. Jean-Georges Vongerichten, who trained at L'Auberge de l'Ill, as I did, can confirm that! When you worked a station, the chef, Paul Haeberlin, would come over and taste the sauces you prepared. He would adjust all of them and you would taste them over again with him. It was the best way to learn. This would not happen every two weeks—it would happen at lunch and dinner every single day, without exception. After several months, you would finally get close, but even after a year at the same station, the chef would come over and taste your sauce.

"When I worked with Paul Bocuse, if you made a pasta dough for him and accidentally put too much salt in it, he would not only make you taste it, he would make you swallow it! He wanted you to always ask yourself, 'Is this right?' After swallowing it, you knew the answer."

Having learned from Bocuse, Keller never turns his back on any cook. "I still have to keep cooks on track when it comes to tasting, especially when I travel [for special events outside his own restaurant]. When I go into a kitchen, the first thing I look for is the salt and pepper. If the cooks have to search for them, we've got a problem! Salt and pepper should be at every station, with a few extra around for convenience. When I don't see salt and pepper, I know no one is tasting in that kitchen. Some cooks know the

technique, and how to produce, but they are robots. I realize that I have to be extra careful if anybody like that is going to be helping me."

Daniel Boulud also spends time teaching his cooks to taste and helping them to produce perfectly nuanced dishes time after time. "We spend the most time helping the cooks to get the balance right," he says. "This goes back to discipline, precision, and consistency. A cook can make something for six people—that is easy. To get it right for fifty and not lose the quality of it is a whole other thing."

"French cuisine is not only taste but discipline as well," echoes André Soltner. "It goes beyond talent. It is getting everything right, every time—and that requires discipline."

Although he himself is one of the top French chefs in the world, Boulud still likes to send his cooks to train in France. "I sent my chef Michael David to France for six weeks, to spend time at Troisgros, Michel Bras, Bernard Loiseau, and Georges Blanc, among others. For him it was a revelation, to be able to see the same cooking principles applied in so many different ways," he says. "Although these restaurants offer different food, they are the same in terms of organization, discipline, and how they buy and treat their products.

"I want them to open up to a culture they don't really know," Boulud continues. "They only get half of it from me here at the restaurant and in New York. They know that I think and cook French. When they get to France, however, they get immersed in an all-French environment. They also meet young French cooks who are talented, with a lot of passion and dedication."

Honoring the Classics

WHEN YOU MAKE A CLASSIC French dish, you are walking in the footsteps of a legion of chefs. By following their route and methodology, you learn both to appreciate what came before you and to look freshly at what you know, or thought you knew. "Dishes are always based on something," says Daniel Boulud. "There is a percentage of established techniques, flavors, and textures in any given dish. When you cook a classic, you are trying to recapture these elements. A classic dish allows you less room for imagination and more room for technique, knowledge, and understanding.

"The cooks at my restaurant love making the classics because they want to understand them," he continues. "For myself, there are so many dishes that I would like to try. For example, from the fall into early spring, it is game season. So in autumn, I start looking forward to making wild hare pâté!

"It is not about trying to be creative; it is about being good at making something that is very traditional. When you cook simply from creativity, you know your own balance, so it is much easier. With a classic, you are looking for clues to find the balance, because you don't know what the point of reference is. I am not a great poet, but it seems that being inspired by Shakespeare is easier than writing like Shakespeare.

"There are some things that I love to rediscover rather than to reinvent. We had an omelet competition at Daniel, and each sous-chef had to make an omelet. It took them back to their apprenticeship days when they learned the basic steps of making eggs and flavoring them differently. I wanted to go back to old times for my omelet, so I made an omelet *roulade,* which is a rolled omelet, with morels. I strained the eggs to make sure there were no clumps, then added a little dice of butter. First I used a third of the eggs to make French scrambled eggs in a double boiler, then added two-thirds of the morels to them with a little *jus de poulet* [pan juices from a roasted chicken]. It was

important to put the morels in the scrambled eggs, because I couldn't have gotten as much flavor if they were just in the omelet. The mixture was cooked very slowly for twenty minutes. As a result, the flavor went up and up into the eggs! Then I made the omelet in a very hot pan and filled it with the scrambled egg mixture.

"The plate was decorated with the remaining morels, a touch more *jus de poulet,* and a morel cream with chervil and chives. This was a very classic omelet with a little refinement. The eggs on the outside were firm, the eggs on the inside soft, buttery, and rich. The dish was very earthy and seasonal, with essentially just two ingredients.

"It was fun to see everyone's 'take' on an omelet. One chef made a lobster omelet with *sauce à l'américaine* [lobster sauce]. Another chef made a *tortilla*, the Spanish omelet with potatoes. Alex Lee, my chef de cuisine, made a Basque omelet with chorizo and peppers. When you are an apprentice, you learn to make eggs in different ways. It is something you never forget."

Making the Classic Contemporary

Just because Escoffier said to serve a dish with certain garnishes on the left or right does not mean that we have to do that for a hundred years.

—HUBERT KELLER

AS WE HAVE DISCUSSED, it is both easy and naive to think of French cuisine as being bound by tradition. The reality is different. Escoffier, for example, was in fact a very innovative cook, condemning two of the four classic sauces of Carême's day—*allemande,* which is *velouté,* already a rich sauce, thickened with egg yolks, and *espagnole,* reduced rich brown stock thickened with a roux. He kept *béchamel* and the basic *velouté,* both of which are still used.

Both André Soltner and Hubert Keller are steeped in, and have great respect for, French culinary tradition but, like Escoffier, they do not feel bound by it. Soltner was the first chef outside France to receive its highest culinary honor, the Meilleur Ouvrier de France. Keller, who was born above his family's pastry shop in Alsace, trained with three of France's legendary chefs. Soltner has changed, among other things, the way he makes stock, which is considered a foundation of French cuisine. Keller is cutting back the fat and increasing the intensity of flavors in his dishes. "I use a classic repertoire of flavors that have been used throughout history, but I can apply new techniques, and that is the challenge to classical cuisine," says Keller. "I feel as though this is my contribution to the cuisine of today."

"I see changes in French cuisine," says Soltner. "When I was young, we spent so much time on our stocks. We would roast the bones, add the vegetables and wine, and then cook them for a day or two. I don't believe in that anymore. What do you really get after twenty-four hours? Stocks and *demi-glace* are too concentrated. Stocks are the fundamentals of French cuisine, but I have changed them. At home, I buy five pounds of chicken wings and sauté them. Then I add a few vegetables, deglaze, and let the liquid reduce to a light pan *jus*. Next I'll add water and reduce a little more—and stop. If I had a restaurant today, I would not use the old style of stocks.

"When I was young, my mother would cook a steak and I would always want more *jus*. She would explain, 'I cannot make a lot of *jus*.' She would sauté the steak and add a little butter, and that would be it for five people. So many chefs reduce stocks for so long, yet they are not as good as what my mother had in that pan. The flavor and simplicity of my mother's *jus* is what I try to capture now."

Cutting Fat, Not Flavor

Looking at a classic Alsatian recipe of sautéed foie gras with apples, Hubert Keller notes how much his preparation of that dish has changed over time. "In the past, I would sauté the apples, then the foie gras, save all the foie gras fat on the side, deglaze the pan with a little stock and wine, add the fat back in, plate the dish, and pour the sauce over it," he recalls. "Now, however, I sauté the apples, then the foie gras, and deglaze. Then I add some blanched ginger and a splash of Gewürztraminer, turning the ginger into a sweet confit. I add just a tiny spoonful of fat, not five tablespoons. I joke that this is a low-fat version of foie gras! If you are having a six- or seven-course meal, I can save you four tablespoons of fat on that dish alone! If I'd cooked it with all the fat of the classic version, you would have absorbed it without even knowing." (See the recipe on page 188.)

Foie gras is not the only meat that Keller has managed to lighten. "A lamb chop renders a lot of fat even when it is trimmed," he continues. "Following the same principle as in the old days, the pan would have a tablespoon or more of fat in it after the chop was removed. It would be deglazed with some lamb stock, butter and roux added, and the sauce reduced.

"Now, instead of using roux and butter to bind the sauce, I do something different: I use garlic cloves that have been blanched three times. I bring the water to a boil and blanch the garlic for two minutes, then repeat the process twice with fresh water. Then the garlic gets panfried in a little olive oil to caramelize it. Next, I put it though a blender, to obtain a smooth, ivory-colored cream of garlic. It is so good and mild that you could eat it by the spoonful!

"At the last moment, the garlic is added to the pan with the lamb *jus* and zapped with a handheld mixer. This in turn makes the sauce lighter visually and texturally because of the air it incorporates. So when I spoon it on the plate, you don't see a dark sauce. You might think it is a lamb *jus* with butter, yet there is no butter in it anywhere. You get up at the end of the meal feeling fine, and I have not compromised anywhere on the flavor. That is the true test."

Vive La Difference

Evolution is not revolution. —ANDRÉ SOLTNER

French chefs are looking beyond cutting fat and lightening dishes to update French food and to achieve more flavor, balance, and consistency. The cuisine is grounded so thoroughly in technique that it is not surprising that they are open to using whatever new equipment is available to achieve their goals. "*Sous-vide* is a technique that has been used a great deal by the French," explains Daniel Boulud. "*Sous-vide* is similar to a vacuum pack; it allows you to capture flavors beautifully. When you braise, you don't do it with a thermometer and high precision. You watch, touch, and baste. When you *sous-vide*, you braise with a thermometer; it is mathematics, no guessing. You could cook something for twenty-four hours at a very low temperature, or you could cook salmon for a half hour without overcooking it—as long as you get the temperature perfect.

"If you are making a rack of lamb, you sear it, leaving it almost raw. Then you put it in the *sous-vide* package and cook until you get the right temperature. The problem when you cook a lamb at 350° to 400°F in the oven is that it may still be cold inside. You are trying to get that perfect medium-rare by stopping the cooking at the exact moment. With *sous-vide*, there is never a risk of overcooking or undercooking. You can cook lamb until it is perfectly pink throughout.

"We are bringing in the foremost expert on this method to give a class to my chefs because I want them to understand its precision," he adds. "Then the cooks and I can take the technique even further. I will not base all my cuisine on this technique, not at all. I just want to have the knowledge of how best to use it when I think it is appropriate."

André Soltner, now in his late sixties, has had no problem changing with the times. "Technology is great!" he enthuses, with the energy of a chef half his age. "The food processor, for example, was a huge revolution for the cook. The only reason Escoffier didn't use one is because he didn't have one! If I'm making a mousse, I'll put everything, well chilled, into the food processor, then blend it for three minutes. It comes out better than any mousse I made before the food processor. The chef who is stubborn and makes his mousse the same way he did fifty years ago is on the wrong track.

"I have changed over the last fifty years," he continues. "When I was an apprentice, there was only one way to make puff pastry. You would make it with one pound of butter and one pound of flour, roll it, and incorporate six turns [rolling out the dough and folding it into a block]. To this day, that is still the standard.

"However, not every dish calls for such fine pastry. Now I'll make a 'quick puff pastry,' combining the flour with water, little chunks of butter, and a pinch of baking powder, and giving it four turns," Soltner says. "Fifty years ago, we had no idea that would work. It is not as good for something like a *mille-feuille*, but for other dishes, it works." (See the recipe on page 190.)

Modernizing Vegetarian Cooking

Hubert Keller looks to the classics even when preparing vegetarian dishes for his West Coast clientele. "Artichokes *barigoule* is a classic dish of the South of France. People ate artichokes because they were poor. They would braise them very slowly with carrots, onions, garlic, and basil, which gets us back to extracting favors. It is very light, and is made with just a little olive oil. The result is a fabulous dish! It has never been labeled a vegetarian dish, because then people would not eat it!

"In the past, depending on what part of France you were in, some people would add butter, or even goose fat or pork fat, to flavor vegetable dishes, because they couldn't afford meat. You would also see people use bacon or something else smoked to give the necessary flavor. I update vegetable dishes by removing the bacon and fat and instead using a wild mushroom reduction. Suddenly, we have the flavor we need. That's another way to update the classical to the contemporary."

Techniques Enable Evolution

Braising, roasting, and sautéing are the basic foundations of French cuisine.
—HUBERT KELLER

THE FRENCH HAVE LONG stressed the importance of classical training to give every cook foundational experience in applying essential cooking techniques, as it is a technique that maximizes the flavor you can get out of your ingredients. Our experts have all emphasized the importance of mastering techniques before attempting to innovate.

"Nouvelle cuisine was meant as a way for young chefs to be able to express themselves and come up with new ideas, presentations, and combinations of flavors. Sadly, it became a bit of a joke," says Hubert Keller. "Everybody jumped on the bandwagon and said they were doing 'nouvelle cuisine,' just to fill their restaurants. It was a catastrophe because many chefs had no foundation; they didn't know how to play with flavors and combine ingredients. Michel Guérard was at the forefront of nouvelle cuisine, show-ing—as a three-star chef then as well as now—how it could be done in an extraordinary way. Why Guérard? Because he was classically trained, he could successfully innovate."

When, for our book *Culinary Artistry*, we asked chefs what techniques they would take to a desert island if limited to using those three for the rest of their lives, grilling, sautéing, and braising were the favorites chosen, with roasting and steaming also given some note. So we asked our experts what makes certain techniques so special.

Braising

"We were starting to lose certain dishes and techniques, but they are coming back," says Hubert Keller. "For example, you have never seen so many beef cheeks on menus as today! Ten years ago in San Francisco, you didn't see them, or things like oxtail, any-where.

"The reason braised dishes were being lost is because they take three to four hours to make. You have to watch them the whole time, and there are a lot of steps that take a great deal of care. You can't put just any cook on a braise. It is not like a *steak frites*, where a cook makes a medium-rare steak, puts a spoon of mustard on the side with French fries, and out it goes! A good cook, just by opening the oven and feeling the heat on his face, will know the temperature is just right. You have to know how much wine to put in, the level of the reduction, the thickness of the sauce, and how to bind the sauce. This is when we have *art culinaire*.

"Techniques such as braising and roasting are incredible ways to get flavor out of a product. These techniques started in the home when people could only afford inex-pensive cuts of meat. They had to cook the meat for three to five hours before it was tender enough to eat. If people had filet mignon, I don't think they would have come up with these great dishes."

Daniel Boulud agrees. "Braising was originally for cuts of meat you couldn't chew. There is no other way to cook shoe leather—a Nike or a shank of meat," he laughs. "Now, braising is for luxury. However, you do need to braise rabbit, because if you served it rare you couldn't pull the meat off the bone. You braise a rabbit for an hour, versus a beef shank or oxtail, which will take three to four hours."

Roasting

"I love slow-roasting, which involves a long-term, compassionate relationship between the cook and the oven," enthuses Jean-Georges Vongerichten. Hubert Keller also favors

DANIEL BOULUD ON THE ART OF BRAISING

Daniel Boulud could be considered a Zen master of braising. Many cooks think the best technique is that which takes place in a sauté pan over high heat, with the adrenaline pumping. Boulud challenges this assumption, while describing his technique for the slow, thoughtful process of making one of his favorite dishes, braised short ribs (see the recipe on page 176):

"I never learned how to make braised short ribs in France, but I did learn how to prepare beef bourguignonne, which is similar. In France, you typically boil short ribs, like a pot-au-feu; you don't braise them in red wine. But for this dish I think short ribs work better than the traditional chuck or bottom round.

THE flavor for a braise starts with the searing of the meat. The more time you take searing and caramelizing the outside, the more flavor will transfer to the dish. The process takes a long time, so you need to be patient.

WE add the *mirepoix* [finely diced onion, carrot, celery, and leek] about three-quarters into the searing of the meat, then pan-roast it until it is lightly caramelized. You need the caramelization because it gives shine to the sauce, and the sweetness it adds

roasting as a cooking technique. "We roast eighty percent of our fish, because it seals in the juices and flavors," says Keller. "We'll also roast small cuts of meat and fish, even scallops. All of our cooks have small spray bottles of oil, to spray whatever is being roasted."

The key steps involved in successful roasting include searing and browning the meat to be roasted, either in a hot oven or in a sauté pan on top of the stove. Then the meat should be placed on a meat rack, so it doesn't come into contact with the juices and fat below while it cooks. And the meat should be basted frequently while it cooks, either with its fatty drippings or another fat (such as the oil Keller substitutes).

There is room for savoir faire in preparing meats for roasting, such as deciding whether to lard the meat (to insert a few pieces of pork fat into the meat, which mois-

brightens the flavor. If you caramelize the vegetables correctly, you won't need to add any sugar later to balance the wine. You are pulling the sugar out of the vegetables to balance the wine.

THEN we drain off the excess fat and dust everything with flour. That is known as "monkeying" it, just as a monkey rolls around in the dust at the zoo. Basically we are making a roux and cooking all the flavors together.

NEXT, you drown the whole thing in red wine. With that, you scrape the flavor off the bottom of the pan.

NEXT, add the spices and seasoning.

NOW you simmer very gently. For the first part of the cooking, the meat is tightening up. Then, the meat relaxes and the flavors permeate. If you stop braising too early, there is no flavor; if you stop too late, it is mush.

DURING all this, you are skimming the fat, just as you would for a meat stock. You want to leave a little fat in for flavor, but you have to skim the fat so that you have flavor but not a greasy sauce.

YOU must let a braised dish cool slowly; that is very important to retain the flavor of the dish. While it's cooling, we trim the meat off the bones, then we put it back in the sauce right away to retain the moistness.

tens the meat as it melts) or to bard it (to cover some or all of it with a layer of fat, ranging from bacon to prosciutto, during cooking). Lamb, for example, could be "larded" with garlic cloves to infuse the flavor into the meat.

The temperature at which to roast will depend on the cut and type of meat being roasted, ranging from beef, goose, ham, turkey, and veal at the low end (i.e., 325 degrees F) to quail (450 degrees F) at the high end. "I typically don't like roasting at high temperatures," cautions Vongerichten. "It too often results in harsh flavors."

Doneness is tested through either high-tech (temperature testing via instant-read thermometer) or low-tech means (simply poking the meat, or puncturing it and seeing the juices of white meats and poultry run clear, or red meats and game run pink).

Sautéing

"Sautéing has not changed much," says André Soltner. "Meat still has to be cooked in a hot pan. If a sloppy chef puts the meat in oil or butter that is not hot enough, he has already ruined the dish.

"I was recently a guest chef on a Greek cruise ship, where I watched Greek cuisine being prepared. Yet the way they cooked was what I learned in my apprenticeship in France. They started a Greek dish with the same sauté technique I had learned. This is one more reason I tell my students to learn the fundamentals—they can apply them almost anywhere."

The temperature for sautéing depends on the fat being used. While, as Soltner points out, the fat must be very hot in order to prevent the meat from sticking to the pan, it shouldn't be smoking hot. Vegetable oil, for example, will start to burn when it reaches 450 degrees F, and regular (nonclarified) butter will burn at only 250 degrees F. After the initial browning, the heat can be reduced for sautéing.

Steaming

Most people don't associate steaming with luxury or skill. "I don't do too much steaming, because people can't picture what is special about it," says Daniel Boulud. "It is the psychology of reading the menu. 'Steamed' is not always the most attractive technique. If I am doing salmon, it is better to talk about the broth with the fish.

"Technically," he explains, "steam is a blanket of heat that is at one temperature and very precise. It's more precise than poaching. It gradually brings a piece of fish, for example, to the right temperature without drying it out. I like to add herbs around the fish, like mint and coriander, and also citrus, like lemon, with a bit of good olive oil. Those things blend very gently and there is no overpowering of the fish. It cooks very delicately.

"The minute the fish is firm, it is done. There is no resting after cooking, as when it is seared. Black sea bass is wonderful for steaming. It firms up nicely, is not too oily, and has a very clean flavor. Cod is also very good."

It's important to know when an ingredient doesn't lend itself well to steaming. "Some fish are better suited for frying than steaming," Boulud points out. "For example, rouget and sardines are more suited to frying because they are fatty fish."

Grilling

Grilling admittedly is not a traditional French technique. Yet that doesn't mean that French chefs don't enjoy and rely on it today. "To me, grilling over fire is some of the best cooking there is," says Daniel Boulud. "You get much more spontaneous and creative with grilling. Wherever you go, whether it is Oregon or the Hamptons, you will see something that will inspire you. Grilling is very natural; it is about simple flavors. You want some herbs and a marinade that will flavor the meat without disguising the wood flavor. Also, you want what you cook to be lightly touched by the flame.

"When I was apprenticing, I didn't see much grilling," says Boulud. "The one thing they would grill would be a tournedos of beef topped with béarnaise—boring! But when I think of grilling, I think of vacation. I also think of a country trip with fishing. It is about being totally relaxed and not having to think about conventional cooking. It is an ancient technique, about instinct. It is very personal, and each person likes it done differently.

"It is easy to be inspired with grilling. The most important thing is the ingredient you choose. You want something slightly firm that you cook rare to medium-rare. Not every fish will work on the grill. Monkfish, for example, needs to be cooked nearly all the way through. But mackerel is great for grilling because all it needs is a quick flash with a char, and it can be left half-raw. You get a warm and cold combination. Scallops also work well for the same reason. Skewer some scallops on a rosemary skewer, add a pinch of black pepper and some nice olive oil, and that is enough for me," he laughs. "I also would not turn down a grilled lobster. Split down the middle, grilled with a drizzle of lemon and a drizzle of butter—I am happy!"

The Culinary Map of France

ANDRÉ SOLTNER'S EYES LOOKED WISTFUL when we asked him about the specialties of the different regions of France. "If you're planning to go to Marseilles, you look forward to eating bouillabaisse," he says. "They have all the ingredients right there to do it as it should be done. If you go there and they serve something else, you will be disappointed.

"When I go home to Alsace, I want to have a 'bakers oven,' which is made with pork, beef, and lamb cooked with onions, potatoes, and white wine. It is put into a terrine and baked for three or four hours. It is a beautiful, regional thing. If you are Alsatian and you have one, you are happy (see the recipe on page 191). I even used to make them on occasion at Lutèce."

Many French chefs, including Daniel Boulud, return to France regularly to visit family and friends, yet they still manage to "work in"—if visiting other top chefs' restaurants can be called work—some time for research. "Two of the stops I am making on my next trip are at the top and bottom of the country," Boulud told us recently. "I'm visiting Regis Marcon in the north at L'Auberge. He is only open from mid-March to mid-November, because after that they get snowed out. I'm looking forward to his food. He is near Le Puy, which is where they grow lentils. Regis works with legumes as well as with chestnuts and lots of local berries and fruit. He draws on the foods of the mountains and, despite how creative he is, he is very grounded.

"In the south, I want to go to Collioure. It is a little seaport near the Spanish border and is known for anchovies. If you want the best anchovy in the world, this is where you have to go! They are great fresh or packed in salt. I want to take a little time to see how they process them."

As is true of many countries, trying to pin down the culinary regions of France is tricky business. Neighboring areas have traded influences with one another over centuries. Nevertheless, it is true that different general patterns characterize different regions. Not surprisingly, the regions mostly break down along ingredient lines—what is available where defines the various regional cuisines. A few examples:

REGION	KEY INGREDIENTS/*CHARACTERISTIC DISHES*
NORTHEAST	
Alsace and Lorraine	charcuterie, fish, game, pork, sauerkraut, sausage, wines/*baker's oven, breads, German-style pastries, kugelhopf, quiche Lorraine*
Champagne	Champagnes, herring, sausage
NORTH CENTRAL	
Île de France/Paris	cosmopolitan melting pot of all the regions
NORTHWEST	
Brittany	apples, butter, chicken, eggs, fish, milk, oysters, potatoes, sea salt (includes *fleur de sel*), shellfish/*buckwheat crepes*
Loire Valley	grapes, pork, trout
Normandy	apples, butter, Camembert, cream, lamb, milk, seafood
SOUTHEAST	
Burgundy	bacon, mustard, onions, red wines/*beef bourguignonne* (beef stew with red Burgundy)
Dijon	crayfish, mustard
Franche-Comté	Bresse chickens, cheese (including Comté, similar to Gruyère), milk
Lyon	Charolais beef, crayfish, onions, potatoes, walnuts/French onion soup/*soupe à l'oignon*
Provence	anchovies, basil, fish, garlic, herbs, lamb, olives, olive oil, tomatoes/*bouilabaisse, tapenade*
SOUTHWEST	
Basque	cod, ham, onions, peppers, tomatoes/*sauce basquaise*
Bordeaux	cèpes, Cognac, oysters, red wines, sausage, truffles/*sauce bordelaise*
Gascony	peppers
Périgord	black truffles, cèpes, chanterelles, chestnuts, duck, foie gras, goose, walnuts

How Wine Builds Character

Traditional French cuisine exists in the regions of France. Despite how food is changing all over the world, it is still there. —ALAIN DUCASSE

THE TECHNIQUES OF THE TRADITIONAL French kitchen are universal throughout the country, but what gives them color is the locale in which they are applied. Chefs throughout France will send their best cooks to work in other regions to learn the full breadth of French cooking and ingredients. Because they take their regionality as seriously as they do their technique, it is vital to understand the nuances of the regions, including their wines.

To understand French wine, you have to understand the regions of France. The food and wines of Alsace, for example, are completely different from those of Provence. For Daniel Boulud, wine helps give French food its character.

"French cuisine is about technique, but it is also about balancing food and wine," he says. "For me, French food without wine is very boring! At every level of French cuisine, you see an emphasis on pairing food and wine, from a bistro with *steak frites* paired with a simple *vin de pays* to haute cuisine served with a grand cru. I believe French food will never go out of fashion—as long as we have wine, we will hold on a little longer!

"French dishes are designed to be paired with wine. A *jus* or sauce with roasted flavors and simple seasonings can match with a Cabernet, Pinot, or Merlot and still be in tune. If you keep in mind the root of the dish, you can make a small deviation and it will still work."

The Bond Between Chef and Guest

No matter who the chef is, cooking always comes from the heart first. Some chefs may cook more from their heads than others, but each chef shares a passion and desire. At the same time, your cuisine must be in harmony with your client and the time period you are living in, so cooking is not entirely just about you. —ALAIN DUCASSE

DANIEL BOULUD LOVES WALKING THE tightrope of the past and the future. He is pragmatic, celebrating traditional dishes while keeping in mind his customers' needs and preferences. "I have to be able to adapt traditional and regional dishes to my kitchen," he says. "However, some dishes are timeless, and for me that type of cuisine will always be appreciated. It will never fade away. Some dishes, like tripe or suckling pig, are esoteric and belong to a certain caste of diner. They are fantastic, but are they right for someone who made a reservation months ago? No—they want something else from me. It is more often the more frequent customer who wants something different.

"We don't always tell all the customers everything that we have," he continues. "We sometimes make things and share them only with the people who are close to us, who understand what we do. It is a way to give them a unique experience. That is the excitement and the curse of cooking. I know other chefs who just stick to their menu and that is it. We may have no one trained to make a particular dish, but we do it anyway just to have fun cooking it!"

Over the years, André Soltner realized that some customers want only expensive things and that there were those who didn't value excellence in the "ordinary." "A *tarte à l'oignon* is delicious, but traditional dishes such as this are being lost because of customer attitudes and the economics of running a restaurant," he laments. "When I was an apprentice, we would make three soups for lunch and three different soups for dinner. At Lutèce, I would make one for each and essentially give them away as an *amuse[-bouche]*. Too many people don't appreciate a great soup; they don't see the value. I like caviar too, but there is nothing wrong with a wonderful soup!

"I could make you a hamburger you would die for," he continues. "I learned how to make *steak haché* fifty years ago: You sauté onions, soak bread in milk, then mix them into the meat. The result is a hamburger that is moist and delicious. Who knows how to make one of those today?

"I put *steak haché* on the menu once at lunch. My partner, André Surmain, loved the idea. Some customers were shocked when they found out *steak haché* was a hamburger! Our adventurous customers, those we knew would 'get it,' couldn't get over how good it was!

"You can't forget that you cook for customers," Soltner says. "If you don't have customers, you close. So you do everything professionally, then you have to do something extra to bring the customer back."

Hubert Keller believes that chefs must cook at another level to set themselves apart from customers who may be talented in their own kitchens. "If you have a dish in a restaurant and can make it the next night at home, then the restaurant has missed something. Dining out should be an experience, it should trigger the 'Oh my God, how did they do that?' response. Culinary art is a bigger challenge than ladling something into a bowl.

"For his special customers, Roger Vergé would prepare pig's feet stuffed with truffles and foie gras. Here is a cut of meat that was for the poor, but in the hands of a three-star chef, it became a peak food experience. All of a sudden, pig's feet were fine in three-star restaurants!"

Cultural Exchange à la Technique

THE WIDESPREAD INFLUENCE OF French cuisine and its techniques cannot be underestimated. Mexican chef Zarela Martinez, for example, believes that training in French techniques has greatly improved Mexican cooking. "In Mexican restaurants, fish used to be overcooked, but not any longer," she observes.

French cuisine has, in turn, been enriched by the cooking of other countries, even China. André Soltner observes, "In Asia, they don't sauté their vegetables the way the French do. The French blanch vegetables before sautéing them, but the Asians just sauté them without blanching. Now that I cook at home, I don't blanch them anymore; I just put them in my Le Creuset [pan] with a little oil and cover it. To me, that is borrowing a little from the Chinese while still cooking French, because I just season them with a little salt."

"I am interested in everything, but I am not influenced by everything," says Alain Ducasse. "For example, I love the flavors of Chinese cuisine, but I don't apply them to my food. I have seen techniques in Asia that have influenced me, however. I like the idea of cooking in a wok, taking something from raw to cooked in a short time. I use a wok at my restaurant Spoon [his multicultural restaurant in Paris].

"In Tokyo, I like the dumplings [pot stickers] that are caramelized on one side and steamed on the other," he adds. "That is a great technique that I also use at Spoon, where I try out all my new ideas. It is a restaurant that offers true freedom of personal expression."

Developing "the Touch"

ALAIN DUCASSE SEES THE KEY to French cooking as savoir faire. "It is not necessarily the taste of French food as we know it. It is the know-how and technique, and how you stamp that on your ingredients. You apply the savoir faire you brought with you. There is a French taste that you are looking for, but first you must think about technique and how you will apply it."

Daniel Boulud knows that sometimes he is leading his cooks down a path they don't see clearly. "Sometimes cooks will do things even though they don't fully understand them. Then, you will see a spark in their eye. They become good at the technique or the dish because they understand that fine point where something happened. It is like a cooking climax—when you feel it, you know it is perfect. Yet it is not always easy for the cook to achieve that.

"When my chef, Alex Lee, and I create a recipe, we know what we are trying to achieve, so we spend the time getting there. When you make a soup, the sweating of the vegetables [cooking them in a little fat and their own juices] is so important. If you go too far or not far enough, you will ruin it. The right ratio of liquids to solids is also important. If you are making something with as few ingredients as a leek and potato soup, and have five cooks prepare it, you will have five different soups. Which one is right? The cook who reaches the climax, voilà!

"I would say two-thirds of the time, vegetables are undercooked," laments André Soltner. "It is easy to understand why cooks undercook vegetables—they stay nice looking that way. However, everything has to be cooked just à point. That is the difference between good chefs and bad chefs: the good chef always hits the mark."

French Savoir Faire on a World Stage

I don't believe anyone should try to classify a chef's cuisine, because it puts limits on their freedom of expression. If you put someone in a box, you miss the big picture.

—ALAIN DUCASSE

HOW DOES DUCASSE DESCRIBE the emerging state of French cuisine? "All French chefs, including myself, have their own personal interpretation of technique," he says. "It is not true that classic French cuisine is being lost. I would say that chefs are creating contemporary classic French cuisine, which is the result of their own personal interpretations. Every French chef has a personal interpretation of French cuisine, and it is very clear. Perhaps not everyone can tell the difference between the cuisines of different chefs, but food lovers can tell one chef's vision from another. I can see and taste the differences clearly.

"My own cooking is influenced by my family and the experience of growing up in Southwest France. My cuisine is the sum of all my life experiences—everything I have tasted and everywhere I have traveled. It is like a 'personal cocktail.' I would say a chef's style is half objective [based on classic French technique and recipes] and half subjective [rooted in personal experience and preferences]."

With restaurants around the globe and France, how does Ducasse stay true to his individual vision? "The common points are my techniques and savoir faire; they are simply applied wherever I am. I try to do something unique for different locations. If I am in Paris, I am touched by modern life and contemporary cuisine. In the city, customers want sexy food or free, liberated food. In New York, you are applying French know-how to American ingredients. In the countryside, people want peasant food, security, and serenity. In Monaco, diners want haute Mediterranean cuisine. Each of my restaurants has its own unique personality, and I cultivate that. If I wasn't one man doing four locations, you would not find common points among them—but I *am* one man, so you will find common points.

"Ultimately, I am led by nature and the products of the area in which I am cooking. It is about doing the best with what is available. Chefs are the interpreters of what nature gives us at any given time. Nature dictates the produce that's available and thus the dishes we do—not our clients. For example, in Monaco, I love the vegetables. There is nowhere else in the world that you can find vegetables like that. I just love the aroma. In markets on the Mediterranean—that is where the pleasure of cuisine starts!"

Applying French technique and savoir faire around the world to other cuisines is possible—with the right reference points, emphasizes Hubert Keller. He muses about how far afield classical French training has taken him and his colleagues now that they are cooking across America and incorporating flavors from different parts of the globe. "Jean-Georges Vongerichten and I trained together in France—we both started out cooking for dogs during hunting season!" he recalls. "Jean-Georges took his classical French training and moved to Asia, and now incorporates those flavors into dishes in his restaurants. Gray Kunz followed a similar path of classical training and living abroad in Asia. Both of them have real reference points—so their cuisines work.

"I draw the line by not ever taking steps that are too extreme with my cuisine," Keller points out. "My style, and that of the restaurant, is contemporary French. I will incorporate things like sesame oil and ginger, but I see them as spices. The world has gotten smaller and people are familiar with more flavors, so by incorporating them into my cuisine, I stay up-to-date.

Nach Waxman's Recommended Reading on French Cooking

Traditionally, what the French mean by "French" cooking is the food of Paris and its schools and its restaurants done in Paris. More marginal, until recently, has been "provincial" cooking, which refers to the cooking of the provinces throughout the rest of France.

There is one book on French cuisine that you ignore at your peril: **The New Making of a Cook** by Madeleine Kamman. It is her statement about cooking, and as her roots are French, it is therefore a statement about *La Cuisine*. If you really want to understand the underpinnings of French cooking, the reason things are done certain ways (whether through mere custom or clear scientific rationale), read this book. It will sharpen and expand your thinking about cooking.

Richard Olney's **Simple French Food** is not quite as rigorous, but it is inspirational, with lots of little essays and discussions, covering everything from sautéing to vinegar-making methods.

The two volumes of **Mastering the Art of French Cooking** by Julia Child can't be waved aside as merely popular works. They are serious resources, with a great deal of information on cooking in general, including how to handle various ingredients, as well as recipes.

Not infrequently, aspiring chefs will come into the bookstore saying that their chef asked them to pick up a copy of Escoffier's **Le Guide Culinaire. Le Guide** is not really a cookbook in the ordinary sense; it is an *aide-memoire*, or a reminder of the outlines of how a dish is made. Recipes are not given in their full form but are highly condensed, and much is assumed about what the cook already knows how to do. On the other hand, the dishes dealt with are the basis of *la grande cuisine*, and knowing this material is like being able to perform the school figures in Olympic figure skating—the basics that are the building blocks of contemporary innovative cooking.

"Some people might think of ginger or star anise as exotic in French cuisine. However, my father, who owned a pâtisserie in Alsace, used to make ginger cookies from French recipes that were two hundred years old. Star anise was used in all sorts of classic Alsatian dishes. Much of the incorporation of spices in French cuisine is not that new—it's just that people have forgotten."

Ma Gastronomie by Fernand Point is not so much a cookbook as the story of a chef and a restaurant in action. Had Point written it himself instead of leaving the task to his wife, it could have been just another chef writing about his cooking. Instead, it is a triumphant tribute to personal cooking in a restaurant setting and a great inspiration.

If you want to expand a bit from the basics, turn to *The Atelier of Jöel Robuchon: The Artistry of a Master Chef and His Protégés* by Patricia Wells and Robuchon. The basic idea is that French chef Jöel Robuchon has inspired a lot of the chefs who passed through his kitchen. It presents a number of recipe concepts, and then his various protégés' differing takes on each of them.

There's one book that was not meant for professional chefs, but the thinking underlying it is so good that I like to recommend it: Michael Roberts' *Parisian Home Cooking: Conversations, Recipes, and Tips from the Cooks and Food Merchants of Paris.* Roberts was at one time a cutting-edge, creative American chef. Here, however, he deals with the way regular French people cook when they come home at the end of the day, describing an approach that is simple, spontaneous, and almost recipe-free. It all begins at the market, where Parisians see what looks fresh and interesting, and then presents a very French sense of the flavor and feel of working with those ingredients.

There've been a number of French regional books, of course, although, except for those published locally (and in French), not as many as might be hoped for. These are a few worth knowing: Paula Wolfert's *Cooking of South-West France* deals with Perigord and Gascony, and it brings together acute observation, historical insights, and meticulous kitchen work; it's really a model of a book about cuisine. Richard Olney's *Lulu's Provencal Table* gives a picture of life in a region and offers the work of one fine cook as a snapshot of the food of Provence. *The Norman Table* by Claude Guermont and Paul Frumkin deals nicely with the culinary creations of France's grape-free zone—the land of calvados and cream. Madeleine Kamman's *Savoie* treats, with her usual thoroughness, the food of her home province, taking us from region's geology to the joys of its kitchens.

Chilled Oyster Velouté with Lemongrass and Osetra Caviar

174

2 cups heavy cream

1 stalk lemongrass, tender heart of the bulb only, coarsely chopped

2 sprigs cilantro

A ½-inch-thick piece ginger, peeled and cut in half

1 sheet gelatin
(or ½ teaspoon powdered gelatin softened in 1 tablespoon cold water, then heated until dissolved)

3 cups chicken stock

2 leeks, white and lightest green parts only, cut into ¼-inch pieces and washed

Salt and freshly ground white pepper

24 North Atlantic oysters, such as Wellfleet, Pemmaquid, or Bluepoint, scrubbed (if you have the fishmonger shuck the oysters for you, make sure to ask for the liquor)

Tabasco sauce

4 ounces golden osetra caviar (optional)

SERVES 4

POUR THE CREAM into a small saucepan and toss in the lemongrass, cilantro, and ginger. Bring to a boil, then adjust the heat so that the cream is at a steady simmer. Let the cream bubble away until it is thick enough to coat the back of a wooden spoon and is reduced to about ⅔ cup. (Patience—this might take as long as 30 minutes.) Pull the pan from the heat, cover, and allow the cream to infuse for 1 hour, time enough for it to take in all the flavor of the lemongrass, cilantro, and ginger.

POUR THE CREAM through a fine-mesh sieve into a large bowl; discard the solids.

SOAK AND SOFTEN the sheet gelatin in a small bowl of cold water. Meanwhile, bring the chicken stock to a simmer.

LIFT THE GELATIN out of the water, squeeze it gently between your hands to remove excess moisture, and whisk it into the warm chicken stock. (Or, if you're using softened and dissolved powdered gelatin, add it to the stock.) When the gelatin has dissolved, whisk the chicken stock into the cream. Let the mixture cool, then cover and refrigerate, whisking from time to time, until the velouté is well chilled.

PUT THE LEEKS in a small sauté pan or skillet with 3 to 4 tablespoons water. Season with salt and pepper, cover the pan, and cook the leeks until tender but still very green, 3 to 5 minutes. Drain and let cool, then cover and chill.

SHUCK THE OYSTERS, putting them in one bowl and their liquor in another. Cover the oysters and refrigerate. Discard the oyster shells. Strain and save 1 cup of the liquor.

LITTLE BY LITTLE, strain the liquor into the velouté mixture—the amount you add will depend on how briny you want the taste to be and how thick or thin the consistency. Season with pepper and Tabasco and refrigerate until serving time—but for no more than 2 hours.

TO SERVE, PLACE A spoonful of the leeks in the bottom of each of six small chilled soup bowls. Top the leeks with the caviar, if you're using it. Pat the oysters dry between paper towels and put 6 oysters around the leeks in each bowl. Stir the chilled velouté very well and pour it into the bowls. Serve immediately.

Short Ribs Braised in Red Wine

Three 750-ml bottles dry red wine

2 tablespoons vegetable oil

8 beef short ribs, trimmed of excess fat

Salt

1 teaspoon black peppercorns, crushed

Flour for dredging

10 garlic cloves, peeled

8 large shallots, split

2 medium carrots, peeled and cut into 1-inch lengths

2 stalks celery, peeled and cut into 1-inch lengths

1 medium leek, white and light green parts only, trimmed, coarsely chopped, washed, and dried

6 sprigs flat-leaf parsley

2 sprigs thyme

2 bay leaves

2 tablespoons tomato paste

3 quarts beef stock

Freshly ground white pepper

Celery Duo (recipe follows) (optional)

SERVES 8

HEAT THE WINE in a large saucepan over medium heat. When the wine is hot, carefully set it aflame, then let the flames die out. Increase the heat and bring to a boil; boil until the wine cooks down by half. Remove from the heat.

CENTER A RACK in the oven and preheat the oven to 350 degrees F.

HEAT THE OIL in a Dutch oven or large casserole over medium-high heat. Season the ribs all over with salt and the crushed pepper. Dust half the ribs with about 1 tablespoon flour and then, when the oil is hot, slip them into the pot and sear 4 to 5 minutes on each side, until well browned. Transfer the browned ribs to a plate, dust the remaining ribs with flour, and sear in the same manner.

REMOVE ALL BUT 1 TABLESPOON of fat from the pot, lower the heat to medium, and toss in the vegetables and herbs. Brown the vegetables lightly, for 5 to 7 minutes, then stir in the tomato paste and cook for 1 minute to blend. Add the reduced wine, the browned ribs, and stock to the pot. Bring to the boil, cover the pot tightly, and slide it into the oven. Braise for 2½ hours, or until the ribs are tender enough to be easily pierced with a fork. Every 30 minutes or so, lift the lid and skim and discard whatever fat may have bubbled up to the surface. (Not only can you make this a day in advance up to this point, it's best to make it ahead. Let cool and refrigerate the ribs and stock in the pan overnight. The next day, scrape off the fat. Reheat before continuing.)

CAREFULLY (the tender meat falls apart easily) transfer the meat to a deep, heated serving platter with a raised rim and cover to keep warm. Boil the pan juices until thickened and reduce to approximately 4 cups. Season with salt and white pepper and pass through a fine-mesh strainer; discard the solids. (The ribs and sauce can be made a few days ahead and kept covered in the refrigerator. Reheat gently, basting the ribs frequently with the sauce, on top of the stove or in a 350-degree oven.)

TO SERVE, POUR the sauce over the meat. If you've made the celery duo, serve it on the same platter—the celery root puree can go under the ribs, the braised celery over them.

Wine Recommendation
A young brawny Médoc, such as a Pauillac or a Saint-Julien

Celery Duo

FOR THE CELERY ROOT

1 quart whole milk

4 cups water

2 tablespoons coarse salt

2 pounds celery root, peeled and cut into 8 pieces

1 pound Yukon Gold potatoes, peeled and cut in half

8 tablespoons (1 stick) unsalted butter, softened, cut into 8 pieces

Salt and freshly ground white pepper

FOR THE CELERY

2 bunches celery

1 tablespoon extra-virgin olive oil

1 carrot, peeled and quartered

1 turnip, peeled and quartered

Salt and freshly ground white pepper

2½ cups chicken stock

SERVES 8

FOR THE CELERY ROOT

PUT THE MILK, water, coarse salt, celery root, and potatoes in a medium saucepan and bring to a boil over medium heat. Lower the heat and cook at a simmer until the vegetables can be easily pierced with the point of a knife, 20 to 25 minutes. Drain the vegetables and return them to the pan.

PUT THE PAN BACK over low heat and toss the vegetables around in it just enough to cook off their excess moisture. Transfer the vegetables to a food processor. Add the butter and process—taking care not to overwork the mixture—just until the puree is smooth and creamy. Season with salt and pepper. Keep the puree warm in the top of a double boiler over simmering water. (The puree can be made up to 6 hours ahead. Let cool, cover it with plastic wrap, pressing the wrap against the puree, and refrigerate. When you're ready to serve, rewarm the puree in the top of a double boiler over simmering water.)

FOR THE CELERY

MEANWHILE, TRIM the bottom of each bunch of celery, but make certain the stalks remain together. Measure 4 to 5 inches up from the bottom and cut the celery tops off at that point; you'll be using the bottom part. Remove and discard the three or four tough outer stalks from each bunch. Run a vegetable peeler over the outer celery stalks to remove the stringy fibers, then cut each bunch of celery lengthwise into quarters.

HEAT THE OIL in a large sauté pan or skillet over medium heat. Add the carrot, turnip, and celery quarters, season with salt and pepper, and cook, without coloring the vegetables, for 3 minutes. Pour in the stock and bring to a boil. Adjust the heat so that the stock simmers steadily, and cook the vegetables for about 25 minutes, or until they can be pierced easily with the point of a knife. When the vegetables are tender, the liquid should be just about gone, so that you have tender vegetables lightly glazed with the stock. Remove and discard the carrots and turnips, and serve the celery with the puree. (If it's more convenient, you can make the celery up to 6 hours ahead, chill it, then rewarm it gently at serving time.)

Note
If not serving the duo with the short ribs, spoon the puree onto one side of a large heated platter and the glazed celery onto the other.

Gratin aux Cerises
Cherry Gratin

FOR THE RED WINE REDUCTION

1½ cups dry red wine

1 cup port

¼ cup sugar

Grated zest and juice of ½ orange

½ vanilla bean, split

Approximately 2 quarts Bing cherries, pitted

FOR THE GRATIN BATTER

2 large eggs, separated

3 large egg yolks

3 tablespoons cornstarch

2 cups milk

½ capful tangerine oil

Pinch of salt

⅔ cup sugar

Confectioners' sugar for sprinkling

SERVES 10

FOR THE WINE REDUCTION

COMBINE THE WINE, port, sugar, orange juice, and zest in a small saucepan. Scrape the seeds from the vanilla bean into the pan, and bring to a boil. Lower the heat to a simmer and allow the liquid to reduce by half, 10 to 15 minutes. Strain through a fine mesh sieve and let cool.

CENTER A RACK in the oven and preheat the oven to 375 degrees F.

ARRANGE THE CHERRIES in an even, tight single layer in ten large crème brûlée dishes. Spoon the wine reduction over the cherries. Cover the dishes with aluminum foil and bake for 15 to 20 minutes, until the cherries are plump and tender. Remove from the oven and let the cherries stand for a few hours to develop their flavors. (The cherries can be made up to a day ahead and refrigerated.)

FOR THE BATTER

WHISK TOGETHER the egg yolks, cornstarch, and ¼ cup of the milk in a medium bowl.

IN A MEDIUM SAUCEPAN, bring the remaining 1¾ cups milk to a boil. Whisking without a stop, very gradually add half the hot milk to the egg mixture to temper the eggs. Pour the mixture back into the saucepan and, still whisking energetically and constantly, cook over medium heat until the pastry cream thickens and starts to boil. Boil for 30 seconds, then scrape into a bowl. Cover the pastry cream with plastic wrap, pressing the plastic against the surface of the cream, and refrigerate until chilled; stir in the tangerine oil. (The pastry cream can be made up to a day in advance.)

CENTER A RACK in the oven and preheat the broiler. Place the cherry-filled dishes on a baking sheet.

THIRTY MINUTES before serving, remove the pastry cream from the refrigerator.

IN A MEDIUM BOWL, whisk the egg whites and salt until soft peaks are formed. Gradually whisk in the sugar and beat until stiff peaks are formed. Fold one-quarter of the egg whites into the pastry cream. Fold in the remaining egg whites. Spoon the mixture over the cherries, making sure to cover them completely.

SPRINKLE THE TOPS liberally with confectioners' sugar and immediately place the dishes underneath the broiler. Bake until the tops have puffed slightly and colored to a nice golden brown. Serve warm.

Roasted Chicken with Herbs under the Skin, Garden Vegetables, and Roasting Jus

1 bunch flat-leaf parsley

1 bunch chervil

Sprig of tarragon

14 tablespoons (1¾ sticks) unsalted butter, at room temperature, plus 7 tablespoons butter, cut into bits

7 ounces white mushrooms, trimmed, cleaned, and finely diced

1 shallot, thinly sliced

Salt and freshly ground black pepper

One 4½ pound roasting chicken

4 cups Roast Chicken Jus (recipe follows)

Stuffed Onions (recipe follows)

½ bunch chives, cut into 1-inch lengths

SERVES 4

PREHEAT THE OVEN to 350 degrees F.

RESERVE THE TIPS of about one-quarter of the parsley and chervil sprigs. Chop the remaining parsley and chervil with the tarragon. In a medium bowl, cream the 14 tablespoons softened butter. Beat in the chopped herbs. Set aside.

COMBINE THE MUSHROOMS with the remaining 7 tablespoons butter until very soft. Add the shallots and mushrooms to the herbed butter. Season with salt and pepper.

USING YOUR FINGERTIPS, carefully lift the skin from the chicken, without tearing it, and spread the herbed butter underneath. Make sure that the skin is covering the meat so that it does not dry out during cooking. Put the chicken in a roasting pan.

ROAST THE CHICKEN for about 1¼ hours. When the chicken is three-quarters cooked, baste with the chicken jus.

WHEN THE CHICKEN is done, strain the pan juices and add the reserved chervil and parsley.

TO SERVE, TRANSFER the stuffed onions to serving plates. Carve the chicken, arrange on the plates, and coat with the jus. Sprinkle with a little pepper and the chives.

YOU CAN ADD OTHER vegetables, such as whole artichokes cooked barigoule style, then stuffed with olive tapenade and braised with the tomatoes in the chicken juices. A few croutons rubbed with garlic and panfried are perfect to garnish.

Roast Chicken Jus

3 tablespoons olive oil

7½ pounds chicken carcasses, cut up with a cleaver or heavy knife

1½ tablespoons unsalted butter

18 garlic cloves, crushed

3 cups water, plus more as needed

1 tablespoon salt

MAKES 6 CUPS

HEAT THE OLIVE OIL in a heavy stockpot or large Dutch oven over high heat. Add the chicken carcasses and cook, stirring occasionally, until golden brown, 10 to 15 minutes.

REDUCE THE HEAT to medium, add the butter and salt, and garlic, and cook, stirring occasionally, until the garlic is golden brown.

ADD 1½ CUPS of the water, bring to a simmer, and simmer until reduced to a glaze. Add another 1½ cups water and simmer until reduced by about three-quarters.

ADD ENOUGH WATER to cover the bones and bring to a simmer. Reduce the heat and simmer gently for 20 minutes.

STRAIN THE BROTH through a fine-mesh sieve, and pour into a saucepan. Skim off the fat and bring to a simmer. Simmer until reduced to 6 cups, skimming occasionally. If not using immediately, let cool, cover, and refrigerate.

Stuffed Onions

12 medium white onions

Olive oil

Salt and freshly ground white pepper

1 small celery stalk, finely diced

2 tablespoons pine nuts, toasted and crushed with the side of a knife

1 tablespoon ricotta

1 tablespoon diced salted pork fat

1 tablespoon freshly grated Parmigiano-Reggiano

1 tablespoon chopped flat-leaf parsley

A little chopped sage

2 tablespoons Roast Chicken Jus

SERVES 4

PREHEAT THE OVEN to 350 degrees F.

SLICE OFF THE TOPS of 8 of the onions; reserve these lids. Scoop out the centers of the onions with a spoon, leaving a shell of two or three layers.

FINELY DICE THE spooned-out interiors and the remaining 4 onions. Sauté the diced onions in olive oil until lightly golden. Add salt and pepper to taste, and remove from the heat. Stir in the celery, pine nuts, ricotta, pork fat, grated parmigiano, parsley, sage, and salt and pepper to taste.

STUFF THE ONIONS and replace their tops. Put them on a baking sheet and drizzle with olive oil. Bake for about 30 minutes, basting them regularly with their juices (this will make them really tasty and fondant—slightly melted). If the onions start to brown too much, cover them with foil. When the onions are cooked, spoon the chicken jus over them and sprinkle with freshly ground pepper.

Vegetables from the Gardens of Provence Simmered in Crushed Black Truffles, with Olive Oil, Balsamic, and Fleur de Sel

12 baby carrots with tops

12 baby turnips with greens

4 baby fennel bulbs

8 baby leeks

8 radishes

1 pound baby peas in the pod

1 pound fava beans in the pod

7 ounces green string beans

4 zucchini flowers

4 artichokes

8 asparagus spears

Juice of ½ lemon

Olive oil

Sea salt

About ¼ cup chicken stock

1 ounce black truffles, crushed

Mature olive oil

A knob unsalted butter

Dash of aged balsamic vinegar

Dash of aged sherry vinegar

12 scallions

Freshly ground white pepper

Fleur de sel

SERVES 4

PEEL THE BABY CARROTS and turnips. Trim them, leaving about ¼ inch of the tops. Trim the fennel bulbs and remove the outer layer of skin. Trim the leeks and radishes. Shell the peas and fava beans. Trim the green beans. Remove the pistils from the zucchini flowers. Remove the leaves of the artichokes, then the chokes. Cut into quarters and place in a bowl of water with the lemon juice. Trim the asparagus to 3-inch tips.

ONE AT A TIME, blanch the peas, fava beans, green beans, and asparagus in boiling salted water. Remove the vegetables from the water while they are still firm and immediately plunge them into an ice bath to cool. Drain thoroughly and let cool.

HEAT A DASH of olive oil in a large wide pot (the pot should be large enough that vegetables are not piled on top of each other) and add all the remaining vegetables except the radishes. Add a little sea salt, cover, and simmer until the moisture from the vegetables has evaporated. Add just enough stock to come nearly to the top of the vegetables and cook, stirring gently from time to time, until the vegetables are nearly cooked. Remove the lid and add the blanched vegetables, the crushed truffle, olive oil, and butter. Let simmer until the vegetables are cooked to your liking, the flavor of the truffle has permeated the dish, and the sauce has thickened.

MEANWHILE, COOK THE radishes in a small saucepan in the same manner as the other vegetables and add tem to the other vegetables.

USING A SLOTTED SPOON, gently transfer the vegetables to a deep serving dish. Add both vinegars to the sauce, check the seasoning, and pour the sauce over the vegetables. Add a drizzle of olive oil, a sprinkling of fleur de sel, and a crack of pepper, and serve immediately.

Hubert Keller

Maine Lobster Tail on Salsify with Pinot Noir Sauce, Vanilla Oil, and Crispy Leeks

¼ cup white wine vinegar

4 live Maine lobsters (about 1¼ pounds each)

FOR THE SALSIFY PUREE

12 stalks of salsify (8 inches long)

¼ cup water

1 teaspoon fresh lemon juice

1½ tablespoons unsalted butter

Salt and freshly ground black pepper

3 tablespoons heavy cream

Pinch of sugar

FOR THE CRISPY LEEKS

1 medium leek

¼ cup vegetable oil

Salt

FOR THE VANILLA OIL

3 plump vanilla beans

1 tablespoon grapeseed or olive oil

This is one of my favorite food combinations! Very quickly, the delicate vanilla perfume will seduce your most critical guests.

FOR THE LOBSTERS

PREHEAT THE OVEN to 400 degrees F. Bring 11/2 gallons salted water to a boil in a large stockpot.

ADD THE VINEGAR to the boiling water, then add 2 of the lobsters, headfirst, cover tightly with a lid, and cook for 6 minutes. Remove the lobsters and set aside to cool. Repeat with remaining lobsters.

BREAK OFF the lobster tails. Using scissors, cut down the underside of the tail and remove the meat, keeping the tails whole. Break off the claws, carefully crack the shells, and remove the claw meat from each in a single piece. Cut the bodies of the lobsters lengthwise in half, then cut them into 4 pieces; reserve the shells.

FOR THE SALSIFY PUREE

PEEL THE SALSIFY and cut into 1-inch pieces (to prevent the salsify from discoloring). Immediately place in a medium saucepan with the water, lemon juice, butter, and salt and pepper to taste. Cover and simmer for 15 minutes, or until tender. Meanwhile, in a small saucepan, bring the cream to a boil. When the salsify is cooked, drain it and add to the cream. Add the sugar and simmer for 2 to 3 minutes. Transfer to a blender and blend until very smooth. Adjust the seasoning with salt and pepper. Transfer to a small saucepan; just before serving, reheat over low heat.

FOR THE CRISPY LEEKS

TRIM OFF THE ROOT and all the green parts of the leek. Cut lengthwise in half. Holding each half together, wash away all the grit under cold

FOR THE PINOT NOIR SAUCE

1½ teaspoons virgin olive oil, separated

3 tablespoons finely minced shallots

1 garlic clove, minced

Lobster shells

½ cup Pinot Noir

1½ cups brown chicken stock

1½ teaspoons cornstarch

1 tablespoon port

Salt and freshly ground black pepper

SERVES 4

running water. Pat dry with paper towels. Lay each half cut side down on a cutting board and slice lengthwise into fine julienne. Pat dry again. Heat the oil in a medium nonstick sauté pan over medium heat. Add the leek julienne and fry for about 3 minutes or until golden and crisp. Using a slotted spoon, transfer to paper towels and drain well. Season with salt. (The leeks can be made early in the day and then reheated for about 5 minutes in a 300-degree oven just before serving.)

FOR THE VANILLA OIL

SPLIT THE VANILLA BEANS lengthwise in half and scrape the seeds into the grapeseed oil. Stir the oil and reserve.

FOR THE PINOT NOIR SAUCE

HEAT THE OLIVE OIL in a large sauté pan over medium heat and sweat the shallots for 5 to 6 minutes. Add the garlic and cook for 1 minute. Add the lobster shells and sweat for another 5 to 8 minutes. Stir in the wine and simmer for 5 minutes, or until the pan is almost dry. Mix the stock, cornstarch, and port in a bowl, then add to the pan and simmer gently for 8 to 10 minutes. Strain the sauce into a small saucepan and season with salt and pepper.

TO ASSEMBLE AND SERVE the dish, split each lobster tail lengthwise. Place the tails and claw meat in a small baking pan. Drizzle with the olive oil, then season with salt and pepper. Place the pan in the oven and roast for 3 to 4 minutes, or until the lobster is just cooked.

SPOON ABOUT 1½ TABLESPOONS of the salsify puree onto the center of each warm serving plate and spread the puree into a 4- to 5-inch circle. Carefully place 2 lobster tail halves and 2 claws on top of the puree. Spoon the sauce generously around the puree. Top the lobsters delicately with the crispy leeks. Stir the vanilla oil and drizzle it between the rims of the plates and the sauce.

Sautéed Foie Gras with Roasted Apples with Gewürztraminer and Ginger Sauce

¼ cup diced carrot

¼ cup diced onion

¼ cup diced leek

¼ cup diced celery

1 cup chicken stock

2 tablespoons unsalted butter, softened

2 small apples (dessert apples), peeled, cored, and cut into 8 wedges each

1 teaspoon finely julienned fresh ginger

One 1-pound fresh foie gras (goose or duck)

Salt and freshly ground black pepper

¼ cup Gewürztraminer

4 sprigs chervil

SERVES 4

This sautéed foie gras dish employs traditional French technique—with all the fat and all the flavor! For techniques to lighten the dish, see page 158.

PLACE THE DICED VEGETABLES in a saucepan with the chicken stock, bring to a boil, and reduce by half. Drain the vegetables in a strainer, reserving the stock, and set aside.

MEANWHILE, PREHEAT the broiler. Generously grease a baking sheet with the softened butter. Place the apple slices on the baking sheet and place under the broiler to brown lightly. Remove from the broiler and keep hot.

BRING A SMALL SAUCEPAN of water to a boil. Add the ginger and blanch for 2 minutes. Drain and refresh under cold running water. (Blanching the ginger reduces its sharpness.) Set aside.

REMOVE ANY MEMBRANES surrounding the foie gras and remove the veins. Cut the foie gras into 4 slices. Season with salt and pepper. Heat a nonstick pan. Fry the slices of foie gras briefly on both sides. Remove from the pan and place on a warm platter. Pour the fat into a bowl and reserve.

DEGLAZE THE PAN with the wine. Add the ginger and bring to a boil over medium-high heat. Reduce the liquid by two-thirds. Add the stock and the vegetables and reduce further to a saucelike consistency. Just before serving, add the foie gras fat, whisking until emulsified. Season to taste.

PLACE A SLICE of foie gras on each plate and garnish the plates with the roasted apples. Spoon the sauce over the foie gras and garnish with the chervil.

Hubert Keller

Garlic and Saffron Soup

1 tablespoon virgin olive oil

2 small leeks, white part only, cut lengthwise in half and thinly sliced (about 1 cup)

3 to 4 garlic bulbs, separated into cloves, peeled, and blanched

4 cups vegetable stock or water

Salt and freshly ground black pepper

¼ cup finely diced peeled white potato

A large pinch of saffron threads

¼ cup heavy cream or half-and-half

3 tablespoons peeled, seeded, and diced tomato (optional)

2 tablespoons finely sliced fresh chives

SERVES 4

This recipe is based on the Provençal soupe d'ail doux (sweet garlic soup). Don't be afraid of the garlic's pungency; after blanching, it becomes quite mild.

To give the soup another dimension, place a warm poached egg on a toasted slice of baguette in the bottom of each bowl and then ladle the soup over. This is a very common addition in the South of France.

HEAT THE OLIVE OIL in a large heavy saucepan over medium heat and sweat the leeks, stirring often, for about 6 minutes, or until soft. Add the garlic cloves, stock, and salt and pepper to taste and bring to a boil. Add the potato and saffron threads, reduce the heat, and simmer for 7 to 8 minutes, or until the potatoes are soft. Stir in the cream and return to a boil. Immediately remove the soup from the heat. Let cool slightly.

TRANSFER THE SOUP to a blender or food processor, in batches if necessary, and puree until smooth. Pour the soup into a clean saucepan and heat through. Adjust the seasoning if necessary. Stir in the diced tomato, if desired.

LADLE THE SOUP into warm bowls, sprinkle with the chives, and serve immediately.

Quick Puff Pastry

1 pound instant flour
(Wondra)

1 teaspoon baking powder

½ teaspoon salt

1 pound cold unsalted butter,
cut into 1-inch cubes

1 cup cold water

MAKES 2½ POUNDS

IN A BOWL OR MIXER, combine all the ingredients just so they come together.

ON A LIGHTLY FLOURED SURFACE, roll out the dough into an 18-by-8-inch rectangle. Fold the dough crosswise in half. Turn the dough so a narrow side end is toward you and roll out into an 18-by-8-inch rectangle again. Fold the dough in half and roll out again. Fold the dough into thirds and refrigerate for 15 minutes.

ROLL OUT THE DOUGH to an 18-by-8-inch rectangle again and fold in half. Roll out again, and fold into thirds. Refrigerate for 30 minutes. The dough is now ready to be used.

André Soltner

Baker's Oven
(Alsatian Stew)

FIRST DAY

1 pig's foot

½ pound lamb shoulder

½ pound pork shoulder

½ pound boneless breast of beef

1 small thinly sliced onion

1 garlic clove, sliced in half

1 bouquet garni

2 cups dry white wine, preferably Alsatian

SECOND DAY

1 pound potatoes, peeled and thinly sliced

¼ pound onions, thinly sliced

Dry white wine, preferably Alsatian, to cover

Salt and freshly ground black pepper

SERVES 6

TO MARINATE THE MEAT, cut all the meats into 1-inch cubes (use a cleaver for the pig's foot). Combine with the onion, garlic, and bouquet garni in a large bowl. Add the wine, cover, and marinate overnight in the refrigerator.

PREHEAT THE OVEN to 300 degrees F.

DISCARD THE bouquet garni. Spread half of the potatoes over the bottom of a large casserole.

COVER WITH THE marinated meats, then the onions, then cover with the remaining potatoes. Add enough wine to cover, and season with salt and pepper.

COVER TIGHTLY and bake for about 2½ hours.

China

EASTERN TECHNIQUES AND
A YING-YANG BALANCE

*China is the mother of Asian cuisine. It is where soy sauce, tea, and
stir-frying were born. Chinese cuisine is the tree from which
Japanese, Korean, and Southeast Asian cuisines grew.*

—BARBARA TROPP, AUTHOR, *THE MODERN ART OF CHINESE COOKING*

CHINESE CUISINE IS ONE OF the world's most ancient cuisines, going back thousands of years. When you consider China's population, migration, and culinary history, it doesn't come as a surprise that its influence on the cuisines of other Asian countries has been tremendous—from what is cooked in other kitchens to how these ingredients and dishes are prepared and enjoyed.

There is obviously a lot to be learned from a people who were already cultivating rice in 4000 B.C.—and by 2700 B.C. were categorizing plants according to their culinary and medicinal values (recalling the Chinese proverb "He that takes medicine and neglects diet wastes the skills of the physician"). Starting in 1100 B.C., they were using ice for refrigeration, as well as pickling and smoking as means of food preservation. During this time, there were (astoundingly) more than three thousand people involved in preparing food for the royal court. By 1000 B.C., the Chinese were documenting their culinary experiments and writing down recipes! (By contrast, the first professional cooks didn't even come on the scene in Rome until 170 B.C.)

"When you look at the cooking in different parts of Asia, you can see the extraordinary influences that China has had," says Nina Simonds, author of *Classic Chinese Cuisine*. "What is exciting and fascinating is to see how those Chinese influences were incorporated into what each culture already had on hand."

China was the spring of life for Asian food, and its influences spread across mountains, plains, and rivers, and through cities and villages. When the Chinese traveled outside their borders, they packed up their pantries and traditions and took them with them. As a result, the Chinese tea code, for example, which had ritualized the serving of tea under the Tang Dynasty (618–907), evolved into the Japanese tea ceremony around the fifteenth century. Though each culture adapted these influences to suit its own personality, the values of Chinese cuisine have remained intact. Who knows how the Chinese came to take food so seriously, but thankfully for the rest of us they did. Whether dispensing wisdom about the pleasures of gastronomic balance or offering a new ingredient for a country's larder, Chinese culinary masters helped shape the methods and enthusiasm with which other nations approach their cuisines.

"It is interesting to experience one cuisine and then look at how neighboring cultures have adapted or changed that cuisine," Simonds observes. "You can see how the neighboring countries' chefs took the basic techniques, ideas, and ingredients from Chinese cuisine and innovated from there. Take noodles or the standard spring roll, which is a traditional Chinese food that is now popular throughout Asia. In Vietnamese cuisine, spring rolls—rice paper wrappers filled with rice noodles, meat, or seafood—are fried, then served so that diners can wrap them with fresh mint, basil, and cilantro in large lettuce leaves before dipping the entire thing in *nuoc cham*. It is a complex experience, in that Vietnamese cuisine has taken something from the Chinese culinary tradition and built on it.

"In China, there are many varieties of noodles, but when you go to Japan, you see that noodle making has been elevated to an art form. The Japanese have taken this medium and expanded it, taking it to another dimension whereby soba noodles are made by 'soba masters.'"

Our experts in other Asian cuisines acknowledge China's influence as well. "China ruled Vietnam for over a thousand years," explains Corinne Trang, author of *Authentic Vietnamese Cooking*. "The idea of sharing food served from multiple dishes comes from the Chinese. Vietnam is the only other place in Asia where people use chopsticks the way the Chinese do." Arun Sampanthavivat, chef-owner of Arun in Chicago, acknowledges that the impact of the Chinese on Thai cuisine has been enormous, including "the use of chiles in sauces from China."

"These cross-cuisine influences can be seen in a dish as simple as soup," Simonds says. "A classic noodle soup in China is the Szechwan cinnamon and beef soup. The meat is braised and then the broth and vegetables are added. Similarly, in Vietnam you'll find the classic noodle soup *pho*, which is beef broth seasoned with star anise and cinnamon. The Vietnamese then add thinly sliced beef and fresh herbs.

"Malaysian cuisine started with Chinese cooking, and then brought in influences from India, Thailand, Portugal, and Vietnam. You see the overlap of techniques and spices, yet the food is not gastronomic chaos. There is a distinct kind of orchestration that comes together in the mouth."

Peace and Harmony Through Food

He did not eat rice which had been injured by heat or damp and had turned sour, nor fish or flesh which was gone. He did not eat what was discolored, or what was of a bad flavor, nor anything which was ill-cooked, or was not in season. He did not eat meat which was not cut properly, nor what was served without its proper sauce. Though there might be a large quantity of meat, he would not allow what he took to exceed the due proportion for the rice. **—CONFUCIUS, *ANALECTS***

FOR CENTURIES, FOOD HAS BEEN so fundamental to Chinese culture that attitudes toward it are downright philosophical. In his texts on government and strategy, Lao-Tzu (around 600 B.C.) used culinary analogies, such as "Governing a great nation is like cooking a small fish—too much handling will spoil it." No less a mind than Confucius

(551–479 B.C.) himself pondered the deep connections between people and food. His conclusion? "The enjoyment of food is one of the things that contributes to the peace and harmony of a society."

Peace and harmony are achieved through applying the principles of yin and yang, which inform all aspects of Chinese culture. According to the Chinese, by consuming a balanced diet, a person will achieve a balanced and healthy body. Food that is yin—embodying dark, feminine qualities—is cooling and mild. Food that is yang—light and masculine—is warming and hot. Yin reduces body heat, whereas yang increases body temperature. Yin foods are often vegetables, fish, or seafood. Yang foods are often meats, fruits such as apricots or cherries, and some vegetables, such as carrots or onions. Yin foods are sweet, like sugar, while yang foods are tart, like vinegar. Raw ingredients may be one of the two and turn into the other when cooked. Eggs are an example of a food that contains both yin and yang—the yolk is yin and the white is yang. Together, yin and yang create the optimal state of balance.

EXAMPLES OF YIN AND YANG

Generally speaking, yin (or cooling) foods are fruits, vegetables, and many types of seafood. Yang (or heating) foods are beef, lamb, eggs, and many pungent spices.

—NINA SIMONDS

YIN FOODS include asparagus, bananas, bean sprouts, celery, coconuts, crab, cucumbers, grapefruit, lemon, lotus root, oranges, pears, tofu, water chestnuts, watercress, and watermelon.

YANG FOODS include apricots, blackberries, butter, carrots, cherries, chicken, chives, ginger, lamb, leeks, litchis, mangoes, onions, scallions, shallots, and strawberries.

YIN COOKING techniques include boiling, poaching, and steaming.

YANG COOKING techniques include deep-frying, roasting, and stir-frying.

A YIN AND YANG MENU

YIN

Cold asparagus

YANG

Red-cooked pork with ginger

YIN

Steamed shrimp with eggplant

YANG

Stir-fried Chicken with ginger

The concept of yin and yang informs the balance of ingredients within each dish, as well as the entire menu, in a Chinese meal. Juxtaposing contrasting ingredients and cooking techniques is key.

While serving three spicy stir-fried fish dishes in one meal might be to your personal taste, it would not be traditional nor would it highlight the distinctive qualities of each dish. Some simple greens would provide a chance for your palate to rest, something stewed would be a way to enjoy slowly developed flavors, and individual stir-fries of pork, chicken, and shrimp would make you look forward to the next bite that much more.

The number of dishes remains the same whether you are serving four people or eight; you just adjust the portion sizes. The one constant at any meal is the centerpiece bowl of rice.

"The key concepts in Chinese cooking are proportion, harmony, and balance," says Nina Simonds. "One of the Szechwan dishes most familiar to Westerners is hot-and-sour soup, a dish that demonstrates this balance [see her recipe on page 224]. In the West, it often has a spicy, one-dimensional flavor: hot. However, if it is prepared properly, chile paste is not used—instead, pepper and ginger provide it with its punch. Those flavors give the soup subtlety, and you can taste the sour flavor as well as the touch of sweetness.

"The soup has an extraordinary texture; tofu and wood-ear mushrooms give it some crunch. Traditionally, chicken blood is also added, which imparts a liver-like quality to the soup. Without that chile paste blast, you can appreciate the diversity of flavors that come together in this one dish.

"This is a dish that teaches you about subtlety without being subtle! When it is done properly, it offers a variety of seasonings, with the heat being only one dimension. It's a prime example of Chinese culinary balance at work."

Rice and the Chinese Meal

MEALS IN MOST PARTS OF China revolve around rice, of which more than forty thousand types are grown. As in many of the countries of Asia, rice is not an accompaniment: it is the main dish. Barbara Tropp notes that the amount of rice that would serve four Westerners in the United States would serve only one Chinese diner. The Chinese divide food into two categories: *fan*, which is primarily starch (most often rice), and *ts'ai*, which is vegetables and meats (or, put another way, things served with rice). Each person has an individual bowl of rice, then picks from the meat, fish, or vegetable dishes on the table with chopsticks.

"When people get into the curlicues or allegros of fusion cuisine, you don't see the bowl of rice or noodles," says Barbara Tropp. "However, if you are Asian, you can't eat your dishes without the base of rice or noodles. It would be like eating the icing without the cake!" The Chinese also cannot eat meals without soup, which serves as a beverage.

And what do the Chinese eat after their rice and its accompaniments? Nothing. Sweets are snacks, not finales to meals. In a formal banquet, desserts are served between some courses, but not at the end.

From the Mountains to the Sea

While Beijing, in the North, was part of the Silk Route and wielded political power, the South had economic power.

—MARK MILLER, CHEF-OWNER, COYOTE CAFÉ, SANTA FE

CHINA'S BORDERS ENCOMPASS TERRAIN from the Himalayas to the tropics. The country includes over three and a half million square miles and has a population of more than one billion. The climate and geography in China vary widely. It's not surprising then, with such diversity of regions and population, that regional differences are a key element of the cuisine.

THE ART OF COOKING RICE

Talk doesn't cook rice. —CHINESE PROVERB

Andrew once worked with a fellow cook who had spent a great deal of time living and cooking in China. When he asked him what the secret to making perfect rice was, he replied, "There is no secret. They put some rice in a pot, rinse it, and cover it with enough water until it comes to their first knuckle on their index finger (or about one inch of water above the level of the rice). Then they bring it to a boil, and cook it covered until it is done. You see, there are not a lot of measuring cups and timers in China!" Ever since, Andrew has continued to dig, and he's found a few more secrets beyond the "first-knuckle rule—which indeed works!"

In China, rice is either steamed or boiled, with the boiled version being the most common. The Chinese primarily consume long-grain rice, but, as we stated earlier, there are thousands of varieties of rice. It is not essential to use imported rice. Great long-grain rice is being grown in Texas as well as the delta area of California, less than seventy miles from the Napa Valley.

Key Steps to Preparing Rice
Boiled Rice

- **WASH THE RICE:** Put the rice in a bowl and rinse it in cold water, stirring with your hand or a spoon, changing the water several times. This not only cleans the rice but also makes it less starchy. (Barbara Tropp describes the washing as a ritual: "Washing rice symbolizes the beginning of preparing the meal.") After talking to our experts and reading countless recipes, many contradicting each other, we came to the conclusion that rinsing the rice was the only thing everybody seemed to agree on. Rinsing three times is typical, but some rinse it even more.

- **TO SOAK OR NOT TO SOAK:** After the last rinse, many cooks like to soak the rice in the water in which it will cook, for anywhere from 15 minutes to an hour. Soaking the rice is believed to make it more tender. Soaking also reduces the cooking time; soaked rice cooks in 15 minutes, compared to unsoaked rice, which cooks in about 30.

- **USE THE RIGHT AMOUNT OF WATER:** The standard American ratio of rice to water is one to two, but all our experts agree that this makes rice that's too soft for Chinese tastes. In the Chinese kitchen, the proper ratio of rice to water is one to one and three-quarters. You can adjust this, depending on how soft you like your rice.

- **COOKING THE RICE:** Combine the rinsed rice in a pot with the water and bring to a boil. Boil for about 5 minutes, uncovered. Turn down to a very low simmer, cover, and cook for an additional 20 to 25 minutes (if you are cooking soaked rice, cook only for an additional 10 minutes). Do not uncover the rice during cooking except to check for doneness near the end of the cooking time. The rice should be soft and not appear "soupy." As with any ingredient, each bag of rice may vary in how long it will take to cook. Make sure the rice is cooked through. It should *not* have a "toothy" feel, like al dente pasta or risotto. The grains should not stick together or clump. Just before serving, fluff the rice with chopsticks or a fork.

Steamed Rice

Steamed rice is a little fluffier than boiled rice.

- Rinse the rice in cold water two to three times.

- Using a ratio of one portion of rice to two to three portions of water, combine the rice and water in a saucepan, bring to a boil, and cook for 3 minutes.

- Drain the rice.

- Put the rice in a steaming basket and steam, covered, over water at a rolling boil for about 30 minutes. Fluff with chopsticks or a fork before serving.

Before preparing a Chinese meal, it is essential to understand the characteristics of the regional cuisines, including those of the north (in and around Beijing, formerly Peking), east (Shanghai), south (Canton), and west (Szechwan, Hunan, and Yunan). That way, you'll have a frame of reference when planning a menu. You can look to the west, for example, if preparing a spicy dish, or the north if cooking moo shu pork. If you happen to have a great piece of fish to cook *and* a desire to make Peking duck, you are already in two different regions.

"Each region has its own philosophy and aesthetic," Mark Miller points out. "So, if you want to know Chinese food, it is not enough to know the food of one area. Shanghai [east] is very different from Hong Kong [south]. They are almost opposites in terms of their attitudes towards subtlety. Southern China has always been subtler philosophically, and in poetry, painting, and music—and even the glaze on their meat is subtler!" (While pork in the eastern region is served in a savory sauce, pork in the south is paired with a sweet sauce.)

The North: Beijing (Peking)

"The north features great street food, as well as the tradition of imperial food, which is more refined," says Nina Simonds. "The cooking of the north is very sensual and gutsy. Dishes are seasoned with garlic chives and leeks. Traditionally, it was a relatively poor area, but the Imperial cooks could afford to import things."

The most striking difference in the north is the use of wheat. Most of China relies on rice, but in the north you see bread, baked buns, dumplings, and wheat noodles. The pancakes served with *moo shu* dishes and Peking duck are also made from wheat flour.

Regional Larder

The weather is extreme in this region, which borders on both the Gobi Desert and the mountains of Siberia. You could say that the yin and yang of weather are represented there! The north does not rely on fresh herbs as other parts of China do. Meat—everything from chicken and goat to lamb, beef, and pork—is especially prized. Smoking meats is very common; one of the classic dishes is smoked chicken. Hearty winter vegetables are frequently preserved or pickled. The north's characteristic strong flavors are provided by garlic, leeks, and onions, as well as vinegars and bean pastes.

Key Dishes and Techniques

The north has the sophistication of the imperial cuisine from the capital, Beijing, with dishes such as bird's nest soup, Peking duck, and beggar's chicken, which is wrapped in lotus leaves and clay and slow-cooked. The flip side is country cooking like dumplings and scallion pancakes. Moo shu pork is a classic northern dish. The most common cooking techniques are braising, roasting, and boiling.

The East: Shanghai

Each region has four or five different cuisines within it. In the east, you have Yangzhou, Suzhou, Hangzhou, and Wuxi. Together they make up what's known as Shanghai cuisine. The soupy dumplings that are so popular are actually from Yangzhou, not Shanghai.

—MICHAEL TONG, OWNER, SHUN LEE PALACE, NEW YORK

"In Shanghai, you see a refinement of all cooking styles and a subtlety in the saucing and techniques," observes Nina Simonds. Carved vegetable and fruit garnishes often accompany dishes, and the region is known for its use of sugar as a flavoring.

DUCK IN CHINA

The preparation of duck also varies throughout the regions. Westerners don't often realize that there is more to duck in China than the famous Peking version.

- **NORTH:** Peking duck is known for its crispy skin, accomplished partly with the use of a bicycle pump to pull the skin from the meat. The skin of the duck is scalded, then the duck is air-dried and roasted.

- **EAST:** In Shanghai, duck is marinated in a variety of sauces and spices, including soy, hoisin, star anise, and cinnamon.

- **SOUTH:** Cantonese duck is marinated in bean paste with garlic, star anise, and peppercorns. However, rather than the usual technique of letting the meat sit in the marinade, the marinade is poured into the cavity, which is then sealed.

- **WEST:** Szechwan duck is also noted for its crispy skin. The duck is rubbed with spices, including salt, Szechwan peppercorns, and five-spice powder, then steamed and finished off by frying.

Regional Larder

Eastern China is coastal, and the region also includes the freshwater West Lake and the Yangtse River. Thus the cuisine features both seafood (saltwater carp, eel, and yellow crab) and freshwater fish (freshwater carp, crab, shrimp, and shad). Where there is water, there is fowl, and duck and other game birds are prevalent in the area. The east

TREKKING THROUGH CHINA: EATING DUMPLINGS WITH NINA SIMONDS

Dumplings are just one type of food you can compare throughout China. They are made almost everywhere, but they differ from region to region—something that is also true for almost any food made across China. With each common food form, you see a diversity.

I once worked on a travelogue covering thirty-two cities, and it was on this trip that I realized the diversity of dim sum.

- **NORTH**: Northern dumplings tend to be coarser than those found elsewhere. They are filled with ground lamb or pork and garlic chives. The dumplings are usually boiled, but are sometimes panfried. They are very substantial.

- **EAST**: When you think of dumplings in New York, everybody thinks of "soupy buns" that squirt all over your shirt if you don't know how to eat them. In fact, Eastern regional dumplings are very diverse. They are more often steamed than boiled, and the ingredients are often opulent. You may find shrimp, water chestnuts, shark's fin, or crab roe in them.

- **SOUTH**: Dumplings here also tend to be more refined with opulent ingredients. Chefs here have applied relatively new, European techniques to traditional ingredients. The dumplings are baked in an oven and are flaky in texture.

- **WEST**: Here, the area of Szechwan, Hunan, and Yunan, there is a diversity of dim sum that you don't see in the United States, such as dumplings in hot oil.

is also very fertile, with crops of everything from corn, rice, and sweet potatoes to melons, mangoes, peaches, and plums. It is sometimes called "the Land of Fish and Rice."

Hoisin sauce and what's considered to be the best rice wine vinegar in the country are used as flavorings. Black vinegar is frequently used as a condiment. The east is known not only for the quality, but also for the quantity of soy sauce it produces, although soy sauce is not commonly placed on the table. (Maybe making it cures your craving?)

Key Dishes and Techniques
Shanghainese cooking includes the technique known as "red cooking," in which meat (such as whole chickens and other poultry, fish, and pork) is braised in soy sauce, rice wine, sugar, and salt. The result is tender meat and a rich, flavorful sauce. The meat and sauce are typically served with crunchy cooked vegetables, to contrast with the texture of the meat, as well as with white rice. Red-cooked meats are typically prepared in clay pots, which can be found in Asian markets. The meats are cooked slowly and can be served hot, but are more often presented cold.

"There is also a repertoire of dishes called 'drunken,'" according to Nina Simonds. "The meat for these dishes (such as chicken) is partially cooked and then left to sit in the liquid to finish cooking. They're then chilled and eaten as appetizers. A famous Cantonese variation is drunken shrimp, for which the shrimp are brought live to the table. Rice wine is poured over them before eating."

Pot stickers and scallion pancakes are other regional favorites. The area is also known for its famous salted pressed pork, *hsiao*. Tea is popular here, as throughout the country, yet it is different from the tea served in the rest of China. It can be compared to espresso in that the tea is made strong, served in a small cup, and consumed in one gulp rather than sipped.

The South: Canton (Guangzhou)

The food of the south is most commonly thought of as Cantonese. Cantonese food is widely considered the finest, most sophisticated, and most innovative cuisine in China. Simple and light, Cantonese cuisine dishes are never heavily sauced, and when something is fried, you note the crispness, not the flavor or texture of oil.

"In Canton, the cooking is even more refined and focused than in the east and the north. Here you see the influence of European cooking," says Simonds. "In Canton, the main ingredient is the star of a dish and the sauce is used just to accentuate the ingredient's extraordinary flavor."

Regional Larder
"The climate is warmer, even subtropical," explains Simonds, "so you see rice and an extraordinary supply of vegetables". In addition, vegetables tend to be served slightly undercooked in order to accentuate their freshness and flavor. The south grows citrus

fruits like oranges, tangerines, and grapefruits, as well as peaches, litchis, melons, and star fruits. Fish and shellfish are used a great deal. Squab (pigeon) and frog's legs are very popular, as are more unusual meats, including snake and dog.

The south preserves a variety of foods, from vegetables to ham to shrimp and fish. Ginger is common, as is rice wine vinegar, which acts as an acid to balance the flavors in dishes. Soybeans in all their variations (from soy sauce to tofu) and mustard sauces are also typical.

Key Dishes and Techniques

Cantonese cuisine employs a wide range of flavors and cooking techniques. Though pork is the most common meat, it is often served in small quantities. A good way to recognize a Cantonese restaurant is to walk by and look in the window; if you see poultry hanging there, that's a signal. The poultry is marinated and roasted, then hung to air-dry. Dim sum also originated in this region.

Many cooking techniques are used in Cantonese cooking—from braising to, roasting, simmering to steaming—but the most popular is stir-frying in a wok. Common dishes include steamed scallops with black bean sauce, crisp skin chicken, soup, egg rolls, egg foo yung, and roast pork.

The West: Szechwan, Hunan, and Yunnan

Szechwan cooking in the West is some of the most bastardized food there is. Most of what's available in the United States and Europe is a far cry from the authentic version.

—NINA SIMONDS

The food of the west, home of a legendary trading route, has been influenced by the many countries that border it. These include India, Laos, Myanmar (Burma), Nepal, Pakistan, and Vietnam. The weather of two geographic extremes, the Himalayas and the tropics, buffet the area. The tropical climate gives rise to rice, as well as citrus fruits, bamboo, and chiles.

The food is a little simpler and less subtle than that of the south. This is the region of spicy food. Two of its cuisines are famous: Hunan and Szechwan, both of which are typified by intense heat, with Hunan food being the spicier of the two, because of the use of more fresh chiles, as opposed to the chile paste predominantly used in Szechwan cooking. This is also the region of multiple cooking techniques applied within one dish.

Regional Larder

Cooking of the west makes use of onions, garlic, ginger, pepper, chiles, peanuts, and sesame seeds. Soy sauce, soy paste, bean curd, and black beans are also essential ingredients. In addition to chiles, ginger, garlic, and onions are other common flavorings.

Meat, especially beef and lamb, smoked duck, and fish (both fresh and dried, with dried most often used in soups and sauces) are also used in many dishes. Spicy peanut sauce, sesame sauce, and hoisin sauce are the most typical sauces.

Key Dishes and Techniques

Classic dishes of Szechwan cuisine include Kung Pao chicken and twice-cooked pork. Among the most popular classic Hunan dishes are orange beef and sweet-and-sour chicken. Meat is often cooked first in water, then cut into small pieces and finished in a wok.

Stir-frying, simmering, steaming, and shallow frying are the most commonly employed cooking techniques. Szechwan duck, green onion pancakes (*cuong you bing*) and cold spicy noodles (*liang ban mian*) are among the most famous Szechwan dishes. Hot-and-sour soup is also very popular.

Hunan cuisine is considered more complex because it tends to combine more than one cooking technique in a dish. Hunan food is often described as being "hot, sour, sweet, and spicy." Popular dishes include chicken with walnuts and hot pepper, diced pork with dried fish, and steamed spicy pork.

Yunnan cuisine is known for its whole cured hams that have a sweet flavor, as well as for its steam pot chicken. Common techniques include frying, simmering, steaming, and stewing.

Getting Started in the Chinese Kitchen

In Chinese cuisine, things are cooked again and again. You may brine something for two days in twenty-seven herbs and spices, then roast it, and finish it by deep-frying. The end result is the development of unique flavor profiles.

—MARK MILLER

Ingredients

Barbara Tropp explains the approach to food and cooking that is typical of the Chinese: "Food is purchased two or three times a day in the local market. There is no tradition of refrigeration in Asia, so there is no holding of dead animals. Chinese cooks are hesitant to buy anything that is not freshly killed. To them, it would be like buying a fish and not looking at the gills!"

Meat

Pork is the most common meat in China. Pigs, unlike cows, serve no function other than food, and pork is cheap. Most of all, pork is extremely versatile. Large cuts are braised in red-cooking, and, combined with various seasonings, the ground meat is stuffed into countless dumplings. Chicken, beef, snake, and frog are also part of the Chinese diet.

Vegetables

Vegetables—stir-fried, steamed, blanched, or pickled—are an integral part of Chinese cuisine. Most techniques aim to cook them quickly in order to preserve their freshness. For reasons of hygiene, vegetables are almost never eaten raw. Even when used in salads, they are usually quickly blanched. However, vegetables are most commonly cooked in a wok.

Preserved Foods

Preserved foods are eaten on their own or used as ingredients in other dishes. Dried beans and their by-products are seen everywhere: mung bean sheets, cellophane noodles, and tofu. The wide variety of dried fish found in every authentic Chinese market (some of which can run up to nine hundred dollars a pound!) is used to enhance flavors. Seeds, particularly sesame and lotus, are also frequently used.

Soy Products

It's hard to imagine Chinese cuisine without the soybean. You could fill a table with it in all its variations: soy sauce and hoisin sauce, raw beans, fried beans, tofu, noodles. Everything on the table could be fried in soy oil or coated in soy flour. (Vegans owe a debt of gratitude to the Chinese for their soy milk and desserts topped with whipped soy.)

"Tamari is a wheat-free soy sauce whose flavor band is about the same as soy sauce," says Barbara Tropp. "I like the artisanal tamari that is imported by the Corti Brothers of Sacramento. Darrell Corti is one of the most extraordinary people on the planet. He got interested in Asian products and traveled to Japan and elsewhere to do research, and he sells incredible products. People should get on his mailing list and buy whatever he is selling. The tamari he has is simply the best liquid soy product I have ever put my lips to."

Flavorings

Some flavorings are universal throughout most of China. When stocking your pantry, "Great things to keep on hand include ginger infused with sherry; sugar, to be used for balance; and scallion and ginger for yin-yang pairings," advises Tropp. "Hoisin sauce, sweet bean paste, and bean paste are also essential. I tend to be a northern, central, and western Chinese cook as opposed to a southern cook, and to cover those regions, you should also have fermented black beans, Szechwan peppercorns, chile products, and toasted sesame oil. If you are a southern cook, you also want oyster sauce."

Tropp makes her own five-flavor oil with ginger, scallion, citron, and peppercorn infused in toasted sesame oil, then mixed with a neutral oil, like corn or peanut. She prefers the Chinese rice wine *shao-hsing*, a brown sherry-like wine that is quite different from the Japanese sake. Tropp finds the Japanese brands of some ingredients better than the Chinese; for example, the toasted sesame oil and rice wine vinegar she prefers are Japanese.

Tools and Equipment

The Wok

The wok is used throughout Asia. From the Himalayas to the sea, from Beijing to Bali, the ingredients may vary, but not the pan. While no longer unique to China, the wok did originate there. The word "wok" means "cooking vessel" or "pot," and most food historians believe that it evolved out of necessity. China, like other Asian nations, has never boasted abundant energy resources, so a way to cook food quickly was essential.

There are two main types of woks: flat-bottomed and round-bottomed. The flat-bottomed wok is designed to be used on electric burners, while the round-bottomed model is meant for gas stoves. Some Chinese cooking experts prefer the flat-bottomed version on American gas stoves.

While she doesn't believe one is essential, Nina Simonds likes the versatility of a wok. "It is a great multipurpose piece of equipment that you can use to stir-fry, steam, and braise. When I first came back from Taiwan," she recalls, "I was poor and didn't have any other piece of equipment, so I used it for everything."

It is very important not to overload a wok, because the whole point of it is to allow you to cook things at high heat. If the wok is too full, your ingredients will steam rather

than sear. This is especially true when cooking on American stoves, because they are never as hot as stoves designed for woks.

The Chinese stir-fry meat and vegetables separately because they take different amounts of time to cook, then combine them at the end. Typically, a mixture of water and cornstarch is added at the last moment of cooking in order to thicken the cooking liquid into a sauce.

Other Essential Tools

According to Nina Simonds, Chinese handled strainer might be the best piece of equipment of all, even if you don't have a wok. Basically a strainer that has a long wooden handle and a wire netting, it is incredibly functional: you can use it as a scoop or for straining." The French have a similar piece of equipment called an *écumoire*, or skimmer.

A cleaver, which serves multiple purposes, can be indispensable. "You can use the sharp edge of a cleaver to cut, the blunt edge as a tenderizer, and the flat side to smash and flatten," Simonds explains. "Cleavers can also serve as scoops; I scoop everything up onto the blade and into the pan. Plus, they look so menacing!" she laughs. "I recommend a medium-sized cleaver, which can be used for everything. There are also small ones, about 11/2 inches across, that are for cutting vegetables. The large ones are closer in weight to a butcher's cleaver.

"Bamboo steamers are not essential, but they are lovely for presentation and absorb steam very efficiently," Simonds advises. "Rice cookers are not essential either, but they are handy for those who are nervous about cooking rice. Personally, I just use a little pot with a lid. I have used a French Le Creuset pot to cook rice in for all these years!"

Key Chinese Techniques

In Chinese cuisine, achieving a pleasing balance of textures has long been especially prized—leading to the development of a variety of unique cooking techniques and procedures resulting in unusual textures.

You can achieve such a balance within a menu by being sure to use techniques designed to soften (e.g., braising, steaming) and crispen (e.g., deep-fat frying, roasting)

food. However, through combining such techniques—for example, frying, then braising—you can produce multiple textures within the same dish (i.e., soft on the inside, crispy on the outside).

Mastering Chinese techniques will help you appreciate the nuanced differences in the Chinese approach, as well as stimulate your creativity in employing multiple techniques to achieve desired flavors and textures in your cooking.

Stir-Frying

Stir-frying allows food to retain its flavor and character. Because it is so practical, stir-frying is an important technique throughout Asia. The process of stir-frying in a wok does not require much fuel. Furthermore, you can use virtually any combination of ingredients in a stir-fry, which makes this cooking style so universal and adaptable.

TIPS

- Because stir-frying is such a fast way of cooking, it is vital to have all your ingredients prepared in advance. Everything should be cut into uniform size so it cooks evenly (an important rule for any type of cooking). Use your judgment when you do your chopping, however—for example, a carrot could be cut a little smaller than an onion because it takes longer to cook. (When following a recipe, however, follow instructions excatly.)

- Stir-frying relies on very high heat, meaning the pan should be smoking. To test its readiness, flick a bead of water into the wok; it should dance for a brief moment before evaporating.

- Use very little oil when stir-frying. Peanut oil is ideal because it has a high smoke point, meaning it can get very hot without burning, and because it is so hot, the oil goes further and keeps the food light.

- Once the oil is hot, cook the meat first, then remove it. Next cook the vegetables, then add your seasonings. Put the meat back in the wok, and add a pinch of thickener (such as cornstarch) to make a thicker sauce.

Deep-Frying

Deep-frying is fundamental to Chinese cooking. The Chinese use deep-frying very differently than non-Chinese cooks do. In most of the West, it is a one-step technique used to cook something through. In China, it is used often at the beginning of the cooking process. As a first step, it is for searing the outside of an ingredient. The Chinese may take a whole five-pound pork shoulder and marinate it, then dip it into a wok of bubbling oil to crisp the skin, and put it into the oven to be braised.

TEACHING THE WEST HOW TO EAT CHINESE

Chinese restaurants paved the way for all ethnic restaurants in the United States, providing the model for other restaurateurs. Experts on other cuisines cite how Chinese restaurants introduced customers to non-Western styles of eating, including the use of chopsticks as well as Chinese banquet-style dining, where all the food is served at once, rather than in courses.

Chinese restaurants were also the first to specialize in particular regions. Today, American diners can decide they're in the mood for Cantonese, Shanghainese, or Szechuan food. However, it is still pretty hard to find regional Mexican food, and it wasn't that long ago that there wasn't the range of Italian restaurants, from Sicilian to Tuscan, we take for granted today.

Michael Tong, the owner of Shun Lee Palace, one of the first Chinese fine-dining restaurants in New York, explains how Chinese cuisine evolved from the food of immigrant laborers to one of the most respected cuisines in America:

"In the 1800s, Chinese immigrants came over from Taiwan to build the railroads, and San Francisco was their first stop. This is where the first Chinese restaurants opened, and they introduced dishes that everyone now knows, such as egg rolls and chow mein. They even invented dishes such as pepper steak and chop suey, which many people still don't realize are not authentic Chinese food.

"Eventually, the Chinese immigrants made it to New York, and now our Chinatown is a hundred years old. For a long time, though, the food in Chinese restaurants remained pretty much the same. It wasn't until the late 1930s that you would find food other than things like egg drop and wonton soups.

"Ruby Foo [the original Ruby Foo, after which the contemporary Ruby Foo restaurants owned by Steve Hanson in Manhattan are named] opened a restaurant in midtown Manhattan in the 1930s, and the restaurant became a hit with the Broadway crowd as well as with midtown diners and business people. It was soon followed by two other restaurants—and as they were the first major Chinese restaurants outside of Chinatown, these restaurants

became pioneers of Cantonese cooking. This in turn led to the acceptance of fine-dining Chinese restaurants.

"Chinese food changed for the better in the early 1950s, when trained chefs from Shanghai arrived in New York. They worked on ships as chefs, and when they got to the U.S., they applied for political asylum. They then started working and opening restaurants. This is when we saw Shanghai restaurants for the first time. We started seeing dishes like lion's head or oversized pork and pork fat meatballs cooked in a clay pot with bok choy, as well as *kung pao* chicken."

Earning Critical Acclaim

"My partner and I opened Shun Lee in 1967, and I ran the dining room. I was working when Craig Claiborne came into the restaurant. In those days, only the French restaurants spotted the *New York Times* food critic, so I didn't know who he was. He kept coming back to the restaurant and since we were not that busy, I would always take care of him. Every time he came in, we would talk about food.

"Six months after I met him, he asked if I knew who he was. I was aware that he was a writer, but nothing beyond that. He told me, 'Buy a copy of the *New York Times Dining Guide* next Monday. Your restaurant will be in it.' We found out that there were five four-star restaurants in New York—and Shun Lee was one of them. The others were La Caravelle, La Grenouille, Le Cygne, and Lutèce. We were the first-ever non-French restaurant to get four stars.

"That changed things overnight. In one week, we went from serving one hundred to three hundred din-

ners a night. It made a difference not just for us, but for the idea that a non-Cantonese restaurant (which is what had been popular for a hundred years) could be celebrated."

Expanding the Cuisine

"In 1971, we had two really talented Hunan chefs. Since we didn't really have room for them, we decided to open the first Hunan-style restaurant. My partner was very cautious, so we opened a small place called Hunan. The *New York Times* restaurant critic at the time [Raymond Sokolov] loved spicy cooking, and gave Hunan four stars after only being open four weeks. That review was the first four-star review of a Chinese restaurant that ever appeared in the paper. [Craig Claiborne's review appeared only in the book, not in the newspaper.]

"Sokolov also gave another Hunan restaurant four stars, and this opened the floodgates for spicy food in New York. You suddenly saw Indian curry at Gaylord's, as well as new Thai and Mexican restaurants opening.

"To me, the main contribution of Shun Lee has been to bring Szechwan and Hunan cooking to the city. We revealed a very different cuisine to people who thought Chinese food was egg foo yung, chow mein, pepper steak, and sweet-and-sour pork. We also contributed all the 'standardized' Hunan and Szechwan dishes that appear throughout the country, so that today in little towns across America, everybody has moo shoo pork, crispy sea bass, or Szechwan shrimp."

Shun Lee Today

"In our restaurant, we have three chefs: one each for Cantonese, Shanghainese, and Szechwan food. We also have one who works primarily on presentation, carving vegetables. For example, he will carve a swan from turnips, a bird from carrots, and a frog from taro.

"It is very hard to compare cuisines. Each has its wonders, so you can't really compare Chinese to French or Italian cuisine. A good Chinese restaurant will have any-where from eighty to one hundred dishes. The Chinese love a big variety. In China, you would order a variety of cooking styles—something steamed, sautéed, roasted, or braised in red-cooking.

"We have two menus: one for Caucasian customers and another for Asians who appreciate Chinese food. The latter has more exotic dishes on it, which might offend some diners who don't want to eat tripe or liver. We offer shark's fin soup for two for $150 (which is steamed for six hours with chicken stock and ham). We may offer sea cucumbers or sea turtle for $70, eel for $30, and abalone in oyster sauce for $100—which to a Chinese person is cheap! We also offer long-cooked items. We have a braised dish that cooks in rock candy, soy sauce, and wine for six hours. While we include these items on the menu for our Chinese customers, we don't want them to appear on the Caucasian menu, because some people would think we are crazy!"

The Chinese are fearless fryers. In addition to frying large cuts of meat, they also deep-fry whole fish. At dim sum restaurants, you will see countless items deep-fried to a golden brown. The Chinese also use the technique of frying something twice: the first time is in oil at a low temperature to seal in the flavors. The food is then left to drain and finish cooking while it cools; the process of resting adds to the crispiness of the final product. Just before serving, the food is popped back into hot oil to crisp and heat. (Apply this method of double-frying to potatoes to make the crispiest French fries!)

TIPS

- The wok is the most-used vessel for deep-frying in China. Its high sides make it perfect for the purpose, but in a Western kitchen, any tall, sturdy pot will do.

- You need to adjust the temperature of the frying oil depending on the food you are cooking. For a piece of meat, for example, the temperature should be at around 375 degrees, while something like shrimp fritters would be cooked at lower temperature, around 350 degrees. An experienced Chinese cook can adjust the temperature by eye, but for the less experienced, we recommend using a deep-fat thermometer.

Steaming

Steaming has multiple purposes in the Chinese kitchen. It rejuvenates the dried food that has traditionally composed much of the Chinese diet, and it also is the most delicate way to cook an ingredient. Steaming gently envelops an ingredient with heat while basting it with moisture at the same time.

Steaming is practical, because it requires little fuel. In addition, most steamers are two or three tiered, making it possible to cook more than one dish at once over the same heat source.

Steaming is best for the most delicate foods. While you wouldn't steam a steak, it's a wonderful way to gently cook a delicate fish or a dumpling.

TIPS

- You can use either a bamboo or a stainless steel steamer, but most experts recommend bamboo because the condensation does not collect on the undersides of their lids the way it does in a stainless steel steamer. Also, bamboo steamers can be used for serving the food.

- When you arrange your foods in the steamer, put the dish that will take the longest in the bottom steamer basket and the one with the shortest cooking time at the top.

- Make sure the bottom basket is at least an inch above the water, and keep the water at a medium boil, not higher.

THE ART OF TEA

Better to be deprived of food for three days, than tea for one.

—CHINESE PROVERB

Lu Tung, an eighth-century Chinese poet, reflected: "The first cup moistens my lips and throat, the second cup breaks my loneliness, the third cup searches my barren entrails but to find therein some five thousand volumes of odd ideographs. The fourth cup rises a slight perspiration—all the wrong of life passes through my pores. At the fifth cup I am purified; the sixth cup calls me up to the realm of the immortals."

It's not known exactly when tea began to be consumed in its native China, but the legends that surround it attest to its almost magical qualities. One has it that tea originated when a sleepy monk cut off his eyelids to stop himself from dozing while praying. The eyelids fell to the ground and blossomed into the first tea tree. Another legend links tea with the origins of Taoism. After drinking a cup of tea offered to him while he was traveling, Lao Tsu, the philosopher poet and founder of Taoism, was so refreshed that he sat down to write the *Tao Te Ching*.

Tea cultivation was almost certainly under way by 350 A.D., but most experts agree that tea was being brewed from wild leaves long before then. By the eighth century, news of the beverage had begun to spread to other cultures. Tea was introduced to Japan at the beginning of that century when the emperor gave tea leaves to one hundred Japanese Buddhist monks. Tea's popularity spread all over Asia and eventually, though not until the seventeenth century, to Europe and the American colonies.

The tea tree is a flowering evergreen that is difficult to cultivate. It thrives in warm, humid climates, but the richest, most complex flavors develop better in cooler temperatures. A temperate climate at an elevation of 5000 feet is optimal for growing delicious tea. The trees can grow to be more than thirty feet tall, but the choicest leaves are the young shoots, so crops are rigorously pruned. At harvest, pickers take care to pluck leaves of fairly equal size so that the

leaves can be dried at an even rate. Differences between teas grown in different places are due not so much to species differences as to differences in climate, elevation, and soil. The difference between green, black, and oolong tea is not in the trees themselves, but in the extent to which the leaves are fermented. The longer that leaves are fermented, the more color they will have and the less pungent their tannins will be. The process of firing the leaves stops fermentation. Green tea is unfermented (and therefore the lightest), oolong is semi-fermented, and black tea is fully fermented. (There is also red tea, which is double-fermented.)

China continues to produce all three kinds of tea, but these days India and Sri Lanka together produce about half of the world's tea. Assam teas from India are full-bodied, rich, and malty. Green tea is produced chiefly in China, Thailand, and Japan. When the Japanese drink tea, it is almost exclusively green tea. The leaves are steamed and rolled to release natural oils and tannins and then immediately fired to prevent

oxidation. Almost all oolong tea is made in Taiwan. The leaves are slightly withered and then fermented, fired, rolled, fermented again, and fired again.

Once processed, the leaves are sifted in order to group them into unified sizes, or grades. Generally, there are whole-leaf grades and broken-leaf grades, but each tea-producing culture has different methods of grading. India and Sri Lanka have three leaf grades and five broken-leaf grades. Green tea grades are related to both leaf size and quality. China has seven grades for green tea, Japan has ten. The eighteen oolong grades are related solely to quality: they are so specific that they include such categories as "Fine to Finest" and "Fully Good." A good tea, of any type, should have leaves or pieces that are consistent in size and that are wellrolled or twisted, but not brittle.

Tea contains more caffeine than coffee per pound, but less of it is extracted per cup.

To prepare tea properly, bring fresh cold water to a boil, then pour

the water over the tea in a warmed (i.e., by rinsing with hot water) pot or cup. Let the tea brew for 3 to 5 minutes; it is important to time it, because color isn't always an indicator. Often tea releases color before it releases flavor, so don't just rely on your eyes to tell you when it's done.

In 1906, Okakura Kakuzo wrote in *The Book of Tea:* "Tea is more than an idealization of the form of drinking; it is a religion of the art of life."

Some Suggestions for Pairing Teas with Food

Just as it is a vast oversimplification to say that "white wine goes with white meats (e.g., fish, chicken), and red wine goes with red meats (e.g., beef, lamb)," it is also an oversimplification to say that "green and oolong teas go with white meats, while black teas and darker oolong teas go with red meats." But it's a starting point!

Continental breakfast	Assam, Ceylon, Darjeeling, Kenya, Yunnan
Full breakfast	Assam, Ceylon, Lapsang Souchong
Egg dishes	Darjeeling
Creamy dishes	Green
Pasta dishes	Ceylon
Rice	Green
Fish	Green, Oolong, smoked tea
Shellfish	Darjeeling, greenish Oolong
Poultry	Darjeeling, Keemun, Lapsang Souchong, Oolong, Yunnan
Meat and game	Assam, Black, Earl Grey, Lapsang Souchong
Spicy dishes	Black, Green, Keemun, Oolong
Strong cheese	Earl Grey, Green, Lapsang Souchong
Sweet dishes	Black, Yunnan
Fruit desserts	Black
Lemon desserts	Lapsang Souchong
Creamy desserts	Darjeeling
After a meal	Darjeeling, Keemun, Oolong

A Last Word

TRADITIONALLY, INNOVATION HAS NOT been part of Chinese cooking. "Just as in classic French cuisine, young Chinese cooks were taught that you have to master the classic dishes. You don't innovate," says Nina Simonds. "Traditionally, the sign of a true Asian master was that he was able to replicate the repertory of classic dishes from a given area. You need to learn the traditions to have a context.

"So when you taste and experience other cuisines, it is important to have a palate built on tradition so you can have a sense of how those cuisines developed. Once you know the original context, then you can go forth and be innovative with your own dishes."

Nach Waxman's Recommended Reading on Chinese Cooking

There are two principal books covering recipes and techniques. The first, **The Key to Chinese Cooking,** was written by Irene Kuo, who was a fine cooking teacher, and it shows. When it went out of print, I feared another book like that might never come along, so I was tickled when **The Chinese Kitchen** by Eileen Yin-Fei Lo was published. It's a good general book, and she's also a good teacher—and I'm sure it didn't hurt to have had a little help from Fred Ferretti [Lo's husband, who also writes about food]. Another book, a personal favorite, soundly assmembled by a highly knowledgeable author, is Nina Simonds' **Classic Chinese Cuisine.** Sadly, there aren't any readily available books that cover the breadth of Chinese regional cooking that I can think of.

Those who want to take Chinese cooking in a slightly more modern direction can turn to **The China Moon Cookbook** by Barbara Tropp. Her little hors d'oeuvres–sized turnovers filled with lamb and flavored with lemon are absolutely delicious—and I don't care if they're technically Chinese or not!

Sour Soup

1 chicken (about 3 pounds), cut into 10 or 12 pieces

3 quarts plus ¼ cup water

½ cup rice wine or sake

8 slices fresh ginger, about the size of a quarter, smashed lightly with the flat side of a knife

8 scallions, trimmed and smashed lightly with the side of a knife

1 pound firm tofu, cut into slabs about 1 inch thick

6 dried Chinese black mushrooms, softened in hot water for 20 minutes, drained, stems removed, and caps cut into thin julienne strips

¼ cup dried wood ear mushrooms, softened in hot water for 20 minutes, drained, hard ends trimmed, and cut into thin julienne strips

2 cups leeks, cut into thin julienne strips (white and pale green parts only)

2½ tablespoons cornstarch

SEASONINGS

4½ tablespoons Chinese black vinegar or Worcestershire sauce, or more to taste

Try this sumptuous soup as a light lunch or dinner. This is a lighter version than the classic recipe, made with chicken rather than pork.

IN A LARGE POT, combine the chicken pieces, 3 quarts water, the rice wine, ginger, and scallions and bring to a boil. Lower the heat and simmer for 1½ hours, skimming the surface to remove any impurities.

MEANWHILE, WRAP the tofu in paper towels, place on a plate, and place a heavy weight, such as a skillet, on top. Let stand for 30 minutes to press out the excess water, then cut into thin julienne strips about 3 inches long and ⅙ inch thick.

REMOVE THE CHICKEN BROTH from the heat, remove the ginger and scallion from the broth, and skim off any fat. Remove the chicken pieces with a slotted spoon. Remove and discard the skin and bones. Slice or tear the meat into thin julienne strips.

STRAIN THE CHICKEN BROTH into a large heavy pot. Add the chicken, tofu, black mushrooms, wood ear mushrooms, and leeks and bring to a boil. Boil for about 2 minutes, skimming the surface to remove any impurities.

MEANWHILE, COMBINE the cornstarch and remaining ¼ cup water, blending well.

SLOWLY ADD THE cornstarch thickener to the broth, stirring constantly to prevent lumps, and cook, stirring, until the broth has thickened. Add all the seasonings and stir. Taste and add

3 tablespoons soy sauce

2½ to 3 tablespoons minced fresh ginger, or to taste

¾ teaspoon freshly ground black pepper

1 teaspoon toasted sesame oil

1 teaspoon salt, or to taste

1 large egg white, lightly beaten with 2 tablespoons water

SERVES 6

any additional seasonings as necessary. Remove the soup from the heat and slowly stir in the beaten egg white, pouring it in a thin stream around the edge of the pot; stir the soup several times in a circular motion so that the egg forms streamers.

LADLE THE SOUP into a serving bowl or bowls, and serve immediately.

Chinese Meat Dumplings

5 cups finely minced Chinese or Napa cabbage

1 teaspoon salt

1 pound lean ground pork

2 cups finely minced Chinese garlic chives (or substitute 1 cup minced leeks plus 1 tablespoon minced garlic)

FOR THE SEASONINGS

2½ tablespoons soy sauce

2 tablespoons toasted sesame oil

1½ tablespoons rice wine

1½ tablespoons peeled and minced fresh ginger

1 tablespoon cornstarch, plus more if needed

50 dumpling or gyoza skins

MAKES 50 DUMPLINGS

Chinese meat dumplings make me feel nostalgic for my days as a student in Taiwan, when we would visit our favorite dumpling shop and fill ourselves with luscious steamed dumplings, plump with juice, and crusty-brown pot stickers. My favorites are the most traditional: they're stuffed with cabbage, pork, and garlic chives and boiled in a big pot. I usually double the recipe and freeze half of them uncooked. Then I can throw them into boiling water for an instant, satisfying meal.

IN A LARGE BOWL, combine the cabbage and salt and let sit for 30 minutes. (This will draw water out of the cabbage.)

SQUEEZE AS MUCH water as possible out of the cabbage and combine with the ground pork and minced chives in a large bowl. In a small bowl, combine the seasonings, mixing well. Add to the pork mixture and stir vigorously. If the mixture seems loose, add another teaspoon of cornstarch.

TO SHAPE THE DUMPLINGS, place a teaspoon of filling in the center of each dumpling skin. Spread a little water along the edge of the skin, and fold the skin over to make a half-moon shape. Use the thumb and index finger of one hand to form small pleats along the edge of the skin. Place the dumplings on a baking sheet lightly dusted with cornstarch.

BRING A LARGE POT of water to a boil. Add half the dumplings, stirring to prevent them from sticking together. Once the water has boiled again, cook for 5 minutes longer. Remove with a handled strainer, drain, and put in a bowl. Cook the remaining dumplings. Serve the dumplings with dipping sauce (see Note).

Note

You can flavor soy sauce in different ways to serve as a dipping sauce with dumplings. To ½ cup soy sauce, add one or more of the following, to taste: 3 tablespoons Chinese black rice vinegar, 1 tablespoon minced garlic, and/or 2 red chiles, thinly sliced.

Michael Tong

Rock Candy–Ginger Short Ribs

3 pounds beef short ribs, cut into 10 pieces about 2½ inches wide

1 teaspoon freshly ground black pepper

⅓ cup all-purpose flour

2 tablespoons peanut oil

⅓ cup soy sauce (preferably Kikkoman)

⅓ cup dark soy sauce (preferably Gold Label)

2 cups shao-hsing rice wine

6 ounces rock candy or sugar

1 piece star anise

Two 1-inch cinnamon stick pieces

4 slices fresh ginger

2 scallions, trimmed

8 cups water

SERVES 6

SEASON THE SHORT RIBS with the pepper and dust with the flour. Heat the oil in a large pot. In batches, add the short ribs and sear until browned. Return all the ribs to the pans.

ADD BOTH SOY SAUCES, rice wine, rock candy, star anise, cinnamon, ginger, scallions, and water to the pot. Bring to a boil over high heat, then lower the heat to medium-high and cook for about 2½ hours, until the ribs are tender when poked with a fork or chopstick.

TRANSFER THE SHORT RIBS to a large plate. Skim off the fat and cook the sauce over high heat until reduced to about 1½ cups. Pour over the short ribs and serve.

Diced Szechwan Chicken Soong
Chicken in Lettuce Leaves

1 large boneless, skinless whole chicken breast (about 1 pound)

1 egg white

½ teaspoon salt

2 tablespoons cornstarch

2 hot or mild long green chiles, cut into small dice

10 to 12 water chestnuts, preferably fresh, cut into small dice

½ cup finely diced celery

1 tablespoon finely diced carrot

1 teaspoon chopped fresh ginger

2 teaspoons finely chopped garlic, or more to taste

1 tablespoon finely chopped scallions

2 teaspoons shao-hsing rice wine or dry sherry

½ teaspoon soy sauce

½ teaspoon chile paste with garlic

1 teaspoon sugar

1 teaspoon monosodium glutamate (optional)

PLACE THE CHICKEN BREAST on a work surface and, holding a sharp knife almost parallel to the cutting surface, cut the breast into the thinnest possible slices. Stack the slices a few at a time and cut into thin strips, then cut the strips into tiny cubes. There should be about 2 cups.

PLACE THE CHICKEN MEAT in a bowl and add the egg white, salt, and 1 tablespoon of the cornstarch. Blend well with your fingers. Refrigerate for at least 30 minutes.

COMBINE THE CHILES, water chestnuts, celery, carrot, and ginger in a small bowl; set aside. In another bowl, combine the garlic and scallions; set aside. Combine the wine, soy sauce, chile paste, sugar, and monosodium glutamate, if using, in a small bowl; set aside. Combine the remaining 1 tablespoon cornstarch and the water in a small bowl and stir to blend. Set aside. Pile the lettuce on a platter and set aside.

HEAT THE PEANUT OIL in a wok or deep skillet over medium-high heat. When it is hot, add the chicken, stirring constantly to separate the cubes, and cook for about 1½ minutes, until just cooked through. Drain in a strainer set over a bowl, then set the chicken aside.

RETURN 2 TABLESPOONS of the oil to the wok, then add the water chestnut mixture. Cook, stirring, for about 30 seconds. Add the chicken. Add the scallion and garlic and cook, stirring, for about 30 seconds, or until the chicken is

1 teaspoon water

1 head iceberg lettuce, separated into leaves

2 cups peanut, vegetable, or corn oil

½ teaspoon toasted sesame oil

SERVES 4

piping hot. Add the soy sauce mixture and the sesame oil. Return the chicken to the wok. Stir the cornstarch mixture until smooth, and quickly add it to the wok. Stir rapidly for about 30 seconds. Transfer to a hot platter.

SERVE THE CHICKEN with the lettuce on the side. Let guests help themselves, placing a spoonful or so of the chicken mixture on a lettuce leaf and folding it before eating.

229

China

Steamed Sea Bass Cantonese-Style

1 sea bass (around 1½ pounds), cleaned and scaled

2 tablespoons white wine

¼ cup chopped scallions (green part included)

2 tablespoons finely minced fresh ginger

3 garlic cloves, coarsely chopped (about 2 tablespoons)

2 teaspoons sugar

¼ cup olive oil

3 tablespoons toasted soy sauce

SERVES 3 AS AN ENTRÉE, 6 AS AN APPETIZER

RINSE THE FISH inside and out with the wine. Place the fish on a heatproof round or oval platter that will fit inside a steamer.

ADD WATER TO THE bottom of the steamer to come just below the steamer basket or rack and bring to a boil. Place the sea bass, on the platter, in the steamer, cover, and steam until the meat at the midsection is firm, 10 to 15 minutes, depending on the size of the fish.

MEANWHILE, FOR THE SAUCE, combine the scallions, ginger, garlic, and sugar in a small bowl; set aside.

WHEN THE FISH IS COOKED, remove the platter from the steamer and pour off the liquid that has accumulated around the fish. Set aside, covered to keep warm.

HEAT THE OIL in a wok or saucepan. When it is hot, add the sauce mixture and cook, stirring, until the sauce boils. Pour the soy sauce over the sea bass first, then pour the sauce over it. Serve immediately.

Chile-Orange Cold Noodles

2½ tablespoons Chile-Orange Oil (recipe follows)

1 tablespoon "goop" (solids) from the Chile-Orange Oil

2 tablespoons black soy sauce (see Note)

2 tablespoons white vinegar

1 tablespoon sugar

1 teaspoon kosher salt

8 ounces fresh bean sprouts

8 ounces very thin (1⁄16-inch-wide) fresh Chinese egg noodles

¾ cup finely shredded carrots

½ cup thinly sliced scallions (green and white parts)

¾ cup slivered cilantro leaves and stems, plus sprigs for garnish

½ cup chopped roasted peanuts

SERVES 3 TO 4 AS A MAIN COURSE, 6 TO 8 AS PART OF A MULTICOURSE MEAL

COMBINE THE chile-orange oil, "goop," soy sauce, vinegar, sugar, and salt in a bowl, whisking to blend. Set this dressing aside.

BLANCH THE BEAN SPROUTS in boiling water for 15 seconds, drain, and refresh in ice water. Drain again, transfer to a bowl, cover with cold water, and refrigerate until ready to use; drain well just before using.

BRING A LARGE POT of water to a rolling boil over high heat. Fluff the noodles in a colander to separate and untangle the strands. Add the noodles to the boiling water and stir gently until they are al dente, about 2 minutes. Drain and plunge quickly into ice water to chill, then drain thoroughly and transfer to a large bowl.

REWHISK THE DRESSING, pour over the noodles, and toss well with your fingers to coat and separate each strand. Scatter the bean sprouts, carrots, scallions, cilantro, and two-thirds of the peanuts on top. Toss lightly to mix. Taste and adjust the seasoning, if needed, with a dash of sugar to bring the heat forward. Garnish with cilantro sprigs and the remaining peanuts and serve.

Note
Black soy sauce has a hint of molasses flavor and is saltier than regular soy sauce. Koon Chung is one brand Tropp recommends.

Chile-Orange Oil

3 large oranges with unblemished skins, preferably organic

½ cup pungent dried red chile flakes

3 tablespoons Chinese black beans, not rinsed, coarsely chopped

1 to 2 large garlic cloves, lightly smashed

2 cups corn or peanut oil

¼ cup Japanese sesame oil

SCRUB THE ORANGES and let dry. Using a vegetable peeler or a sharp paring knife, peel away the thin layer of orange zest, being careful not to remove the white pith. Finely mince the zest. (Reserve the oranges for another use.)

COMBINE THE ZEST with the rest of the ingredients in a medium heavy nonreactive saucepan. Heat over medium-low heat to 225° to 250°F on a deep-fry thermometer, stirring occasionally. Let bubble for 15 minutes. Remove from the heat and allow to cool.

SCRAPE THE OIL and solids (the "goop") into a glass or plastic container, cover, and store in a cool place.

Pearl Balls

1 cup plus 2 tablespoons sweet (glutinous) rice

4 large Chinese dried black mushrooms

6 to 8 large fresh water chestnuts, to yield about ½ cup (chopped; substitute jicama or, as a last resort, high-quality canned water chestnuts if fresh are unavailable)

1 walnut-sized piece fresh ginger

1 scallion, trimmed and cut into 1½-inch lengths

12 ounces ground pork butt

1 large egg

1 tablespoon soy sauce

1½ teaspoons kosher salt

½ cup unsalted chicken stock

Sesame, corn, or peanut oil for brushing

FOR THE GARLIC-SOY DIPPING SAUCE

1½ tablespoons soy sauce

1 tablespoon white vinegar

¼ teaspoon toasted sesame oil

A pinch of sugar

1 teaspoon finely chopped garlic

SERVES 4 TO 5 AS AN ENTRÉE, 6 TO 12 AS AN APPETIZER

IN A MEDIUM BOWL, cover the rice with 4 cups cold water. Soak for at least 1 hour, stirring occasionally to loosen the talc. Shortly before using, drain the rice in a colander, rinse under cold running water until the water is clear, and set aside. (The rice should still be moist so that it will adhere more easily to the meat.)

MEANWHILE, FOR THE MEATBALL MIXTURE COVER THE MUSHROOMS with water in a small bowl and soak until soft and spongy, 20 minutes to an hour; drain. Snip off stems, rinse the caps, and chop into peppercorn-sized bits.

IF USING FRESH WATER CHESTNUTS, peel them. If using canned, drain and blanch in boiling water for 15 seconds, then drain and immediately chill in cold water. Chop into peppercorn-sized bits. (The mushrooms and water chestnuts can be prepared ahead: sprinkle lightly with water, seal airtight, and refrigerate up to overnight, if desired.)

COMBINE THE GINGER and scallion in a food processor and finely mince. Add the pork, egg, soy sauce, salt, and stock and pulse just until well combined; do not process to a paste. (If you don't have a processor, mince the ginger and scallion by hand and finely chop the pork, then mix.) Scrape the mixture into a bowl. It will be very loose. Add the mushrooms and water chestnuts and stir, in one direction only to keep mixture light, until blended. (The mixture can be refrigerated, covered in plastic wrap to keep airtight, for up to 24 hours if desired; stir again just before using.)

SPREAD THE RICE in a thick even layer in a baking pan. Place the meat mixture, a bowl of cold water, and a tablespoon alongside. If steaming the meatballs immediately, liberally oil the steaming rack with sesame oil; if refrigerating, line a baking sheet with wax paper.

DIP YOUR PALMS and the spoon in the cold water, so that meat will not stick. Scoop up 1 tablespoon of the mixture, roll it in the rice as if you were forming a snowball, and hold the loose ball in one hand while gently shaping with the other: do not press rice into meat, but rather pat the loose ball into shape. Repeat with the remaining meat mixture, placing the balls about one inch apart on the rack or lined sheet. If refrigerating, cover airtight; bring to room temperature before steaming, and arrange on the oiled steaming rack.

CHOOSE THE LARGEST POT you have that will hold a steamer rack, so that you don't have to refill it constantly during the lengthy steaming. Fill with water to come 1 inch below the rack and bring to a boil over high heat. Place the rack in the pot, reduce the heat to medium-high, cover, and steam the meatballs for 1½ to 2 hours, replenishing with boiling water as required.

FIFTEEN MINUTES PRIOR TO SERVING, PREPARE THE DIPPING SAUCE
COMBINE THE SOY SAUCE, vinegar, sesame oil, and sugar in a small bowl. Add the garlic and stir to blend. Let stand for 5 to 10 minutes before using to allow the garlic to permeate the soy.

TO EAT THE MEATBALLS Chinese-style, hold a small porcelain spoon in one hand and chopsticks in the other. Scoop the meatball onto the spoon with the help of the chopsticks, then bring it almost to your mouth on the spoon and use the chopsticks to lift the meatball into your mouth. Keep the spoon just below your mouth, to hold what you can't take in one mouthful and to act as a face-saver, or lap-saver, should the meatball slip from your grasp.

Barbara Tropp

Steamed Whole Fish with Seared Scallions

1 extremely fresh 1½-pound fish, sea bass preferred, cleaned and scaled

2 teaspoons salted Chinese black beans, not rinsed, coarsely chopped

1 tablespoon soy sauce

1 tablespoon Chinese rice wine or dry sherry

1 teaspoon toasted sesame oil

½ teaspoon sugar

1 to 1½ teaspoons kosher salt

½ tablespoon fine julienne threads fresh ginger (cut 1½ inches long and as thin as possible)

2 medium scallions, trimmed, 1 cut into 2-inch lengths, the other cut into shreds 2 inches long and ³⁄₁₆ inch thick

2 tablespoons corn or peanut oil

SERVES 2 OR 3 AS AN ENTRÉE, 4 TO 6 AS PART OF A MULTI-COURSE MEAL

CLEAN the fish well. Lay flat on a work surface and and score it crosswise at 1-inch intervals from neck to tail on both sides, cutting to within ¼ inch of the bone.

COMBINE THE BLACK BEANS, soy, wine, oil, and sugar, stirring well to blend.

RUB THE SALT EVENLY over fish, inside and out, rubbing it into the score marks with your fingers. Lay fish in a Pyrex pie plate or shallow bowl at least 1 inch smaller in diameter than your steamer, ideally one the fish can be served in after it has been cooked. If the fish is too big, curl it gently to fit.

STIR THE LIQUID SEASONINGS to recombine, and pour evenly over the fish. Scatter the ginger threads on top. Crush the scallion lengths slightly and array over the fish.

BRING WATER FOR STEAMING to a full boil over high heat. Set the pie plate on the steamer rack or in a steamer basket, cover tightly, and steam over medium-high heat for 12 to 15 minutes, until the flesh at bottom of the score marks in the thickest part of the flesh is white.

WHEN THE FISH is within several minutes of being done, heat the oil in a small saucepan over low heat until hot but not smoking.

REMOVE THE PIE PLATE from the steamer and transfer the fish and cooking liquid to a warm plate if necessary; discard the cooked scallions. The "natural sauce" that is rendered by the fish during steaming is delicious and should be eaten with the fish. Sprinkle the shredded scallions on top of the fish, then drizzle the hot oil evenly on top, standing at arm's length from the fish and averting your face, because the oil will splatter. Serve at once.

India

THE MASTERFUL USE OF SPICES

*If an Indian ever invites you home for
a meal, don't say no! The best Indian
food is eaten at home.*

—FLOYD CARDOZ, CHEF, TABLA, NEW YORK CITY

Indian is one of the cuisines that has had the greatest impact on a large part of the world.

—BARBARA TROPP, AUTHOR, *THE MODERN ART OF CHINESE COOKING*

IN NEW YORK CITY, if you walk south on Lexington Avenue below 30th Street, you would be entering an area affectionately known as "Little India" or "Curry Hill." You would be tipped off well beforehand, however, by the pungent aroma of spices. The food of India is slow-simmered curries and long-marinated meats. Spices permeate the air in this neighborhood, and it's almost impossible to locate a vent that is not exhaling their beautiful perfume.

To sample how the spices are used, you might go to a restaurant specializing in *dosai*, foot-long rolled crispy crêpes filled with spiced potatoes. Or you might enjoy the sight of cooks working the tandooris, placing chunks of marinated chicken on skewers, or slapping *nan* bread onto the sides of the clay ovens. Or you could venture into one of the spice shops, searching your memory bank for that elusive aroma, finally to place it as cardamom. The whole area is intoxicating. By the time you leave, you will have been transported halfway around the world without going beyond a three-block radius.

This small pocket in Manhattan reveals an essential aspect of Indian cuisine—that a cuisine can celebrate the blending of native spices and herbs. To work with the Indian palette, it's fundamentally important to understand how and why the various spices are used.

As long as three thousand years ago, Sanskrit scriptures were proclaiming the importance of spices as medicines and preservatives. (Today, of course, their flavors are at least as important.) European exploration in part was spurred by craving for Indian spices, which were so eagerly sought—and so highly prized—that the Dutch still use the expression, "It's as costly as pepper!"

"Many spices have dual functions, both coloring and flavoring at once, or perhaps thickening while imparting fragrance," explains Floyd Cardoz, chef of Tabla restaurant in New York City. "Many combinations of spicing and food are related to how the two work together, not only on the palate but also in the rest of the body. Ginger, for example, is added to legumes to impart flavor, but also to aid digestion."

"The rule of thumb in cooking with any spice is that it should be an integral part of the dish but never stand out, whether the spice is toasted, ground fresh, or made into an infusion," says Raji Jallepalli, chef-owner of Maison Raji in Memphis. "Bouquet and lightness are very important in Indian cooking."

"You find several great things with Indian spicing," observes Nina Simonds, author of, among other books, *A Spoonful of Ginger: Irresistible Health-Giving Recipes from Asian Kitchens*. "The spices are very fragrant, and as the American public gets more sophisticated, people are looking beyond curry. Also, the seasonings have health-giving properties. As baby boomers age, they want food that prolongs life. Garam masala [the principal spice mixture of northern India] is directly related to health. Cinnamon alone is a great digestive and helps the blood circulate. Cardamom combined with cinnamon and bay leaf naturally helps the absorption of medicine.

"I have a strong background in Chinese food, and when I was studying Indian food, I saw similarities between the evolution of the classic cuisines of India and China. Classic Indian cooking evolved from the Ayurvedic principles of wholeness and balance in exactly the same way as classic Chinese cuisine evolved from yin-and-yang philosophy. In both countries, spices were used for their flavors, but more important, for their health-giving properties."

In India, spices are categorized as "cool" or "warm," a practice dating from ancient Hindu scriptures. Spices that generate heat in the body are known as "warm." "Cool" spices induce perspiration and therefore act as cooling agents, making them especially useful in India's hot climate.

"The summers are pretty severe in India, and some spicing traditions have grown out of this," says Cardoz. "In summer, you don't combine green cardamom and mace, because it generates a lot of heat in the body. Fennel is a good summer spice because it generates cooling. You see chiles in many hot climates because they make you perspire, which cools you."

How to Work with Spices

Toasting spices is a very important technique in Indian cooking. It intensifies the flavor of the spice.
—RAJI JALLEPALLI

WHILE THERE ARE, OF COURSE, exceptions, in Indian cooking, most spices should be cooked or toasted, then crushed or ground before they are used. This helps release their aromatic oils and makes them easier to digest. There are a variety of steps to follow before the raw spices make it into the dish, so that all flavors are maximized.

"Buy your spices whole and in small quantities," recommends Floyd Cardoz. "Spices have a lot of oils. When you buy them ground, they have already lost some of those fragrant oils, so you end up using more of the spice than you need. Use a coffee grinder (or spice grinder) to grind them fresh, and you will have a much better flavor from your spices and for your food."

"You should also have a mortar and pestle for working with your toasted spices," adds Julie Sahni, author of *Classic Indian Cooking*. "The mortar is really handy when you just need a half-teaspoon of something."

FLOYD CARDOZ ON SPICING FOR THE INGREDIENT

It is not difficult to understand why amateur cooks might want to buy a tin of curry powder and call it a day. Yet why should they deny themselves so much pleasure? Imagine if you'd stopped learning about wine after white Zinfandel!

Since many different wines are made from the same grapes, what defines a wine is the manner in which the grapes were treated and the types of grapes with which they were blended. Pairing wines with complementary foods is both an art and a science. Similarly, in order to prepare authentic Indian meals, you must understand how to work with spices. You must have a grasp of what spices to blend well and, ultimately, what foods and beverages to pair with them.

"It really gets back to the question, 'What is best for the individual ingredient?'" says Cardoz. "For instance, halibut is delicate, so I might poach it in duck fat and serve it in a sun-dried ginger broth. The broth is very delicate, so you can taste the ginger but it does not overpower the halibut. I would never put black cardamom, for example, with vegeta- bles, because it is too strong and would overpower their flavors. Nor would I pair it with fish, because it would 'fight' with the fish. However, I would pair it with meat, such as venison, lamb, or beef.

"When it comes to spicing, I don't believe that 'one spice fits all,'" says Cardoz. "However, I do like coriander because it is so versatile; you can use it with almost anything and it will taste good. These are some of my favorite pairings:

- **I LIKE DUCK** with star anise, black pepper, clove, fennel, and mace. Citrus-flavored spices are great with duck.

- **WITH FISH**, I like using coriander seed, sometimes cumin. Black pepper, mustard seed, and chile also work well with fish.

- **BEEF IS GREAT** with clove, chile pepper, a little bit of cinnamon, and black pepper.

- **WITH CHICKEN**, some of my favorites are coriander, green cardamom, and mace.

Neela Paniz, chef-owner of Bombay Café in Los Angeles, credits her aunt with teaching her the age-old techniques for getting the most flavor out of spices. "You can taste the difference," she explains. "Tempering spices in hot oil before adding vegeta-bles—as opposed to simply adding ground spices directly to the vegetables you're cooking—makes such a difference to your food. Sprinkling a dish with mustard seeds that have not been tempered in oil is a big mistake," Paniz warns. "Mustard seeds do not impart their flavor until they have been heated through. Fresh curry leaves also have to be cooked first, whether in a little oil or added to lentils or curry."

"Julie Sahni likes to roast her spices in a wok." "This method distributes heat so well and provides room for the spices to dance around, which helps them get more evenly roasted. But if your spices come out a little unevenly toasted, that is OK because it will give the dish a slightly different flavor. It is like the difference between a light roast and a dark roast of coffee," she explains.

"Because my food has layers of spices, it gives you layers of sensations," observes Floyd Cardoz. "If the food is too hot, then you don't taste all the flavors. The heat is always an aftereffect. It is a complement. I work hard at balancing acid, bitter, and sweet flavors."

Without an inherent knowledge of spices, it's essential to experiment in order to learn their different qualities. "The key is that when you experiment, you should follow the protocol of science by writing notes about what you taste. You note the effects of the cooking and the how, when, where, and why," advises Raji Jallepalli. "It is similar to tast-ing wine, when you ask yourself questions like, 'Where on my palate am I tasting the wine? What does it remind me of? What would go best with it?'"

The Culinary Map of India

"THE FOOD OF INDIA IS much more diverse than what's represented in the U.S.," says Floyd Cardoz. "There are twenty-two states in India, and each state has different religious groups: Hindu, Muslim, Catholic, and Sikh, just to name some of the main ones. Then you take an area like Bombay, where you have the ocean on one side, contrasted with the inland area, which creates another variable. You now have at least eight groups of people with twenty-two different styles of food. And because some people are strict vegetarians, you end up with 176 variations of food, which is still only the tip of the iceberg! You can go to three different families and have three completely different meals."

Not only is India culturally diverse, but its regions' climates and geography differ as well. The country—only one-third the size of the United States—is neighbored to the north by some of the world's highest peaks, to the west by the Arabian Sea, to the east by the Bay of Bengal, and at its southern point by the Indian Ocean.

India has sixteen provinces and the food is distinct in each one, despite the fact that the same spices are used throughout the country. Neela Paniz observes, "It is how cooks put spices together combined with local ingredients that gives the food completely different tastes. Because the North has a colder climate, you see more cold climate vegetables there. In the South, it is always summer, so a lot of squashes are grown there."

The distinctions between the regions are marked. Madras cuisine, for example, is known for its creative use of lentils and grains; Maharashtrian cooking is considered very sophisticated; and Gujarati cuisine is considered by many to be mild, even bland. In a basic way, though, the cuisine of India can be broken down into two regions: North and South. "Picture the country of India, and draw a line across the middle," says Julie Sahni. "A huge mountain range divides the North from the South. The Moghuls, who lived in the north, could never penetrate the mountains and move south."

Northern India

Much of the cooking in the North, with some religious exceptions, is meat-based, characterized by braising and subtle spicing. According to Julie Sahni, "Northern food draws on flavors and ingredients such as cardamom, cinnamon, cloves, mace, nutmeg, saffron, fruit, cream, and yogurt. Bread, not rice, is the staple." The food of the North is considered more refined and luxurious than that in the South.

"The North is where all the foreign invasions took place, and as a result, its food was influenced," Sahni continues. "In the North, you can see the influence of the Mediterranean in the prevalence of such things as tomatoes, gravy with lamb, cumin, cilantro, and garlic, which are flavors native to that area, not India."

In northern cuisine, one can also see the influence of the Moghuls, who ruled the area for several centuries. As a result of their presence, sauces in northern India often contain yogurt, cream, fruit, or nut butters and may be made with a seasoning base of garlic, onion, and ginger. Pot roasts, kebabs, pilafs, and *koftas* are common.

Biryani is a popular northern dish for which boiled rice is sprinkled with saffron-infused milk and layered with meat in a large dish, which is then sealed and baked. The North is also the home of tandoori cooking, which is more often associated with restaurants, because most people don't have a tandoor (essentially, a vertical coal oven) in their home.

Neither pork nor beef is particularly popular, due to the religious observances of the Muslims and Hindus. The Muslims consider pork unclean. For the vegetarian Hindus, the cow is sacred. Consequently, lamb, chicken, and goat are the typical meats. Tea is the beverage of choice. Indians drink it milky, and in the winter it is sometimes steeped with cloves, cinnamon, honey, and ginger.

Southern India

"I wanted to learn the beneficial properties and use of spices, so I went to Kerala, which was one of the main ports along the ancient Spice Route," says Nina Simonds. "In that port city, you see influences from Asia and Europe mingling with those of India. We went to a spice farm there, and in one small plot you could find black pepper, chile pepper, nutmeg, ginger, cardamom, and vanilla beans!"

As a general rule, unlike northern Indian cuisine, southern Indian cooking does not use meat. Yet the term "vegetarian" is rather loosely defined in southern India, and in some areas it does not apply at all. "Some vegetarians eat fish, since the South is coastal like Southeast Asia," explains Julie Sahni. "They refer to fish as 'cucumbers of the sea,' counting them as vegetables. To me, eating fish and calling yourself a vegetarian is cheating a little! There is also a large Christian population in Kerala, where they eat pork as well as beef."

The South is wet and fertile, and fresh ingredients are readily available year-round, except for the brief monsoon season. Fresh spices play much more of a role in southern cooking than they do in the North, where spices are usually toasted. Fresh spices (e.g., chiles, ginger) are typically mixed into a wet paste with some sort of liquid, such as coconut milk, vinegar, water, or lemon juice.

Nevertheless, southern cooks do prepare spice blends. "Southern India was the birthplace of spice blends," explains Julie Sahni. "Every home in southern India makes its own curry powder. The North Indians used to tell foreigners that there was no such thing as curry powder, but that was simply because they didn't use curry powder.

"Southerners also employ a lot of coconut, lime, tamarind, and herbal flavors to spice their food," she continues. "In the South, the coconut palm—referred to as 'the

tree of wealth'—is revered, and every part of the tree is used. Shredded coconut might be added to a chutney or a curry, while coconut oil is commonly used as cooking oil."

Southern Indians also like to steam rice with coconut milk. Rice is such an important staple grain that it's often eaten three times a day, in one form or another. "It is important to note that in the South they don't eat basmati rice [which is from the Himalayan mountains], but rather jasmine and red rice," Sahni points out. "Jasmine rice sticks together a little, letting sauces soak in, so it is easier to eat than basmati."

Regional Spicing in India

THE SPICES EMPLOYED THROUGHOUT India do not vary much. "Cayenne is a given in almost every dish," says Neela Paniz. "Indian cayenne, from Kashmir, is richer, sweeter, and redder than what you see in the U.S. Turmeric is another given—you will see it in most dishes.

"The North and South use the same spices, but in different proportions," she adds. "For example, cumin and mustard seed are used throughout India. However, in the North, they like to use a lot of cumin, while in the South they use less cumin but a lot of mustard seed. Curry leaf is something you will see in almost every dish in the South but only occasionally in the North.

"The North uses more garam masala, a combination of, generally, cinnamon, clove, cardamom, black peppercorn, and cumin. Those spices are roasted and ground to get the most flavor. Garam, which is often used as a garnish, is considered a hot spice blend because it generates heat in your body. In the South, it is never a ground spice mix; the spices are used whole in the cooking process.

"In the area of Gujarat in South India, people are prohibited from eating roots. [The predominant religious sect, Jainism, prohibits killing any living thing, and it is feared that the process of pulling food from the ground might cause the death of earthworms or grubs.] The Jains cannot, as a result, eat ginger or garlic. Instead, they use a spice called *asafetida*, which is a combination of resins from various plants and trees. When it is added to a hot medium, asafetida emulates the flavors of garlic and ginger. Asafetida smells like rotten eggs, so you need to keep it wrapped five times to disguise its odor, and you should only use minuscule specks of it. When you add it to hot oil, it is just incredible. You can add it to dishes containing garlic and onion because it will add a little zing to the cooked-down flavors. It is also a nice addition to potatoes and carrots."

American Misconceptions about Indian Food

"INDIAN FOOD HAS COME ALONG slowly in America," explains Julie Sahni. "It helps that Americans have absorbed interesting flavors from other cultures, such as Thai or Chinese. Within America itself, Southwestern and Floridian foods have also helped pave the way for the Indian palette. Let's face it, once you start eating spices, it's a one-way journey, a 'river of no return'! Americans have come to accept chiles and other distinctive flavors."

Nevertheless, Americans have many misconceptions about Indian cuisine. "One of the problems," continues Sahni, "is that as Indian restaurants got better, they didn't teach Americans how to order, as the Chinese, Italian, and French restaurants did. Indian cuisine is not necessarily mix-and-match food. Rice does not go with everything in Indian cooking!"

"Indian food has not been exposed enough," says Floyd Cardoz. "Unfortunately, the Indian food in New York and the rest of the U.S. in general is not very good, nor does it represent what millions of people in India eat at home. The food that people eat at home is much lighter, less fatty, and more seasonal than what you find in most restaurants. I was born in India, but the first time I saw a tandoori oven was when I was eighteen!"

Part of the problem stems from the lack of a restaurant tradition in India, in the manner of other countries such as France and Italy. Thus, some of the first to stray from authentic Indian cooking were early Indian restaurateurs themselves. Sahni points out, "A lot of the meat in the early Indian restaurants was cooked in advance and sat soaking in curries. When you ordered, cooks would figure out what color the dish needed to be and add the appropriate spices. If the dish was supposed to be yellow, they would add dry mustard, and then they would adjust the heat level. It was an assembly line."

"People have ideas about Indian food that they don't want to change," observes Cardoz. "They will complain when their tandoori chicken is not red because they have always had red tandoori chicken, but what they don't know, and don't want to know, is that the red comes from dye. I have my own spices for tandoori chicken and they are not red. People will also complain that their curry is not yellow. Well, curry can be many colors, including green," he points out. "Unfortunately, most restaurants make the same thing. A lot of restaurants don't want to make something authentic; they just keep serving chicken *makhni*, which is chicken in orange sauce, or chicken *tikka masala*. I didn't have chicken *tikka masala* until I was twenty-five years old!"

Getting Started with Indian Cooking

DESPITE CURRENT MISCONCEPTIONS, remaining true to Indian cooking outside of India is entirely possible. Even if you are using American instead of Indian squash, the basic repertoire of spices—the backbone of the cuisine—can remain the same. All the individual ingredients needed to make a curry or other spice blend or a tandoori sauce can be found at the supermarket.

It's simply a matter of applying Indian flavorings to ingredients local to your area. "While you won't find salmon in India, I love to work with it," says Neela Paniz. "Growing up in India there was no broccoli either, and the squash that we had there is different from what we have here. Now I experiment with the best ingredients I can get in the U.S. to find the best spicing matches."

No elaborate equipment is necessary to make Indian food. "You can make flatbreads in a skillet or heavy sauté pan," Julie Sahni points out. "While Indians use a special wok, having one is not key. I like to use one because they're good to fry in, and frying is a technique we use a lot in Indian cooking. But you can use a Chinese, a Korean, or an Indian wok. An Indian wok, called a *kadhai*, is distinct because it has straighter sides and is deeper. It's worth buying one because they are so beautiful!"

After you return from your neighborhood grocery and your first sack of Indian booty is sitting on your kitchen counter, what do you do next? "Start with one ingredient and build from there," advises Floyd Cardoz. "Start with the basics you have at home, like clove and black pepper, and then boost them with coriander seed. Build on that by adding cumin, then a chile, then turmeric. You could sprinkle these spices on a piece of meat and sauté it, put them into a stew, or add a squeeze of lime to them to make a marinade for some meat that you want to grill. By building slowly, you'll eventually get more comfortable using spices. The important thing is to not use too much spice, as you don't want to lose the flavor of whatever you're seasoning."

RAJI JALLEPALLI ON STOCKING YOUR INDIAN KITCHEN

My favorite tools for experiments in cooking are simple and, for the most part, universal. I have pots, pans, knives, and a stove. Then I have my coffee grinder, which is indispensable for grinding spices, and a VitaMix blender for pureeing my blends, sauces, and chutneys. I recommend the following spices and flavorings.

Black pepper
Cardamom
Chiles (three to four varieties)
Cinnamon
Cloves
Coriander seeds
Curry powder
Cumin seeds (including black cumin seeds)
Fennel seeds
Garam masala
Onion seeds
Palm sugar
Saffron
Star anise
Tamarind
Turmeric

I also have a variety of oils. Olive oil is a great bridge between Eastern and Western cuisines. It doesn't fight with other ingredients. I prefer to use extra-virgin olive oil, and Moroccan oil is my favorite. It is intensely flavored and unbelievable! I treat it like gold. I also have peanut oil for cooking. Mustard oil is especially useful to me when I am making wilted mustard greens, and it also makes a great vinaigrette.

NEELA PANIZ'S GUIDE TO MAKING CURRY

Tinned curry powder should not exist! The word "curry" applies to a stew. You choose a spice blend to make a curry. A traditional North Indian curry includes a minimum of nine spices.

First, you need all your garam masala spices, which I recommend using whole:

- Cassia (which is not as sweet as cinnamon, but cinnamon can be substituted)
- Cloves
- Black peppercorns
- Black cardamom seeds
- Bay leaf

Next you need two spices which are traditional in every browned onion–based curry:

- Coriander
- Cumin

The finishing spices are

- Cayenne
- Turmeric

The cooking process:

- Brown the onions.
- Add pureed ginger or garlic.
- Add meat and whole spices and brown them.
- Add tomatoes.
- Add the ground spices.

That is a simple curry. I like to leave the spices whole so a person can experience all the flavors. Note that Indians don't eat meat rare. The meat of choice in the North is kid [goat], but since that is not easily available in the U.S., lamb can be substituted. Because lamb can be gamy, it would be added to the spices to cook out some of the gaminess.

You can vary your curry by adding tomato, yogurt, or cream, or a combination of these ingredients, depending on what part of the North you want to go to. If you want to prepare a South Indian curry, add fennel and fenugreek and skip the tomatoes. It comes out with a lighter sauce, almost a *jus*.

We do not feature six different chicken curries at our restaurant. Rather, we prepare one chicken curry each day. That way, we can showcase many types of curry over a period of time. One dish consists of chicken marinated in minced ginger, garlic, and yogurt. It is simmered until it is tender, then we add green chiles and ginger while it is still hot. It's finished with clarified butter and fresh-cracked pepper. The dish is smooth, soft, and flavor-intensive.

Another important thing to keep in mind when cooking Indian dishes is that there are three primary ways to season. "You add your spices at the beginning, in the middle, or at the end, depending on the dish," explains Neela Paniz. "For example, if you are cooking vegetables, you start with oil and spices, then add your vegetables. You brown them together to permeate the whole cooking process.

"As another example, a traditional northern Indian curry is started by browning onions in a small amount of oil. You stand over the onions, stirring, until you get a caramelized brown color, which is one of the secrets to a good curry. Only then do you add your other ingredients and spices.

"Finally, you'd finish a dish of lentils by drizzling a mixture of spices tempered in hot clarified butter on top at the very last moment," she adds. "When cooking, I will add whole garam masala spices to a dish, because I don't happen to like to cook with a garam masala mix of toasted and ground spices. It gives you heartburn! If I have not added the spices whole, I will wait until the end and add the ground mixture as a garnish in the last two minutes."

Planning an Indian Menu

Herbs are almost always fresh. Coriander, mint, curry leaves, and basil are the most frequently used herbs in Indian cooking. —JULIE SAHNI

THE GUIDELINES TO AN Indian meal are few and simple. Indian food, like Chinese food, is all served at once, in the middle of the table, and people eat with their hands. For every dish, there is a contrasting dish or accompaniment to balance the textures and spices. Within these guidelines, the ingredients vary depending on the region, but of course you will find similarities throughout India.

Though you may be served an appetizer in an Indian restaurant in the U.S., you would not find them in India. "The closest we get to appetizers in India are the little things like *samosas* that we serve with tea," says Neela Paniz. "The appetizers you see in Indian restaurants in America are the snacks that are eaten all day long in India."

"If you were to serve an Indian dinner Western-style with courses, the same principles would apply as with any good menu," says Raji Jallepalli. "You don't want to start with something too strong, which would kill the palate for any more delicate dishes to follow. Among Indian dishes, this would include anything spiced with fenugreek."

Our experts may have adapted to Western dining by necessity, but they still don't stray far from the principles of home.

Contrasts

An Indian meal is all about contrasts. —NEELA PANIZ

The menu for an Indian dinner, any good meal, relies on contrasts, considering everything from flavors to textures to degrees of richness.

"If you serve meat in a sauce, you would not also serve sauced vegetables," says Neela Paniz. "I would pair a chicken curry with some simply cooked green beans with mustard seed or potatoes and peas." A bowl of soup, on the other hand, is an example of a dish to which contrast would be added. "*Rasam* is the word for 'soup,' and mulligatawny is the most popular," points out Julie Sahni. "Mulligatawny is a pepper water. It typically contains cumin, lentil, and tamarind. Then it is flavored with mustard seeds, curry leaves, and coriander. With this soup you will be served rice, which you mix in with your finger, turning the soup into a porridge. You will also be served wafers called *pappadam*, or *papad* in the North. The wafers provide a textural contrast to the soup."

Staples

Every night I was in India, we ate rice and dal. The dal would be made with mung beans, lentils, or chickpeas, and it would be finished in a different way, such as with buttermilk, garlic, or mustard seeds. Each night, the food had a whole different taste, but it was still essentially "rice and beans." To me, there was something grounding about that.

—SUSAN FENIGER, CHEF/CO-OWNER, BORDER GRILL AND CIUDAD, LOS ANGELES

The colorful dishes and variety of accompaniments cloak the fact that Indian cuisine revolves around humble staples: lentils, rice, bread, and potatoes. "When you visit someone's home for dinner, the whole meal can very easily consist of lentils, rice, bread and potatoes," says Julie Sahni. "Indians consider potatoes as a vegetable, not a starch. Very rarely will you have a meal without potatoes. Rice and bread are always on the table; that's a given."

"During a trip to India, I had the most amazing lentils I have ever had in my life," recalls Mark Miller. "I asked the cook what the secret was, and he told me, 'I cooked them in *ghee* [clarified butter] for two days.' As a chef, it was very humbling. There is something about seeing people with little money, no fancy kitchens, and no budgets to buy fancy farm-raised animals. You think to yourself, 'How much do I really know?'"

"Lentils are a great example of the variations in Indian cooking," says Neela Paniz. "There are about eight different kinds of lentils. They come whole with husks, split with the husks, split with the husks removed, or whole with the husks removed, so with one bean you have four different variations. Each one cooks up to a different level of creaminess."

Julie Sahni shares her strategy for cooking lentils: "For a dinner, you want to soak your lentils while you are browning your onions for the curry. Then you cook them in water with some turmeric, or maybe some ginger, garlic, or onion."

Bread

The fact that almost all bread in India is made with whole wheat flour has not hindered Indians' creativity with dough. Bread is cooked in a wide variety of ways: over a flame, on the sides of tandoori ovens, deep-fried, and on a flat-top griddle. "When I was young, I was very good at making bread," remembers Julie Sahni. "My father liked his puffy, so I would make the bread that way and my sisters would run them out to him from the kitchen!" (See her recipe on page 268.)

Rice

Though rice is universal throughout India, it is somewhat less popular in the North than in the South. "To make perfect rice, I recommend that it be soaked for twenty minutes before cooking," says Julie Sahni. "When it is finished cooking, the grains should be elongated and separate. At the last moment before serving it, you should add a little clarified butter."

Accompaniments That Add Counterpoints

Chutneys, curries, and pickles are popular throughout the country, providing contrasting flavor notes within meals. "Chutney is optional, however," points out Neela Paniz. "You would not make a chutney every night, but if you have company or are serving something special, you would make some chutney. You may have five or six dishes at a meal, and then you'll have chutneys that add additional flavor.

"When you make a raw chutney, you make a small amount just for that meal. Chutneys are freshly made with herbs, green fruit, spices, and ingredients that are zesty and tart. For example, tamarind is added to a coconut chutney. Chutney is also very seasonal. If small mangoes are in season, everybody is making mango chutney!

"What we call chutney in the U.S. is more like a preserve in India," continues Paniz. "You dry out ripe fruit, then cook it into a chutney. Chutney is about the contrast of flavors. You add it to your spoonful of food. It is the contrast to the cooked spices in

WINE WITH INDIAN FOOD?

"People will sometimes complain that our food is not hot enough, but it doesn't need to be hot to be Indian," says Floyd Cardoz. "In addition, food that's less hot leads to better wine pairing. Our food does not overpower the right wines, plenty of which work very well. The wines need to be strong-bodied in order to match the food well. Syrahs, Cabernets, Merlots, Sauvignon Blancs, and Alsatian whites all work with Indian food. There are layers of flavors in my food, so there is always something the wine can pick up. People sometimes say that we don't have old wines on our list, but you don't want to pair an old Petrus with Indian food."

"I love wine, and the marriage of spices with it," says Raji Jallepalli. "They are so complementary. I had a Margaux that was one hundred percent sauvignon blanc grapes. It was just pure flavor. And I thought, this wine deserves a dish!

So, I created a dish with lobster, coconut milk, lemongrass, and toasted poppy seeds [see page 261], which I could taste with the Margaux in my mind before I made and paired it.

"Bordeaux works well with spices, and Pinot Noir goes well with tandoori food," she says. "To me, Champagne is also a great match. There is nothing it doesn't work well with! My choice would be Billecart-Salmon, because I love its flavor and effervescence."

your food. You might be eating a dish with dried cayenne, coriander, and cumin, among other spices. Then you'll have a chutney made of freshly ground cilantro, peanuts, green chiles, garlic, and lots of lemon juice. A few drops of that will take your food to another level."

"In the U.S., we think of chutneys as pickled," agrees Nina Simonds. "However, in southern India, chutneys are more like fresh herbal pestos. The base will be coconut, to which cilantro, mint, and garlic are added. I was recently at a spa there that came recommended by the author Andrew Weil, and at every meal we had a different chutney."

In the North, most tandoori dishes are served with a fresh mint chutney as a dipping sauce. In the South, if you order a *dosa*, you will get *sambar* (spicy lentil soup) and coconut chutney with it.

"We also like pickles, but we don't eat ones anything like the American dill," says Neela Paniz. "If your food is lacking zing, you'll have a pickle with it. They are highly spiced, which is a nice contrast, because not every dish is highly spiced." Pickles vary widely: cauliflower, carrots, chiles, green mangoes, limes, and turnips are all pickled. Fruits are frequently preserved in oil, while crunchy vegetables are usually preserved in brine. Ground mustard, turmeric, and chile powder are common pickle seasonings.

A few other accompaniments are fixtures of the condiment tray at even the most casual Indian restaurants: relishes, sauces, and *raita*. Mint relish, composed mainly of pureed mint, ginger, and chile, has a spicy edge. Mint and cilantro sauce is milder, with just a hint of chile. There is also tamarind sauce, which resembles molasses and has a sweet, aromatic edge. *Raita* is an accompaniment consisting of yogurt mixed with spices and either raw or cooked vegetables, or sometimes fruit. And *cachumbar* is the term for a category of salad-type accompaniments composed of chopped raw vegetables and fresh herbs.

Indian Flavors: The Next Frontier?

A fellow chef heard that Danny Meyer wanted to open a high-end Indian restaurant, Tabla, and I got the call. It was a huge commitment to me and Indian cuisine.

—FLOYD CARDOZ

OUR EXPERTS SEE INDIAN INGREDIENTS and spicing increasingly working their way into the American palate. "I believe that Indian culture is becoming more and more popular, from our fascination with yoga to our involvement with the food," asserts Nina Simonds. "If you go to a McDonald's in England, you will see Indian choices on the menu! Chinese, Thai, and Vietnamese foods have had huge influences in America, and Indian food is sure to be the next frontier, because the spices have extraordinary flavor!"

Chefs here have developed ways to take the complex spicing of India and meld it with the subtleties of their own specialties. "I like to combine French technique and Indian flavors," says Raji Jallepalli. "The guiding principle in fusion is that the ingredient can't lose its integrity. You don't want diluted Indian or French cuisine, yet a little cumin can take a French dish to the next level or dimension."

"Gray Kunz was open to using Indian spicing and techniques when he was chef at Lespinasse [a four-star French restaurant in New York]," says Floyd Cardoz. "We would do lentil crusts on fish and braised lamb with Indian spices."

"One technique that is very effective with Indian spices is a cold infusion, which produces a very delicate flavor," says Jallepalli. "This method is similar in principle to the making of coffee. Coffee beans are too bitter by themselves, so you make an infusion by pouring water over the beans through a filter. With a cold infusion, I put Indian spices with ice in a cheesecloth and let the ice melt through the spice. What you get is a very light liquid that is flavored with the essence of the spices. Since the ice takes a long time to melt, the water has time to absorb the flavor of the spice. This liquid is perfect to add to something like a bisque."

Chinese cuisine expert Nina Simonds laments, "I went to India to get exposed to the power of spices and I did. But the food is so great there that after I left, I felt deprived!" With ever-expanding Indian influences in cosmopolitan restaurants—seen in dishes from Hubert Keller's Curried Split Pea Soup at Fleur de Lys in San Francisco to Michael Romano's Sautéed Shrimp Goan-Style at Union Square Café in New York City—these flavors are becoming increasingly accessible. Best of all, you can now create them yourself in your own kitchen!

Nach Waxman's Recommended Reading on Indian Cooking

The first ninety pages of Julie Sahni's **Classic Indian Cooking** are a short course on the ingredients, techniques, equipment, and basic preparations that are central to Indian cooking. The pantry is critical because many of the items used in Indian cooking—from the spice blends to ghee—are made in advance. This book is a terrific introduction to Indian cooking, although some are disappointed that there are no color photographs.

I'd also recommend a vegetarian book: **Lord Krishna's Cuisine** (also known as **The Art of Indian Vegetarian Cuisine**) was written by Yamuna Devi, an American woman who has won the respect of Indians, much as Carol Field has won the respect of Italian bakers. This is a large, brilliant, and important book covering both North and South Indian cuisine, which doesn't appear in most Indian cookbooks.

Savoring the Spice Coast of India by Maya Kaimal is a book of stunning tastes and flavors, presenting the food of the southern state of Kerala. I can report this from firsthand experience, as Indian cooking is my passion and I've cooked my way through most of the recipes in this book.

A more modern take on Indian cooking—an enriched blend of methods and materials from east and west—is **Raji Cuisine** by the late Raji Jallepalli. It is fusion at its best.

Chilled Tomato Soup with Celery, Fennel, and Ginger

FOR THE SPICE MIX

1 teaspoon cumin seeds

1 teaspoon coriander seeds

⅛ teaspoon fenugreek seeds

½ teaspoon black peppercorns

½ teaspoon red mustard seeds

1 teaspoon fennel seeds

FOR THE SOUP

Extra-virgin olive oil

½ carrot, diced

¼ onion, diced

1 celery stalk, diced

A 1-inch piece of ginger, peeled and finely chopped

2 garlic cloves, minced

1 red bell pepper, cored, seeded, and diced

½ fennel bulb, trimmed and diced

4 tomatoes, chopped

FOR THE SPICE MIX

TOAST THE SPICES, one type at a time, in a small skillet over medium heat, shaking the pan frequently, until fragrant. Transfer to a plate to cool, then finely grind in a spice grinder.

FOR THE SOUP

IN A LARGE SKILLET, heat a thin film of extra-virgin olive oil over medium heat. Add the carrot, onion, and celery and sweat until the vegetables soften. Add the ginger and garlic and sweat until aromatic. Add the pepper and fennel and sweat until softened. Add the tomatoes and salt. Cook until the tomatoes begin to break down.

ADD ENOUGH VEGETABLE STOCK to cover by 1 inch. Bring to a simmer and cook until all the vegetables are tender.

PURÉE THE SOUP, in batches if necessary, in a blender. Return to skillet. Add the spice mix and bring to a boil. Remove from the heat and let stand for 20 minutes to marry the flavors.

STRAIN THE SOUP through a fine-mesh sieve. Chill in a bowl over ice, or cover and refrigerate until cold.

SEASON THE SOUP with lemon juice, Tabasco sauce, salt, a pinch of sugar, and pepper. Ladle into bowls. Garnish with the celery, celery leaves, radish, chives, and fennel seeds, and serve.

1 teaspoon salt, or more
to taste

About 8 cups vegetable stock

Fresh lemon juice to taste

Tabasco sauce

Sugar

Freshly ground black pepper

1 tablespoon tender inner
celery stalk, thinly sliced

1 tablespoon chopped celery
leaves

1 tablespoon thinly sliced
radish

2 tablespoons chopped fresh
chives

1 tablespoon Lucknow fennel
seeds (see Note), toasted in a
dry skillet until fragrant and
pounded

SERVES 4

Note
**Lucknow is a sweet aromatic type of fennel; if not avail-
able, substitute regular fennel seeds.**

257

RECIPES INSPIRED BY India

Curry Leaf–Marinated Flank Steak with Smashed Potatoes, Haricots Verts, and Ginger-Horseradish Raita

FOR THE MARINADE

8 sprigs curry leaves

2 teaspoons freshly ground black pepper

1 tablespoon ground cumin

1 dried ground chile

A 1½-inch piece of ginger, pureed

1 tablespoon pureed garlic

½ cup canola oil

6 tablespoons soy sauce

1 flank steak (approximately 1½ pounds), trimmed of excess fat

FOR THE GINGER-HORSERADISH RAITA

1 cup yogurt

A 1-inch piece of ginger, juiced

1 tablespoon grated horseradish

Salt and freshly ground black pepper

Sugar

Smashed Potatoes (recipe follows)

Haricots Verts (recipe follows)

SERVES 4

FOR THE MARINADE

COMBINE ALL THE INGREDIENTS in a blender and blend until smooth. Put the flank steak in a shallow dish and rub all over with the marinade. Cover and refrigerate for at least 4 hours, but no more than 7 hours.

FOR THE RAITA

COMBINE THE YOGURT with the ginger and horseradish, folding them in with a rubber spatula. Season to taste with salt, pepper and sugar. Cover and refrigerate until ready to serve.

PREHEAT A GRILL to medium-high.

GRILL THE STEAK, turning once, to the desired temperature. Transfer to a platter and let rest for 10 minutes, then thinly slice against the grain.

PLATE, and serve.

Smashed Potatoes

4 Yukon Gold potatoes, peeled and quartered

1 teaspoon turmeric

1 tablespoon canola oil

1 tablespoon chana dal (yellow split peas)

1 teaspoon red mustard seeds

1 sprig curry leaf

4 roasted garlic cloves

COOK THE POTATOES in boiling salted water, seasoned with the turmeric, just until partially cooked; they should still be firm in the center.

MEANWHILE, PREHEAT the oven to 375 degrees F.

TRANSFER THE POTATOES to a large bowl and smash with a potato masher or wooden spoon. Cover with aluminum foil to keep warm.

HEAT THE CANOLA OIL in a small sauté pan over low heat. Add the chana dal and cook until golden brown and fragrant. Add the mustard seeds and curry leaf. Cook until the mustard seeds pop and the curry leaves wilt, about 2 minutes. Turn off the heat and stir in the roasted garlic.

ADD THE GARLIC MIXTURE to the potatoes and toss until well combined. Spread the mixture out on a sheet pan or a baking pan and bake for 30 minutes, or until golden brown and crusty. Serve warm or at room temperature.

Haricots Verts

1 tablespoon canola oil

1 teaspoon yellow mustard dal (split mustard seeds)

2 garlic cloves, thinly sliced

¼ onion, thinly sliced

A ½-inch piece of ginger, julienned

10 ounces haricots verts

¼ cup chicken stock, heated

¼ chile pepper, thinly sliced

Salt and freshly ground black pepper

HEAT THE OIL in a large skillet over medium heat. Add the mustard dal and toast until fragrant. Add the garlic, onions, and ginger and sweat until translucent.

ADD THE HARICOTS VERTS, hot stock, and chile, increase the heat, and boil rapidly until the beans are tender. Season to taste with salt and pepper. Transfer to a bowl, set over a larger bowl of ice, and let cool, stirring occasionally. Serve at room temperature.

Seared Day-Boat Cod, Brown and White Basmati Kanji, Baby Artichokes, and Kokum

FOR THE CARROT PICKLE

2 carrots

A 2-inch piece of ginger

3 chiles, split

1 tablespoon salt

2 tablespoons white vinegar

1 tablespoon sugar

Water to cover

FOR THE KANJI

2 tablespoons canola oil

2 cloves

1 bay leaf

2 tablespoons unsalted butter

2 tablespoons minced shallots

A 1-inch piece of ginger, peeled and chopped

1 cup brown basmati rice

¼ cup dry white wine

2 ounces salt cod, thinly sliced and toasted (not soaked)

3 cups chicken stock

1 sprig rosemary

1 cup white basmati rice

8 baby artichokes, trimmed and quartered

One 14½-ounce can unsweetened coconut milk

Four 6-ounce pieces cod fillet

Salt and freshly ground black pepper

8 pieces kokum, julienned

SERVES 4

Kokum is the fruit of an evergreen tree that is native to South India. Also known as black deshi, or flower plum, it has a tart, fruity flavor. If not available, substitute eight slices of green mango.

FOR THE CARROT PICKLE

COMBINE ALL THE INGREDIENTS in a saucepan and bring to boil. Remove from the heat and let cool, then drain. Dice the carrots and reserve. Discard the remaining solids.

FOR THE KANJI

IN A MEDIUM POT, heat the oil. Add the cloves and bay leaf and cook until fragrant. Add the butter, shallots, and ginger and cook until translucent. Add the brown basmati rice, wine, salt cod, chicken stock, and rosemary. Simmer until the rice is almost done.

ADD THE WHITE BASMATI RICE and the artichokes. Bring to a boil and simmer for 15 minutes. Add the coconut milk and continue to cook just until the rice is tender.

MEANWHILE, SEASON THE COD with salt and pepper on both sides. Coat the pan with oil and pan-roast for approximately 6 minutes to desired firmness.

REMOVE THE GINGER, chiles, and rosemary from the rice, and add the kokum.

TO SERVE, SPOON THE RICE onto plates. Place the fish on top and garnish with the diced carrot, sprinkled over the fish.

Raji Jallepalli

Coconut Milk Soup with Lobster and Toasted Poppy Seeds

¼ cup canola oil

2 tablespoons finely chopped shallots

¼ cup chopped fresh cilantro

1 tablespoon minced fresh ginger

½ teaspoon poppy seeds

¼ teaspoon toasted and ground cloves

¼ teaspoon ground cinnamon

¼ teaspoon turmeric

Two 2-inch pieces tender inner lemongrass stalk, tied together with a chive

1 pound fresh lobster meat, cut into chunks

One 14½-ounce can unsweetened coconut milk

2 cups heavy cream

Coarse salt

SERVES 6

HEAT THE OIL in a large heavy saucepan over medium heat. Add the shallots and sauté for 2 to 3 minutes, or until the shallots have wilted and begun to take on some color. Stir in the cilantro, ginger, poppy seeds, cloves, cinnamon, turmeric, and lemongrass. Sauté for 5 minutes, lowering the heat if necessary to keep from burning.

ADD THE LOBSTER and continue sautéing for 3 minutes. Stir in the coconut milk and bring just to a simmer. Cook at a bare simmer for 5 minutes.

STIR IN THE CREAM and bring to boil. Immediately lower the heat and gently simmer for 15 minutes, or until the flavors are well blended and the soup has reduced slightly. Season with salt if necessary.

LADLE INTO BOWLS and serve immediately.

Chicken with Sweet Spice

FOR THE MARINADE

2 tablespoons coriander seeds

1 tablespoon black cumin seeds

1 tablespoon black peppercorns

1 tablespoon whole cloves

1 cinnamon stick

6 tablespoons canola oil

2 tablespoons minced onion

1 tablespoon minced garlic

1 tablespoon minced fresh ginger

1 tablespoon minced serrano chile

½ cup nonfat yogurt

3 tablespoons fresh lime juice

Coarse salt

Six 6-ounce boneless, skinless chicken breast halves

1 cup chopped leeks (white and pale green parts only)

1 cup heavy cream

4 tablespoons unsalted butter, softened

Coarse salt and freshly ground black pepper

2 cups cauliflower florets

1 cup tiny fresh peas

SERVES 6

This recipe has a long list of ingredients, but it is easy to make. If you don't have time to make the whole dish, the marinated chicken is great right off the grill, with just a crisp green salad and crusty bread. This dish goes well with a velvety Pinot Noir, like a Beaune Les Boucherottes or a Morgon, wines that pair well with the sweet spices.

FOR THE MARINADE

COMBINE THE CORIANDER, cumin, peppercorns, cloves, and cinnamon in a small nonstick pan and cook, stirring frequently, over medium heat for about 4 minutes, or until the spices are nicely toasted and aromatic. Remove from the heat and allow to cool. Put the spices in a spice grinder and process until very fine. Set aside.

HEAT 2 TABLESPOONS of the oil in a large sauté pan over medium heat. Add the onions, garlic, ginger, and chile and sauté for about 5 minutes, or until golden. Add the spice powder and stir to blend. Remove from the heat and allow to cool.

STIR THE YOGURT, lime juice, and salt to taste into the vegetable-spice mixture. Place the chicken in a baking dish and pour the yogurt mixture over the top. Cover and refrigerate for at least 1 hour.

MEANWHILE, BLANCH the leeks in a small saucepan of rapidly boiling salted water for 30 seconds. Drain and pat dry. Combine the leeks with the heavy cream in a medium saucepan over medium heat. Bring just to a boil. Immediately whisk in the butter and salt and pepper to taste. Gently simmer for 4 minutes, or until the sauce coats the back of a spoon. Pour into the top half of a double boiler over very hot water, cover loosely, and keep warm.

REMOVE THE CHICKEN from the refrigerator and scrape off the marinade.

PREHEAT THE OVEN to 375 degrees F. Heat 2 tablespoons of the oil in a large ovenproof sauté pan over medium heat. Add the chicken and cook for about 5 minutes, turning once, until it begins to brown. Place the pan in the oven and roast the chicken for 10 minutes, or until cooked through.

WHILE THE CHICKEN is cooking, heat the remaining 2 tablespoons oil in a sauté pan over medium heat. Add the cauliflower and sauté for 2 minutes. Add the peas and cook for 5 minutes, or until the vegetables are crisp-tender. Season with salt and pepper.

TO SERVE, PLACE VEGETABLES in the center of six plates. Nestle a chicken breast on top of each and drizzle the warm leek sauce over the chicken.

Spiced Basmati Rice with Fruit and Pine Nuts

3 tablespoons ghee (see Note)

½ cup minced onions

1 teaspoon finely minced ginger

½ teaspoon minced garlic

3 whole cloves

3 cardamom pods

One 2-inch cinnamon stick

2 cups basmati rice, rinsed and drained

1 teaspoon turmeric

2½ cups water

½ cup fresh coconut milk (see Note)

Coarse salt

¼ cup golden raisins

¼ cup finely diced dried apricots

½ cup pine nuts, toasted

SERVES 6

This rice dish can be served with almost any meat or poultry. Traditionally the whole spices are left in the dish, but not eaten. For wine, the spice and fruit flavors of the rice call for a fruity-style wine, like a Syrah. Two that I recommend are Rosemount and Qupé.

HEAT THE GHEE in a heavy sauté pan over medium-high heat. Add the onions, ginger, garlic, cloves, cardamom pods, and cinnamon stick and sauté for 5 minutes. Stir in the rice and turmeric and sauté 3 minutes, or until the rice is shiny.

RAISE THE HEAT and add the water, coconut milk, and salt to taste. Bring to a boil. Immediately reduce the heat to low, cover, and cook for 10 minutes. Stir in the raisins and apricots. Cover and cook, without lifting the lid, for 10 minutes. Remove the pan from the heat (without lifting the lid) and allow the rice to steam for 5 minutes.

REMOVE THE LID and stir in the pine nuts. Remove the whole spices if you wish, and serve.

Note
To make ghee, slowly melt 1 pound unsalted butter in a heavy saucepan over low heat. Bring to a low boil and cook for about 20 minutes, or until the milk solids separate. Remove from the heat and strain through a triple layer of cheesecloth. Cover and store at room temperature for up to 1 week. (Prepared ghee is available in many ethnic markets.)

To make fresh coconut milk, combine 1 cup tightly packed grated fresh coconut with 1 cup boiling water in a bowl and let stand for 30 minutes. Puree the mixture in a blender, then strain through a sieve lined with a double layer of cheesecloth, squeezing out as much of the liquid as possible. You can use frozen grated coconut if fresh is not available, but sweetened flaked coconut or canned coconut cream *cannot* be substituted.

Braised Lamb Shanks with Masala Raan

6 lamb shanks (approximately 12 ounces each)

12 garlic cloves

A 2-inch piece of ginger, peeled

½ cup yogurt

1½ teaspoons garam masala (see Note)

¼ cup vegetable oil

8 small onions, halved and sliced into thin half-moons

6 medium tomatoes, coarsely chopped

1½ tablespoons ground coriander

1 tablespoon ground cumin

1½ teaspoons cayenne

¼ teaspoon turmeric

1 ½ teaspoons salt

1 cup dark rum

1 teaspoon saffron threads

Chopped fresh cilantro for garnish

SERVES 6

Note

Garam masala is a North Indian spice blend containing cumin, coriander, cardamom, cinnamon, cloves, and black pepper. It is available in specialty and Indian grocery stores.

Lamb shanks are closest to the small legs of lamb we get in India.

TRIM ANY EXCESS FAT off the shanks, being careful not to pull the meat away from the bone. With the point of a knife, pierce holes in the meat.

IN A MINI BLENDER, grind the garlic, ginger, and ¼ cup of the yogurt to a smooth paste. Transfer to a bowl and mix in the remaining yogurt and the garam masala. Put the lamb in a shallow dish and rub the marinade into the lamb. Set aside.

HEAT THE OIL in a large Dutch oven. Add the onions and sauté until dark golden brown, about 10 to 15 minutes, stirring frequently so as not to burn them. Add the tomatoes, mixing well, and continue to sauté until incorporated. Add the coriander, cumin, cayenne, and turmeric to what is now *masala raan*. Cook until the oil separates and the mixture pulls away from the sides of the pan.

CAREFULLY ADD 3 of the shanks to the pot and brown them on all sides for about 5 minutes. Return them to the dish with the marinade and repeat with the remaining 3 shanks. Return all the shanks, with their marinade, to the pot and cook for another 4 to 5 minutes over high heat, turning the shanks every so often. Add the salt, mixing well, lower the heat, cover, and simmer for 1 hour, turning the shanks once or twice so they absorb the masala evenly.

ADD THE RUM and saffron threads and cook for another 45 minutes, or until the meat is very tender.

PLACE ON A SERVING PLATTER, topping off with the masala remaining in the pot. Garnish with cilantro and serve.

Murghi Masala Tikka
Chicken Tikka in Green Spices

FOR THE MARINADE

10 cloves garlic

A 2-inch piece of ginger, peeled and coarsely chopped

4 to 6 serrano chiles, coarsely chopped

1 bunch cilantro, roots trimmed

1 tablespoon ground coriander

1 tablespoon ground toasted cumin seeds

½ teaspoon cayenne

¼ teaspoon freshly grated nutmeg

¼ teaspoon mace

2 pounds skinless, boneless chicken breasts, cut into 1-inch chunks

1 teaspoon salt

1 tablespoon corn oil

Lime wedges for garnish

SERVES 4

FOR THE MARINADE

COMBINE THE GARLIC, ginger, chiles, and cilantro in a blender and blend to a smooth puree, adding a little water as needed. Transfer to a bowl and mix in the rest of the spices.

IN A LARGE BOWL, season the chicken pieces with the salt. Coat well with the marinade. Set aside for at least 30 minutes at room temperature, or marinate in the refrigerator for up to 6 hours.

STIR THE OIL into the marinade, mixing well. Thread the chicken pieces onto skewers. Grill or broil for 6 to 8 minutes on each side, until cooked through. Serve with lime wedges.

Julie Sahni

Jheenga Chat
Shrimp Madras-Style

1½ pounds jumbo or large shrimp, peeled, deveined, and rinsed

1 teaspoon curry powder

1 teaspoon garam masala (available in specialty and Indian groceries) or ground cumin

24 fresh curry leaves, cut into chiffonade; or 1 tablespoon coarsely ground dried curry leaves

1 teaspoon minced garlic

1 tablespoon vegetable oil

1 tablespoon tomato paste

¼ cup unsweetened coconut milk (fresh or canned)

Coarse salt

1 tablespoon lemon juice

1 bunch (6 to 7 ounces) watercress, trimmed, rinsed, and patted dry

SERVES 4

This is a wonderful recipe of the Chettinad (the business community) from Madras, whose food often reflects a fusion of northern and southern flavors. In this preparation, for example, both curry powder and garam masala are used to achieve intriguingly complex results.

PLACE THE SHRIMP in a bowl. Add the curry powder, garam masala, curry leaves, garlic, and oil, and rub all over the shrimp.

HEAT A LARGE SKILLET over high heat until very hot. Add the shrimp and sear, shaking and tossing, for a minute, or until they turn pink and begin to curl up. Whisk the tomato paste into the coconut milk and add to the shrimp. Continue cooking until the sauce is reduced to a glaze and shrimp are cooked through. Sprinkle with salt, drizzle with the lemon juice, and remove from the heat.

SPREAD THE WATERCRESS on a platter and mound the shrimp on top of it. Serve immediately.

267

India

Chapati
Puffy Whole Wheat Bread

1 cup aata/chapati or whole wheat flour (or a combination of ½ cup whole wheat flour and ½ cup all-purpose flour)

⅓ cup water, or more as needed

Additional aata or all-purpose flour for dusting

Ghee for garnish (optional)

MAKES EIGHT TO TWELVE
6-INCH CHAPATI

Chapati are a wholesome and earthy-tasting whole wheat bread staple of North India. They are similar to flour tortillas except they are always made with whole-grain flour, with the bran and germ intact. The soft and pliable breads are made by rolling out the dough into thin circles and baking them on a hot griddle. Chapati go well with any Indian dishes.

PLACE THE FLOUR in a bowl. Add enough water to form a rough dough, then knead the dough until soft and pliable. Alternatively, place the flour in a food processor. With the machine running, add the water in a thin stream until the mixture comes together into a mass and a dough ball forms on the blades, then process for 1 minute to knead the dough. Transfer the dough to a work surface. (The dough can be placed in a zipper-lock plastic bag and refrigerated. Bring to room temperature before using.)

PINCH OFF SMALL PORTIONS of dough and roll them into smooth 1-inch balls. Dust the balls lightly with flour to prevent sticking. Keep the dough covered with a damp towel or plastic wrap to prevent it from drying out.

HEAT A GRIDDLE or a large skillet over medium-high heat. Pick up one dough ball, dust it with flour, and place it on the work surface. Press firmly to flatten, turning once. Roll the dough into a thin circle with a brisk back-and-forth motion, working around the dough to keep it circular. Dust often with flour to prevent sticking.

LIFT THE BREAD and gently place on the hot griddle. When it develops several small puffed spots and the bottom is cooked, with several light brown spots, flip the bread, using a pair of unserrated tongs, and bake the other side the same way. (If the griddle temperature is right, the first side will take about 30 seconds and the second side 10.) Remove the pan from the heat. Pick up the bread with the tongs and, holding it directly over the flame, toast, turning, until the bread is covered with dark brown spots, about 30 seconds. The bread generally will puff during toasting but it is still perfectly acceptable if it doesn't. Brush the bread with ghee, if desired, and serve, or set aside in a warm place. Continue with the remaining breads in the same way.

Mexico

WHERE CHILES REIGN SUPREME

Chiles are one of the most widely cultivated spice crops today.

—JILL NORMAN, AUTHOR, *THE COMPLETE BOOK OF SPICES*

IT IS UNFORTUNATE HOW LITTLE most Americans know about authentic Mexican food—and how much they think they know! Chain restaurants serving molded corn tortillas and burritos the size of footballs, touting what they are offering as Mexican food, have led many Americans to believe that tacos are supposed to be made with ground beef and shredded American cheese. How can the United States—a country whose citizens famously consume more salsa than ketchup—be so lacking in its knowledge of authentic Mexican food? How can the food of a country that shares our border and once extended into much of what is now the American Southwest and California still be so foreign to us?

Fortunately, thanks to the efforts of our experts in Mexican cuisine, among others, more and more Americans are learning that the range of Mexican cuisine encompasses far more than the bastardized tacos and salsa offered by chain restaurants would suggest. Rick and Deann Bayless established a beachhead with Frontera Grill and Topolobampo in Chicago, widely considered to be two of the best Mexican restaurants in the world. Zarela Martínez opened Zarela in New York City to introduce people to the food she ate while growing up in Mexico. Susan Feniger and Mary Sue Milliken of Border Grill and Ciudad in Los Angeles were among the first to serve authentic regional Mexican food in a place you'd least expect to have been without it: Southern California. And after years in the Frontera Grill kitchen, Mexican native Priscila Satkoff opened her own Chicago restaurant, Salpicón, to share her take on Mexican cuisine.

These chefs and restaurateurs are all still pioneers, deliciously educating us while spinning dishes from different regions of Mexico. They take our palates on an adventurous ride with a diverse array of stews, ceviches, street food, dishes for celebrations, and more. Yet there is one ingredient that unites all of these chefs and truly defines Mexican food: chiles.

Chiles are the soul of Mexican cuisine. The country produces a far greater volume and variety of chiles than any other place on earth. Throughout history, they have been used as medicines, ritual objects, even pigment. While chiles play an important role in other countries—including China, India, and Thailand—in Mexican cooking, chiles are not just a flavoring, they are often the main ingredient. "That is the big difference," attests Zarela Martínez. "Chiles are used in many ways, and their varieties and the ways they are used vary throughout the country."

Used fresh in a salsa or roasted and simmered in a *mole*, chiles can be brightly flavored or earthy. "To start, you have to decide how you will cook a chile," says Mark Miller of the Coyote Café in Santa Fe. "Some dishes call for grilling, some for roasting, and some for frying in oil. If you are using a poblano chile, all three techniques are used and all affect the final sauce differently.

"It is even very important how you peel them," he continues. "After roasting a chile, you put it in a bowl and cover it to loosen the skin. If you put too many chiles together and let them sit for too long, you get chiles with a vegetal quality as opposed to a smoky, anise quality. You have lost all the subtlety of why you are using a poblano."

Knowing the context of when, why, and how a chile is used is the essence of the artistry of Mexican cuisine. For a salsa, a chile is a splash of color and heat. In a *mole*, it blends with the other ingredients to turn into a multilayered sauce playing off garlic, chocolate, and ground seeds. In every dish, it manages to dazzle the palate in ways ranging from subtle to bold.

American Misconceptions about Mexican Food

INTRODUCING AUTHENTIC MEXICAN FOOD to America has not been an easy task. Just as Italians have had to overcome the perception of pizza and pasta with red sauce as the only foods of Italy, our Mexican experts have had to work past what Americans *think* Mexican food is, versus what it *really* is.

Zarela Martínez recalls that when she opened her restaurant in 1987, people would complain that they did not serve nachos: "I would have to explain that we wanted to serve *real* Mexican home food."

"When we opened Salpicón, people would come in asking for burritos and fajitas," echoes Priscila Satkoff. "We'd try to explain that that was not our style of Mexican food. I would tell them that I am Mexican, that I grew up in Mexico, and that what we were serving was Mexican food. But they'd find it hard to believe that there are no 'chimichangas' in Mexico. I am over forty, and I've never had a burrito in Mexico!"

Another common misperception is that cheese is a vital part of any Mexican dish. "Cheese is not that popular in Mexico," explains Martínez. "You don't see gloppy dishes with cheese. When you order enchiladas in Mexico, you get a little crumbled cheese on top—that's it." Satkoff agrees. "Some 'Mexican' restaurants put cheddar cheese on top of everything to please the American palate. In Mexico, we eat vegetables. We put lettuce on top of things, not cheese."

If a visitor came to the United States and ate only hamburgers and French fries, he would no doubt get the wrong idea about American food. If he added cheese to both of those items, he might also feel a little weighed down. "It is a big misconception that Mexican food is heavy," says Martínez. "People confuse snack foods with traditional foods. Tacos and enchiladas are the hamburgers and hot dogs of Mexico. They are not something the average person eats that often. The main meal of the day is lunch. So tacos and such are something you might have for supper in the evening."

"I am not sure what some restaurants are adding to refried beans," laughs Satkoff. "Lard? Butter? There is so much in there that it doesn't taste like fresh beans anymore."

"The biggest of all misconceptions is that Mexican food is spicy," adds Martínez. "Some dishes are, but intrinsically the food is not. You have condiments and table sauces to make it spicy if you choose. In the hottest areas of Mexico, you'll find the spiciest food."

Mexican Culinary History

TO GET A PROPER PERSPECTIVE on Mexican food, just look to the history of the country. Foods that were eaten by the Aztecs before the arrival of Cortés are still consumed today: beyond the native ingredients, such as squash and pumpkin, such things as gorditas, tamales, tortillas, and *mole* and *pipián* sauces, to name just a few. Mexican culinary history changed with the arrival of Cortés from Spain in 1519. Cortés brought things from the Old World that one would have a hard time imagining Mexican cuisine without: chickens, cows, and pigs, as well as sugar, wheat, onions, and, serendipitously, garlic (which, as Rick Bayless explains in our book *Culinary Artistry*, are key to enhancing the flavor of chiles).

Mexico held up its part of the culinary bargain by sending back to Spain chocolate, beans, chiles, sweet potatoes, and tomatoes, to name just the tip of the historical iceberg. As Bayless points out, "Despite all these influences crisscrossing the Atlantic, it wasn't until 1910 that the two cultures really united to form Mexican cuisine. Until that time, the Spaniards living in Mexico adapted some local ingredients out of necessity, but essentially they made 'their' food in Mexico."

Food in Mexico evolved two ways. "Both the Spanish and native Mexicans adopted the new ingredients that were introduced to them. Yet both cooked them their own ways. They adopted each other's ingredients—not dishes," explains Priscila Satkoff.

Culinary Map of Mexico

ONE OF THE PRACTICES THAT Mexican culinary experts rail against is the ubiquitous use of cumin in Mexican dishes in America, when cumin is, in fact, only used in the north of Mexico. Understanding the country's culinary regions will help prevent your seasoning from suffering a negative fate.

If you were to visualize Mexico, you would see that its northern border runs from California to Arizona and New Mexico to Texas. It dips down, framing the Caribbean and West Indies across from Cuba, then begins the bridge of Central America. So, we have a country with deserts in the north and tropical weather and jungles in the south—a diversity of climate and geography that make for distinctive regional cooking styles and ingredients.

As with any country, it is possible to divide Mexico into small and even smaller regions and micro-regions. To avoid getting carried away, we turned to Rick Bayless for a broad-brush picture. He divides the country into the following regions: Mexico City and central Mexico (*Chilango*), Guadalajara and west-central Mexico (*Tapatío*), Veracruz and the Gulf Coast (*Jarocho*), the North (*Norteño*), the Yucatán Peninsula (*Yucateco*), and Oaxaca and southern Mexico (*Oaxaqueño*). (The words in parentheses are the Mexican adjectives applied to these regions, similar to the American use of terms like "Southerner" or "Yankee"). These categories are fairly general, but they reflect areas of distinct cultural differences.

Central Mexico

The central part of the country is characterized by the coexistence of opposites that Bayless sees as both "the Spanish and the Aztec, the modern and the primitive." The area is incredibly fertile, producing vegetables and dairy products for much of the country.

West-Central Mexico

West-central Mexico is characterized by a blend of Spanish, Aztec, and regional traditions. This region includes the mountainous state of Michoacán. As the home of tequila and tacos, it is the region whose food is probably the most widely known outside of Mexico. Meat is extremely popular. West-central Mexico produces more corn than any other region, and many tropical fruits, including pineapples, bananas, papayas and coconuts, are also grown. In general terms, the food found along the coast is spicier, while that in the mountains is milder.

The Gulf Coast

The cuisine of the Gulf states is typically simple, and European culinary traditions have visibly influenced the spicing and garnishing here. Sugar cane, coconuts, plantains, and pineapples are all grown in the Gulf states. "Veracruz is the most strongly Spanish-influenced area of Mexico," says Zarela Martínez. "You see *bacalao* in white garlic sauce. You see a garlic-and-olive-oil sauce, which is strictly Mediterranean. They have a rice dish that is a cross between risotto and paella, as well as a dish that is a cross between an omelet and a tortilla with seafood. The soups of the region are nut-based, which you see in Spain, and *escabeche* is also from a Moorish/Spanish legacy. In Veracruz, very few spices are used, similar to Spain. What you do find is a lot of herbs and greens. Many dishes are finished with fresh oregano, mint, parsley, cilantro, or chives."

Northern Mexico

Open fires impart a smoky flavor to food in the north. Unlike the rest of the country, where pork and chicken are popular, beef is the most common meat. The northern states also use much more wheat, and their tortillas are made with wheat rather than corn. The food of the North is substantially less spicy (hot) than that of other regions.

"The spice palate varies depending on who settled in the region," explains Martínez. "The North is like a separate country, because it was very influenced by the United States as well as Spain."

The Yucatán Peninsula

The Yucatán Peninsula was the "seat" of Mayan culture, and retains arguably the strongest regional identity. Yucatán Mexicans are known for their diverse cuisine, but really the diversity lies in the preparations, not the ingredients, which are themselves fairly limited. Achiote (annatto) is used heavily, as are various spice pastes, known collectively as *recados*. People of the Yucatán have a long tradition of cooking pork or chicken rubbed with a *recado* and wrapped in banana leaves in a *pib* (an underground pit). Sour orange juice often flavors pork or fish, black beans are more commonly served than pinto beans.

Oaxaca and the South

Oaxacan cuisine is quite complex, influenced by the region's strong Indian tradition. Food is characteristically well seasoned and well spiced; allspice, cinnamon, cloves, and a wide variety of dried chiles are used. Sauces and stews are common preparations. The

region is known as "the land of seven moles," all of which are made with different combinations of dried chiles, except for *mole verde*, which is made with herbs and fresh chiles. The other six are *amarillo, chichilo, coloradito, colorado, mancha manteles,* and *negro.* Oaxacans also make extensive use of seeds, nuts, herbs, and chocolate.

Staples of Mexican Cuisine

DESPITE THE REGIONAL VARIATIONS, Mexican cuisine features some universals. "Mexican food is like barbecue," says Rick Bayless. "I grew up in my family's barbecue restaurant and I've realized that like barbecue, Mexican food is not afraid of acidity and spiciness and it includes earthy things like beans and potatoes. In both Mexican cuisine and barbecue, the meat used has smoky aspects—and it is not steak. Both use cuts that are cooked a really long time and take on a wonderful texture. But although Mexico's cuisine can be likened to barbecue, it is much more complex. In Mexican cuisine, I discovered the heights to which flavors could be taken."

Rick's wife and partner, Deann, admits that her love of Mexico came a little more slowly. "I had traveled a great deal growing up. I had lived in Taiwan for a year and traveled the Trans-Siberian Railroad; I'd visited Africa and India; and I'd been around the world with my family when I was fifteen. I loved travel and foreign things, but I'd never been to Mexico. At first, I didn't find Mexican cuisine that exotic, but I was really attracted to the deep, long-cooked flavors with their bright counterpoints. That is one of the great distinguishing things about the cuisine. A *mole* is not a *mole* to me without the raw onion and cilantro over the top. The bright counterpoint is such a big part of the food. I like the contrast of all of the acidic salsas and the pickled onions."

"Mexico, like so many countries, has a vegetable-based cuisine," says Zarela Martínez. "The diet is made up of corn, beans, and tortillas, with potatoes, tomatoes, and chiles filling out the list. Most people eat soups and stews with lots of vegetables. It is only on special occasions that they eat meat."

"Mexican flavors are very down to earth," add Susan Feniger and Mary Sue Milliken. "We stuffed some raw masa dough with poblano peppers and potatoes, fried it, topped it with roasted tomatoes and crema—and it was unbelievable. It is a cuisine where you can spend thirty-one cents on ingredients and make something great."

If you were to serve their dish with stewed black beans you would be presenting the staples of Mexican cuisine in one meal. Their dish also uses two techniques that give the cuisine its characteristic flavor: frying and roasting.

Chiles

In Mexico, you will see more than one hundred varieties of chiles!

—MARK MILLER

It is surprisingly easy to compare chiles with wine grapes. There are many varieties, and the soil and climate of a particular area dictates the difference in flavor. Each chile will vary in its intensity of flavor depending on when it was picked, its tannin level, and how it was stored. We could just as easily be describing cabernet grapes!

Chiles grow throughout the country, but some climates are better suited to them than others—Oaxaca can grow many chile varieties, while other areas can only grow a few. "There is very distinct regionality for some chiles," explains Zarela Martínez. "In Oaxaca, you will find *chilhuacle, chilcosle rojo*, and *negro*, as well as small fruity chiles like *serrano seco* and tons of wild chiles. In Veracruz, you will find smoked chiles. Chipotles and *moritas* are pickled, stuffed, fried, and made into paste. In the Yucatan, you will find mostly habanero. In the North, Mexicans use long green chiles, jalapeños, and serranos."

"When buying a particular chile, ask where it was grown," advises Mark Miller. "If you are in a market in Mexico, buy pasilla chiles from four or five different regions and see how regionality affects their flavor. You also want to sample the chiles at different price levels. You may think that the only reason a chile is more expensive is because it is bigger, but there is more to it. It is not just quantity you are buying. It is more expensive because it is thicker, plumper, and has less tannin."

Fresh and dried chiles are as different as fresh and dried herbs. They are not used in the same way and do not give the same results. Fresh chiles may be pickled or chopped into fresh salsas, while dried chiles are commonly used in sauces.

"I like fresh chiles, but I prefer dried chiles because they give more flavor," says Priscila Satkoff. "When a jalapeño is fresh, it is hot and herby. When it becomes a chipotle, it is sweet, spicy, and smoky. I like many chiles, but I will go with chipotle in a heartbeat. You can use them so many ways. I like them in eggs and salsa, or with fish."

The topic of chiles is immense, and it has spawned entire books. Our goal is to provide you with a "toolbox" of fresh and dried chiles that is easily accessible and will provide a wide variety of flavors to enhance your cooking.

Fresh Chiles

Fresh chiles can be stored for several days to several weeks in the refrigerator, loosely wrapped in paper towels and placed in an open paper bag. (Plastic bags cause the chiles to "sweat," which accelerates spoilage.) While some books suggest rinsing chiles prior to storage, Mark Miller cautions, "If you wash a fresh chile, you lose a lot of the flavor because you are washing away the oils. There is not enough emphasis on the importance of *not* washing them." To seed and devein a fresh chile, slice off the stem, cut it open, then cut away the seeds and veins. Be careful not to touch your eyes or nose when doing so, as the seeds and veins are packed with the chile's heat and can cause burns. In fact, when working with fresh chiles, you might consider using disposable plastic gloves. Remember to wash your hands well afterward.

Roasting chiles is no different from roasting bell peppers. Rub the outsides with a little oil, then roast them in your broiler or, for more fun, over the flame on your gas stove; rotate the chiles until they are entirely blackened but not burned through. Put them in a bowl, cover with plastic wrap, and let cool (be sure not to overcrowd them, or they will steam). When they have cooled, scrape off the blackened skin with your fingers or the back of a knife. Cut off the top and scrape out the inside, or slit open down the side and scrape out the seeds and veins.

We list some of the more common fresh chiles below.

	SIZE	COLOR	HEAT	USAGE
Anaheim	4 to 5 inches long/2 inches wide	Green or red	Mild to medium hot	rellenos, stews
Güero	4 to 5 inches long/2 inches wide	Yellow	Medium hot	sauces
Habanero	2 inches long/1 inch wide	Orange	Among the hottest of hot	salsas
Jalapeño	2 to 3 inches long	Green	Hot	salsas, soups
Poblano	3 to 5 inches long	Green to red-brown	Mild; almost fruity	rellenos
Serrano	2 to 3 inches long	Green to red	Medium to very hot	salsas
Thai	Up to 4 inches long/1 inch wide	Red to green	Medium to very hot	salsas

Dried Chiles

"Always use high-quality dried chiles," emphasize Susan Feniger and Mary Sue Milliken. Dried chiles are commonplace now, found next to other Mexican ingredients in supermarkets all around the country.

Some of the more common dried chiles are listed below.

	SIZE	COLOR	HEAT	USAGE
Ancho	3 to 5 inches long	Brown	Mild to medium hot	sauces, soups
de Árbol	2½ inches long	Bright red	Hot	soups, stews
Cascabel	1½ inches long	Reddish brown	Medium hot	salsas, soups
Chipotle	2 to 3 inches long	Brown	Hot; smoky flavor	sauces, soups
Guajillo	2 to 3 inches long	Reddish brown	Medium hot	sauces
Mulato	3 to 5 inches long	Brownish black	Medium hot	*moles*
Pasilla	5 to 7 inches long	Dark brownish black	Mild to medium hot	*moles*, with seafood

Dried chiles need to be cleaned, toasted, soaked, and patted dry before being used. Begin by removing their seeds and veins. For a small chile, simply roll it between your fingers, then tear off the stem and dump out the seeds. For a large chile, cut off the stem, slice it down the side, and split it open. Scrape out the seeds and cut away the veins.

Toasting dried chiles imparts a great deal of flavor. Simply put the chiles in a hot pan and press down on them for a few seconds, then flip them over and repeat. If the chiles smoke, you are using too hot a flame. (If they do smoke, be careful to avoid the fumes coming from them, because they can be very powerful.)

After chiles have been toasted, they must be rehydrated. Put them in hot water and let soak for about 30 minutes. Then drain and pat dry.

Chill with Your Chiles

"The worst things that North American cooks do to Mexican food is make it too hot," complains Zarela Martínez. "Then, you can't taste the flavor of the other ingredients, much less the chile. You need to be careful with chiles, for example, when cooking fish. A red sauce is going to overwhelm a piece of red snapper. But a red chile sauce works fine with tuna, because the fish is fatty and rich."

Corn

Many countries have one key staple for which they are known and on which much of their food is based, such as wheat in Italy and rice in Asia. For Mexico, it is corn. All parts of the corn plant are used. The kernels are treated as a fresh vegetable, dried and ground to make tortillas or masa for tamales, or soaked in brine for hominy, used in soups such as *posole*. The husks are saved for wrapping tamales. A by-product of Mexican corn is *cuitlacoche*, also known as "corn smut." A rich-tasting delicacy that looks like a black, squishy tar on the kernels, *cuitlacoche* is not corn, but a mushroom that grows on it.

"You can find almost every ingredient you see in Mexico in America except for corn," laments Zarela Martínez. "I have seen live worms [eaten in tacos in Mexico] in Queens, but not the corn. Even the masa in the U.S. is different. The corn here is grown for sweetness, while corn in Mexico is grown for starchiness. Starchy Mexican corn gives the dishes a chewiness. Since the corn is so sweet here, I do not prepare a lot of corn dishes in my restaurant, because the dishes would be so dramatically different from the dishes in Mexico."

Tortillas

Anywhere you go in Mexico, even in the fanciest restaurants, you will be served tortillas.
—PRISCILA SATKOFF

Tortillas are eaten throughout Mexico, with some regional variations. "Flour tortillas are only eaten in the north of Mexico," says Priscila Satkoff. "Corn tortillas are eaten in central and southern Mexico." The tortillas are far more varied than in the United States. "Some tortillas are made with plantains," says Zarela Martínez. "Some are pinched, while others puff up like Indian *poori*."

"My grandmother and I would make tortillas from scratch," reminisces Satkoff. "She wouldn't even use a tortilla press for the tortillas. A tortilla has a top, bottom, and skin. A good tortilla should be thin, with the first side down being the better side because it has a thinner skin.

"We make our own tortillas at the restaurant and the temperature of the *comal* [flat grill] is very important. If it is too cold, they stick; if it is too hot, they burn. In the movie *Like Water for Chocolate*, there is a scene where they throw a few drops of water on the *comal* to check the temperature. That was the way my grandmother taught me. If the water jumps, it is the perfect temperature. It is the technique I still use today!

SETTING UP YOUR MEXICAN KITCHEN

WHEN you are ready to create the complex and deep flavors of authentic Mexican food, where do you start?

"Don't be afraid," Priscila Satkoff says reassuringly. "Start with one serrano chile. Next time, you might buy two. Use a little epazote [a pungent herb] at the end of cooking your beans. Next time, you might add more chile and epazote. Just start slow. There are so many ingredients to play with."

"People will say their food doesn't taste like mine," says Zarela Martínez. "Then, I'll find out that they didn't use canela [true cinnamon], or they poached their seafood or chicken in water. I poach seafood in fish stock and chicken in chicken stock."

ZARELA MARTÍNEZ'S TOP TEN INGREDIENTS

1. **CANELA, CLOVE AND CUMIN:** These three spices are used together all the time. One would use one part each canela, cumin, and clove.

2. **MEXICAN OREGANO:** a little stronger than the European type.

3. **FRESH HERBS:** thyme, bay leaf, marjoram, parsley, cilantro, and mint.

4. **A SMALL HOT CHILE.**

5. **WHITE ONION:** used in countless dishes, cooked and/or raw as a garnish.

6. **SMALL GARLIC:** garlic in Mexico is picked very young. You may see a recipe that calls for a hundred cloves. The large garlic in the United States has less flavor.

"The person who makes our tortillas now makes them perfectly, but she did not at first. In the beginning, they would be too thick, or overcooked or undercooked. I had to teach her how to test the *comal* to see if the water jumps.

"To me, a packaged tortilla is dry," she continues. "To make a great tortilla, you have to use fresh corn dough. The masa harina flour you buy in the store is not as good. We have factories in Chicago that make fresh masa dough and we get deliveries every day. When the dough is coarse, it is used for tamales. When the dough is ground fine, it is for tortillas. I only use a little water and salt in the tortilla dough. You work it until it becomes soft, smooth, and takes on a texture that is almost light."

7. **MASA HARINA:** ground corn dough, for making tortilla and tamale and other doughs.

8. **HOMEMADE LARD:** there is a huge difference in quality and flavor between this and commercial versions.

9. **ACIDS:** lime juice and vinegar—I use a Swiss vinegar called Kressi; in Mexico, vinegars are made at home and are much milder. If I use an American vinegar, I use half as much.

10. **OLIVE OIL:** for Veracruz cooking.

MARY SUE MILLIKEN AND SUSAN FENIGER'S TOP TEN INGREDIENTS

ONCE you learn how to work with the basic ingredients, you can pick up any book and go."

1. **DRIED CHILES.**

2. **FRESH CHILES.**

3. **ACHIOTE:** a dark red seed also known as annatto.

4. **MASA AND TORTILLAS.**

5. **BEANS:** pinto, black, and red, as well as lentils; beans are a huge part of the Mexican kitchen.

6. **CITRUS:** bitter oranges, limes, and lemons.

7. **FIDEO NOODLES:** these get toasted.

8. **CONDENSED MILK:** we recommend making it from scratch (see page 305).

9. **TAMARIND.**

10. **CHEESE:** our favorites are Manchego, panella, and cotija.

Beans

Beans, *frijoles,* are another staple throughout Mexico. They are typically prepared with lard for more flavor. In general terms, pinto beans are popular in the north, while black beans are more common in the south. Fried beans most often accompany masa-based snacks, and soupier beans are served at the main meal of the day.

Beans are best cooked in *ollas,* clay pots traditionally used for this purpose. Rick Bayless notes that cooking beans in clay *ollas* gives them an earthy flavor that metal pots cannot impart.

Sauces—Salsa and *Mole*

Salsa and *mole* are both considered sauces in Mexican cuisine. A salsa can be cooked or raw. A *mole,* on the other hand, is always cooked, and often contains ingredients not found in salsa, such as nuts and seeds, and—as in the dish *mole poblano*—chocolate.

Salsa

"Much of the food is finished with a salsa of some sort," say Susan Feniger and Mary Sue Milliken. "So you'll have a rich dish with a fresh salsa on top, or a hot dish finished with something cold. The flavors of Latin food are very simple, but great."

A salsa of chiles, garlic, and tomato is a cornerstone of Mexican cooking, one that Rick Bayless, among others, cites as a classic Mexican combination of flavors. The flavor combo does change from region to region, with different acids like lime or other fruits, instead of vinegar, giving it its local flair.

"*Salsa de molcajete* is a salsa made with roast tomatoes that is also emblematic of Mexican cuisine," Rick Bayless points out. "This salsa teaches you to dry-roast ingredients—a technique that most non-Mexican people aren't familiar with. The salsa is made with roasted garlic, roasted tomatoes, and roasted green chiles, but it opens you to a whole host of new ingredients and textures. You can use different tomatoes, lightly or heavily roasted, and you can experiment with chiles from serrano to habanero to jalapeño."

"The first thing I learned how to make was salsa," says Deann Bayless. "It was exciting because I learned that through approaching it with different techniques, I could make it all these different ways. I could use tomatoes raw, roasted a little, roasted until they were charred, or roasted until they were completely cooked."

Adds Rick Bayless, "If you make one salsa in a food processor and another in a stone mortar and pestle, you will realize what a huge difference the stone mortar makes. In the mortar, you'll find you have a communion with the ingredients that you've never had before. This dish shows the first step to the heart of the cuisine. If I have a knife, a mortar, a pestle, and a pan, I can make great food!"

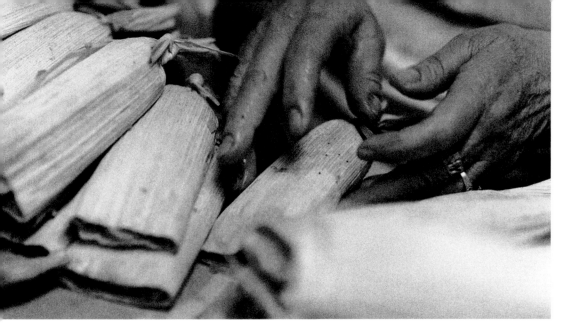

Mole

Moles, which, according to Rick Bayless, are Mexico's national dish, are sauces with strong native roots. "These sauces are almost always served on special occasions. *Moles*, as well as *pipiáns*, similar sauces in that they are made with chiles and thickened with nuts, are the centerpieces of many dishes," says Zarela Martínez. "I categorize both *mole* and *pipián* as main-dish sauces. The sauce *is* the dish."

"Making a *mole* was a ritual for my grandmother," says Priscila Satkoff. "We would start at seven in the morning and finish at six in the evening. We would do it all by hand. She did not have a blender, so everything would be ground in the *metate* [stone mortar]. By the end of the day, my back would be so sore! To be honest, I use a blender now. I cook for a hundred or more people a day!"

Time to Eat

The Mexicans have a saying, "Alone, one cannot share life. Others must be there." That is a very Mexican attitude. —**ZARELA MARTÍNEZ**

"THE ROLE OF FOOD in Mexican culture is pretty astonishing," says Rick Bayless. "I have been with people making food that was not all that great, yet in the midst of the party, and the serving of it with love, the food's taste was transcended. That is difficult to explain to people, and one of the great wonders of food."

"If you visit a village as an expected guest, you will be offered one of two things: *mole* or *barbacoa* [barbecue], whether it's lamb, pork, or beef," says Zarela Martínez. "*Mole* is labor-intensive and *barbacoa* is expensive. When you are going to honor your guest, you make everything by hand—a philosophy I use when I entertain at home, no matter what kind of food I am serving."

To live in Mexico is to live with the possibility of it always being mealtime: one meal or another is appropriate at almost any time of day. But few people eat every meal, and not all meals are large. Breakfast, *desayuno*, typically consists of coffee and a roll or sweet tamale. A midmorning snack, or *almuerzo*, is popular: it is usually something like *menudo* (tripe soup) or *chilaquiles* (simmered tortilla casseroles). The midday meal, or *comida*, is the largest. Usually eaten at about 2 P.M. it typically starts with soup, followed by a rice course, a meat course, beans, vegetables, and then a dessert of fruit.

Afternoon tea, *merienda*, typically consists of something sweet, like fruit or pastry. The late-night supper, or *cena*, is usually something light like soup or bite-sized foods.

Street foods are staples in Mexico, and the typical choices are more elevated than the American pretzel or hot dog. Chilaquiles, empanadas, enchiladas, soup, and tacos are all popular street-stall snacks. Known collectively as *antojitos*, these snacks will on some occasions become a meal-on-the-run.

Techniques of the Mexican Kitchen

Make sure to have textural contrast. It is very important in Mexican cuisine.
—SUSAN FENIGER AND MARY SUE MILLIKEN

As mentioned earlier, roasting and frying are pillars of Mexican cooking. Of course there are other techniques that are also important to achieving the harmony of flavors that is Mexican cuisine. But despite finding techniques you may be familiar with, the Mexican kitchen has its own twists and turns on how to achieve the ultimate balance, textures, and flavors.

"My flavors have gotten simpler because I have spent years cooking and thinking about Mexican food," says Rick Bayless. "I see the thrust of the cuisine as being about roasting vegetables, pureeing them and putting them into sauces, then cooking them in a way that brings them all together. That is the essence of the cuisine."

"I use many newer techniques today, but some I haven't changed," states Priscila Satkoff. "Roasting is a very important technique, especially for chiles. Roasting brings out so much flavor. My grandmother would roast different types of seeds like sesame,

A MEXICAN MEAL FOR FIRST-TIMERS

SUSAN FENIGER AND MARY SUE MILLIKEN

This menu is perfect for a fun celebration. We like casual-style eating and plan our menus that way. Mexican food lends itself to party food. We have lots of large parties at our restaurant! Our place is not Italian romantic. Come here for fun!

Appetizers

- Make some salsas. Everybody loves salsa! Salsa is the base for so many other things. With salsa on hand, you can also make red rice, and you have the base for tortilla soup. When you make a chicken soup, you can add some of your great smoky chipotle salsa. It's a great way to enjoy those flavors. (See Red Tomato Salsa, page 302.)

- Guacamole made with roasted tomatillos is great.

- Make some snack foods, such as tortillas and quesadillas, to go with the guacamole.

- Ceviche is another easy dish. It really impresses people because they think it is hard, but all you need is good fish.

Snack food is great with margaritas, so you don't get too loaded too fast.

Sopas or tamales require some effort, but they are fun and festive!

Entrée

Mexican food, like Chinese cuisine, is great for communal eating.

Carnitas are a great party food (see page 301). We did the food for the movie *Tortilla Soup,* and we made carnitas for it. Make a huge pot, then bring it to the table garnished with fresh lime and cilantro. Have some salsas, guacamole, rice, beans, and fresh tortillas on the table. Then let everybody dive in family-style. Or make a seafood pozole or stew. These are easy and are also hearty.

Dessert

Tres leches (a cake made with three different milks) and flan (see the recipe on page 304) are traditional. We have also done candied pumpkin with vanilla ice cream.

pumpkin, or chile. When she would roast chiles and chile seeds, you could not breathe in her kitchen! The chile seeds were used in a dish called *pipián*, which I still prepare a few times a year in the restaurant."

Grinding is another essential technique in giving Mexican cuisine its depth. Two tools have traditionally been used for this: the *metate* and the *molcajete*. A *metate* is a flat slab of rock on which ingredients, such as nuts, seeds, and cacao beans, are crushed with a hand-rolled pin. A *molcajete* is a stone mortar, with a pestle, used to crush spices and vegetables. Today, blenders and food processors are widely used for these jobs, but the results are not the same. Electric appliances chop food into small bits, but they can't achieve the same smooth pastes that *metates* and *molcajetes* can.

Asar, toasting or dry-roasting, is widely used. Chiles, garlic, meats, tomatoes, and tomatillos, as well as masa in its many forms, are cooked on a hot, dry surface, usually iron or clay. The technique, which intensifies flavors and adds smokiness, is believed to date back to the Aztecs. (The Aztecs didn't have much cooking oil or grease, as they lacked olives, cows, chickens, and pigs before the Spanish arrived.)

Quickly sautéing or searing sauce ingredients is common. Pureed chiles and/or tomatoes are cooked in hot fat to concentrate their flavors. And boiling—or, more often, a long, slow simmer—is employed to soften and/or cook beans, corn, and meats.

One of the major differences between Mexican and European cuisines is the use of stock. "We don't use French cooking stocks in Mexico. We use light broths," points out Satkoff. "In Mexican cooking, you never use a reduced meat stock. You would use the broth from cooking a chicken. Maybe you would enrich it with some sautéed tomato, onion, garlic, and chile. What you want, though, is a lively flavor."

What to Drink with a Mexican Meal

IN MEXICO, DRINKING WINE with everyday food is not all that common. "Mexicans more often pair their food with beer, margaritas, or sweet soft drinks," says Rick Bayless. "We don't have a taste for Mexican sodas, and we hate Corona beer!" say Susan Feniger and Mary Sue Milliken. "We do like Pacifico, Bohemia, and Negro Modella beers. The last is especially good served with ice, lime, and salt."

But Zarela Martínez loves wine with Mexican food. "In Mexican households, you do drink wine," she points out. "While you would drink beer with casual fare like carnitas or *carne asada* [grilled steak], I can't imagine *mole* with a beer. In fact, there is a great resurgence in Mexican wine making. I recommend Château Camou. They developed a blanc de blancs that is similar to a viognier. Monte Xanic is a trail-blazing wine maker.

The wines are very expensive in Mexico. Cetto is also very good. All three wines are in the French style, produced with French wine makers."

At Salpicón, Priscila Satkoff's husband and partner Vincent is also the restaurant's sommelier. "He spent a great deal of time choosing wine that would not fight with the chiles in our food," she says. "This food needs fruity, light-bodied, low-tannic wines. We tried countless Cabernets, because if you are serving venison it is a logical match—until you taste the sauce. Then, the wine becomes terrible. We do like Pinot Noirs and Rieslings. We must be onto something, because we won a *Wine Spectator* award. It is encouraging, because people are not just looking to drink tequila and beer anymore."

Passing on the Traditions

LEARNING A CUISINE IS A precious thing, and learning from your grandmother may be the ultimate way. However, Priscila Satkoff, who worked at Frontera Grill for seven years before opening her own restaurant, had the benefit of both her grandmother *and* Rick Bayless. "I was inspired by my grandmother when it comes to authentic Mexican food," she says. "When I was older, I would go back to Mexico, sit next to her, and have her recite her recipes. She didn't cook with anything written down and had no quantities. At least now I have the basic ingredients!"

Bayless himself pursued a course of learning that honored the traditions of the families who shared their recipes with him. "When you taste a great soup or *mole*, you realize that time-honored techniques have been employed to make it," says Bayless. "I have the advantage of not having a Mexican grandmother—so I can learn from everyone's grandmothers! Better yet, I can distill the best of all of them. Because food is so tied to family in Mexico, Mexican cooks are dedicated to the recipes that have been passed down in their family, good or bad. When someone teaches me that *this* is the way it is done, and there is no other, I have great respect for that," he says. "I realize, too, though, that for tradition's sake they may be holding onto something in their hearts with great sacredness."

"During our first trip to Mexico, we stayed with the family of a kid who worked in our restaurant," recall Susan Feniger and Mary Sue Milliken. "We would go to the market every morning with the family cook, eating in the little stalls, and shop for all this great food. The cook thought we were nuts!

"At night, the parents would take us to the best fancy 'continental' restaurants, and the food would be terrible. It was with the cook that we were learning. She would translate for us what everybody was doing in the market. Then we would come back with a truckload of food. Anything we didn't understand, we would buy. We don't speak much Spanish except for the swearing we learn in our restaurants' kitchens, but somehow we communicated enough that she would just turn it loose and start cooking. We would watch everything she did and take notes. It was so fun, and we got the best overview of Mexican food. By the end of the week, the parents had stopped taking us out."

"It is important to try to learn from people who can show you the techniques," adds Milliken. "I know how many pitfalls there are in making a dish, so I don't want to prepare it unless someone learned it from their grandmother or the equivalent and has made it a hundred and fifty times." But, she points out, "you don't have to just learn from the older generation. You can't always find that old sage woman or man. You can find people who are passionate about food of any age. I take my learning where I can get it."

Tradition versus Innovation

Mexican was the original fusion food. Things changed once Spain and Mexico started exchanging ingredients. Why should Mexican food have to remain stagnant?

—ZARELA MARTÍNEZ

"THE SCHOLAR JEFFREY PILCHER looked at cookbooks about Mexico, and found that North Americans are traditionalists and want to save this or that, which is an incredible contribution," relates Martínez. "However, native-born Mexicans want to play with the ingredients. In fact, I actually got some resistance from the staff at The Culinary Institute of America when I first started teaching there because I did things a little differently."

There is, as we emphasize throughout this book, room for both approaches. "Without Rick Bayless, other authentic Mexican restaurants and mine would not exist," says Priscila Satkoff. "Rick was the pioneer who opened our eyes and the doors to Mexican food. I once asked him about an herb from Oaxaca. He did not answer with just one or two words. He knew where it grew, how it was grown, in what season, the authentic name, and more! He may be an American, but his mission, like mine, is to educate people about the flavors of Mexico."

However, it's not everybody's approach to educate. "We are not anthropologists, and we don't take a scholarly approach to Mexican cooking like Rick Bayless does," explains Susan Feniger. "We are interested in cooking at more of a gut level," emphasizes Mary Sue Milliken. "We love the regions of Oaxaca and Mérida especially, and that is the food that influences us, but we are not concerned with making a perfectly tradi-

tional Oaxacan dish. We just want the food to taste wonderful." "We filter in all the information, let it simmer and percolate, then go in the kitchen and cook," adds Feniger. "What results is a little fusion of all the experiences we've had."

And while their restaurants do serve authentic Mexican dishes, Feniger and Milliken don't limit themselves to only food that is strictly authentic. "Our dishes are authentic in that they are inspired by Mexico; however, our ingredients will be different," Milliken explains. In general, though, Feniger and Milliken don't mix cultures. "However, we may use a French technique or some other technique if it will elevate the dish a little," says Feniger. "When we were in Mexico, we were taught to make *pozole* with a pork tenderloin that had been boiled to hell, which did not taste that great. At the time we smiled, but when we got home, we made the dish with braised pork butt instead, which was great.

"When we modify a dish," Feniger continues, "we always stress to our cooks to keep it as Latin as possible. We always want some traditional dishes, to be true to what grandmothers have done forever. We also want our chef to work with the best ingredients in season and to cook from a Latin starting point, even if it's poblano-chile mashed potatoes with chopped tomatillo salsa."

"I served on a panel on the subject of authenticity with Robert Del Grande of Café Annie," says Milliken, "and I don't define authentic as 'traditional and old-fashioned.' Authentic to me means that something is true to the feeling and culture and inspiration you experience when you are in Mexico. It does not have to be old to be authentic."

"When I first opened my restaurant, I was criticized by people in Mexico because I was playing with ingredients and doing a more contemporary version of Mexican food," says Zarela Martínez. "But certain French techniques greatly improve the quality of Mexican food. Many times in Mexico, people overcook fish. Or *mole* is served with boiled pork—and in America, people just don't like boiled pork. So, incorporating some new techniques is very good for the cuisine.

"At Zarela, my favorite dish is duck with *mole*. In Mexico, they would boil the duck. Here, we roast it. But the sauce—not the cooking technique—is traditional. There is a dish from Veracruz in which boiled pork is paired with pumpkin that has been added into the boiling liquid. In our version, we add an extra dimension by frying the pork, which gives the dish more depth. I also like to take a local fish from here in the U.S. and combine it with a sauce from Mexico. Once again, the fish would be boiled in Mexico. Here, we grill or sauté it.

"I don't see this as experimentation. I see this as evolution," she asserts. "Why should we boil things to death just because Mexicans traditionally did—because they didn't have refrigeration?"

In the end, finding the right line to walk between authenticity and experimentation is a matter of personal taste. "There are times when my cooks cut across boundaries that I would never cut across," admits Rick Bayless. "It is important to always be able to identify our food as reminiscent of Mexican cooking. However, I do believe that all cuisines have to innovate, or they will die."

Nach Waxman's Recommended Reading on Mexican Cooking

My personal pick for an overall Mexican cookbook is Rick Bayless's first book, **Authentic Mexican.** He's done a good job with his others, but this book is a standout, with terrific notes, sidebars, and background on ingredients and methods.

To understand the "classical" cuisine of Mexico, as contrasted with authentic "home cooking," turn to Diana Kennedy's **The Essential Cuisines of Mexico,** which draws on her first three books, **The Cuisines of Mexico, Mexican Regional Cooking,** and **The Tortilla Book.** This work as well as Kennedy's later **From My Mexican Kitchen: Techniques and Ingredients** are very sound, and the newer book avoids some of the more uncompromising attitudes of her earlier work. On the other hand, her admonishments that without procuring a particular obscure ingredient one should abandon one's effort altogether can be fearsomely forbidding!

Patricia Quintana, a fine chef, has done some nice, even gorgeous, books on Mexican cuisine, including **The Taste of Mexico.**

Books on regional Mexican cuisines are starting to emerge, such as Zarela Martínez's **The Food and Life of Oaxaca: Traditional Recipes from Mexico's Heart,** and there have also been some very bright, entertaining north-of-the-border efforts, such as Mary Sue Milliken and Susan Feniger's **Mesa Mexicana.**

Tacos de Puerco y Papas al Guajillo
Guajillo-Spiked Pork-and-Potato Tacos

8 medium (2 ounces total) guajillo chiles, seeded, and torn into flat pieces

4 cups water

12 ounces (4 to 6 plum or 2 medium-small round) ripe tomatoes, roughly chopped, or one 15-ounce can good-quality whole tomatoes in juice, drained

3 large garlic cloves, roughly chopped

1½ tablespoons vegetable oil or rich-tasting pork lard

1 pound lean boneless pork (preferably from the shoulder), cut into ½-inch cubes

Salt

4 medium (about 1 pound total) boiling potatoes, such as red-skins, cut into ½-inch cubes

3 tablespoons chopped fresh cilantro

12 to 16 warm fresh corn tortillas

MAKES ABOUT 4 CUPS FILLING FOR 12 TO 16 TACOS, SERVING 4 AS A CASUAL MEAL

FOR THE CHILE SAUCE BASE

TOAST THE CHILE PIECES a few at a time in a dry heavy skillet or on a griddle heated over medium, pressing them flat against the hot surface with a metal spatula until they are aromatic, about 10 seconds per side. (If the heat is right, you'll hear a slight crackle when you press them down, but you shouldn't see more than the slightest wisp of smoke; the inside surface of the chiles should look noticeably lighter.) In a bowl, rehydrate the chiles for 20 minutes in hot tap water to cover; place a small plate on top to keep the chiles submerged.

USE A PAIR OF TONGS to transfer the rehyrated chiles to a food processor or blender. Measure in 1 cup water, add the tomatoes and garlic, and process to a smooth puree. Leave in the food processor or blend while you brown the meat.

FOR THE FILLING

IN A MEDIUM (3- to 4-quart) pot (preferably a Dutch oven or a Mexican cazuela), heat the oil over medium-high heat. When the oil is quite hot, add the pork in a single layer (do this in batches if necessary; don't crowd the pan or the meat will not brown nicely). Cook, turning the pieces, until richly browned all over, about 10 minutes. If working in batches, transfer the browned pork to a plate while you brown the rest; when all the meat is browned, return all the pork to the pot. Push the chile puree through a medium-mesh strainer directly into the pot. Cook, stirring frequently, until the sauce mixture is as thick as tomato paste, 6 to 8 minutes.

STIR IN THE REMAINING 3 cups water and 1 teaspoon salt. Partially cover and simmer over medium-low heat, stirring often, for 20 minutes. Stir in the potatoes. Partially cover and cook, stirring often, until the potatoes and meat are both thoroughly tender but not falling apart, usually 20 to 30 minutes more. By that time, the sauce should have thickened to the consistency of canned tomato sauce—if it is too thick, add a little water; if too thin, cook uncovered to reduce. Taste and adjust the seasoning with salt if necessary.

TO SERVE, SCOOP the hot pork-and-potato mixture into a serving bowl, sprinkle with the chopped cilantro, and carry to the table, along with the warm tortillas.

Rick and Deann Bayless

Tacos de Pollo en Salsa Verde
Tacos of Tomatillo Chicken with Greens and Fresh Cheese

FOR THE SIMMERED TOMATILLO-SERRANO SAUCE (MAKES 1¼ CUPS)

8 ounces (5 to 6 medium) tomatillos, husked and rinsed

Serrano chiles to taste (roughly 2), stemmed

1½ tablespoons olive or vegetable oil

½ medium white onion, roughly chopped

1 garlic clove, roughly chopped

1 cup chicken stock

3 tablespoons roughly chopped fresh cilantro

¼ to ½ teaspoon salt, depending on the saltiness of the stock

12 corn tortillas (plus a few extra, in case some break)

2 cups firmly packed sliced chard leaves, lamb's quarters, sliced amaranth greens, purslane (remove thick bottom stems), or spinach (all pieces should be about ½ inch wide and no more than 2 inches long)

1⅓ cups coarsely shredded cooked chicken (you'll need, for instance, 1 very large chicken breast for this amount)

FOR THE TOMATILLO-SERRANO SAUCE

ROAST THE TOMATILLOS and chiles on a baking sheet 4 inches below a very hot broiler until blackened and soft on one side, 5 to 6 minutes, then turn them over and roast the other side. Transfer (including all the juices) to a food processor or a blender.

HEAT 1 TABLESPOON of the oil in a large (10- to 12-inch) heavy skillet over medium. Add the onion and cook, stirring regularly, until deep golden, about 8 minutes. Stir in the garlic and cook for 1 minute, then scrape into the food processor or blender. Process to a medium-coarse puree.

HEAT THE REMAINING ½ tablespoon oil in the skillet over medium-high. Add the puree all at once and stir for about 5 minutes, until noticeably darker and thick. Stir in the stock, partially cover, and simmer over medium-low for 10 minutes. (The sauce will be a little soupy.) Stir in the cilantro and generously season with salt.

TO FINISH THE DISH, set up a steamer (a vegetable steamer in a large saucepan filled with ½ inch of water works well); heat to a boil. Wrap the tortillas in a heavy kitchen towel, lay in the steamer, and cover with a tight lid. Boil 1 minute, then turn off the heat and let stand, without opening the steamer, for 15 minutes.

½ to ¾ cup crumbled
Mexican *queso fresco* or
pressed salted farmer's
cheese

MAKES ABOUT 3 CUPS FILLING,
FOR 12 TACOS

BRING THE SAUCE to a boil and add the greens.
When the mixture returns to a boil, stir in the
cooked chicken and simmer until the greens are
done (lamb's quarters will take the longest, about
5 minutes; spinach the least amount of time,
about 2 minutes.) Taste and season with additional salt if necessary.

THE MOMENT YOU'RE ready to serve, make the tacos one at a time,
spooning a portion of the filling into a warm tortilla, sprinkling on
cheese, and folding it over. As with all tacos, these are informal
morsels, intended to be filled, folded, and eaten on the spot.

Guacamole de Chile Poblano Asado
Roasted Poblano Guacamole with Garlic and Parsley

2 medium (about 6 ounces total) poblano chiles

6 ounces (1 medium round or 2 plum) ripe tomatoes

2 garlic cloves, unpeeled

3 tablespoons chopped fresh flat-leaf parsley

3 medium-large (about 1¼ pounds total) ripe avocados

Salt

1 to 2 tablespoons fresh lime juice

2 tablespoons finely crumbled Mexican *queso añejo* or other dry grating cheese, such as Pecorino Romano or Parmigiano-Reggiano

A few slices of fresh radish for garnish

MAKES 2½ CUPS; SERVES 6 AS AN APPETIZER, 8 TO 10 AS A NIBBLE

LAY THE POBLANOS, tomatoes, and garlic on a baking sheet and set 4 inches below a very hot broiler. Roast, turning every couple of minutes, until the chiles and tomatoes are soft, blistered, and blackened in spots and the garlic is soft, 12 to 13 minutes total. Place the chiles in a bowl, cover with a towel, and let stand 5 minutes, then wipe off the blackened skin. Pull out the stems, seed pods, and seeds; rinse quickly to remove any stray seeds and bits of char.

WHEN THE TOMATOES are cool, peel off and discard their skins. Slip the papery skins off the garlic. In a mortar and pestle or with a food processor, make a coarse puree of the roasted garlic and poblanos (with both mortar and processor, it's best to start with the garlic, then add the poblanos). Place in a large bowl. Chop the tomatoes and add to the poblano mixture, along with the parsley.

CUT THE AVOCADOS lengthwise in half around the pit, twist the halves apart, and remove the pits. Scoop out the flesh into the bowl with the chiles. Using a potato masher or the back of a large spoon, coarsely mash everything together. Taste and season with salt, usually a scant teaspoon, then add enough lime juice to enliven all the flavors. Cover with plastic wrap, placing it directly on the surface, and refrigerate until you're ready to eat.

TO SERVE, SCOOP into a decorative bowl or Mexican mortar, sprinkle with the *queso añejo,* and stud with radish slices.

Carnitas Norteñas

2 pounds boneless pork shoulder or butt, cut into 2-inch cubes

Salt and freshly ground black pepper

1½ pounds lard, pork fat, or vegetable shortening

1 medium red onion, diced

1 bunch trimmed and chopped (½ cup) cilantro

5 serrano chiles, chopped

3 avocados, pitted, peeled, and mashed

Corn tortillas, warmed

SERVES 6

Pork chunks slowly simmered in fat develop a heightened pork flavor and silky-smooth texture. Carnitas are delicious in tacos or burritos, with spicy salsa.

GENEROUSLY SEASON the pork all over with salt and pepper. Melt the lard in a large deep saucepan or Dutch oven over medium heat. Add the meat and simmer, uncovered, over medium-low heat for 1 hour and 15 minutes, or until fork-tender. With a slotted spoon, transfer the pork to a cutting board. (The fat can be refrigerated for future use.)

PREHEAT THE OVEN to 400 degrees F.

WHEN THE PORK is cool enough to handle, shred it by hand or with two forks.

IN A BOWL, toss the pork with the onion, cilantro, and chiles. Transfer to a casserole, cover tightly, and bake until heated through, about 15 minutes. Serve hot, with the mashed avocados, corn tortillas, and Red Tomato Salsa (page 302).

301

Mexico

Red Tomato Salsa

1 tablespoon vegetable oil

½ medium onion, thinly sliced

2 cups diced canned Italian plum tomatoes

½ cup tomato juice

1 garlic clove, peeled

1 small jalapeño chile, stemmed, seeded if desired

1 teaspoon salt

MAKES 3 CUPS

HEAT THE VEGETABLE OIL in a medium skillet over medium heat. Cook the onion until soft, about 10 minutes. Transfer to a food processor or a blender.

ADD THE REMAINING ingredients except the salt, in batches if you are using a blender, and puree until smooth. Pass through a medium strainer, pressing with a spatula or wooden spoon to push through as much pulp as possible.

POUR THE PUREE into a saucepan, and add the salt. Bring to a boil, reduce to a simmer, and cook, uncovered, 20 minutes. Adjust the seasonings. Set aside to cool for table salsa, or use warm for rice or chilaquiles. (The salsa can be stored in the refrigerator for 2 to 3 days or in the freezer for weeks.)

Vegetarian Red Bean Stew

2 cups dried red beans, rinsed and picked over

8 cups water

⅓ cup olive oil

1½ medium white onions, diced

2 teaspoons salt

½ teaspoon freshly ground black pepper

4 garlic cloves, crushed

2 ancho chiles, wiped clean, stemmed, seeded, and lightly toasted (see Note)

2 medium parsnips, peeled and cut into ½-inch chunks

2 medium carrots, peeled and cut into ½-inch chunks

2 celery stalks, peeled and cut into ½-inch chunks

1 medium zucchini, trimmed and cut into ½-inch chunks

1 medium yellow squash, trimmed and cut into ½-inch chunks

SERVES 4 TO 6

PLACE THE BEANS AND WATER in a saucepan and bring to a boil. Cover, reduce to a simmer, and cook until the beans are creamy, not powdery, 45 to 60 minutes. Remove from the heat; set aside.

HEAT THE OLIVE OIL in a large stockpot or Dutch oven over medium heat. Cook the onions with 1 teaspoon of the salt and the black pepper until golden, 10 to 15 minutes. Add the garlic, reduce the heat, and cook, stirring frequently, until fragrant.

POUR THE RED BEANS, with their liquid, into the stockpot, and add the toasted anchos, parsnips, and carrots. Turn the heat up to medium and cook at a low boil for 10 minutes. Add the remaining vegetables and 1 teaspoon salt. Simmer until all the vegetables are soft, about 15 minutes longer. Remove and discard any chile skin that floats to the top. Ladle into large bowls and serve hot, with a dollop of salsa.

Note
Dried chiles such as anchos are lightly toasted just to soften and develop flavor, never to blacken. Place over a low gas flame or on the grill and heat for a few seconds on each side, just until soft.

303

Mexico

Vanilla Flan

FOR THE CARAMEL

2 cups sugar

1¼ cups water

6 large eggs

6 large egg yolks

½ cup sugar

2 teaspoons pure vanilla extract

2 cups half-and-half

1 recipe Homemade Condensed Milk (recipe follows)

1 vanilla bean

SERVES 8 TO 10

FOR THE CARAMEL

HAVE READY A 9-INCH round cake pan. Combine the sugar and ½ cup of the water in a medium saucepan. Use a pastry brush dipped in cold water to wash down any sugar granules from the sides of the pan. Cook over medium heat, swirling the pan occasionally, until the mixture is dark brown and has a distinctive fragrance of caramel, 10 to 15 minutes. Pour enough of the caramel into a the cake pan to coat the bottom and sides, swirling to coat evenly. Set aside.

SLOWLY AND CAREFULLY ADD the remaining ¾ cup water to the caramel in the saucepan. Bring to a boil and cook over medium heat until the caramel dissolves, about 5 minutes; occasionally stir and brush down the sides with the pastry brush dipped in cold water to prevent crystallization. Set this caramel sauce aside to cool, then chill until serving time.

PREHEAT THE OVEN to 325 degrees F.

IN A LARGE BOWL, gently whisk together the eggs, egg yolks, sugar, vanilla extract, and half-and-half, without incorporating any air.

POUR THE CONDENSED MILK into a saucepan. Split the vanilla bean lengthwise and, using the tip of a paring knife, scrape the black seeds into the milk. Add the bean and bring to a boil. Gradually pour the hot milk into the egg mixture, whisking constantly. Pass through a strainer into the caramel-coated cake pan. Place inside a large roasting pan and pour in hot tap water to come halfway up the sides of the cake pan.

BAKE FOR 1 HOUR AND 10 minutes, or until the center just feels firm when pressed. Set aside to cool in the pan of water, then remove from the water bath, cover with plastic wrap, and refrigerate for at least 6 hours, or overnight.

TO SERVE, RUN A KNIFE along the inside of the pan and gently press the center of the bottom to loosen the flan. Cover with a platter, invert, and lift off the pan. Any excess caramel in the cake pan can be added to the caramel sauce. Cut into wedges and serve with the cold caramel sauce.

Homemade Condensed Milk

6 cups nonfat milk

5 tablespoons sugar

MAKES 3 CUPS

POUR THE MILK into a medium heavy saucepan and bring to a boil. Reduce to a simmer and cook for 45 minutes, stirring occasionally.

STIR IN THE SUGAR and continue simmering for 10 to 15 minutes, or until reduced to 3 cups. Strain. (The condensed milk can be refrigerated for up to a week.)

Manchamanteles de Pato
Roasted Duck with Spicy Fruit Sauce

One 5-pound duck

Salt and freshly ground black pepper

1 medium carrot, peeled and cut into thirds

1 small onion, unpeeled

2 garlic cloves, unpeeled

6 bay leaves

1 true Ceylon cinnamon stick (canela), or 1 regular cinnamon stick

FOR THE MANCHAMAN-TELES SAUCE

2 tablespoons vegetable oil

1 medium onion, sliced into thin half-moons

2 large garlic cloves, minced

One 28-ounce can whole tomatoes, with their juice

2 bay leaves

1 to 2 teaspoons salt, to taste

½ to 1 teaspoon freshly ground black pepper, to taste

¼ to ⅓ teaspoon ground cloves

1½ teaspoons ground true Ceylon cinnamon or ½ teaspoon ground regular cinnamon

1 teaspoon ground cumin

1 teaspoon dried Mexican oregano, crumbled

¾ cup pitted prunes, whole or sliced

½ cup dried apricots, sliced

½ cup golden raisins

PREHEAT THE OVEN to 400 degrees F.

WITH A SHARP FORK, prick the duck all over. Salt and pepper the cavity and stuff with the carrot, onion, garlic, bay leaves, and cinnamon stick. Place on a rack in a heavy-duty roasting pan and roast for 2 hours. Drain off the fat as it accumulates.

MEANWHILE, FOR THE SAUCE

HEAT THE OIL in a medium heavy saucepan over high heat until hot but not quite smoking. Add the onion and garlic and cook, stirring, until golden and translucent, 3 to 4 minutes. Add the tomatoes, breaking them up with your hands. Add the bay leaves, 1 teaspoon salt, ½ teaspoon pepper, the cloves, cinnamon, cumin, and oregano. Bring to a boil, then reduce the heat to low and simmer, uncovered, for 10 to 12 minutes. Remove from the heat.

WORKING IN BATCHES if necessary, puree the tomato mixture in a blender. Transfer to a large Dutch oven or saucepan and bring to a boil over high heat. Add the prunes, dried apricots, raisins, pineapple, with its juices, sherry, and vinegar. Let simmer for a minute, then add the adobo. Season with salt and pepper if necessary. Reduce the heat to medium-low and simmer, uncovered, for about 10 minutes. Add the apple pieces, let the sauce return to a boil, and then simmer for 20 minutes. Keep warm over very low heat, or reheat before serving.

One 20-ounce can unsweetened pineapple chunks, with their juice

½ cup dry sherry or red wine

1 tablespoon cider vinegar

1 cup Adobo de Chile Colorado (recipe follows)

1 to 2 medium tart apples, such as Granny Smith, cored and cut into eighths

SERVES 2

WHEN READY TO SERVE, cut the duck lengthwise in half. Place on two plates, and serve with the sauce.

Adobo de Chile Colorado Red Chile Adobo

2 tablespoons lard or vegetable oil

4 medium-hot dried red chiles (ancho, guajillo, or Anaheim), stems intact

1½ cups boiling water

1 large garlic clove, finely minced

1 teaspoon dried Mexican oregano

1 cup water

MAKES ¾ TO 1 CUP

HEAT THE LARD in a heavy small or medium skillet over medium heat until rippling. Fry the chiles, one at a time, turning several times with tongs, until puffed and red or slightly orange in color, 30 to 60 seconds—be careful not to let them burn! As the chiles are done, place them in a bowl and cover with the boiling water. Let soak until softened, about 20 minutes (push them down if they float); drain.

PULL OR CUT OFF the chile tops and scrape out the seeds; discard the tops and seeds. Place the chile pods in a blender, with the garlic, oregano, and 1 cup water. Process to a smooth puree. Add a little more water if necessary to facilitate blending, but the sauce should be thick.

PLACE A MEDIUM-MESH sieve over a bowl. Pour the paste into the sieve and force it through with a wooden spoon, scraping and rubbing to push through as much of the solids as possible. Discard any bits that won't go through.

Ensalada de Camarones
Shrimp Salad

6 cups fish stock or water

1 small white onion, unpeeled

2 garlic cloves, unpeeled

3 bay leaves

10 to 12 black peppercorns

1½ teaspoons salt, or to taste

1 pound medium shrimp (16 to 20 count), in the shell

Juice of 1 lime

3 tablespoons olive oil

Freshly ground black pepper

1 fresh white bulb onion (see above) or 1 medium-small red onion, sliced into thin half-moons

3 jalapeño chiles, seeded if desired (to mitigate the heat—I don't bother), finely julienned

1 ripe avocado, pitted, peeled, and finely diced (Hass or Fuerte, which are buttery)

10 cilantro sprigs, leaves only

SERVES 4 TO 6

In dishes like this that are garnished with raw onion, I really value the freshness of Mexican onions, which are used much sooner after pulling than are common storage onions. Often they are like the middling-sized pearly white onions with green tops still attached that you'll find in some ethnic groceries as "bulb onions" or "spring onions" (don't confuse them with scallions). Red onions make a good substitute, especially the kind that are new looking and shiny, without papery skins.

PLACE THE FISH STOCK, onion, garlic, bay leaves, peppercorns, and 1 teaspoon of the salt in a medium saucepan or small stockpot. Bring to a boil over high heat and cook, uncovered, for 10 minutes to infuse the flavors. Add the shrimp and cook, uncovered, for about 2 minutes, or until they turn pink. Quickly cool by emptying into a colander set under cold running water. Drain thoroughly.

PEEL THE SHRIMP and cut lengthwise in half.

IN A SMALL BOWL, combine the lime juice, olive oil, a generous grinding of black pepper, and about ½ teaspoon more salt.

PLACE THE SHRIMP in a large bowl, along with the onion, chiles, avocado, and cilantro. Pour the lime juice dressing over the salad and toss to distribute evenly. Taste for seasoning and add a little more salt and pepper if desired. Serve at once.

VARIATION

The same recipe works well with virtually any kind of seafood, though each has to be cooked by its own optimum timing. For Ensalada de Calamares (Squid Salad), start with about 1 to 1½ pounds squid (cleaned weight). Peel off the outer membrane and cut the meat into ½-inch squares or rings. Cook as directed for shrimp, or until tender. Continue as directed.

Priscila Satkoff

Sopa de Tortilla
Tortilla Soup

3 quarts water

6 medium plum tomatoes

4 garlic cloves, minced

½ medium yellow onion, finely diced

2 sprigs epazote

Salt

6 corn tortillas (preferably a day old), cut into 3-by-½-inch strips

1 cup canola oil

1 medium avocado, pitted, peeled, and diced

1 cup grated *queso añejo* (aged Mexican cheese)

2 pasilla chiles, toasted (see Note, page 303), deveined, and cut into pieces (optional)

Salt

SERVES 6

IN A LARGE SAUCEPAN, bring the water to a boil. Add the tomatoes and boil gently for 20 minutes.

ADD THE GARLIC AND ONION, then strain the broth into another saucepan. Puree the tomatoes, onion, and garlic, and add to the broth.

BRING THE BROTH to a boil. Add the epazote and salt to taste. Boil for 5 minutes.

MEANWHILE, HEAT the oil in a large skillet and fry the tortilla strips, in batches, until crisp.

TO SERVE, DIVIDE the tortilla strips among six bowls. Add the broth and garnish with the avocado, cheese, and peppers, if using. Serve immediately, so the tortilla strips don't get soggy.

309

Mexico

Camarones al Carbon
Grilled Tiger Shrimp with Two Salsas

FOR THE AVOCADO SALSA

½ medium avocado, peeled

2 medium tomatillos, husks removed and rinsed

½ cup fresh cilantro leaves

1 cup cold water

½ teaspoon salt

FOR THE TOMATO-CHIPOTLE SALSA

3 medium plum tomatoes, roasted, peeled, and seeded

3 to 7 canned chipotle chiles in adobo (depending on how spicy you like the dish), seeds removed

1 cup cold water

½ teaspoon salt

1 pound tiger shrimp (16 to 20 count), peeled and deveined

1 medium fresh mango, peeled, pitted, and cut into thin wedges

SERVES 4

FOR THE AVOCADO SALSA

IN A BLENDER OR food processor, blend the avocado, tomatillos, cilantro, water, and salt to a smooth puree. Set aside.

FOR THE TOMATO-CHIPOTLE SALSA

IN A BLENDER OR food processor, blend the tomatoes, chipotle chiles, water, and salt to a smooth purée. Set aside.

PREPARE A FIRE in a grill or preheat the broiler.

SEASON THE SHRIMP with salt. Grill or broil, turning once, until they are pink and just opaque throughout; be careful not to overcook them.

SPOON SOME AVOCADO salsa onto one side of each plate and some tomato-chipotle salsa onto the other side. Set the grilled shrimp between the two salsas, and garnish with the mango slices.

Flan de Naranja
Orange Flan

FOR THE CARAMEL

2 cups sugar

1 cup water

FOR THE CUSTARD

2 cups whole milk

2 cups half-and-half

1 cup sugar

Grated zest of 6 oranges

8 large eggs

SERVES 8

FOR THE CARAMEL

IN A HEAVY SAUCEPAN, combine the sugar and water and bring to a boil over high heat. Cook until the mixture becomes a deep golden brown caramel, about 8 minutes.

POUR THE CARAMEL into eight individual ramekins. Let cool.

FOR THE CUSTARD

IN A MEDIUM SAUCEPAN, combine the whole milk, half-and-half, sugar, and orange zest. Bring to a boil, reduce the heat, and simmer for 3 minutes. Remove from the heat. Let stand at room temperature for 10 minutes.

PREHEAT THE OVEN to 325 degrees F.

IN A MEDIUM BOWL, whisk the eggs. Meanwhile, return the milk mixture to a boil; remove from the heat.

WHISKING CONSTANTLY, slowly pour 1 cup of the hot milk mixture into the eggs to temper them. Whisk in the rest of the milk mixture. Strain through a fine sieve.

POUR THE CUSTARD into the caramel-lined ramekins. Arrange the ramekins in a baking pan and add enough hot water to the pan to come halfway up the sides of the molds. Cover the pan with foil and bake for 22 to 25 minutes, until a knife or toothpick inserted in the middle of a custard comes out clean. Let cool to room temperature in the water bath.

REMOVE THE FLAN from the molds by gently running a small knife around the sides and inverting them onto individual plates.

Thailand

BALANCING STRONG FLAVORS AND AROMATICS

Harmonizing is essential in Thai cooking because we work with such bold flavors.

—KASMA LOHA-UNCHIT, AUTHOR, *IT RAINS FISHES*

EATING THAI FOOD MEANS immersing yourself in a world of spicy, perfumed red, yellow and green curries. This world also features salty pungent fish sauce, which makes your eyes water and your lips pop, and the citrusy tang of lemongrass, whose exotic aroma transports you straight to Asia. And then there is coconut, which complements the heat of chiles in curry and adds sweetness to desserts. Because the flavors and fragrances of Thai cuisine are so intense, they need to be seduced and coaxed into well-balanced dishes.

"I was my mother's helper from the age of five, so I started balancing flavors at an early age," recalls Kasma Loha-unchit. "Balance is essential in Thai cuisine because when you add something to a dish, it does not act in isolation; it interacts with everything else. Westerners don't think like that, because they don't have the same background of playing with flavors."

Balancing flavors is always difficult, and balancing strong flavors is even more of a challenge. With Thai food, you are not exactly balancing parsley with veal. You're using many intense flavors, ones that can set off a chain reaction and ruin a dish if you're not careful. On the other hand, big flavors hitting each other can create big sparks—in a great way.

In Thai cooking, you can achieve the desired balance among salty, sweet, sour, bitter, and/or hot flavors in myriad ways. For example, fish sauce is the primary source of saltiness. Palm sugar, cane sugar, and coconut sugar act as the sweet components. Tamarind, lime, and kaffir lime are used to add sour qualities to a dish. Bitterness—not to mention aroma—may come from a variety of herbs, such as cilantro, Thai basil, and spearmint leaves, while chiles impart heat.

Leading and Supporting Flavors

Common throughout Thailand is the delicate balance of taste and texture, fresh chiles with dried chiles, or fresh herbs with lime juice and fish sauce.
—SAIPIN CHUTIMA, CHEF, LOTUS OF SIAM, LAS VEGAS

SO, HOW DOES BALANCE play itself out in Thai cuisine? How do these strong flavors work together to create unified dishes? "A dish must feature elements of surprise and balance," says Kasma Loha-unchit. "By surprise, I mean that if a dish has three primary flavors—such as sweet, salty, and sour—one of these flavors will be predominant, though it will always be balanced by the secondary taste. Or the real surprise might be how that second taste reminds you of some element of nature, such as the sea, or a forest after it has just been rained upon, or a flower after it has just blossomed. There must be something beyond hot, salty, sweet, and sour. A dish must have you asking, 'What's that flavor element?' There should be a surprise of some sort and it can be a flavor, texture, or aroma."

What few Western cooks appreciate is how well Thai cooks can perceive the nuances of their bold flavors. "Thai dishes do not rely on just one taste," explains Su-Mei Yu. "We do not have a dish that just tastes salty. If you tell me that a dish tastes salty, I will ask, 'What do you mean by salty? Is it salty like the sea, or salty-metallic?'"

"The limes in the U.S. are not as intense or as sweet as Thai limes," adds Loha-unchit. "That's why sometimes here we add a little sugar to the lime juice to intensify the flavor. You need to be careful, however, because too much sugar can neutralize the lime. The sugar has to balance the other flavors."

The Thai rely on smell to discern these subtleties of flavor. While a common saying in American restaurants is that "you eat with your eyes first," the Thai believe that aroma—as opposed to appearance—comes first. "Aroma always takes precedence," explains Loha-unchit. "We will never comment first on how great a dish looks; we will comment on how great it *smells*. The smell has to hit you first. Then we say it looks good, and finally we taste it."

"I have taken advantage of the fact that Thai cuisine has a great classical foundation with great variety too," says Arun Sampanthavivat, chef-owner of Arun's in Chicago. "Using herbs as a main ingredient in dishes makes them lighter, healthier and multi-layered. The cuisine is also very beautiful because of its color composition. So I will have six flavors with beautiful colors to combine into a whole with which to express myself."

Curry School

Curry? I could give you a whole chapter on curry! —ARUN SAMPANTHAVIVAT

CURRIES, AMONG THE MOST popular dishes in Thailand and a standard in Thai restaurants in the United States, are often the centerpiece of a meal. The simple soups and salads that accompany curries act as foils to balance out their intense flavors. But curries themselves are also perfect examples of harmonizing flavors into a sum that is greater than its parts. A curry is a formula interpreted through a painter's eye: the ingredients are fairly standard, yet the results always vary.

"There are technically three kinds of Thai curry—red, green, and yellow—with the distinctions being very apparent," explains Arun Sampanthavivat. "They all share similar ingredients, from as few as three to as many as twenty, depending on the curry. In general, they will include chile peppers, garlic, shallots, kaffir peel, lemongrass, galangal, cilantro, and definitely shrimp or fish paste. These elements are key to a classic Thai curry." (Kaffir peel can be found dried in Asian stores; it has a different flavor from kaffir leaves.)

It may be helpful to think of curries as being similar to tomato sauce: Everybody makes them. All tomato sauces are likely to contain tomatoes, garlic, and onion, but after that, it can be a free-for-all, with one cook's version doubtless different from another's. Yet, you would never mistake a tomato sauce for anything else. "Almost all curries, except for *masamun,* have essentially the same eight or nine ingredients," agrees Su-Mei Yu. "What determines a curry and makes for some variation is the choice of meat, vegetable, or fish you cook in the paste."

Preparing a curry, though often thought of as daunting, is actually quite simple. These days, however, many time-pressed cooks, both in restaurants and in homes, start with prepared pastes that, like most canned and processed products, lack the character of the original.

The steps to making a curry from scratch are straightforward: Begin by creating a pungent paste of chiles, lemongrass, galangal, shrimp or fish paste, shallots, kaffir lime, and garlic. The way to achieve an authentic paste is to mash and pound these ingredients with a mortar and pestle, rather than using a blender. Then add seasonings such as cumin or coriander seed to further individualize the mixture. The ingredients that are added next will determine the character of the resulting curry. Most—but not all—curries contains coconut cream, which transforms the paste base into a sauce. If meat or chicken is part of the dish, it is usually first boiled in coconut milk, added to the paste and coconut cream mixture, and then slowly cooked longer to thicken the sauce. Fresh herbs are added at the very end.

"Don't take shortcuts," cautions Arun Sampanthavivat. "If you are making a curry paste, you could just toss it in a blender. However, you would sacrifice both intensity and texture, because to blend it, you will need to add water. The resulting mixture is not the desired thick and sticky paste, but rather a watered-down, diluted mixture."

"The sauce of a good curry is thick enough to cling to your rice and not run all over your plate, but it should not be as thick as gravy," elaborates Su-Mei Yu. "When it is placed in front of you, you should be able to smell it! You should be able to pick up all the spices, and in the back of your mouth, you should detect the aroma of fresh coconut cream. When you taste it, nothing should be predominant. You should experience a balanced blend of contrasts. That's good curry!"

Types of Curry

Red and green curries take their names from the colors of the peppers that are used to make them. "Red curry is made from dried red chiles," says Arun Sampanthavivat. "It has a mellow flavor, and it can be sweet, hot, or mild—it is simply up to the cook. Red and green curries are eaten mainly in central Thailand, especially in Bangkok.

"With a green curry, you use fresh green chile peppers. The color also comes from green chile leaves, which some Thai chefs in America don't even know. In addition, green curry contains toasted and ground cumin and caraway seeds, which add an aromatic element. It is a misconception that green curry is hotter; that is just a matter of taste. However, the curry is a little sharper tasting because of the fresh chiles. The Thai name for green curry literally translated means 'green and sweet curry,' so by definition it has a note of sweetness."

Su-Mei Yu points out the confusing fact that, in this case, "the word for 'sweet' also means 'savory' in Thai, depending on who you talk to. While everybody agrees that the curry has to be green, few agree about whether it should be sweet or savory; I prefer savory.

"Every cook makes curry differently and is very strong-minded about it," she continues. "The sweet school adds palm sugar to the paste. So with that paste, you get hot, spicy, creamy, and sweet. My friend who is a professor at the Royal Cooking College in Thailand says that green curry has been ruined by the new generation because they have such sweet palates. Now green curry is *really* sweet!"

Yellow curry, which contains turmeric, is popular in the far north and far south. "In the north, it was influenced by the Burmese, while in the south, it was influenced by the Malaysians," explains Sampanthavivat. "Both the northern and southern versions include chile and garlic. In the south, the curry is cooked with coconut milk and, in some cases, has sour notes. It is paired mainly with fish, not meat."

According to Sampanthavivat, yellow curries can be prepared in a variety of ways: "One version that is cooked in coconut milk is soupy and eaten in central as well as southern Thailand. In the north, though, they don't use coconut milk, so the curry is more saucy as opposed to soupy. Stir-frying the curry paste can be done with or without coconut milk. No matter how you will eventually use the curry, however, it is always a good idea to stir-fry it a little to bring out the aroma," he advises, echoing our experts on Indian cuisine.

A type of yellow curry, *masamun* curry is a result of Persian influences. According to Su-Mei Yu, "Most *masamun* curries in the U.S. have chicken, potatoes, and roasted whole peanuts. However, that is just one version and not even the most famous. If you're making a beef *masamun* curry, there should be no peanuts. It should be matched with a sour or savory fruit, like apples or grapes."

Beyond Curry

Thai food is immediate. It is hot. It is emotional. It doesn't have the depth and flavor bases of Chinese cuisine, or the separate dimensionality that Vietnamese food has.

—MARK MILLER, CHEF-OWNER, COYOTE CAFÉ, SANTA FE

Most Americans' knowledge of Thai food unfortunately does not extend much beyond *pad Thai* and a few curries. "In general, the dishes you see in American Thai restaurants tend to be sweeter and richer than they are in Thailand," says Kasma Loha-unchit. "The food in Thailand is very light. *Pad Thai* is really good street food—basically the Thai equivalant of a hot dog—but unfortunately, it has been Americanized, becoming over-simplified to the point of being made with ketchup in some Thai restaurants in America.

"If you combined all the dishes in all the Thai restaurants in the United States, you would see a representation of only about ten percent of what exists in Thailand. My colleagues have jokingly wondered if all the Thai restaurant owners in the U.S. got together to come up with a master menu!"

Thai food encompasses far more than curries and the limited repertoire of dishes typically seen in America. "Thai cuisine is multilayered, in that the high cuisine is very different from what is eaten by the regular people," points out Saipin Chutima. "While the high cuisine tends to focus on preparation and presentation, the majority of the population enjoys simpler food on a regular basis. In a restaurant, you might see a beautiful giant freshwater prawn cooked separately and served atop a spicy soup, while at home it would simply be spicy shrimp soup."

Salads: *Yum*

Yum is the Thai name for cold, tangy salads. Chile, lime, and fresh herbs are the basic flavors, which are then expanded with noodles, meat, vegetables, and fish. Lemongrass, shallots, and lettuce are also typical ingredients. *Yum wun sen* is a salad of mung bean noodles, fresh lime juice, chiles, ground pork, dried or fresh shrimp, and seasonings. "In Thailand, there is a much larger variety of salads than in the U.S.," says Loha-unchit. "Thai salads are very different from what you see in Western cooking, where you simply have leafy greens tossed in a dressing.

"In Thailand, a typical salad consists of seafood or spiced meat with raw vegetables," she continues. "At times, the vegetables are grilled or blanched and the dressing is spicy and pungent. Salads in Thailand are typically eaten at room temperature. Thai people will take almost any green leafy vegetable and use it to make a hot and sour salad."

Soups

The Thai have a soup that is similar in style to the Vietnamese pho, although ours is lighter. You can judge noodle soups by their aroma and the clarity of their broth.
                                                        —SU-MEI YU

Tom yam is the name for a host of rich, velvety broth-based soups that are eaten with rice. Lemongrass and/or lime and chiles provide the key flavors, but many other ingredients—including galangal and tamarind—are often added to enhance the soup's complexity. Other than shrimp or straw mushrooms, often nothing garnishes the soup but cilantro leaf. *Kaeng jeurn* are milder broths, often seasoned with simply black pepper and fish sauce. Mung bean noodles, ground pork, and tofu are among the numerous items that may be added to *kaeng juern*. *Kaeng liang* are spicier vegetable soups, seasoned with liberal amounts of black and green pepper, and may include chicken or pork and leafy greens, baby corn, and squash. In the north, where it is cooler, stew-like soups are popular, frequently seasoned with such Chinese ingredients as soy sauce, five-spice powder, cinnamon, and star anise.

Rice and the Thai Meal

The northern regions eat sticky rice, and they eat with their hand. In the central region, they eat with a fork and spoon, using the fork to push the food onto the spoon. Chopsticks don't work, because the rice there does not stick together.   **—KASMA LOHA-UNCHIT**

Rice, or *khao,* is *the* fundamental staple of Thai cuisine. Archaeologists have uncovered agricultural evidence dating back to 8000 B.C. that what is now Thailand was the site of the first rice-growing culture. Thai jasmine rice is considered one of the premium rices in the world. Most Thai prefer long-grain rice, and if jasmine is not available, they use Indian basmati or American long-grain rice. Some Thai, especially in the north, prefer sticky rice. And sticky rice, or occasionally long-grain, is used in many desserts.

"Rice is actually the main feature of a meal," explains Loha-unchit. "The Thai word for food translates as 'rice.'" As in other parts of Asia, "when you announce that a meal is ready, you say, 'It's time to eat rice.' All nonrice dishes are equal in importance, and none is more important than rice. As it is the centerpiece of the meal, the quality of the rice is critical." "If you don't have good rice, your meal won't taste good," echoes Su-Mei Yu.

"Like most Asian meals, a Thai meal is shared," says Loha-unchit. "It is served all at once, so we don't really have courses. We don't serve soups or salads separate as a course; they are served with everything else and are collectively called 'things to eat with rice."

The Thai do not use chopsticks. They prefer to eat sticky rice with their right hand, and, for virtually everything else, they use a Western-style fork and spoon. However, the fork is never placed all the way into the mouth. It may be used to spear pieces of meat or fruit, but most times is used to push food onto the spoon, which is then brought to the mouth.

"To start the meal, you place a scoop of rice on your plate," Loha-unchit explains. "Then you do what we call 'nibble eating.' You take one or two bite-sized portions from one of the dishes on the table and put them on your rice. Once you eat them, you serve yourself the next thing. We never pile a plate with food. We never pass dishes around. It is OK to reach over or have someone 'dish you' some. If you are not sitting next to the food, you will have someone 'dish' for you."

"A typical Thai meal consists of four or five dishes: a soup, a salad, a protein such as fish or chicken, a mild stir-fried vegetable, and a dipping sauce with vegetables, along with rice served from a pot," she continues. "The dishes will be chosen so that two or three are spicy, and the others are mild. If you serve a curry dish with coconut, you will serve a light soup to balance it. The key thing is not to have one particular flavor over-power the meal. An overly strong sour or hot flavor can wipe out everything else."

Noodles are also popular in Thailand, though not to the extent of rice. There are four types: *kuaytiaw*, flat rice noodles; *khanom jiin*, rice noodles pushed through a sieve; *ba-mii*, whole wheat noodles, sometimes made with egg; and *wun sen*, mung bean noodles.

The actual components of a meal are surprisingly flexible. "The meal is planned around seasonal vegetables and how you feel," says Su-Mei Yu. "You have your array of dishes with the rice, then finish the meal with fresh fruit for dessert." She points out that although fried bananas are often served for dessert at Thai restaurants in the U.S., "In Thailand, fried bananas are eaten for breakfast, with strong Thai coffee."

ARUN SAMPANTHAVIVAT ON PAIRING SAUCES AND DISHES

Sauces are very important. When someone asks for hot sauce, we don't just bring them anything: we carefully choose what will pair best with the dish. The customer only thinks about a generic spiciness and heat, but sauces work differently.

- **FOR DUMPLINGS**, I recommend a sweet chile sauce. You don't want one that is heavy or too garlicky, because dumplings are delicate.

- **FOR GRILLED MEAT OR FISH**, I recommend something with lime to freshen the flavor.

- **WITH CURRY**, I would use a fish sauce with chopped chile peppers and possibly a pinch of lime.

- **FRIED DISHES** are often Chinese-influenced, so I'd do something sweet and sour. If you used fish sauce here, it would be the wrong direction.

Dipping Sauces

Dipping sauces are a key component of a Thai meal, and are ever-present on the table. Balance and harmony are again important: one sauce does not fit all. An individual dipping sauce will be slightly altered to suit the foods with which it is being paired.

"The most classic sauce in Thai cooking is *nam prik*, which dates back nearly four hundred years," explains Saipin Chutima. "The name essentially translates as 'chile dip.' *Nam prik*, often eaten with vegetables, is usually a mixture of roasted fresh or dried chiles, garlic, fish sauce, vegetables, roasted onion, and dried or fresh shrimp or another type of fish. The combinations among these ingredients are as endless and varied as people's palates." Other possible ingredients in *nam prik* include cilantro, sugar, rice vinegar, and peanuts.

Some variation of *nam prik* is served at virtually every meal. For example, the sauce can be transformed into a seafood dipping sauce by adding lime juice, garlic, and sugar. When stir-frying was originally introduced by the Chinese, the Thai made it their own by replacing the soy sauce with *prik nam pla*.

A Map of the Thai Palate

Thailand is the same size as France. It is shaped like an elephant's head: the north is the ear, the central area is the head, and the south is the trunk.

—KASMA LOHA-UNCHIT

THAILAND HAS FOUR DISTINCT regions—the northeast, north, central, and south—each with its own distinctive palate. While all the regions share many of the same dishes and ingredients, they have varying emphases to suit each region's climate and tastes.

"The regional flavors of Thai cooking are very distinct because of the different chile pastes," says Saipin Chutima. "The north uses a lot of dried chiles and dried spices, for example, while chile paste mixed with coconut cream makes the dishes of the central region famous."

"One of my favorite Thai dishes, calamari salad, features all the elements of hot, sweet, salty, sour, and bitter or aromatic," says Loha-unchit. "It contains all five flavors with these ingredients: chiles for hot, sugar for sweet, fish sauce for salty, lime for sour, and herbs for bitter and aromatic." These five flavors, although present throughout Thai cuisine, are emphasized to different degrees by various regions.

Northeast Thailand

The Northeastern area, which has been influenced by Laos and Cambodia, uses fresh herbs, fresh and dried chiles, lime juice, and pickled fish.

—SAIPIN CHUTIMA

"Thai cuisine in general is light, yet very hot," says Kasma Loha-unchit. "The heat comes from chiles. On a scale of 1 to 10, I like my food to be 10 in spiciness, though we make sure that the heat doesn't overpower the other flavors. The food in northeastern Thailand, however, is a 20! They are poor, and the spiciness adds more flavor to the rice—plus the spice works as a preservative for the food.

"The food in the northeast region has been influenced by the large numbers of Laotians and Cambodians who live there," she adds. "Northeasterners don't use much shrimp paste and rely instead on fermented fish, or what others call 'rotten fish.' It does smell, but it tastes great once it is cooked. People in the northeast also eat a lot of raw food. The soil is not that great for planting, so they eat anything that moves, including snakes, frogs, and insects."

ASIAN INFLUENCES ON THAI CUISINE

"Thai cuisine has been affected by the cooking of its neighbors. Nevertheless, when a dish enters our borders, we change its intensity—the dish becomes uniquely Thai," explains Arun Sampanthavivat. "Thai influences can be seen in Western cuisine as well. It was not long ago that tamarind, lemongrass, and kaffir were virtually unheard of in the United States. Now they are commonly employed by American chefs.

"From Burma, we get some curry influences," he continues. "The Burmese as a rule do not eat spicy food. They hardly eat chile peppers, so when I visit, it is hard for me to find hot sauce! The curries are pretty bland and oily and include dried ingredients like turmeric, which shows up in Thai yellow curries as well. The Burmese also influenced northern Thailand with the use of tomatoes.

"The impact of Chinese food on Thai cuisine is enormous. One example is the use of chiles in sauces. When we serve a plain steamed chicken as they do in China, we will accompany it with a variety of sauces, many with chiles.

"We see influences of Laos in the consumption of spicy salads prepared with chile, fish sauce, and lime," Sampanthavivat explains. "The Thai make them a little milder and add lots of herbs, like mint and lemongrass.

"Throughout Malaysia and Indonesia, you see satays and marinated meats and curry peanut sauce. Thai peanut sauce, however, is more aromatic. We also add tamarind to marinades and curries borrowed from these countries.

"And," he concludes, "our crepes can be traced back to the Vietnamese. Theirs are kind of plain: stuffed with bean sprouts and pork, with no sauce and just a little sliced cucumber on the side. In Thai cooking, we make a cucumber salad and enrich the stuffing with coconut, shrimp, diced tofu, and bean sprouts. Thai crepes are also more delicate, as are our dumplings. While Vietnamese dumplings tend to be very simple, with pork, soy sauce, and maybe onion, Thai dumplings also contain cilantro, lettuce, and chile pepper."

Northern Thailand

"The north is influenced by Myanmar, South China, and eastern India, and uses dry ingredients like chiles, herbs, and spices in most dishes," says Saipin Chutima. Rice and vegetables thrive in the cooler climate and hilly terrain, and bitter and sour flavors characterize much of the food.

"The North is a thickly forested area," Kasma Loha-unchit explains. "It was difficult to access in the old days, because you had to cross mountains, rivers, jungles, and waterfalls. Since the area is landlocked, northerners only eat fish during the rainy season [when they are abundant in rivers]. They also ferment fish to use in curries. You see a lot of pork and pork sausage dishes. The sausages are spicy or sour.

"You have a mix of spicy and mild dishes," she adds. "The rich curry dishes and dried spices are legacies of the Burmese (who ruled for two hundred years) and are not typical of most of Thailand. You also see some spicy curries in the north, but they are not made with coconut milk, as they are in the rest of Thailand. Northern Thai curries are brothy and resemble soups."

Mexican cuisine expert Rick Bayless has found surprising similarities between Mexican and northern Thai cuisine. "In the north of Thailand, they make a dish called *nam prik numm*, that consists of roasted tomatoes, chiles, and garlic, ground in a mortar and pestle. They use a chile that is similar to the Mexican Anaheim. It was fascinating to watch them dry-roast chiles, just like they do in Mexico."

Central Thailand

The central area is the melting pot, with complex chile pastes, coconut cream, and more well-rounded flavors.
—SAIPIN CHUTIMA

The sweet cuisine of central Thailand is in many ways considered classic Thai cooking. Because Bangkok is located smack in the middle of the country, virtually any ingredient from any corner of Thailand is available there. The terms "central" and "middle" could also describe the palate of central Thailand: the food in this area is more balanced than anywhere else in the country.

"The food in the central region is the most mainstream," says Kasma Loha-unchit. "Dishes are richer and sweeter. This is the area of green, red, and *masamun* curry and a lot of hot-and-sour dishes with a touch of sweetness. You see many rather sweet desserts."

"Because the central region uses coconut cream in both its sweet and savory dishes, its food is considered the heaviest," says Saipin Chutima. "There are many rivers here, so fish is used in many dishes. Fish in Thailand is almost always freshwater, and it is cooked on the bone to add more flavor."

Southern Thailand

Southern Thai cuisine is influenced by Malaysia. It features fresh seafood, chiles, and lots of fresh vegetable garnishes. —**SAIPIN CHUTIMA**

The South is dominated by tropical beaches, and their waters provide many of the region's most prominent foodstuffs. "Rainfall is heavier here than anywhere else in Thailand," says Kasma Loha-unchit. "As parts of the land are still covered in lush jungle, not surprisingly, fish and seafood dominate the menu in the South." Given the predominance of Muslims in the south, less pork is consumed than in other regions. The area grows coconuts and cashew nuts, and incorporates both in many of its dishes—which are also served with locally harvested and favored jasmine rice.

The South's cuisine incorporates both Chinese and Malaysian influences. While salty and sour flavors are especially appreciated, like their fellow countrymen the southern Thai do not shy away from chiles.

Setting Up Your Thai Kitchen

BETTER GROCERY STORES MAY HAVE the majority of what you need to prepare Thai food, as most Thai ingredients are not that "exotic." However, you may want to stop by an Asian market for certain specialty items, as well as a mortar and pestle.

"In truth, Thai food is not hard to cook," says Su-Mei Yu encouragingly. "It takes time to prep, but then it cooks very quickly. It is historically stove-top cooking, with lots of knife work.

"Freshness is fundamental to Thai food," she emphasizes. "Even the curries are made mainly with fresh ingredients. Dried and powdered spices don't have much of a place in the Thai kitchen.

"Before you start cooking, it is important to taste your ingredients," Yu advises. "Crush them, smell them, taste them, then cook with them. This is key with spices you are not familiar with. Then, in no time, you'll understand what other flavors they pair well with. After you get to know them, then it is time to play. Don't be afraid!"

Chiles

Roasted chile paste adds tons of flavor to stir-fried vegetables, soups, and salad dressings. —**KASMA LOHA-UNCHIT**

Before the arrival of chiles in Thailand, natives spiced their food with black pepper, galangal, ginger, and garlic. After their arrival from the New World, chiles were added to almost every dish. In fact, chiles acquired the name—*prik*—that had previously been used for the native black pepper, which then came to be known as *prik Thai*. And Thailand is now one of the leading consumers, producers, and exporters of chiles in the world.

About a dozen chiles are prevalent in Thailand, but three, which are named for their shapes, are the most common: *prik chii faa* ("sky-pointing chile"), which may be red, green, or yellow; *prik khii nuu* ("mouse-dropping chile"), a tiny, extremely hot Thai chile, which is often eaten raw; and *prik yuak* ("banana-stalk chile"), the largest common chile, which is usually cooked.

Ready-Made Curry Pastes

Although our Thai experts recommend making curry paste from scratch (see page 337), they understand that there may be times you'll want to use a prepared product. On those occasions, you can enhance the flavor of your dishes by following their tips.

"If you use store-bought curry paste, I recommend one from a plastic container. The flavor of canned curry isn't as vibrant," says Kasma Loha-unchit. "You can enhance the taste of store-bought curry paste by frying it first, or adding a little sugar, which brings out the subtleties of flavor. Adding some basil at the end also makes a difference."

Fish Sauce: *Nam Pla*

Nam pla is made from small fish—mostly anchovies—that are packed in barrels, covered in salt and water, and left to ferment. The resulting liquid is then strained, pasteurized, and bottled. "Choose a sauce in a glass bottle," advises Su-Mei Yu. "I believe the plastic ones affect the flavor. Also, you don't want the sauce to be too dark. You want it to be the color of light tea, so that you can almost see through it."

The taste you're after is a sharp salty flavor that dissipates quickly. "You should go 'Emph!' and get a little sweetness," says Kasma Loha-unchit. "Then you should get the smell of the ocean, like sand baked by the sun. The scent should be pleasant. When they become dark, and have foam floating on top and sediment at the bottom, throw them out. A couple of brands I like are Golden Boy and Tra Chang. I recommend buying a few different brands so you can compare them. Most are made in Thailand and China. The Thai ones are a little sweeter, while the Chinese like them strong and salty. I always taste fish sauce before I use it."

Fruits and Vegetables

"Thailand has tremendous open-air markets. More people are involved with food per capita than anywhere else," says Kasma Loha-unchit. "Some markets open at 4 A.M., and when people visit them from other countries, they are overwhelmed."

Tomatoes, potatoes, corn, and a host of other vegetables from the New World, including chiles, have had a huge impact on Thai cuisine. The Thai also eat numerous varieties of eggplant. Leafy greens, such as Chinese kale, various cabbages, long beans, onions, gourds, and mushrooms are all popular.

Many different fruits are grown in Thailand, including bananas, mangoes, papayas, melons, coconuts, oranges, and pineapples. Fruits are usually eaten fresh or dunked in a bit of sugar mixed with salt and chile. Some fruits are preserved, dried, pickled, salted, or candied. Coconuts, tamarind, pineapple, lime, and jackfruit are used as ingredients in many dishes.

Techniques

OVENS ARE NOT USED OFTEN in Thailand, so you don't see much roasting. "We do more grilling over charcoal, which makes meat and fish nice and juicy," says Arun Sampanthavivat.

Fish, which are usually cooked with their heads on to yield the most flavor, are often steamed or fried. When stir-frying shrimp, many cooks remove the heads from the bodies and cook them first. This releases the fat from the heads, enhancing the flavor and texture of the dish.

Meat is less common than fish, but is still quite popular, as is poultry. Portions tend to be smaller than they are in the West. If the meat or poultry is used as an ingredient in a dish such as a soup, stir-fry, or salad, it will be cut into strips.

"Most Thai cooking is done with a wok, on the stove top, or a char-broiler," says Saipan Chutima. "A clay pot and a mortar and pestle are the other two key pieces of equipment."

THE MOST IMPORTANT TOOL IN THE THAI KITCHEN

A mortar and pestle is the first thing you should buy to make Thai cuisine.

—SU-MEI YU

"A mortar and pestle is very important in Thai cooking and really cannot be replaced by anything else. You can't get the same outcome from a blender; pounding produces a very different result. When you pound, you smell, and in order to be a good cook, you must be able to smell. If you aren't smelling the food, you can't adjust along the way.

"I recommend a mortar with an inner diameter of six or seven inches. You can find them in Chinatowns around the country. A granite mortar is best. Then, you want to get two pestles, one made of stone and one made of wood. The pestles produce different consistencies. Wood does not pound ingredients as fine; it breaks them up, but it does not turn them into a paste like a stone pestle."

What to Drink with Thai Food

NONALCOHOLIC FRUIT DRINKS are popular in Thailand and are usually served slightly salted. Sugarcane juice is also common, sometimes blended with crushed ice. Beer and rice whiskey are the alcoholic beverages of choice. Yet, a simple glass of water is the most common beverage with meals.

In the United States, Arun Sampanthavivat has found, many customers ask for wine. "We used to sell more beer, but it's rare now," he says. "We serve far more wine, especially Rieslings from Germany and Austria. Since Thailand does not produce wine, this is a new chapter for Thai food. You don't even see wine in Thailand, because there is no market for it."

Carrying Curry Further

I love the cuisine because it is limited only by my imagination. If I apply the philosophies of Thai cooking to a new ingredient, I have another opportunity to discover the beauty of the cooking.

—SAIPIN CHUTIMA

HOW DO OUR THAI EXPERTS navigate preserving authentic Thai cuisine while adapting to an American context? They sometimes struggle to overcome the expectations of customers who are used to seeing the typical limited repertoire of dishes and getting them to experience something new they have created or are introducing. But Saipin Chutima stresses the importance of making sure that the Thai kitchen remains Thai. "Fusion cooking is new to us," she says. "What Americans call Thai- or Asian-influenced dishes are questionable to us when they use rice wine vinegar, sesame oil, or ginger, which are all components of Chinese and Japanese cooking, not Thai."

"I am trying to strike a balance between classical cooking and innovative cooking," says Arun Sampanthavivat. "Food is an important part of our culture and we Thai want to preserve our traditional classic cuisine. If a dish is hot, for example, we believe it should always be that way to be exactly right. So, there has not been much encouragement for change. Our food needs to branch out, but its roots must be strong. You must have an integrity of flavors and techniques, but interpretation can be a chef's freedom.

"A chef should be able to take things as far as his or her imagination allows. I am between the two poles, classic and innovative. There is no clearcut line. When I make a curry, I tend to be pretty classical. For example, if I make green curry, it must convey the flavor of kaffir lime and have some sweetness. However, one way I express my freedom though is through presentation.

"A good example would be Thai pasta with a sweet curry sauce. A Thai would expect a certain type of vegetable, such as banana blossom or water spinach, which is almost a prerequisite. However, I might use a different spinach, or a fried vegetable as a contrast to the pasta.

"One of the dishes I prepare," he continues, "is a traditional *hunglay* curry [see page 337], which has its origins in Burma. Traditionally, it is cooked in a very oily base, almost floating in oil. Cooked that way, the dish is not very appealing to me, or digestible. The curry is for pork, and it's made with pork fat. In Thailand, they make the curry with a little less fat than in Burma, but it is still heavy. My version has the traditional elements of turmeric and salt, but I cut back on the fat further and use a better cut of pork. Then I add tamarind, which cuts the fat even more. Finally, I finish it with a little kaffir lime to add some aroma in the background.

"Three years ago, I demonstrated this curry at a food forum in Thailand. The Thai were actually a little shocked that I chose this curry for such distinguished Thai and other chefs from around the world. When they tasted it, they commented that the curry was beautiful. The aim of the conference was to maintain the tradition of keeping dishes the same, but even this group was able to see that a dish could be refined and taken further."

Nach Waxman's Recommended Reading on Thai Cooking

There should be a law that no one cooking food from Southeast Asia should be allowed to do so without first consulting **Hot Sour Salty Sweet** by Jeffrey Alford and Naomi Duguid. At every level I can think of, it's a brilliant book. The well-travelled husband and wife team present the social context of cooking and eating in these regions, from food eaten by the Thai royal family to street-stall food.

There's an unprepossessing older book I recommend called **The Original Thai Cookbook** by Jennifer Brennan, an Australian who has lived throughout Southeast Asia. She knows the food well, and writes not only about the ingredients and their basic methods of preparation, but also about how dishes are put together to make a meal.

The ultimate work on Thai cooking, however, is the dazzling **Thai Food** by David Thompson—more than 670 pages on all there is to know on the subject, from history and tradition to the basics of techniques to menu planning.

Salmon Panang
Grilled Salmon in a Creamy Red Curry Sauce

334

Two 8- to 10-ounce skinless salmon fillets

One 19-ounce can good-quality coconut milk (*not* shaken)

1 tablespoon vegetable oil

1 tablespoon Thai red curry paste, or a dash more for a spicier dish

1 tablespoon Thai fish sauce (*nam pla*)

2½ teaspoons sugar

1 teaspoon Cognac

2 kaffir lime leaves, julienned

1 sprig basil for garnish

SERVES 2

PREPARE a hot fire in a grill.

PLACE THE UNSEASONED FISH on the grill and cook to your liking, approximately 6 to 9 minutes on the first side and 4 to 6 minutes on the second.

MEANWHILE, WITHOUT SHAKING the can, open the coconut milk. Spoon off and reserve the cream on top; save about a tablespoon of it for garnish.

IN A SAUTÉ PAN, HEAT the oil over medium heat. Add the curry paste and cook until fragrant. Add the coconut cream, turn up the heat to high, and stir constantly until the sauce has a nice sheen.

SLOWLY ADD ½ CUP of the coconut milk (reserve the remaining coconut milk for another use). Add the fish sauce and sugar and stir until incorporated. Add the Cognac and stir for 3 seconds. Remove from the heat.

TO SERVE, STRAIN THE SAUCE and ladle it onto a platter. Place the fish in the center. Top the salmon with the reserved coconut cream, kaffir lime leaves, and basil.

Saipin and Bill Chutima

Thum Kha-Noon
Stir-Fried Green Jackfruit Northern Thai–Style

4 to 5 slices (about the size of a quarter) fresh galangal

1 shallot, sliced

8 garlic cloves

1 teaspoon chile powder, or more to taste

One 15-ounce can young green jackfruit, drained

8 ounces ground pork

6 cherry tomatoes

3 tablespoons vegetable oil

1 tablespoon Thai fish sauce *(nam pla)*

1 teaspoon sugar

¼ cup chicken stock

2 tablespoons chopped scallions

2 tablespoons chopped fresh cilantro

2 kaffir lime leaves, julienned

4 to 8 dried Thai bird chiles, pan-roasted until fragrant

GARNISH

1 garlic clove, thinly sliced

1 shallot, thinly sliced

SERVES 2

POUND THE GALANGAL in a large mortar with a pestle until finely broken down. Add the shallot, 4 garlic cloves, and the chile powder, and pound until well mixed.

SQUEEZE THE EXCESS LIQUID from the jackfruit and add to the mortar, a few pieces at a time, pounding until well combined. Add the ground pork and pound to incorporate well. Add the cherry tomatoes and pound for about 30 seconds. Set aside.

FINELY CHOP the remaining 4 garlic cloves. In a small skillet, heat 2 tablespoons of the oil over low to medium heat. Stir in the chopped garlic and cook until almost golden. Set aside.

IN A WOK or another skillet, heat the remaining 1 tablespoon oil over high heat. Stir-fry the jackfruit-pork mixture, adding the fish sauce and sugar, until the mixture is brown and dry. Add the chicken stock and fry until dry again.

ADD 1 TABLESPOON of the scallions, 1 tablespoon of the cilantro, and the kaffir lime leaves. Stir to combine the ingredients well, and take the pan off the heat.

TO SERVE, PLACE the jackfruit on a platter or individual plates, and sprinkle with the fried garlic, the remaining 1 tablespoon each scallions and cilantro, and the dried chiles.

GARNISH WITH THE sliced garlic and shallot. Serve with Thai sticky rice.

RECIPES INSPIRED BY Thailand

Stir-Fried Cellophane Noodles with Shredded Chicken and Vegetables

2 tablespoons corn oil

1 garlic clove, crushed and minced

1 small white onion, very thinly sliced

¼ cup dried shrimp, soaked in warm water for 2 hours and drained

½ cup raw shredded or julienned chicken or pork

Pinch of salt

2 tablespoons dried cloud ear mushrooms, soaked for 2 hours and drained

2 tablespoons very thinly sliced shiitake mushroom caps

2 tablespoons dried lily buds, soaked for 2 hours, drained, and each one tied into a knot

¼ cup small fresh shrimp, peeled and deveined

2½ cups dried cellophane (glass) noodles, soaked for 2 hours and drained (about 4 cups soaked)

1 cup chicken stock, vegetable stock, or water

4 cups shredded green cabbage

⅓ cup julienned carrots

⅓ cup very thinly sliced celery

3 tablespoons light soy sauce

1 teaspoon sugar

¼ teaspoon freshly ground black or white pepper

2 tablespoons finely julienned scallions

2 tablespoons fresh cilantro leaves

SERVES 4

The smooth glass noodles paired with shredded chicken and crispy fresh vegetables make this delicate dish a delightful contrast of textures. The flavor is light and mildly peppery, with a subtle sweetness from the juices of the very thinly sliced vegetables. For a balance of flavors, serve this dish with a richer, spicier curry, such as the Hunglay Curry that follows.

HEAT A WOK or large sauté pan over medium heat. Add the corn oil. When the oil is hot, add the garlic, turn the heat down slightly, and sauté the garlic very briefly, being careful that it does not brown. Add the onion and sauté for about 1 minute. Add the dried shrimp, shredded meat, and salt, and continue to sauté until the meat is nearly done.

ADD THE CLOUD EAR MUSHROOMS, shiitake mushrooms, and lily buds and sauté for a few seconds. Add the fresh shrimp and cook until pink and opaque throughout, about 2 minutes.

ADD THE CELLOPHANE NOODLES and about 2 tablespoons of the stock and toss briefly. Add the cabbage, carrots, and celery, cooking for about one minute. Add the soy sauce, sugar, and pepper.

GRADUALLY ADD THE remaining stock, adding more as it is absorbed, until all the stock has been absorbed and the noodles are cooked. Add the scallions and cilantro leaves and toss gently. Serve immediately.

Hunglay Curry

2 pounds "five-flower" pork (pork belly), cut into 1-inch cubes

FOR THE MARINADE
2 teaspoons dark soy sauce
1 tablespoon Thai fish sauce
1 teaspoon turmeric
2 tablespoons finely minced fresh ginger
1 tablespoon corn oil
1 teaspoon minced garlic
Pinch of salt

FOR THE CURRY PASTE
7 red guajillo chiles, soaked in water for at least 2 hours and drained
2 shallots, chopped
10 garlic cloves, chopped
2 thick slices galangal, chopped
2 tablespoons finely chopped lemongrass
1 tablespoon finely chopped fresh cilantro stems and/or roots
2 teaspoons shrimp paste
1 teaspoon salt
About ½ cup water

2 tablespoons corn oil
3 cups chicken stock, vegetable stock, or water
2 tablespoons Thai fish sauce
2 tablespoons palm sugar
1 tablespoon tamarind juice
1 tablespoon dark soy sauce
1 teaspoon turmeric
About 10 kaffir lime leaves

SERVES 4

BLANCH THE PORK in a pot of boiling water for 2 minutes. Drain immediately and rinse with cold water.

FOR THE MARINADE
COMBINE ALL THE marinade ingredients in a shallow baking dish, mixing well. Add the pork, tossing to coat with the marinade, and marinate, covered and refrigerated, for at least 3 hours, or up to overnight.

FOR THE CURRY PASTE
GRIND TOGETHER THE curry paste ingredients in a blender, adding only as much water as necessary to form a smooth, thick paste.

HEAT THE CORN OIL in a medium pot or large sauté pan. Sauté the curry paste until deep red in color and fragrant, about 3 minutes. Add the pork and stir well. Gradually add the stock, continuing to stir. Then add the fish sauce, palm sugar, tamarind juice, soy sauce, and turmeric. Cover and simmer over low heat for 1½ to 2 hours, until the pork is very tender.

GARNISH THE CURRY with the kaffir lime leaves and serve with steamed white rice.

337

Thailand

Yum Makeua Yao Pow
Mesquite-Grilled Eggplant Salad with Shrimp

FOR THE HOT-AND-SOUR DRESSING

10 to 15 Thai chiles (*prik kee noo*), finely chopped

Juice of 2 limes, or to taste

3 to 4 tablespoons Thai fish sauce (*nam pla*)

2 to 3 teaspoons sugar

½ cup peeled and butterflied small shrimp

4 long Asian eggplants—Thai long green, Filipino, Chinese, or Japanese

4 jalapeño or Fresno peppers

2 shallots, thinly sliced

1 tablespoon small dried shrimp

1 hard-boiled egg, peeled and cut into 6 to 8 small wedges

A small handful of small cilantro sprigs

2 bamboo skewers, soaked in water

SERVES 6 TO 8 WITH RICE AND OTHER DISHES IN A FAMILY-STYLE MEAL

START A BATCH of mesquite charcoal; for a stronger smoked flavor, soak a small handful of mesquite wood chips.

FOR THE DRESSING

MIX TOGETHER THE Thai chiles, lime juice, fish sauce, and sugar in a small bowl. Let stand for the salty, sour and slightly sweet flavors to mingle.

COOK THE SHRIMP in boiling water for 20 to 30 seconds. Drain well and set aside.

CUT THE STEMS OFF the eggplants. Grill them whole, turning occasionally, until slightly charred on the outside and softened—for a stronger smoked flavor, add the damp wood chips to the coals and cover the grill as you cook. At the same time, skewer the jalapeños whole and roast; turn frequently until they are lightly charred, softened, and cooked through. Place the eggplant and peppers in a sealed paper sack for a few minutes to steam.

WHEN THEY ARE COOL enough to handle, peel off the charred skin from the eggplant and peppers. Cut each eggplant crosswise into segments about 1½ inches long, cut each segment lengthwise in half, and then cut each half into 2 to 3 strips, depending on the size of the eggplant. Arrange on a serving platter and scatter the sliced shallots over the top. Cut the peppers into long thin strips. Leave the seeds in if you want an extra-hot salad. Arrange in an attractive design over the eggplants and shallots and top with the cooked shrimp.

SPOON THE DRESSING evenly over the salad, then sprinkle with the dried shrimp. Garnish with the egg wedges and cilantro. Serve at room temperature.

Yum Hua Bplee
Banana Blossom and Chicken Salad with Toasted Coconut, Peanuts, and Roasted Chile Dressing

1 small chicken breast half (on the bone)

⅛ teaspoon sea salt

2 tablespoons fresh lime juice mixed with 2 cups water

1 medium to large banana blossom (see Note)

8 small shrimp, peeled and butterflied

¼ cup unsweetened dried shredded coconut

1 to 2 tablespoons small dried shrimp

FOR THE ROASTED CHILE DRESSING

6 to 8 dried red Thai chiles (see Note)

Pinch of salt

1 tablespoon roasted chile paste (see Note)

2 tablespoons fresh lime juice

1½ to 2 tablespoons Thai fish sauce (nam pla)

1 to 2 teaspoons palm or coconut sugar

¼ cup unsalted roasted peanuts, coarsely chopped

3 tablespoons crisp-fried shallots (see Note)

6 tablespoons unsweetened coconut cream (see Note), heated until smooth

1 tablespoon coarsely chopped fresh cilantro

SERVES 4 TO 6

RUB THE CHICKEN BREAST evenly with the sea salt and place in a small heatproof dish. Set the dish on the rack of a steamer, cover, and steam for about 20 minutes, until cooked through. Remove from the heat and let cool.

FILL A SMALL BOWL with 2 cups water and add the lime juice. Remove the dark burgundy outer petals of the banana blossom and the rows of baby bananas in between them. You want only the very pale pink and light ivory petals at the heart of the blossom for the salad. Cut off the exposed stem by first removing the outer leaves, then cut the heart lengthwise into quarters and immediately submerge in the lime water mixture to keep the petals from turning dark. Take one section at a time out of the water and pull the petals off the core, removing all the baby bananas except for the smallest near the center. Line up several petals together at a time and cut on a diagonal into very thin strips about 1½ inches long; immediately return the cut petals to the lime water. (The blossom should yield approximately 2 cups shredded petals.)

COOK THE SHRIMP in boiling water for 20 seconds, or until just cooked. Drain and set aside.

PULL THE CHICKEN MEAT off the bone and tear into small shreds, or dice into small chunks (smaller than bite-size), to make ½ cup. (If desired, save the bone, skin, and the sweet juices released from steaming for soup stock.)

IN A SMALL SKILLET, toast the coconut over medium heat, stirring frequently, until evenly browned and very fragrant. Remove from the pan. Wipe the pan clean and return to the heat. Add the dried shrimp and toast until fragrant and crisped. Remove from the pan, and roast the dried chiles with the salt until dark red and lightly charred; make sure there is good ventilation, and take care not to burn the chiles.

FOR THE DRESSING

GRIND THE ROASTED CHILES to a fine powder in a clean coffee grinder or a stone mortar. Mix with the roasted chile paste, lime juice, fish sauce, and palm sugar in a small bowl, stirring until well blended.

DRAIN THE CUT BANANA BLOSSOM well, shaking off excess water, and place in a bowl. Add the chicken, shrimp, and dressing. Mix well. Add the toasted coconut, chopped peanuts, crisp shallots, dried shrimp, and ¼ cup of the coconut cream. Toss lightly and transfer to a serving plate. Spoon the remaining coconut cream over the top and garnish with the cilantro.

Notes

Banana blossoms are now readily available in many Southeast Asian markets. If you are not able to locate the fresh, you can substitute the canned blossoms, though this will not produce the same result, as they tend to be soggy and to have less flavor. Because the canned blossom has already been cooked, and therefore is no longer laced with the astringent sap, it is not necessary to soak it in lime water after shredding.

The outer leaves of fresh banana blossoms are not used because they are very astringent. Even the lighter inner leaves can be astringent if eaten by themselves, but the spiced coconut cream dressing takes away the astringent taste, so that you are able to enjoy the other unique flavors of this exotic flower.

Dried red Thai chiles, *prik kee noo haeng*, are smaller, skinnier, and more crinkly in appearance than other dried red chiles. They have their own particular flavor. To be sure you are getting the right kind, buy a package imported from Thailand. If you absolutely can't find them, other intensely hot small dried red chiles with a spicy fragrance can be substituted.

Roasted chile paste, *nam prik pow*, is a staple in the Thai kitchen and can be made from scratch, or purchased ready-made in jars or plastic tubs in Southeast Asian markets. A thick paste with a very dark burnt red color, it is made from a roasted mixture of dried red chiles, garlic, shallots, dried shrimp or fish, and fermented shrimp paste, seasoned with fish sauce, tamarind, and palm sugar. Prepackaged products are usually labeled "chile paste in soybean oil" (Pantainorasingh and Maesri brands in jars) or "chile in oil" (Mae Ploy brand in plastic tubs). Because the different brands vary in level of sweetness, make adjustments as necessary with the amount of palm sugar used in this recipe, so that the salad does not become overly sweet.

Prepackaged crisped shallots are available in many Asian markets, usually labeled as "fried onion." Shake the plastic container to make sure they are still fresh and crispy—the pieces should be loose and make a rattling sound. If you prefer to make your own, allow yourself about half an hour to properly crisp the shallots. Western shallots contain more moisture than the small red shallots used in Thailand and, therefore, must be allowed to dry out during frying before they brown and crisp.

Slice the shallots crosswise into thin rounds, then fry in plenty of oil (enough to submerge the shallots) over low to medium heat, so that they sizzle very gently. Stir occasionally. The mass will soon reduce down as the moisture cooks out. Adding a little salt to the oil helps keep splattering down, as well as drawing moisture from the shallots. When the pieces begin to turn brown, stir more frequently to brown them evenly. When most of them are a rich shade of brown, drain in a fine-mesh strainer placed over a bowl to catch the oil (reserve the fragrant shallot-infused oil for stir-frying). Drain the shallots on paper towels and let cool. The pieces will turn crispy when cooled—rather than soggy as they would if fried and browned quickly over higher heat. American shallots usually reduce down to about a quarter of their bulk when crisped, and it usually takes about 20 to 30 minutes from start to finish.

To get coconut cream without milking your own coconut, use either the Mae Ploy or Chao Koh brands of unsweetened canned coconut milk. Do not shake the can before opening—the cream will be floating on top. On cool days, or if refrigerated, this cream will coagulate. Spoon the thickest cream off the top and use it for this recipe. Save the remaining milk to make coconut soup—or use it to make your hot cereal in the morning.

Bplah Doog Gkrawb Nahm Dtok
Spicy Northeastern-Style Crispy Catfish Salad with Lemongrass, Mint, and Toasted Rice

1 pound catfish fillets

Salt and freshly ground white pepper

FOR THE LIME-CHILE DRESSING

12 to 20 dried red Thai chiles (see Note)

4 garlic cloves, finely minced

2 to 3 tablespoons Thai fish sauce *(nam pla)*

3 to 4 tablespoons fresh lime juice

2 to 3 teaspoons sugar

1 stalk lemongrass

2 to 3 cups peanut oil for deep-frying

2 to 3 tablespoons tapioca starch

2 small shallots, halved lengthwise and very thinly sliced crosswise

1 scallion (white and half of green part), cut into very thin rounds

2 tablespoons coarsely chopped fresh cilantro

¼ cup coarsely chopped fresh mint, plus 5 to 6 sprigs

2 to 3 tablespoons ground toasted rice (see Note)

2 to 3 green-leaf lettuce leaves

CUT THE FISH FILLETS into thin bite-sized pieces. Sprinkle lightly with salt and pepper, rubbing the seasoning evenly over fish. Set aside at room temperature while you prepare the remaining ingredients.

FOR THE DRESSING

ROAST THE DRIED CHILES in a dry skillet over medium heat, stirring frequently, until they turn evenly dark red and are slightly charred. Let cool, then grind to a fine powder in a clean spice or coffee grinder. Place in a small serving dish and add the minced garlic and enough fish sauce, lime juice, and sugar to make a dressing that is intensely hot, equally salty and sour, and with only a slight hint of sweetness. Stir well to melt the sugar and blend the flavors. Set aside.

TRIM AND DISCARD the woody bottom tip and fibrous outer layers of the lemongrass. Slice the stalk into very thin rounds from the root end to about 2 inches below where the grass blades fan out.

HEAT THE OIL in a wok over high heat until smoking hot. Coat the fish pieces lightly with the tapioca starch, shaking off the excess. Drop into the hot oil a piece at a time, so that they do not stick together in one big lump. Reduce the heat to medium-high and fry until the fish is golden brown, crispy, and dried through (see Note), 8 to 12 minutes. Remove from the oil with a wide-mesh wire scooper and let cool for a few minutes on a wire rack. (Reserve the oil for future fish frying.)

5 to 6 long beans, cut into 3-inch segments, or substitute green beans

2 small wedges cabbage

A few Thai basil sprigs

JUST BEFORE SERVING, toss the crisped fish with the lemongrass, shallots, scallion, cilantro, mint, lime–chile dressing, and ground toasted rice. Arrange on a bed of the lettuce leaves on a platter, edged on one side with the long beans, cabbage wedges, and mint and basil sprigs. Serve immediately, while fish is still crispy. Nibble on the raw vegetables and herbs along with the fish as desired to temper the heat and clean the palate.

Notes

For this recipe, it is important to fry the fish longer than you imagine fish should be cooked—until it is completely dried, without any moisture remaining in the flesh. This will yield fish pieces that are not only extra crispy in texture, but nongreasy and light as well.

Dried red Thai chiles, *prik kee noo haeng,* are smaller, skinnier, and more crinkly in appearance than other dried red chiles. They have their own particular flavor. To be sure you are getting the right kind, buy a package imported from Thailand. If you absolutely can't find them, other intensely hot small dried red chiles with a spicy fragrance can be substituted.

Ground toasted rice is available in small plastic pouches from Southeast Asian markets, often labeled as "roasted rice powder." You can also make your own supply by browning uncooked white rice (preferably glutinous rice) in a dry skillet over medium heat. Toast the grains, stirring frequently, until they are an even dark brown color and fragrant, about 15 minutes. Do not toast at high heat, as this would brown the outside of the grains quickly but not allow enough time for the interior of the grains to cook and brown. Set aside to cool before pulverizing in a spice or clean coffee grinder. The result should be a powder the color of cappuccino. Make extra while you are at it, as the ground toasted rice stores well in a dry sealed jar for a few months.

Miang Gai
Chicken Bundles

20 green cabbage leaves

1 cup minced grilled chicken

1 garlic clove, minced

1 shallot, minced

2 scallions, white and green parts, finely chopped

1 teaspoon or more red pepper flakes

3 to 4 red bird chiles or 2 to 3 red serrano chiles, seeded and slivered

1 teaspoon sugar

¼ teaspoon sea salt

1 tablespoon Thai fish sauce (*nam pla*)

A 1½-inch piece of young ginger, peeled and diced (see Note)

¼ lime, with peel, slivered

¼ cup dry-roasted peanuts

MAKES 20 BUNDLES

A fermented tea leaf, miang is chewed like tobacco. Many savory dishes, like miang gai, *were invented to imitate this addictive substance. Serve this as finger food or as a snack.*

PLACE A 3-INCH ROUND biscuit cutter in the center of a cabbage leaf. With a paring knife, using the biscuit cutter as a guide, cut a round from the cabbage leaf. Repeat with the remaining cabbage leaves. Set aside.

COMBINE ALL THE remaining ingredients except the ginger, lime, and peanuts in a bowl, mixing well to combine. Let sit for about 15 minutes.

TO ASSEMBLE, SCOOP A rounded teaspoon of the chicken mixture into the center of a cabbage leaf. Garnish with a nugget of ginger, a sliver of lime, and a peanut, and place on a platter. Repeat with the remaining ingredients. To eat, pick up a whole leaf, fold it over the filling, and enjoy.

Note
Mature ginger, diced, tossed with 1 teaspoon sea salt, and allowed to stand for 10 minutes, then rinsed and dried, can be substituted for the young ginger.

Su-Mei Yu

Yum Mah Muang
Green Mango Salad

1 green (unripe) mango, peeled

1 Granny Smith apple

1 tablespoon fresh lime juice

½ cup cherry tomatoes, halved

½ teaspoon sea salt

1 garlic clove, crushed to a paste (ideally using a mortar and pestle)

3 to 4 bird chiles or 2 to 3 serrano chiles (or more for a spicy salad), sliced very thin

2 tablespoons brown sugar

1½ tablespoons Thai fish sauce (*nam pla*)

¼ cup dry-roasted peanuts, coarsely chopped

SERVES 6

This salad is a variation of the popular extremely spicy green papaya salad traditionally served with grilled chicken or sausage. This version is less pungent, but equally delicious with any grilled dish.

GRATE THE MANGO and apple with a coarse grater and transfer to a large bowl. Add the lime juice and toss lightly. Add the tomatoes and toss again.

COMBINE THE SALT, garlic, chiles, brown sugar, and fish sauce in a bowl. Mix well, then add to the mango, apple, and tomatoes. Toss to combine, and pound lightly with a pestle to bruise the fruit. Add the peanuts and toss to combine.

TRANSFER THE SALAD to a serving platter and serve.

Pad Keuy Teow Kee Maw
Drunken Stir-Fried Rice Noodles

1 to 2 tablespoons vegetable oil

1 to 1½ tablespoons Drunken Chile Paste (recipe follows)

3 ounces thinly sliced beef, pork, or chicken, firm tofu, or medium (peeled and deveined) shrimp

1 teaspoon sugar

1½ cups fresh wide rice noodles (2½ ounces) or softened dried noodles

1 tablespoon soy sauce

1 tablespoon oyster sauce

½ cup Chinese broccoli cut into bite-sized pieces (or substitute broccoli florets, parboiled)

¼ cup cherry tomatoes, halved

¼ cup fresh Thai basil leaves (or substitute fresh mint leaves)

SERVES 1

The dish is named for the condition of the eater—either before or after eating it. The spicy noodles are believed to cure a hangover, but they can also make one drunk from drinking the amount of liquor needed to extinguish the fire.

Fresh or dried rice noodles can be used for this recipe. Whichever you use, it's best to stir-fry them in a nonstick skillet. The noodles should be cooked a single serving at a time. This is essential for a perfect plate of noodles, which can be customized to the taste of the guest.

HEAT THE OIL in a large nonstick skillet over high heat for a minute. Add the chile paste and stir until it is fragrant, about 1 minute. Add the meat of your choice (or tofu) and stir-fry until cooked, 30 seconds to 1 minute. Add the sugar and mix well, then add the noodles and continue to stir-fry. If the skillet becomes dry and the noodles begin to clump, add 1 to 2 tablespoons water, 1 tablespoon at a time. For softened dried rice noodles, you will need 4 to 5 tablespoons.

WHEN THE NOODLES are soft, add the soy sauce and oyster sauce. Stir constantly to loosen the strands and toss to mix; try not to break the strands. Add the broccoli and tomatoes; stir-fry until the colors brighten, 30 seconds to 1 minute. Add the basil and stir until limp, about 10 seconds. Transfer the noodles to a plate and serve hot.

Drunken Chile Paste

½ teaspoon sea salt

4 garlic cloves, minced

10 chiles de árbol, softened in warm water and minced, with seeds (or more for a spicier paste)

10 bird chiles or 6 serrano chiles, minced, with seeds (or more for a spicier paste)

1 tablespoon minced galangal (or substitute 1½ tablespoons minced fresh ginger)

1 stalk lemongrass, green parts and outer hard layers removed, minced (⅓ cup)

1 shallot, minced

MAKES ⅓ CUP (ABOUT 3 TO 4 SERVINGS)

PLACE THE SALT and garlic in a mortar and pound with a pestle into a paste. One at a time, add the chiles, galangal, lemongrass, and shallot, adding each new ingredient only after the previous one has been pureed and incorporated into the paste. Transfer to a bowl, or store in a glass jar with a tight-fitting lid in the refrigerator for up to a week.

Note
Blocks of oiled fresh ½-inch-wide white rice noodles, packaged in cellophane, are sold in Asian markets. Each package will make 6 servings. To use, separate the noodles into individual strands.

Dried rice noodles are labeled "dried rice sticks." Buy the widest cut. An 8-ounce package will make about 4 servings. To prepare, soak the noodles in warm water until pliable, about 20 minutes. Rinse in cool water and dry. Keep wrapped in a dish towel until ready to use.

Vietnam

ENCOURAGING TACTILE AND TASTEFUL INTERACTION

The last time I was in Vietnam, I counted twenty-four different fresh herbs on the table. It makes the food much more interactive than Thai or Chinese. Vietnamese food has a personal expression that you don't get with other cuisines.

—MARK MILLER, CHEF-OWNER, COYOTE CAFÉ, SANTA FE

ANYONE READING THIS BOOK will doubtless agree that food should be fun! So you'll be happy to know that the Vietnamese approach to cuisine intrinsically encourages diners to play with their food.

When Jean-Georges Vongerichten recommended Pho Bang in New York City to us while we were researching chefs' favorite restaurants for *Chef's Night Out*, it took us less than twenty-four hours to check it out. On our first visit, we followed his advice, ordering *pho* (a beef noodle soup) and a plate of spring rolls.

First our waiter brought over large plates of Thai basil, cilantro, lime wedges, and bean sprouts, which he placed next to the bottles of hot sauces and hoisin sauce already on the table. Then he brought over a plate of lettuce leaves, fresh mint leaves, and a dipping sauce for the spring rolls. Sitting at the table, we felt as if we were at a farmers' market, yet we had no appetizers or entrées before us.

When the food arrived, the staff showed us how to wrap a hot spring roll in a large lettuce leaf, tucking in a mint leaf or two, and dipping the entire concoction in the sauce before taking a bite. The rolls were a revelation: wrapping something almost too hot to hold in a cool lettuce leaf, then dipping it in a clear sweet and spicy sauce seemed as if it would defeat the crispness of the roll. In fact, it turned out to be a trinity of textures and flavors—hot/cold, crispy/soft, sweet/spicy—that led to an inevitable fourth: joy/ecstasy!

We were also invited to tear up the herbs to flavor our soup and to adjust the balance of flavors with a squeeze of lime, a dash of hot sauce, and/or hoisin sauce. Eating *pho* involves thinking like a chef. You keep adjusting the soup until you get exactly the flavor balance you're looking for. The kitchen puts a great deal of work into an intensely flavorful broth with paper-thin slices of beef and rice noodles. Then they turn the power over to the customer, who gets to season it just the way he or she likes it. This is completely unlike dining in a four-star restaurant (where there might not even be salt on the table), and it offers an extraordinary experience all its own.

One of the exciting aspects of eating Vietnamese food is that it involves all the senses. You smell the aromatic freshly torn herbs and the clove-scented broth of *pho*. The dish itself is a contrast of deeply colored soup, glistening seared meat, bright greens, and pristine white rice noodles. You hear a crunch when biting into the spring rolls or when tearing the lettuce for wrapping. The rolls are eaten with your hands, so you feel the heat making its way through the cool leaves. No other cuisine is as tactile or offers so many juxtapositions of temperature and texture.

It is such a different experience that first-time diners may need a little guidance. "Sometimes our staff needs to help people understand how to eat Vietnamese food," says Hoc Van Tran, chef of Le Colonial in New York City. "A spring roll is finger food. Enjoying it is about wrapping that hot roll in a cool, fresh, crisp lettuce leaf and then dipping it into the sauce. Doing that transforms the roll. It becomes textural, nuanced, and even more delicious! Guests may be nervous at first to try it this way, but if they use a knife and fork on a spring roll, they really miss the whole experience of the food."

Vietnamese food shares many ingredients with the rest of Asia, but nowhere else will you have so much freedom and experience such a contrast between fresh and cooked food. "When a person eats Vietnamese food, they do not take it for granted, because they take part in preparing it," says Corinne Trang, author of *Authentic Vietnamese Cooking*. "It is a ritual in Vietnamese dining to participate with the food. You will always do something to the food yourself, like wrap it or add fresh herbs or a squeeze of lime. You appreciate it that much more because you've worked hard for it."

Balancing a Dish

Vietnamese cooking involves a lot of technique. You will get a sour herb, a sweet herb, salty fish sauce, and then something rich. There is brightness and a lot of dimensionality to its dishes. —**MARK MILLER**

HOC VAN TRAN OBSERVES, "While the Chinese use the concept of yin and yang to compose their food, Vietnamese cooks employ four different elements as their guiding principles: salty, sour, sweet, and spicy." That way, the food is always balanced. "When it is sweet, it is also sour. As a result, no one flavor is ever overwhelming," explains Corinne Trang. "In a bowl of *pho*, for instance, you have cinnamon, star anise, onion, clove, and sugar—and at the end, you squeeze in a little lemon or lime juice to counterbalance the sweetness."

Playing with the seasonings to reach a pleasing balance for yourself makes cooking Vietnamese food an intensely personal experience. "When I teach at the Culinary Institute of America, I don't give proportions and I don't give recipes," says Charles Phan, chef-owner of The Slanted Door in San Francisco. "What I want is for the students to match my flavors. In Vietnam, you don't have recipes; you just watch and learn. I can't say that a quarter-cup of fish sauce will always be right, because I don't know the salt content of the fish sauce you happen to be using. So, a recipe is irrelevant—it is up to your palate."

What are the basic ingredients those cooking Vietnamese food get to play with? Corinne Trang identifies the five main flavors of Vietnamese cuisine as fish sauce, sugar (to counterbalance the saltiness), lime or lemon juice, lemongrass (which is very widely used), and garlic. "With these ingredients, you can marinate almost anything: pork, beef, chicken, shrimp, lobster," she says. "The marinade may sound strong, but the flavor mellows as the food cooks."

Three Cuisines That Shaped Another

VIETNAMESE CUISINE HAS THE DISTINCTION of having been shaped in part by some of the most influential cuisines in history: primarily Chinese and French, with a dash of Indian. A meal of spring rolls that were fried in a wok, a plate of soupy chicken curry served with a baguette, followed by crème caramel may sound strange in a vacuum, yet the combination works beautifully in Vietnamese hands.

The French, who occupied Vietnam for almost a hundred years, introduced bread, butter, coffee, and milk. The latter two ingredients evolved into espresso and condensed milk, the basis of Vietnamese coffee. Bread became the basis for the "Vietnamese sandwich," which melds Vietnamese ingredients with the Chinese and French influences. "When you take a bite of the sandwich, you get all three countries!" explains Charles Phan. "A Vietnamese sandwich is served on a baguette, although the baguette is softer and sweeter than a traditional French baguette. (It is not quite as soft as a Philly cheese steak roll, but close.) The French have been gone for over seventy years, but the brick ovens are still there and bread is made in a very traditional manner.

"Inside the sandwich is pâté, though it is not as refined as French pâté," adds Phan. "The sandwich also has a different version of ham. Vietnamese ham has been pulverized into a paste, wrapped in a banana leaf, and steamed. It's closer to bologna. The sandwich also includes fresh aïoli [garlic mayonnaise], pickled carrots, daikon, fresh cilantro, and chile pepper sprinkled inside, and it's finished off with a drizzle of soy sauce."

Chinese Everyday Influences

Vietnam, which sits at the bottom of China, facing out into the South China Sea, was—like the majority of Asia—most heavily influenced by its neighbor to the north. "Vietnam is largely Buddhist, a religion that was brought by the Chinese," says Hoc Van Tran. "On the first and fifteenth day of the month you don't eat meat, according to the Chinese calendar. These are religious days, so people stay at home and eat very simple foods like tofu or steamed vegetables."

Corinne Trang notes that the Vietnamese custom of sharing food from multiple dishes comes from Chinese cooking. "And Vietnam is the only other country in Asia that uses chopsticks the way China does," she explains.

While Vietnamese cuisine echoes Chinese cuisine in such ways as cooking in a wok and employing a liquid version of salt, Charles Phan points out that the Vietnamese made those techniques their own. "For example, unlike the Chinese, we don't use cornstarch in a stir-fry," he explains. "And instead of soy sauce, we use fish sauce."

These customizations have made Vietnamese cuisine lighter than other Asian cuisines. "It is not oily like Chinese food and it's not spicy like Thai food," points out Corinne Trang. "It is healthy, with lots of vegetables, and it is very fragrant. The food is light and simple, but the flavors are bold."

Culinary Map of Vietnam

As with all the other countries we have profiled, there is no single cuisine in Vietnam. The national dish is the beef noodle soup called *pho,* but beyond that, history has dictated some regional differences, largely according to what ingredients are available locally and through trade. As with any cuisine, the more you know about the regions of its mother country, the more flavorful and authentic your cooking will be.

The North

The north is primarily cattle country; cows were introduced by the Mongolians. Less fish is consumed here than in other regions. As for technique, China's influence is evidenced by the fact that northerners use woks more extensively, for frying and steaming, than other Vietnamese do.

"The cuisine of the north is mild," explains Corinne Trang. "There are hardly any spices and very few herbs. The herbs that are used are specific to each dish. You don't mix a bunch of herbs together like you would in the south."

The Central Region

The food of the central region is considered the most complex. "The central region is where the Emperor has traditionally been located," says Trang. "The imperial cuisine is similar in scale to *dim sum*, consisting of very delicate bite-sized pieces. As the story is told, one emperor liked the food of the north and the south, but he did not want to eat like the commoners. So, he asked his chefs to create a cuisine that combined northern and southern elements. The food of the central region is a little spicier than that of the north and a little milder than that of the south."

The South

The cuisine of the south is the spiciest. Food is typically cooked quickly in sauté pans, not in woks. "The south is where you'll find curries, because of the Indian trade routes," explains Trang. "The curries are made from powders, not pastes like they use in Thailand. They are not spicy like the Thai curries. Southerners also use coconut milk and like a touch of sourness in their food."

Setting Up Your Vietnamese Kitchen

Vietnamese food in America is actually very similar to what you would find in Vietnam because the ingredients are so similar. —CORINNE TRANG

PREPARING A VIETNAMESE MEAL does not require hard-to-find equipment or trips to exotic stores. The herbs and greens can likely be found in your local farmer's market. In an average supermarket, you can find fresh lettuce, cilantro, and mint. If you are near a Chinatown, then you should have no problem finding Thai basil or fish sauce or the few pieces of equipment that our experts recommend.

Fish Sauce (*Nuoc Nam*)

Fish sauce is essential to Vietnamese cuisine, so it is important to know what to look for when purchasing it. "There are several grades of fish sauce," explains Corinne Trang. "The Vietnamese use the strongest and the Thais the mildest. Fish sauce is made on the island of Phu Quoc, south of Cambodia and Vietnam. They take anchovies, which are about the size of your pinkie finger, put them into wooden barrels, and top them with

salt. The first extraction is taken after about two weeks, then it is poured back on top of the fish. Three months later, the first pressing occurs. It's similar to olive oil in that the first pressing, labeled 'fuqua,' is very expensive. It is very strong and you just use a few drops at the last moment for flavor.

"Fish sauces are somewhat interchangeable," she continues. "Tiparos brand Thai fish sauce is good, well rounded and not sharp. If I were making *nuoc cham* dipping sauce and using Vietnamese fish sauce, I would dilute it. If I were using Tiparos, it would not be necessary. This is a matter of knowing your ingredients."

"I find that the darker the color of the fish sauce, the less flavorful and more salty it tastes," says Charles Phan. "The darker ones are cheaper and are for the most part used in marinades. You want a fish sauce with a golden brown color that will have more flavor and less salt. I like the Three Crab brand."

Herbs

"Herbs are used in many ways, from an ingredient in soup to a plateful brought to the table," Phan explains. "We don't cook with our herbs, but use them to add flavor at the last moment."

"You must learn the herbs," counsels Hoc Van Tran. "Twenty years ago, you could not find many of the herbs necessary for Vietnamese food in the U.S., but now they are widely available."

According to our experts, this is the must-have group of herbs for Vietnamese cooking:

- **Asian mint:** "Vietnamese mint does not resemble most mint; it looks more like a bamboo leaf," says Charles Phan.

- **Fresh coriander:** "In Vietnam, the local coriander has pointy leaves; it is similar to the cilantro found here, but more pungent," says Corinne Trang.

- **Lemongrass:** "Lemongrass is key to the marinades of Vietnamese cooking," says Hoc Van Tran.

- **La lob:** "It looks like a grape leaf and is used for wrapping and grilling meat," explains Van Tran. "It is so distinctive that if we do not have any in the kitchen, we pull the dish off the menu rather than try to substitute something for it. To substitute for the leaf would mean to change the flavor of the dish completely."

- **Thai basil:** "You should never substitute Italian basil for Thai basil, or holy basil, as it is also known," says Trang. "The flavors are too different. Holy basil tastes more like licorice and works better with the cinnamon and lemon flavors of Vietnamese cooking. Italian basil is more connected to European cuisine and goes better with garlic."

- **Thai chiles:** "Although chiles are not an herb, they are also key. Thai chiles have more of a piercing heat than most other chiles," says Charles Phan.

Fish and Meat

"Meat is not that popular in Vietnamese cooking," Phan says. "Twenty years ago, it was not much eaten. In restaurants, it was used more as a condiment, because it was expensive." Still, the Vietnamese consume all types of meat and game, of which pork is the most popular. Before grilling meat, they slice it thin and marinate it, using the same marinade for different meats.

"People do eat a great deal of fish," continues Phan. "I recall the fish being lighter flavored in Vietnam. In the U.S., you don't want to use snapper or halibut in Vietnamese cooking—they are too heavy. I like rockfish from Maryland and pompano from Florida. Sea bass works really well. Even Vietnamese customers like it."

"I was in Vietnam and had a great adventure," recalls Mark Miller. "I was taken out into the ocean about a hundred feet offshore, where they have baskets in the water filled with live fish and squid. You choose your fish, then row back and they cook it for you."

Rice and Rice Noodles

Rice is a staple in much of Asia, and Vietnam is no exception. The country is actually the world's second largest producer of the grain. Rice appears on the table at meals, and it is also fried, added to soups, and ground into flour for baking or making noodles. Rice noodles are served in *pho* as well as stir-fried as a base for such foods as barbecued pork.

Low-Tech Equipment

The Vietnamese need very few cooking vessels and utensils to create their delightfully sophisticated cuisine.
—CORINNE TRANG

VIETNAMESE COOKING BEGINS WITH the simplest of tools. "At The Slanted Door," says Charles Phan, "My goal is to recapture the food I remember from my home in Vietnam. When the restaurant started getting busy, we began buying the standard restaurant equipment, such as a hand-held mixer, food processor, and so on. Then it dawned on me that for some foods, you just can't use that equipment. You have to follow the traditional method.

"A general rule of thumb is the fewer machines the better, because there is no fancy high-tech equipment in Vietnam. When we prepare ground pork, that means hand chopped. We don't use the food processor. We found that the processor pulverized the meat too much. This food is peasant food and it tastes a certain way because of the subtle variations.

"When I taught a class at the Culinary Institute of America Greystone campus, in Napa, to professional cooks and I asked them to chop something, they would return it in perfectly uniform pieces. When a chef chopped some herbs, he'd roll them up and julienne them precisely," observes Phan. "To me, it was as if he had just killed the herbs! This is not how the food is traditionally handled in Vietnam. There, you want the variations in size, because the bigger pieces add flavor.

"These chefs were doing things as they had been taught, which for them meant in a European fashion. I had them make a fish sauce dressing, and they would prepare it so quickly. When they finished, the sauce was topped with a huge layer of foam as a result of its being made in a blender. It looked like a milkshake! In Vietnam, when you make a dressing, you just stir the liquid gently and it comes out clear. No one has a mixer!"

Corinne Trang also takes a traditionalist approach to the use of kitchen equipment. "I cook my rice only in a clay pot. I don't use stainless steel pots. Steaming comes from the Chinese, who also use clay pots. The clay pots you find in Chinatown are glazed only on the inside. Somehow, the water evaporates differently in clay. It keeps the rice separate and moist. In stainless steel, the rice gets sticky and mushy, even when I use the same amount of water—one cup of rice to one and three quarters cups of water. To wash my clay pot, I just use hot water and table salt, which I rub gently into the pot. I never use soap. If you cannot find a clay pot, I recommend using the simplest electric cooker you can find. Do not use the super-fancy $100 Japanese kind. They come with a warming cycle that dries out the rice, turns it yellow, and takes out the flavor."

CHARLES PHAN'S RECOMMENDED VIETNAMESE KITCHEN TOOLS

These are the tools that my chefs and I use the most:

BAMBOO STEAMER: I recommend spending $10 to $15 on a set of stacked steamer baskets with a cover. If you take care of them, they'll last forever.

JAPANESE MANDOLINE: Buy one in your local Chinatown, where it will run only $20, as opposed to $40 at a fancy place. We have a $180 French mandoline that we never use. I will give you a word of caution: we call this tool the "finger slicer" in our kitchen!

CLEAVER: You can use these for everything. I purchased eight different types in Hong Kong. A cleaver is not just for chopping. The small ones called "hotel cleavers" are used for intricate slicing. Cleavers are all the same shape, but the thickness varies, so you can sharpen them differently.

WOK: For all sorts of cooking, from stir-frying to deep-frying.

Time to Eat

IN A TYPICAL VIETNAMESE MEAL, all dishes are served at the same time. "Asians are not romantics when it comes to food," says Corinne Trang. "In France, you will sip your wine and sit for hours, then have a little cheese, but in most of Asia, it is eat-and-go.

"In Vietnam and most of Asia, you don't have appetizers and main courses. Anything goes! The table rituals in Asia are basically that you always have a bowl of rice or rice noodles in front of you, and that you will pick from the multiple dishes set out communally at the same time on the table."

Yet when our experts are serving guests who are more familiar with Western dining customs, they make accommodations to honor them as well as Vietnamese traditions. "The notion of appetizer and entrée is Western," says Charles Phan. "We don't eat that way in Asia, but that is how people like to eat in the U.S., so at our restaurant we still serve the food family-style, but in courses."

Corinne Trang agrees. "If I were entertaining people other than my family, I would serve authentic Vietnamese food in a European way, with appetizer, entrée, and dessert," she says. "I would have small serving bowls and small plates like dessert plates. I would put out glasses in case someone wanted beer, water, or wine instead of broth to drink. I would also offer condiments: chile paste or fresh chiles, fish sauce, *hoisin*, and, always, *nuoc cham*."

A Western Vietnamese Menu

To set the mood at a Vietnamese dinner party, I would play music from Vietnam or Cambodia or Bali. Tropical-sounding music also works.

—CORINNE TRANG

WE ASKED OUR EXPERTS how they would go about melding the East with the West when it came to designing a Vietnamese menu.

Starters

"I would start the meal by serving things that are light," says Charles Phan. "For instance, some street foods, like a classic spring roll, followed by some carpaccio, which is from south Saigon. Then I would serve salads," he continues. "Vietnam is one of the few Southeast Asian countries that serve lots of salads. I would prepare a jicama, red cabbage, and grapefruit salad (see page 375). A street vendor would add shrimp or pork to the salad, but I don't think that adds much, so I wouldn't."

"You don't want to miss a spring roll or a Vietnamese ravioli," Hoc Van Tran says enthusiastically. "Growing up, my favorite dish was spring rolls. You can make them at home, even though it can be tricky to make them the first time because the rice paper skin is delicate. You have to roll them gently but tightly so that the stuffing won't come out when you fry them. Then you wrap them with lettuce, cilantro, mint—and it is the best!"

Corinne Trang offers an elegant alternative: "I would start with shrimp on sugarcane and the lacy crêpes known as *bánh xèo,* which are light and delicate."

Main Course

What should the guests expect next? "For the main course, I would serve sautéed water spinach and lemongrass pork tenderloin with garlic-and-ginger-flavored rice, and I would compose the three dishes together on a single plate for each guest," continues Trang.

"I like to serve monkfish with peanut, basil, lemongrass, and garlic along with rice crackers," says Hoc Van Tran. "Vietnamese crackers melt in your mouth. When we can't get them, we take this dish off the menu."

"I would prepare a whole fish, stuffed with some aromatics like ginger and basil," says Phan. "I would pan-sear it to give it a nice crisp skin. Thai snapper or a delicate black bass from Maryland would both work well, cooked until the meat is just barely stuck to the bone. Another option would be a steamed Chilean sea bass stuffed with wild mushrooms, such as tree ears, lily buds, and shiitake [see the recipe on page 374], and served

BEGINNING WITH JUST ONE DISH

If you are not up for preparing an entire Vietnamese meal, our experts recommend starting with just one dish and building from there.

"I would recommend marinating something," advises Hoc Van Tran. "The key to a Vietnamese marinade is using lots of lemongrass and letting whatever you are marinating sit overnight. Then, with those flavors on a piece of meat hitting the grill—oh my!"

"I would not start with *pho*, which takes hours," says Corinne Trang. "Start with ingredients that are very easy to find, such as fish sauce, cucumbers, carrots, mint, rice vermicelli noodles, sugar, lime or lemon, cilantro, shrimp or prawns, and garlic. With those ingredients, you can make a meal. Or you can make something like *bun* [rice vermicelli]. Vietnamese is one of the easiest of Asian cuisines."

"*Pho* is more advanced," agrees Van Tran. "You need to take the time to make the beef broth, but then it's easy because you just need a few ingredients to serve it. The traditional broth is flavored with oxtail and cooked for up to seven hours. Then we add five-spice mix. Our five-spice is made with clove, anise, cinnamon, Szechwan pepper, and fennel."

with glass noodles steamed with some soy sauce. I like to serve fish with a ginger dipping sauce on the side.

"Then I'd serve a meat course, such as the classic dish called 'shaking beef,' which is filet mignon cut into small cubes, seared on all sides, and served with a vinaigrette dressing. When you serve it, it is shaken out of the pan, but the name does not come from that. In Vietnamese, it is called 'bo luc lac,' after gaming dice that you shake in your hand. I recommend serving lots of vegetables too, maybe sautéed with a little shrimp or pork. I also like to prepare different mushrooms."

Accompaniments are always served with the food: dipping sauce for spring or summer rolls, fresh herbs for soup, and pickled vegetables such as daikon, shallots, and carrots for meat dishes.

Originally pho was eaten for breakfast, but now it is eaten throughout the day.

"Most people rarely finish a bowl of *pho*, because there is so much broth. The broth's main purpose is to keep the other ingredients warm. That is why you have so much! After a bite, you sip a little broth, which in turn cleanses your palate. To season *pho*, spoon hoisin sauce and chile sauce side by side into a small dish. Then hold a spoonful of *pho*, with meat, noodles, and broth, in one hand; with the other hand, dip your chopsticks into the sauce mixture, and then dip the chopsticks in your spoonful of *pho*. Don't put the sauces directly into the soup, because their flavor dissipates."

Dipping Sauces

Dipping sauces are key components of a Vietnamese meal, no matter what country it is served in. *Nuoc cham* is a common sauce throughout Vietnam. It varies from palate to palate and region to region, with the spiciest typically being from the South.

Corinne Trang explains, "*Nuoc cham* is a dipping sauce for things like fried spring rolls. It is basically made from lime juice, fish sauce, garlic, chiles, sugar, and rice wine vinegar. It will also have carrot for sweetness and crunchiness, and sometimes shallots. In the U.S., most restaurants strain the sauce so you do not see the garlic and the chiles, but in Vietnam they keep everything in. One of my parents likes it spicy and the other mild. I like it right in the middle. *Nuoc cham* is always on the table," Trang continues. "If you have nothing but a bowl of rice, you may drizzle some *nuoc cham* onto the rice, and that will be lunch."

Another very common sauce is peanut, yet it has lost some of its authenticity since arriving in the United States. "Peanut sauce is used for dipping summer rolls and pork meatballs," explains Trang. "Peanut sauces in Vietnam are made with hoisin that has been diluted with water or fish sauce, then topped with chopped peanuts. Authentic peanut sauce is thinner and more delicate than the version served in most restaurants here."

Dessert

One of the most popular desserts in American Vietnamese restaurants is *crème caramel*, but it is only a small representation of what is eaten in Vietnam. Our experts often prefer something lighter.

"For dessert, I always serve fresh fruit to cleanse the palate," says Corinne Trang. "Exotic Asian fruits such as rambutan, mango, or papaya are particularly good for this. If my guests were still hungry, I would serve *cha choi*, which is very Vietnamese. It is a soup made with coconut milk, tapioca, and banana and is typically served hot, although you can serve it cool or at room temperature." *Che chuoi* is also one of Hoc Van Tran's favorite desserts (see the recipe on page 382).

"To finish the meal, I would serve Vietnamese coffee or tea, both of which are made with sweetened condensed milk," Trang concludes.

What to Drink with Vietnamese Food

When we offer "Vietnamese Voyage" menus at Café Boulud, we will pair German and Austrian wines that are refreshing and "perky." They have a sweetness to them and a nice acidity, which marries well with the spiciness of Vietnamese food. —DANIEL BOULUD, CHEF-OWNER,
CAFÉ BOULUD, DANIEL, AND DB BISTRO MODERNE, NEW YORK CITY

THE COMMON PERCEPTION IS that beer or Riesling wines work best with Asian food. Though neither fights with the strong flavors of the food, they are not the only appropriate accompaniments to consider.

"To drink, I would recommend a Vietnamese beer, like a 33 or a Saigon," says Hoc Van Tran, "but if you don't want beer, have lemonade."

"A clear broth soup is typically used for a beverage, although beer is also consumed," explains Corinne Trang. "Personally, I never drink beer. Even at home with just my husband, I serve soup. I will even have soup in 90- or even 100-degree weather! I might also serve a broth on the side as a palate cleanser. I really like to serve sour fish soup or a pineapple soup. If there is too much food coming out, I may serve a tofu soup, which is purely vegetarian and even lighter.

"When I entertain at home, a lot of my friends—many of whom are French—want wine. For the French, it is not a meal without wine! So I usually serve a semi-dry white, such as a Tokay from Alsace. Or I serve a California Chardonnay that is fruity and semi-dry and does not taste too much of oak. You could also serve a light young red that is not too complex, such as a Chinon or Morgon from France."

"People in Vietnam do not drink wine," says Charles Phan. "They drink tea, fruit juices, or Cognac with meals. I love wine, so I told our wine director, Mark Ellenbogen, that I wanted the wine list to be well thought out and matched with the food. I also told him that I wanted a tea list that no one had ever seen before.

"For wine, we felt German and Austrian Rieslings are a perfect match. Vietnamese food is very complex, hot and sweet. California Chardonnay, with its high alcohol content and strong oak, is too conflicting with the pepper and heat of the food. The same is true of red wines: Cabernets and Bordeaux are not suitable matches for Vietnamese food. A lighter red—a Cabernet Franc, a Chinon, or a Zinfandel—will work though. In general, the rule of thumb is to drink wines with an alcohol level of fourteen percent or under. If the level is higher, the food will turn the wine.

"We are so close to the Napa Valley, and I have a home in the Valley, and yet their wines don't work with our food," he laments. "They're too high in alcohol content and heavy on the oak."

CHARLES PHAN'S PASSION FOR TEA

It's unfortunate that so many Asian restaurants offer free tea, because the tea is usually not very good and not much thought goes into it.

When I am not in the mood for wine, I like tea with a meal, because it is cleansing to the palate. I tend to like oolong, which harnesses aroma and body. Black tea has more body but is less fragrant. Spicy food will overpower a green tea, so you need to be conscious of your tea and food pairings. A tea called Puur is good for cutting fat and grease—so I like it after Mexican food. I also like a dark oolong with chocolate cake, which is a perfect match!

Tea is comparable to wine, in that its character depends on how and where the leaves (versus grapes) were grown. It is very difficult to make a quality tea. We serve an oolong tea called Iron Goddess that costs $180 a pound wholesale. Every year in China, there is a competition around the production of Iron Goddess. I met someone who paid $10,000 for two pounds of this tea!

I once tasted a tea from a seven-hundred-year-old tree. (Most tea trees are around twenty years old.) We brewed the same leaves seven times, and each time they still had flavor. Again, it is like wine: the intensity and flavor are so different when the tea begins with an old vine.

We divide our teas into three categories: green, oolong, and black. Most tea goes through an oxidation process. Green tea is never oxidized. Oolong is oxidized anywhere from 10 to 90 percent. Black tea is 100-percent oxidized.

Our staff puts a lot of work into each pot. The teas are steeped at different temperatures—as opposed to the traditional English method of pouring boiling water over the leaves. The ratio of tea to water is also very important. Also key is at what point you stop the brewing process. If you want strong tea, don't brew it longer. Instead, start with more tea. Tea should never brew for more than three minutes.

Create Cuisine, Not Confusion

IN THIS AGE OF CROSS-CULTURAL culinary experimentation, our Vietnamese experts, like the others in this book, emphasize respecting the culinary traditions of their country. "With all this fusion going on lately, people are forgetting what has been developing over thousands of years," says Corinne Trang. "I have seen people misuse raw ingredients. I was once a guest chef and sent my recipes ahead so the products would be on hand when I arrived. The chef, who was from Saigon, had changed them without consulting me. I ordered fatty meat, because I was going to cook it down and the purpose of the fat was to moisturize. The chef had gotten the leanest meat possible because, to his mind, Americans would not like the fat. Well, in the cooking, the fat rose to the top, to be skimmed off, so the meat was too dry. I mention this because it is not just Americans who make mistakes, but Asians as well. They do not trust themselves."

"It is important for people to understand the traditional way to serve a dish," says Charles Phan. "You need to figure out what people are trying to do with the dish before you can deviate.

A spring roll is a perfect example. You can change the components inside. I have seen restaurants put mango inside to make it vegetarian and I don't have a problem with that.

"However, I try not to change food too much. I believe that if something is called Vietnamese, it should pay respect to the original. If a Vietnamese person orders the dish, he or she will be expecting certain flavors. If my cooks want to change ingredients, I will make sure they also change the name. If they make a spring roll with mango, I don't want them calling it a Vietnamese spring roll—in a 'Vietnamese spring roll,' I would expect to see pork and shrimp. So if a cook does one thing and it is actually another, I am disappointed. Consequently, we are also careful with our translations.

"Certain foods and flavors don't translate so well to the U.S., unfortunately, because a lot of our clientele doesn't always know what authentic Vietnamese food is. When I try to serve a Vietnamese sandwich on a baguette, it won't sell, because the customers think I am trying to do fusion food! It is sad, but the few people who do get it *love* it."

TWO CHEFS' LONG JOURNEYS TO YOUR TABLE

Restaurant kitchens are like mini–United Nations. The best good cooks anywhere have a passion for cooking. They may not have set out to become cooks, but it was the work they could get—work they often needed to support their families back home—and they gave it their all.

Hoc Van Tran of Le Colonial and Vu Bang of Pho Bang are two of the countless immigrants who have forged new lives in the United States. They have overcome hardship, worked hard, and educated themselves, persevering, despite setbacks, to eventually end up on top. Their food can be eaten throughout Manhattan—as a break from shopping on the Upper East Side (at Le Colonial), or from jury duty ten minutes from City Hall (at Pho Bang), or while grabbing a bite in Grand Central Terminal on your way to catch a train (at Nem).

HOC VAN TRAN

"I come from a large family, with nine brothers and sisters. When I was growing up in Vietnam, my mother went to the market every day, because we had no refrigeration. Then she would return and cook lunch and dinner. She was always very busy cooking! I found it very interesting to accompany her to the market and watch her cook.

"In 1975, I tried to escape the war in Vietnam. It took me seven tries before I made it, on a small boat with twenty-six people. I was at sea for seven days and nights, not knowing where we would land. We were raided by pirates three times and they took everything. Eventually we landed in Thailand, where I spent three days without food and water before being taken to a camp. Next, I spent three months in the Philippines, where I learned English.

"My cousin, who escaped before me, sponsored my trip to America. I finally arrived in Seattle on October 26, 1981, with what I was wearing and a pair of shoes. I started working as hard as I could in order to sponsor the rest of my family to come to America.

"It was very difficult to get work in Seattle, so my cousin and I moved to New York City. Two days later, I got a job in Chinatown, at the first Vietnamese restaurant in Manhattan, called Vietnam. I took a job as a waiter because I could speak both Vietnamese and English, and it didn't require the long hours of the kitchen.

Plus, it paid better! I also began working a second job every day at Indochine restaurant. During my shift, I watched all the cooking and started picking things up.

"Eventually, one of the owners left Indochine to open what was to become the first of the Le Colonial restaurants. I was hired away from Indochine to become the sous-chef. Three years later, as head chef, I opened branches in Chicago and Philadelphia, eventually returning to New York as chef. We then opened Nem, a Vietnamese take-out restaurant featuring Vietnamese sandwiches and salads, in Manhattan's Grand Central Terminal."

VU BANG

As mentioned earlier, Pho Bang is a favorite of Jean-Georges Vongerichten (and ours). Vu Bang is the co-owner, manager, and chef of the Pho Bang national chain of Vietnamese restaurants.

The Journey, Part 1:
A Country Divided

"I was born in North Vietnam. In 1954, the country was divided into North and South at the 17th parallel. My family did not like the Communists, so we moved south, along with one million others, and settled in Bien Hoa.

"My father worked for the government information news service, and when I was in high school, he, my brother, and I moved into the city. My mother and sisters stayed outside the city in a rural area. After school every day, he would take us to the market to go shopping. Previously my mother had done all the cooking and shopping.

"My father was a very good shopper. He could choose the best vegetables or fish, and over time he showed us how. He also taught us how to cook, including the order in which ingredients should be added to the pan so that they would cook evenly. Sometimes we would even buy a live pig and butcher it. I learned a great deal from him; he was actually a better cook than my mother. Mostly though, since the country was so poor, we ate a great deal of rice with vegetables and fish sauce. There simply was not that much to choose from.

"I was a student until I was twenty years old and was then required to enter the military. My two older brothers served in the army. I entered air force military school because the air force men were so striking and it seemed that they got all the girls. I had a love of food, so during my military training, on the weekends, I would spend my money to go to the best restaurants. I would pay attention and try to figure out every ingredient in the dishes I tasted.

"In the air force, I learned English, and in 1963 I came to the U.S. for pilot training school in Florida. I studied with Americans in the flight program and returned to Vietnam in 1964. My orders were to fly reconnaissance missions with the U.S. military.

"In 1968, I was transferred to the operations room at the air control center in Saigon. I would oversee flights from around the Pacific. Then, in 1969, I returned to the U.S. for more training. After that, I went back as chief of air intelligence and then was promoted to captain. I was involved in Special Forces fight work over the Ho Chi Minh Trail, in which I would monitor troop and armor build-up. By the end of the war, I had been promoted to major."

The Journey, Part 2: An Eleven-Year Setback

"After the war, I returned to Bien Hoa to run the Air Support Center. Still single, I moved in with my parents. During this time, my father chose my wife from a family he knew, and I got married.

"When the Communists from the North took over, I was afraid every day that I would be arrested and killed. The North then announced that military and government workers had to report for thirty days of 're-education.' At this time, I had only spent nine months with my new wife. The 'thirty days' of reeducation turned into three years, then three more years, which eventually turned into eleven years. I was afraid I would spend my whole life in jail. (The last officer was released after seventeen years in prison.)

"The first year, I was in prison in the South, but the Communists feared that we had too many friends and relatives in the South and that holding us there was a safety threat.

We were sent far up north to a forest near the border of China.

"The Communists imprisoned one million people, with each camp holding four hundred officers. Life was very difficult: we had only a hand saw and knife with which to clear the land. With the cut bamboo, we made huts, then used the leaves for bedding. We planted some food, but there was never enough. There was also no medicine, and in the end, nearly thirty percent of us did not survive.

"I was not allowed any contact with my family—we could not even write letters. For the first three years, my wife had no idea whether I was even alive. After five years, my family was allowed to send food and then visit.

"For my family to visit, they would have to travel the length of the country, which took a week. After all that travel, they were only allowed to spend thirty minutes with me. It was also a long way from the train station to the prison, and no transportation was available. My wife would bring two bicycles—one for her and one carrying food for me.

"When I was released in 1985, I was put on probation for one year.

During my probation, while I was waiting to come to the United States, life was very difficult. I had to work many different jobs. Fortunately, I had a motorcycle, so I would go out and buy things to sell in the market. I would haul up to 250 pounds of cashews! I would also buy medication, coffee, or other goods from arriving ships to sell in the countryside."

The Journey, Part 3: Hard Work and a Great Palate

"My brother, Chuong, had come to the U.S. in 1975. He was very lucky and got out when the North invaded the South. When my brother arrived here, he had a difficult time because he did not speak English. Yet he worked very hard at lots of jobs and sent money back to my family in Saigon. He started a restaurant with some investors in 1987. When I was granted asylum, having him here helped a great deal.

"I arrived in Dallas in 1991. After a month there, my brother asked me to come to New York City. After serving as a major in the air force, I could not even be hired by the airport because I was a refugee. So I went to work in my brother's restaurant as a busboy.

"The restaurant was in Chinatown, and within six months, I had learned to speak Chinese and moved up to manager. Being a manager was easy—I knew management from the military, and the other work was not too challenging.

"One year later, I went to work at another restaurant, Pho Bang, that was losing money. After a month, the chef, assistant manager, and manager all quit. I told the company not to worry. I took samples of all the food from the restaurant's refrigerator home with me. I worked on the dishes at home, trying some four or more times. I worked on them until my family and friends liked them!

Then I wrote down exact recipes.

"I replaced the old versions of the dishes with my new recipes, and fortunately, other people loved the new dishes. People were telling their friends about the restaurant, and the *New York Times* came to visit. We went from losing money to making a profit. The company expanded in New York City and opened branches in Philadelphia, Houston, and Arizona. I now divide my time among all the Pho Bang restaurants in New York.

"I work from 9 A.M. to 9 P.M., six days a week. Every morning, I come in to make sure that the cooks are here. If they are not, I will get the

Nach Waxman's Recommended Reading on Vietnamese Cooking

Vietnamese cooking seems to have been particularly attractive to chefs lately, both because of its rich variety and the easy way it plays host to other cuisines. Its well-known fusion with French food was a product of colonial experience, but the new ways in which it cozies up with European or New World cuisines are much more benign.

Mai Pham's *Pleasures of the Vietnamese Table* gives good background. It's geared to the traditional Vietnamese courses and styles, and it gives the culture and context that

cooking started for the day. The reason our company is so successful is because everybody knows how to cook. The managers and waiters start out in the kitchen, then work their way into the dining room. That way, they know how to perform every job in the restaurant. As a result, we never suffer when we lose an employee. I have seen restaurants where the chef and others quit and the restaurant has to close. Not us!

"I still eat out. If a new Vietnamese restaurant opens, I will investigate the quality. If a dish is better than ours, I will keep tasting their food and our food until I figure out why, and make adjustments to ours.

"I continually change the menu and add new dishes. Much of the food is very traditional, often dishes I grew up with. However, sometimes I will incorporate some ingredients or techniques from Chinese cuisine. Every Vietnamese person knows *pho,* so it is important to make the best version! Fortunately, as the Chinese also like *pho* [and given the restaurant's Chinatown location], I would estimate that we now sell three hundred bowls a day.

"I have two sons and a daughter now. My sons work on the weekends and make good money, but none of my children have an interest in the business. They think it's too hard."

underlie them. ***Food of Vietnam*** by Thi Choi Trieu is in the excellent Periplus Books series, and it gives useful descriptions of ingredients and good cultural background. And there's a bonus; the book has a kind of restaurant sensibility, so there are some respectable photographs of plating. Surely worth knowing is Corinne Trang's ***Authentic Vietnamese Cooking***. It's a good, strong treatment distinguished from other books by its regional organization. With Vietnam's gastronomic diversity one of its important features, it's worth paying attention to a book that puts local variety front and center.

Steamed Sea Bass with Lily Buds

20 dried lily buds

½ cup dried wood ear mushrooms

6 medium dried shiitake mushrooms (1½ inches in diameter)

1 ounce of glass noodles

½ shallot, thinly sliced

1 tablespoon vegetable oil

2 tablespoons light soy sauce

½ cup water

1½ teaspoons sugar

10 ounces sea bass fillets

Salt and freshly ground black pepper

A small piece of fresh ginger, peeled and cut into thin julienne

SERVES 4

SOAK LILY BUDS, wood ears, shiitake mushrooms, and glass noodles in hot water for 30 minutes. Rinse well and squeeze dry. Trim off any hard knobs from the wood ears, then cut into small pieces. Remove and discard the stems from the shiitake mushrooms, then slice them ¼ inch thick.

IN A SMALL SKILLET, sauté the shallot in the oil until brown. Set aside.

IN A SMALL BOWL, combine the soy sauce, water, and sugar, mixing well. Set aside.

ARRANGE THE LILY BUDS, wood ears, shiitake mushrooms, and glass noodles on a deep heat-proof serving dish that will fit in your steamer. Place the fish on top of the bed of noodles. Pour shallot-oil mixture and the soy mixture over the fish, then sprinkle the fish with salt and pepper. Place the ginger on top.

BRING ABOUT 2 INCHES of hot water to a boil in a steamer. Put the fish in the steamer, cover, and steam over high heat for about 25 minutes, until just cooked through. Do not open the steamer too often to check doneness, but make sure that the water in the steamer does not boil away. Serve with rice.

Grapefruit Salad with Jicama and Candied Pecans

FOR THE DRESSING

5 garlic cloves

2 Thai chiles

¾ cup sugar

1 cup light soy sauce

1 cup water

½ cup rice vinegar

FOR THE SALAD

1 pound red cabbage

1 large grapefruit

8 ounces jicama, peeled and cut into ⅛-inch julienne strips

1 cup Candied Pecans (recipe follows)

1 tablespoon olive oil

¼ cup chopped Vietnamese mint *(rau ram)*

SERVES 4

FOR THE DRESSING

IN A MORTAR, pound together the garlic, Thai chiles, and sugar to a paste. Add the soy sauce, water, and vinegar. (The leftover dressing will keep well in the refrigerator.)

FOR THE SALAD

CUT THE CABBAGE into ⅛-inch-wide strips. Wash well, then rinse twice; set aside. Slice off the top and bottom of the grapefruit, exposing the flesh. Stand it on a cutting board and slice off the peel and pith in strips. Using a thin sharp knife, slice between the membranes to release the grapefruit sections.

IN A LARGE BOWL, combine the cabbage, grapefruit, jicama, pecans, olive oil, rau ram, with dressing to taste. Toss well, and serve.

Candied Pecans

½ cup egg whites (from about 4 large eggs)

½ cup sugar

¼ teaspoon salt

2 cups pecan halves

MAKES 2 CUPS

Preheat the oven to 325 degrees F.

IN A LARGE BOWL, with an electric mixer, beat the egg whites on medium speed till soft peaks form. Slowly beat in the sugar and salt. Continue beating for 2 more minutes.

FOLD THE PECANS into the egg whites. Spread the mixture on an ungreased baking pan. Bake for 15 minutes, or until the egg whites are puffed and golden brown. Toss to deflate the whites, spread the mixture out again, and bake until the nuts are lightly toasted, about 15 minutes.

Bun Suon Nuong Xa

Grilled Lemongrass Pork Skewers with Rice Vermicelli

¼ cup Vietnamese fish sauce (nuoc nam)

3 tablespoons sugar

Freshly ground black pepper

1 stalk lemongrass, trimmed, tough outer leaves removed, and inner 5- to 6-inch stem finely ground

2 large garlic cloves, crushed and minced

10 to 12 ounces pork tenderloin, thinly sliced against the grain

¼ cup vegetable oil

4 scallions, white and light green parts only, thinly sliced

8 ounces dried rice vermicelli, soaked in warm water until pliable, and drained

1 small cucumber, peeled, halved lengthwise, seeded, and thinly sliced

2 medium carrots, peeled, and finely julienned

1 head Boston lettuce, separated into leaves, tough ribs removed, and shredded

16 medium to large fresh mint leaves

16 medium to large fresh Thai basil leaves

⅓ cup Vietnamese cilantro or regular cilantro or saw leaves

This classic dish is a healthy rice noodle, grilled pork, fresh vegetable, and herb salad. You'll notice that there is not much marinade, but you work the flavors into the meat with your fingers; there is no need to drown the meat—it will be very flavorful.

It looks as if it takes a long time to make this dish, but really in less than an hour you have a great lunch or dinner. It is perfect for spring and summer, when you can grill the meat outside.

MIX TOGETHER THE fish sauce, sugar, and pepper to taste in a bowl until the sugar has completely dissolved. Stir in the lemongrass and garlic. Add the pork and mix well to coat the slices evenly. Marinate for 30 minutes at room temperature.

HEAT THE OIL in a small saucepan over medium heat until hot. Add the scallions and cook until fragrant and lightly golden, 1 to 2 minutes. Remove from the heat and set aside to cool.

BRING A POT of water to a boil. Divide the rice vermicelli into 4 portions. Working with one portion at a time, place the vermicelli in a sieve, lower into the boiling water, and cook for 3 to 5 seconds only, then rinse under cold running water to stop the cooking. Drain the vermicelli completely and place in a bowl. Toss with some of the scallion oil (including the scallions) until well combined. Add a loosely packed cup each of the cucumber, carrots, and lettuce, tossing until evenly distributed. Divide among four large individual bowls or deep plates.

THREAD THE PORK SLICES onto bamboo skewers, twisting the slices around the skewers.

⅓ cup unsalted roasted peanuts, finely crushed

Nuoc Cham (page 378)

Short bamboo skewers, soaked in water for 20 minutes

SERVES 4

HEAT A WELL-OILED grill pan or nonstick pan over high heat. Grill the skewers until the pork is crispy on the edges, 1 to 2 minutes per side.

TO SERVE, PLACE 3 to 4 skewers on top of each portion of rice vermicelli. Instruct your guests to add freshly torn mint, basil, and cilantro to their individual servings, along with a good sprinkle of crushed peanuts, then drizzle *nuoc cham* to taste over the vermicelli and pork. Serve the remaining cucumber, carrots, and lettuce on the side to pick from.

Note
Traditionally the vegetables are layered at the bottom of the bowl and then topped with the vermicelli—so you cannot see the beautiful colors beneath. My guests always forget to toss well before eating, so my new approach is to toss prior to serving. That way they can enjoy each bite the way it should be.

Nuoc Cham

5 tablespoons sugar

3 tablespoons water

⅓ cup Vietnamese fish sauce (*nuoc nam*)

½ cup fresh lime or lemon juice

1 large garlic clove, crushed and sliced paper-thin, chopped, or minced (see headnote)

1 bird's eye chile or more, to taste, seeded and thinly sliced

MAKES ABOUT 2 CUPS

The very first recipe I ever mastered was nuoc cham, *the ubiquitous sour, sweet, spicy, and salty fish sauce dip. I became the official* nuoc cham *maker—but not until I'd mastered slicing, chopping, and mincing garlic. Everyone in my family hated chopping garlic because it was sticky, so they made me do it because I was a kid.*

Some fish sauces are saltier than others, so you may have to adjust the sugar and lime or lemon juice in this recipe accordingly. This sauce is also open for interpretation, as some like it sweeter, others prefer it saltier, or more sour, or spicier. There are as many versions as there are cooks, but the basic ingredients stay the same. In the North, where the food is milder than in the south, they slice the garlic and chile. In the south, they chop or mince both, for a more powerful flavor. Some cooks strain the sauce, so you have just a clear liquid, free of citrus pulp, garlic, and chiles. And some add finely julienned carrot to contribute another layer of sweet flavor.

WHISK TOGETHER the sugar, water, fish sauce, and lime juice in a bowl until the sugar is completely dissolved. Add the garlic and chile, and let stand for 30 minutes before serving.

Che Chuoi
Sweet Coconut Soup with Banana

1½ cups canned unsweetened coconut milk

1½ cups water

¼ cup pearl tapioca

¼ to ⅓ cup sugar

Pinch of freshly ground sea salt

2 ripe bananas, peeled and diced

1 tablespoon sesame seeds, toasted

SERVES 4 TO 6

This soup can be served hot, warm, at room temperature, or chilled. In Asia we always eat fruit for dessert, so this sweet soup would be served as a snack. You can, however, have it for breakfast or dessert if you wish. This is a favorite among the kids in my family, who have it with shaved ice in the afternoon as a snack on hot summer days.

BRING THE COCONUT MILK and water to a boil in a pot over high heat. Reduce the heat to medium-low, stir in the tapioca, sugar, and salt, and cook until the tapioca pearls are translucent, about 30 minutes. The consistency should be that of a slightly thickened soup (but definitely not thick like pudding).

REMOVE THE TAPIOCA from the heat, stir in the bananas, cover with a lid, and let stand for 20 minutes to steam the bananas.

DIVIDE THE SOUP among four bowls, sprinkle with the toasted sesame seeds, and serve.

Canh Chua Tom
Spicy Tamarind Prawn Soup

2 tablespoons vegetable oil

3 garlic cloves, finely chopped

2 stalks lemongrass, trimmed, tough outer leaves removed, and finely chopped

1 teaspoon cayenne

5 cups chicken stock

2 ounces tamarind paste

16 small (36 to 40 count) shrimp, peeled, shells reserved

1 cup diced pineapple

2 medium tomatoes

4 okra pods, cut into 4 pieces each

1 tablespoon sugar

1 teaspoon salt, or to taste

2 tablespoons Vietnamese fish sauce (nuoc nam)

Fresh lime juice (optional)

2 cups loosely packed bean sprouts

10 fresh Thai basil leaves

SERVES 4

HEAT THE VEGETABLE OIL in a medium saucepan. Add the garlic, lemongrass, and cayenne. Stir briefly until the garlic starts to brown. Add the chicken stock, tamarind, and shrimp shells. Bring to a boil, reduce the heat, and simmer for 10 to 15 minutes.

STRAIN THE STOCK into another saucepan and bring to a boil again. Add the shrimp, pineapple, tomatoes, okra, sugar, salt, and fish sauce.

ADJUST THE SEASONING if necessary with lime juice and more salt.

ADD THE BEAN SPROUTS and basil. Serve immediately.

Ca Chien Saigon

Crisp Red Snapper with Chile-Lime Sauce

FOR THE CHILE-LIME SAUCE

¼ cup Vietnamese fish sauce (*nuoc nam*)

½ cup water

2 tablespoons sugar

3 tablespoons fresh lime juice

2 teaspoons prepared chile paste, or more to taste

2 cups vegetable oil

One 1- to 1½-pound red snapper, cleaned and scaled

Salt and pepper

2 tablespoons all-purpose flour

2 teaspoons rice flour

2 teaspoons minced garlic

2 stalks scallions, trimmed and chopped

Cilantro sprigs for garnish

Lime wedges for garnish

SERVES 2

FOR THE CHILE SAUCE

COMBINE THE FISH SAUCE, water, sugar, lime juice, and chile pepper paste in a bowl. Set aside.

HEAT THE OIL in a sauté pan large enough to hold the fish. Season the fish with a little salt and pepper. Combine the two flours and sprinkle the fish with flour; shake off the excess flour. Place the fish in the hot oil and cook for about 5 minutes on each side. Transfer to a platter.

POUR OFF ALL BUT 1 tablespoon oil from the pan and return the pan to the heat. Add the garlic and brown lightly. Add the scallions and the chile-lime sauce. Bring to a boil, and remove from the heat.

POUR THE SAUCE over the fish. Garnish with cilantro and lime, and serve.

Che Chuoi
Banana-Coconut Tapioca

5 ounces (scant 1 cup) small pearl tapioca

2 cups water

Three 13½-ounce cans unsweetened coconut milk

1 cup sugar, or to taste

1 teaspoon kosher salt

10 ripe bananas, peeled and cut into bite-sized pieces

1 teaspoon pure vanilla extract

SERVES 10

IN BOWL, MIX THE tapioca with 1 cup water. Let stand for 10 minutes to absorb the water.

IN A LARGE POT, BRING the coconut milk and the remaining 1 cup water to a boil. Stir in the tapioca and cook until it swells and becomes translucent, about 30 minutes.

STIR THE SUGAR AND SALT into the tapioca. Bring to a boil, and remove from the heat. Stir in the bananas and vanilla. Let stand until thickened slightly.

SERVE THE TAPIOCA HOT or at room temperature. It will be soupy at first, but it will thicken as it cools.

Pho

FOR THE MEAT BROTH

3½ pounds oxtails, cut into pieces

2½ pounds beef shanks

1 pound beef tendons (see Note)

4 quarts water

1 onion, peeled

3 carrots

4 ounces ginger, thinly sliced

4 whole star anise

4 whole cloves

2 cinnamon sticks

FOR THE SOUP

8 ounces dried rice noodles (rice sticks), soaked in warm water for 20 minutes to soften

1 onion, thinly sliced

8 ounces boneless beef round, sliced paper-thin (see Note)

FOR GARNISH

1 cup bean sprouts

1 cup cilantro leaves

1 cup fresh Thai basil leaves

½ cup fresh mint leaves

3 scallions, trimmed and cut into julienne

3 red Thai chiles, thinly sliced

1 lime, cut into wedges

Hoisin sauce

Hot sauce, such as Sriracha

FOR THE BROTH

TRIM ALL THE MEAT of excess fat. In a large stockpot, combine the meats and water. Bring to a gentle boil, skimming two or three times. Add the vegetables, ginger, and spices. Reduce the heat and simmer for about 3 hours, skimming occasionally, until reduced by about a third.

STRAIN THE STOCK. Reserve the beef tendons to add to the soup upon serving, if desired. Let cool, then skim the fat one more time. (The stock can be made up to 1 day ahead; cover and refrigerate.)

JUST BEFORE SERVING, bring a large pot of water to a boil.

BRING THE BROTH to a boil; keep warm.

BLANCH THE NOODLES in the boiling water for about 10 seconds, to heat through. Drain well, and divide among four bowls.

TO SERVE, TOP THE NOODLES with the sliced onion and pour the broth over noodles. Top with the sliced beef and tendon, if desired. Place the bean sprouts, fresh herbs, scallions, chiles, lime, and sauces in the middle of the table so each guest can flavor the soup to his or her own taste. Serve with chopsticks and Asian soupspoons.

Note
Order beef tendons through your local butcher, or purchase in your local Chinatown. To make slicing the beef easier, put the meat in the freezer for 10 minutes before slicing.